FOR EVERYONE

PRACTICE BOOK

BUSINESS ENGLISH

FREE AUDIO
website and app
www.dkefe.com

Authors

Thomas Booth worked for 10 years as an English-language teacher in Poland and Russia. He now lives in England, where he works as an editor and English-language materials writer, notably of course books and vocabulary textbooks.

Trish Burrow worked for seven years as a teacher and teacher trainer in Poland and UK summer schools. After a year working in a UK college as an ELT lecturer, she worked as an editor of exams materials and then English-language teaching materials. She lives in the UK and is a freelance writer and editor.

Course consultant

Tim Bowen has taught English and trained teachers in more than 30 countries worldwide. He is the co-author of works on pronunciation teaching and language-teaching methodology, and author of numerous books for English-language teachers. He is currently a freelance materials writer, editor, and translator. He is a member of the Chartered Institute of Linguists.

Language consultant

Professor Susan Barduhn is an experienced English-language teacher, teacher trainer, and author, who has contributed to numerous publications. In addition to directing English-language courses in at least four different continents, she has been President of the International Association of Teachers of English as a Foreign Language, and an adviser to the British Council and the US State Department. She is currently a Professor at the School for International Training in Vermont, USA.

ENGLISH
FOR EVERYONE

PRACTICE BOOK **LEVEL 1**

BUSINESS ENGLISH

US Editors Jenny Siklos, Allison Singer
Project Editors Lili Bryant, Laura Sandford
Art Editors Chrissy Barnard, Paul Drislane, Michelle Staples
Editor Ben Ffrancon Davies
Editorial Assistants Sarah Edwards, Helen Leech
Illustrators Edwood Burn, Michael Parkin, Gus Scott
Managing Editor Daniel Mills
Managing Art Editor Anna Hall
Audio Recording Manager Christine Stroyan
Jacket Designer Ira Sharma
Jacket Editor Claire Gell
Managing Jacket Editor Saloni Singh
Jacket Design Development Manager Sophia MTT
Producer, Pre-production Andy Hilliard
Producer Mary Slater
Publisher Andrew Macintyre
Art Director Karen Self
Publishing Director Jonathan Metcalf

DK India
Senior Managing Art Editor Arunesh Talapatra
Senior Art Editor Chhaya Sajwan
Art Editors Meenal Goel, Roshni Kapur
Assistant Art Editor Rohit Dev Bhardwaj
Illustrators Manish Bhatt, Arun Pottirayil, Sachin Tanwar, Mohd Zishan
Editorial Coordinator Priyanka Sharma
Pre-production Manager Balwant Singh
Senior DTP Designers Harish Aggarwal, Vishal Bhatia
DTP Designer Jaypal Chauhan

This American Edition, 2019
First American Edition, 2017
Published in the United States by DK Publishing
1745 Broadway, 20th Floor, New York, NY 10019

24 10 9 8 7 6 5 4
004–312649–Jan/2019

A catalog record for this book is available from the Library of Congress.
ISBN 978-1-4654-5268-9

Printed and bound in China

www.dk.com

This book was made with Forest Stewardship Council™ certified paper - one small step in DK's commitment to a sustainable future.
For more information go to www.dk.com/our-green-pledge

Level 1 Contents

Level 2 Contents see page 180

How the course works

English for Everyone is designed for people who want to teach themselves the English language. The Business English edition covers essential English phrases and constructions for a wide range of common business scenarios. Unlike other courses, *English for Everyone* uses graphics to help you learn as easily as possible. The practice book is packed with exercises designed to reinforce the lessons you have learned in the course book. Both levels of the course are contained in this one volume. Work through the units in order, making full use of the audio on the website and app.

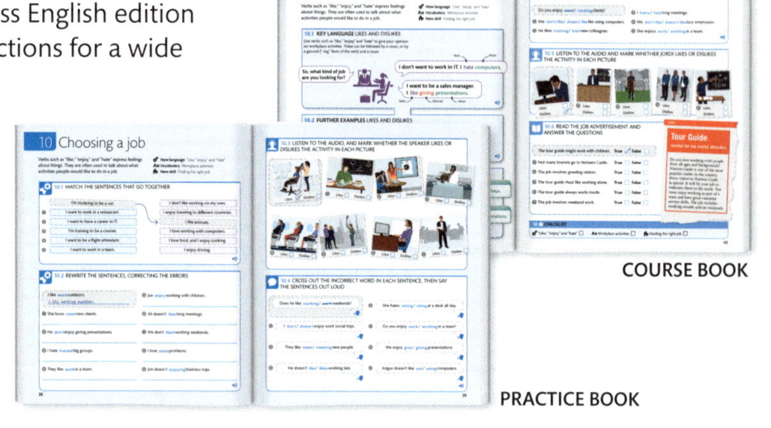

Unit number The book is divided into units. Each practice book unit tests the language taught in the course book unit with the same number.

Practice points Every unit begins with a summary of the key practice points.

Modules Each unit is broken down into modules, which should be done in order. You can take a break from learning after completing any module.

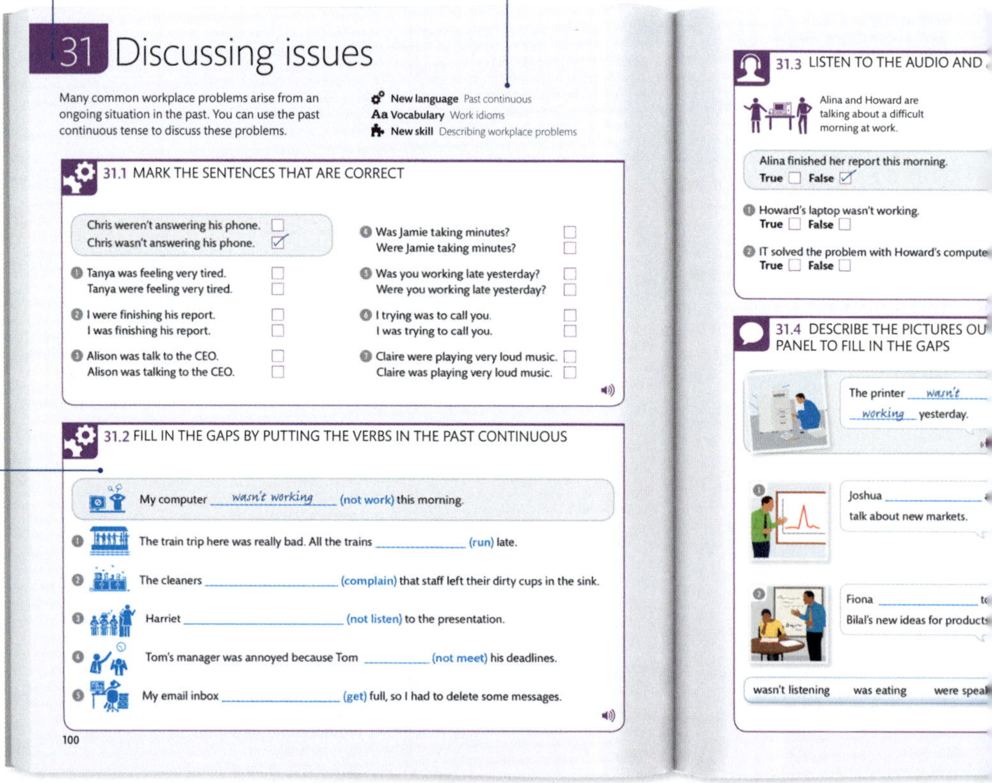

31 Discussing issues

Many common workplace problems arise from an ongoing situation in the past. You can use the past continuous tense to discuss these problems.

New language Past continuous
Aa Vocabulary Work idioms
New skill Describing workplace problems

31.1 MARK THE SENTENCES THAT ARE CORRECT

Chris weren't answering his phone. ☐
Chris wasn't answering his phone. ☑

1 Tanya was feeling very tired. ☐
Tanya were feeling very tired. ☐

2 I were finishing his report. ☐
I was finishing his report. ☐

3 Alison was talk to the CEO. ☐
Alison was talking to the CEO. ☐

4 Was Jamie taking minutes? ☐
Were Jamie taking minutes? ☐

5 Was you working late yesterday? ☐
Were you working late yesterday? ☐

6 I trying was to call you. ☐
I was trying to call you. ☐

7 Claire were playing very loud music. ☐
Claire was playing very loud music. ☐

31.2 FILL IN THE GAPS BY PUTTING THE VERBS IN THE PAST CONTINUOUS

My computer *wasn't working* (not work) this morning.

1 The train trip here was really bad. All the trains ______ (run) late.

2 The cleaners ______ (complain) that staff left their dirty cups in the sink.

3 Harriet ______ (not listen) to the presentation.

4 Tom's manager was annoyed because Tom ______ (not meet) his deadlines.

5 My email inbox ______ (get) full, so I had to delete some messages.

100

31.3 LISTEN TO THE AUDIO AND

Alina and Howard are talking about a difficult morning at work.

Alina finished her report this morning.
True ☐ False ☑

1 Howard's laptop wasn't working.
True ☐ False ☐

2 IT solved the problem with Howard's compute
True ☐ False ☐

31.4 DESCRIBE THE PICTURES OU PANEL TO FILL IN THE GAPS

The printer *wasn't working* yesterday.

1 Joshua ______ talk about new markets.

2 Fiona ______ t Bilal's new ideas for product

wasn't listening was eating were speal

Vocabulary Throughout the book, vocabulary pages test your memory of key business English words and phrases taught in the course book.

Visual practice Images act as visual cues to help fix the most useful and important English words and phrases in your memory.

Audio support Most modules have supporting audio recordings of native English speakers to help you improve your speaking and listening skills.

FREE AUDIO
website and app
www.dkefe.com

Practice modules

Each exercise is carefully graded to drill and test the language taught in the corresponding course book units. Working through the exercises alongside the course book will help you remember what you have learned and become more fluent. Every exercise is introduced with a symbol to indicate which skill is being practiced.

GRAMMAR
Apply new language rules in different contexts.

READING
Examine target language in real-life English contexts.

LISTENING
Test your understanding of spoken English.

VOCABULARY
Cement your understanding of key vocabulary.

SPEAKING
Compare your spoken English to model audio recordings.

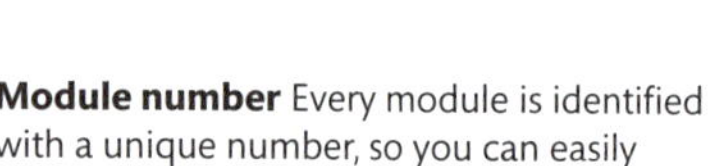

Module number Every module is identified with a unique number, so you can easily locate answers and related audio.

Exercise instruction Every exercise is introduced with a brief instruction, telling you what you need to do.

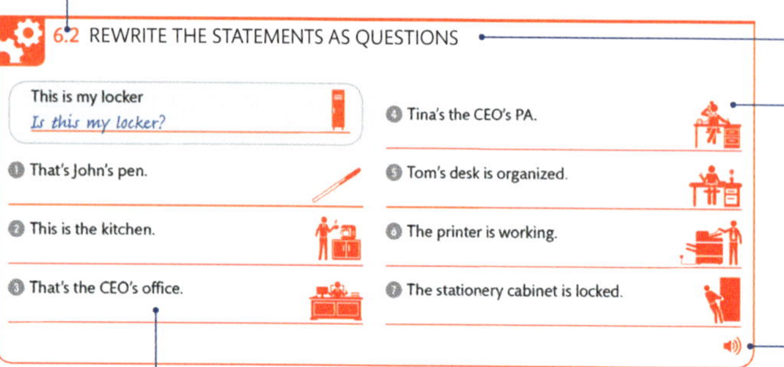

Supporting graphics Visual cues are given to help you understand the exercises.

Supporting audio This symbol shows that the answers to the exercise are available as audio tracks. Listen to them after completing the exercise.

Space for writing You are encouraged to write your answers in the book for future reference.

Speaking exercise This symbol indicates that you should say your answers out loud, then compare them to model recordings included in your audio files.

Listening exercise This symbol indicates that you should listen to an audio track in order to answer the questions in the exercise.

Sample answer The first question of each exercise is answered for you, to help make the task easy to understand.

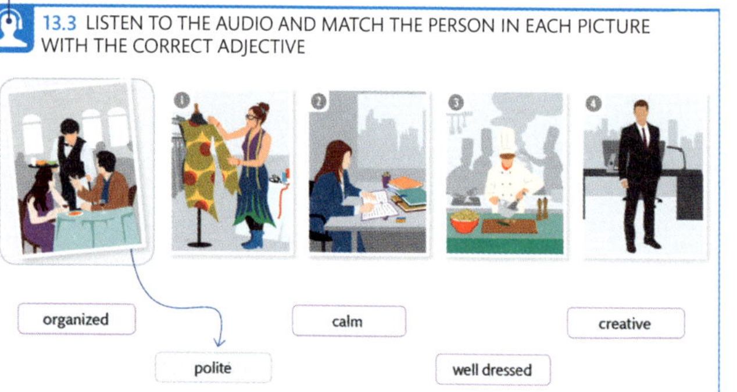

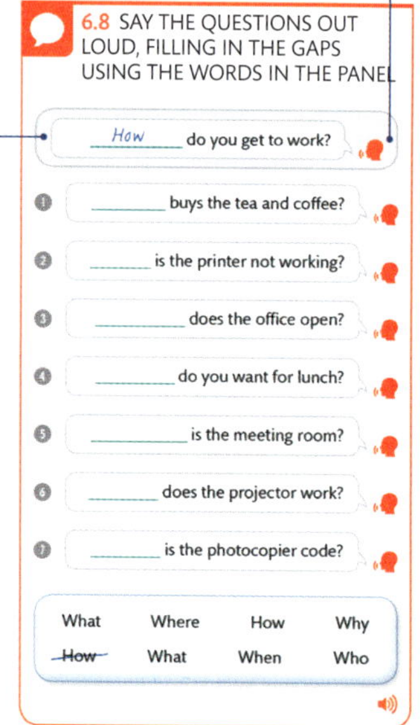

Audio

English for Everyone features extensive supporting audio materials. You are encouraged to use them as much as you can, to improve your understanding of spoken English, and to make your own accent and pronunciation more natural. Each file can be played, paused, and repeated as often as you like, until you are confident you understand what has been said.

LISTENING EXERCISES
This symbol indicates that you should listen to an audio track in order to answer the questions in the exercise.

SUPPORTING AUDIO
This symbol indicates that extra audio material is available for you to listen to after completing the module.

Answers

An answers section at the back of the book lists the correct answers for every exercise. Turn to these pages whenever you finish a module and compare your answers with the samples provided, to see how well you have understood each teaching point.

32

32.1

1. I am so sorry I was late for the meeting with our clients today.
2. I would like to apologize for not finishing the report yesterday.
3. I'm really sorry. I forgot to charge the office cell phone and it has no power.
4. I'm really sorry this line is so bad. I hope we don't get cut off.
5. I'm afraid that's not good enough. I want a full refund on my ticket.

Answers Find the answers to every exercise printed at the back of the book.

32.2

1. No problem. I'll help you finish it now.
2. That's not good enough. Please heat it up.
3. Never mind. We're not very busy today.
4. No problem. I'll have tea instead.
5. Don't worry. I'll print off some more.

32.3

A 4
B 3
C 1
D 5
E 2

Exercise numbers Match these numbers to the unique identifier at the top-left corner of each exercise.

32.4

1. I'm really **sorry**. I forgot to send the agenda for the meeting.
2. I would like to **apologize** for the rudeness of the waitress.
3. I'm **afraid** that's not good enough. You missed an important meeting.
4. That's all **right**. I'll make you a copy right now.
5. Please **make** sure it doesn't happen again.

Audio This symbol indicates that the answers can also be listened to.

01 Meeting new colleagues

You can use formal or informal English to introduce yourself and greet colleagues or co-workers, depending on the situation and the people you are meeting.

New language Alphabet and spelling
Vocabulary Introductions and greetings
New skill Introducing yourself to co-workers

1.1 MARK THE SENTENCES THAT ARE CORRECT

It's pleasure to meet you. ☐
It's a pleasure to meet you. ☑

1. My name Ali Patel. ☐
   My name's Ali Patel. ☐
2. Hi, I'm Jeff. ☐
   Hi, I Jeff. ☐
3. It good to meet you, Jane. ☐
   It's good to meet you, Jane. ☐
4. Pleased to meet you. ☐
   Please to meet you. ☐
5. I'm name is Deepak Kaur. ☐
   My name is Deepak Kaur. ☐
6. Great to meet you, Tanya. ☐
   Pleasure to meet you, Tanya. ☐
7. It's nice to meet you, too. ☐
   It's nice meet you, too. ☐
8. Good hello. My name is Ben Lewis. ☐
   Good morning. My name is Ben Lewis. ☐
9. It's a great to meet you, Gill. ☐
   It's great to meet you, Gill. ☐
10. Good evening. My name is Karen. ☐
    Great evening. My name is Karen. ☐

1.2 REWRITE THE SENTENCES, PUTTING THE WORDS IN THE CORRECT ORDER

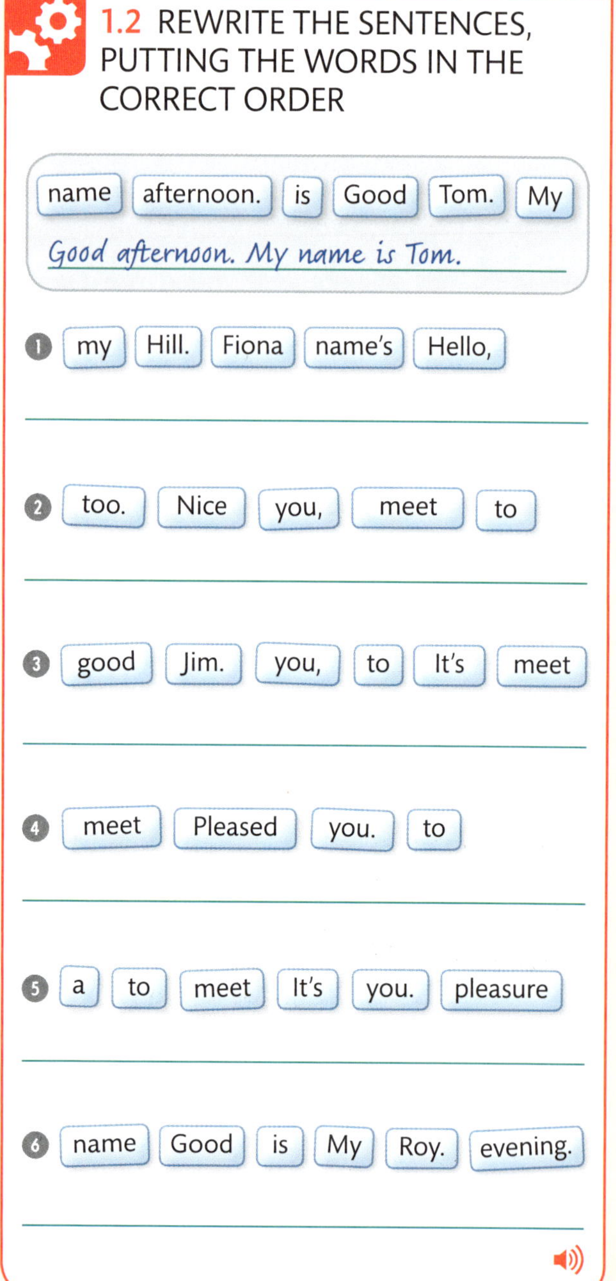

1.3 LISTEN TO THE AUDIO AND MARK THE NAMES THAT ARE SPELLED OUT

A George
B Jorge

1
A Jayne
B Jane

2
A Adam
B Alan

3
A Sarah
B Saleh

4
A Mick
B Mike

5
A Carrie
B Kerry

1.4 SPELL THE NAMES OUT LOUD

Alisha Sharma

A-L-I-S-H-A S-H-A-R-M-A

1 Alex Hann

2 Dev Singh

3 Francis Palmer

4 Hansa Sya

5 Zandra Fellini

6 Raj Dhabi

7 Katy Adenova

1.5 REWRITE THE SENTENCES, CORRECTING THE ERRORS

May you introduce Amy Daniels?
May I introduce Amy Daniels?

1. This our new designer.
2. Raj and I works together.
3. I like you to meet our CEO.
4. Hi, I'm name's Lola.
5. It's great to meet to you, Emily.
6. I may introduce Ewan Carlton?
7. Farah, this my colleague, Leon.

1.6 CROSS OUT THE INCORRECT WORD IN EACH SENTENCE

Hi, Luke. This is / ~~meet~~ Emiko.

1. Good morning. I'm / My name's Saira Khan.
2. Bye / I'm Harry.
3. I'm / I's Andrew Shaw.
4. It's / It good to meet you.
5. Pleased to / I meet you.
6. It's a pleased / pleasure to meet you.
7. May / This I introduce our new HR assistant?
8. Keira, meets / meet John.
9. Great / Greater to meet you.
10. I would / had like you to meet Dan.
11. Colin and I works / work together.

1.7 LISTEN TO THE AUDIO, THEN NUMBER THE SENTENCES IN THE ORDER YOU HEAR THEM

Julia has recently started a new job. She meets some of her new co-workers at a company party.

A. Meet Jim. He's our CEO. ☐
B. It's nice to meet you, Julia. ☐
C. Hi, Jim. It's great to meet you, too. ☐
D. And this is Gary, our Marketing Manager. ☐
E. May I introduce Julia Parker? 1
F. It's a pleasure to meet you, too, Claire. ☐
G. Pleased to meet you, Julia. ☐

02 Everyday work activities

Use the present simple to talk about things that you do regularly, such as your daily tasks or everyday work routines.

New language Present simple
Vocabulary Work activities
New skill Talking about workplace routines

2.1 MATCH THE PICTURES TO THE CORRECT SENTENCES

2.2 REWRITE THE SENTENCES, CORRECTING THE ERRORS

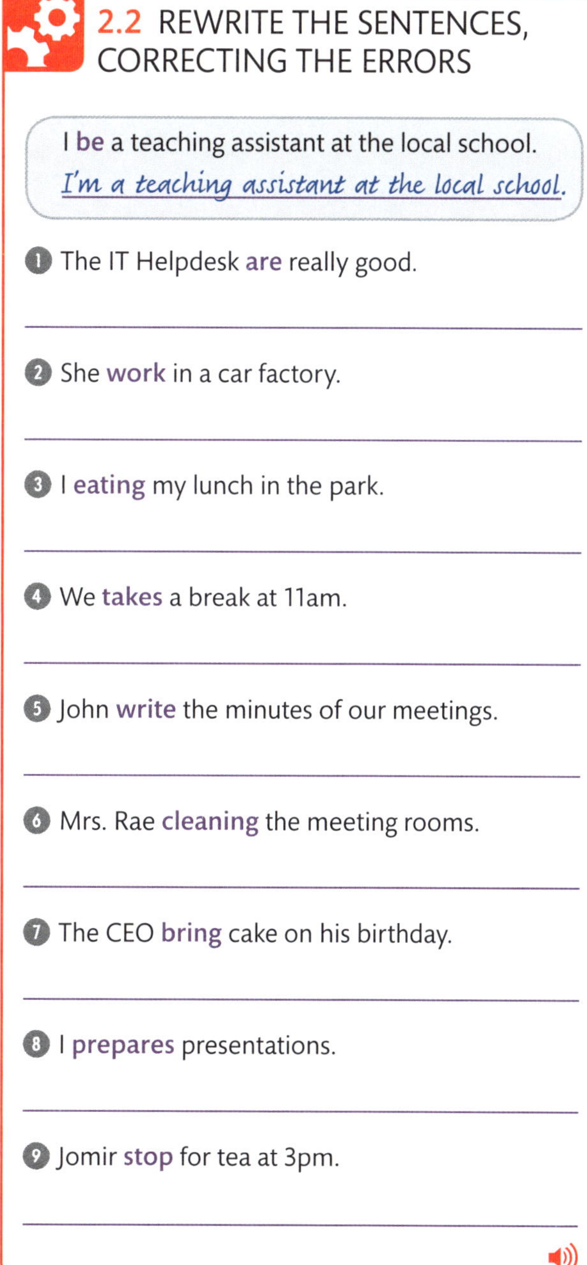

2.3 MARK THE SENTENCES THAT ARE CORRECT

The office close at 7 o'clock. ☐
The office closes at 7 o'clock. ☑

1. The CEO arrive at work early. ☐
   The CEO arrives at work early. ☐

2. We have a hot-desking policy. ☐
   We has a hot-desking policy. ☐

3. My assistant opens my mail. ☐
   My assistant open my mail. ☐

4. Shazia be an engineer. ☐
   Shazia is an engineer. ☐

5. Hal working for his uncle. ☐
   Hal works for his uncle. ☐

6. I start work at 8:30am. ☐
   I starts work at 8:30am. ☐

7. They finish at 5pm. ☐
   They finishes at 5pm. ☐

8. They eating lunch in the cafeteria. ☐
   They eat lunch in the cafeteria. ☐

9. Kate only drinks coffee. ☐
   Kate only drink coffee. ☐

10. I calls the US office every Monday. ☐
    I call the US office every Monday. ☐

11. Andrew helps me with my PC. ☐
    Andrew help me with my PC. ☐

12. I replies to emails at 11am and 3pm. ☐
    I reply to emails at 11am and 3pm. ☐

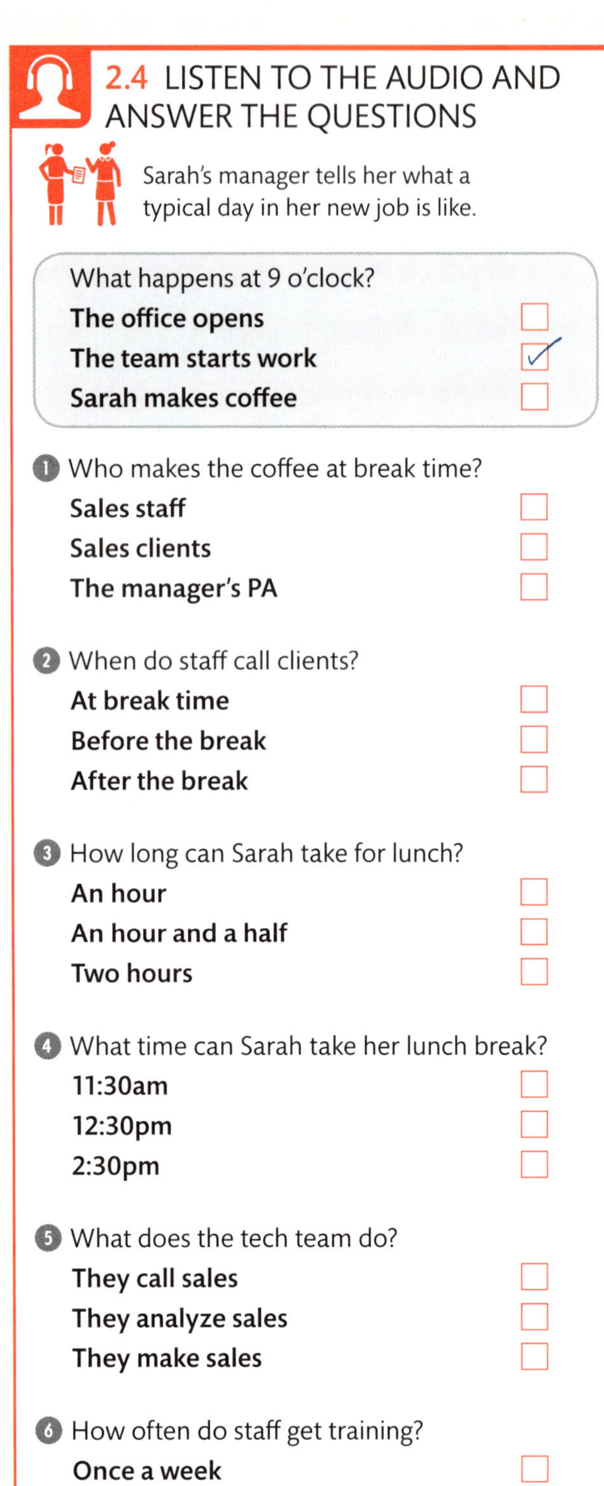

2.4 LISTEN TO THE AUDIO AND ANSWER THE QUESTIONS

Sarah's manager tells her what a typical day in her new job is like.

What happens at 9 o'clock?
The office opens ☐
The team starts work ☑
Sarah makes coffee ☐

1. Who makes the coffee at break time?
   Sales staff ☐
   Sales clients ☐
   The manager's PA ☐

2. When do staff call clients?
   At break time ☐
   Before the break ☐
   After the break ☐

3. How long can Sarah take for lunch?
   An hour ☐
   An hour and a half ☐
   Two hours ☐

4. What time can Sarah take her lunch break?
   11:30am ☐
   12:30pm ☐
   2:30pm ☐

5. What does the tech team do?
   They call sales ☐
   They analyze sales ☐
   They make sales ☐

6. How often do staff get training?
   Once a week ☐
   Twice a week ☐
   Three times a week ☐

2.5 CROSS OUT THE INCORRECT WORD IN EACH SENTENCE

Samia **takes** / ~~**take**~~ notes in our meetings.

1. The director **has** / **haves** an open door policy.
2. I **deal** / **deals** with all his emails.
3. Gavin **leaves** / **leave** work at 7pm.
4. They **works** / **work** evenings and weekends.
5. She **ride** / **rides** her bike to work.
6. Tim and Pat **bring** / **brings** their own lunch.
7. Deepak **turn** / **turns** off his phone after work.
8. Sobek and Kurt **plays** / **play** tennis after work.
9. My boss **plan** / **plans** my work for the week.

2.6 SAY THE SENTENCES OUT LOUD, FILLING IN THE GAPS USING THE WORDS IN THE PANEL

I *write* a list of my tasks every day.

1. Lulu always ______ to work early.
2. Our reps ______ clients at their office.
3. The CEO ______ to all new staff.
4. He's a nurse and he ______ weekends.
5. Imran ______ with all the contracts.
6. The printer ______ working late in the day.
7. The staff ______ to a nearby café for lunch.
8. Raj ______ a break at 11am.
9. Sophie ______ a travel agent.

deals go meet stops takes
talks gets ~~write~~ works is

03 Vocabulary

Aa 3.1 **COUNTRIES AND CONTINENTS** WRITE THE WORDS FROM THE PANEL UNDER THE CORRECT PICTURES

1 ______

2 ______

3 ______

4 ______

10 ______

11 ______

12 ______

13 ______

14 ______

20 ______

21 ______

22 ______

23 ______

24 ______

30 ______

31 ______

32 ______

33 ______

34 ______

5 ______ 6 ______ 7 ______ 8 ______ 9 ______

15 ______ 16 ______ 17 ______ 18 ______ 19 ______

25 ______ 26 ______ 27 ______ 28 ______ 29 ______

Canada Netherlands Thailand China Japan Poland Russia India Singapore
Mexico Australia New Zealand Spain France Brazil Asia Africa Germany Europe
South Africa Turkey Argentina Australasia North America Egypt South Korea
South America Austria United States of America (US / USA) Republic of Ireland (ROI) Switzerland
United Kingdom (UK) Pakistan Mongolia United Arab Emirates (UAE)

04 Business around the world

English uses "from" or nationality adjectives to talk about where products or people come from. "From" can also refer to your company or department.

New language Negative statements
Aa Vocabulary Countries and nationalities
New skill Saying where things are from

Aa 4.1 FIND FIVE MORE COUNTRIES IN THE GRID THAT MATCH THE FLAGS

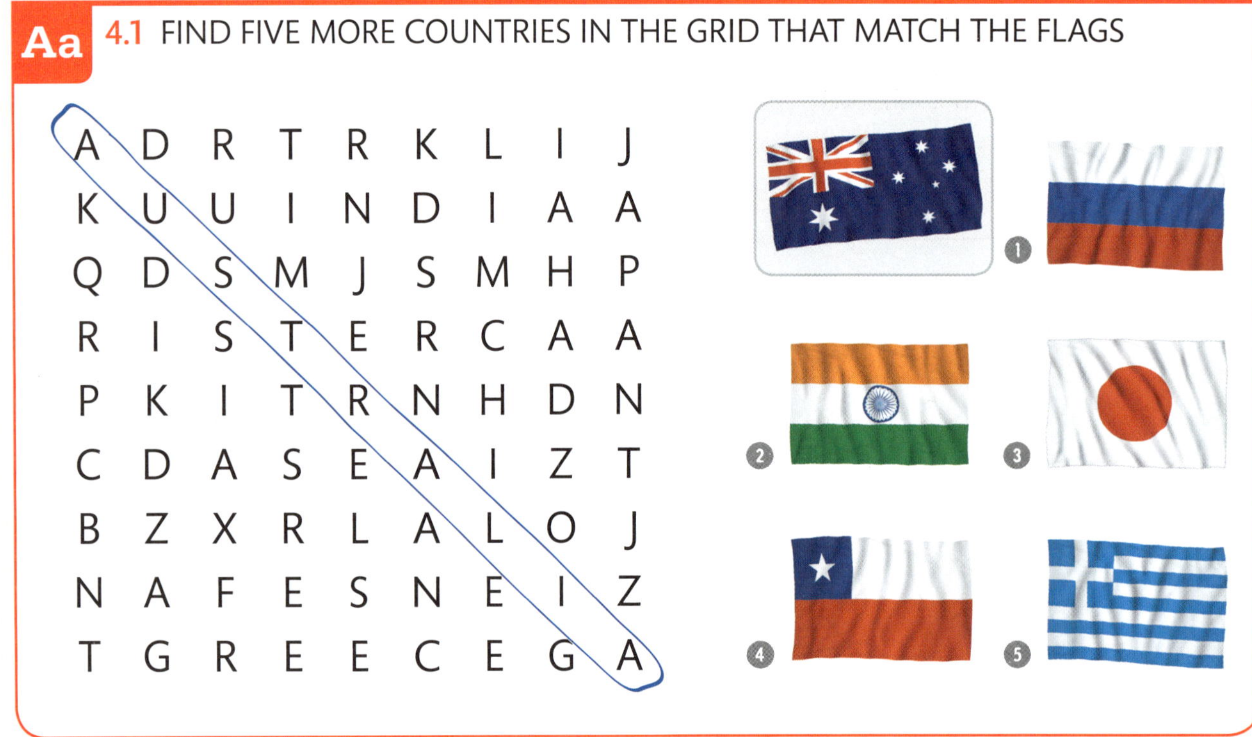

Aa 4.2 WRITE THE WORDS FROM THE PANEL IN THE CORRECT GROUPS

COUNTRIES		NATIONALITIES	
South Africa		Brazilian	

France ~~South Africa~~ British Greek Italy Canadian
Vietnam Japanese Switzerland ~~Brazilian~~ Spanish China

4.3 REWRITE EACH SENTENCE IN ITS OTHER FORM

	These new tablets are from China.	*These new tablets are Chinese.*
1		The new CEO is Australian.
2	These new robots are from Japan.	
3		We sell Portuguese leather bags.
4		I'm Argentinian, but I work in the US.
5	The designer is from Britain.	
6		Our sales director is South Korean.
7	Our best-selling rugs are from India.	
8		These beautiful clothes are African.

4.4 MARK THE SENTENCES THAT ARE CORRECT

Our restaurant serves Japan food. ☐
Our restaurant serves Japanese food. ☑

1. Our CEO is America. ☐
   Our CEO is from America. ☐

2. I've got a flight to Italy next Monday. ☐
   I've got a flight to Italian next Monday. ☐

3. These sports cars are from French. ☐
   These sports cars are from France. ☐

4. Most of our fabrics are from Africa. ☐
   Most of our fabrics are from African. ☐

5. My PA is from Spanish. ☐
   My PA is from Spain. ☐

4.5 CROSS OUT THE INCORRECT WORD IN EACH SENTENCE

Our best products are from Russia / ~~Russian~~.

1. We sell smartphones from Japan / Japanese.
2. The HR manager is from America / American.
3. My team follows the China / Chinese markets.
4. Travel to the Greece / Greek islands with us.
5. Our products are from Vietnam / Vietnamese.
6. Our CEO is Canada / Canadian.
7. Most of the sales team is from Spain / Spanish.
8. I'm British, but I work in Italy / Italian.
9. I have a lot of Mexico / Mexican co-workers.
10. My new assistant is from France / French.

4.6 REWRITE THE SENTENCES, CORRECTING THE ERRORS USING SHORT FORMS

The photocopier works not!
The photocopier doesn't work!

1. I am'nt very tall.

2. He works not in an office.

3. We not sell French cars.

4. They not are from Italy.

5. The fruit in the supermarket not local.

6. I work not for an Asian company.

7. You be not happy.

8. She are not from China.

9. We produce not robots.

10. You not have any meetings today.

11. It aren't a steel factory.

4.7 SAY THE SENTENCES OUT LOUD, USING SHORT FORMS

I am not Mexican.
I'm not Mexican.

1. These dresses are not made in India.

2. She does not come from Russia.

3. The workers in this factory are not American.

4. They do not sell energy to South Korea.

5. He is not from Chile.

4.8 LISTEN TO THE AUDIO AND ANSWER THE QUESTIONS

Nadia, Tim, and Carlos are attending a conference.

What department does Nadia work in?
Finance ☐ Sales ☑ IT ☐

1. What department does Carlos work in?
Finance ☐ Sales ☐ IT ☐

2. Who hasn't Nadia met before?
Carlos ☐ Tim ☐ Neither of them ☐

3. What department does Tim work in?
Finance ☐ Marketing ☐ IT ☐

4. Who has to report back to their team?
Tim ☐ Nadia ☐ Carlos ☐

5. Where will Tim's company launch a brand?
China ☐ Chile ☐ Japan ☐

4.9 READ THE ARTICLE AND ANSWER THE QUESTIONS

The company sells food from one country.
True ☐ False ☑ Not given ☐

1. The CEO has visited many different countries.
True ☐ False ☐ Not given ☐

2. He stayed with local people in each country.
True ☐ False ☐ Not given ☐

3. All Fairtrade coffee comes from Chile.
True ☐ False ☐ Not given ☐

4. Some Fairtrade products come from Kenya.
True ☐ False ☐ Not given ☐

5. Food always tastes better if it's Fairtrade.
True ☐ False ☐ Not given ☐

6. "Tasters" choose the food that the company sells.
True ☐ False ☐ Not given ☐

7. "Selectors" find new foods to sell.
True ☐ False ☐ Not given ☐

COMPANY PROFILES

Foods from around the World

Founded in 2005, Foods from around the World brings you food from every corner of the globe. Their CEO, Johnathon Medway, had the idea for the company after he spent a year traveling around the world, eating exotic foods in each country that he visited.

Johnathon says, "We buy directly from our producers and all the food you buy from us has the Fairtrade guarantee. That means the food is from small-scale farmers in countries like India, Chile, and Egypt. Workers are treated fairly and paid a living wage. So Costa Rican coffee growers and Kenyan tea growers all earn enough to live on if you buy our products."

So, how does the company find new products to sell? They have a team of "tasters" who travel around a different region of the world, trying food in markets, cafés, and from shops and factories. The "tasters" then make a shortlist of their favorite products for the "selectors" to choose from at the head office. Finally, the "selectors" talk to the producer and agree a trade deal. So, next time you want to eat something interesting, go to Foods from around the World.

05 Vocabulary

5.1 OFFICE EQUIPMENT WRITE THE WORDS FROM THE PANEL UNDER THE CORRECT PICTURES

1 ______

2 ______

3 ______

4 ______

8 ______

9 ______

10 ______

11 ______

12 ______

16 ______

17 ______

18 ______

19 ______

20 ______

24 ______

25 ______

26 ______

27 ______

28 ______

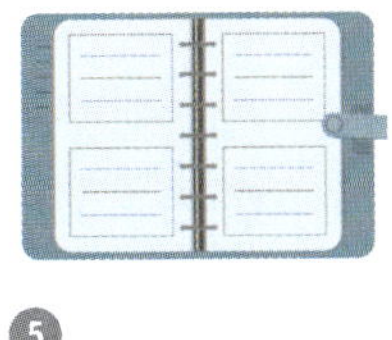

5 ______

6 ______

7 ______

13 ______

14 ______

15 ______

21 ______

22 ______

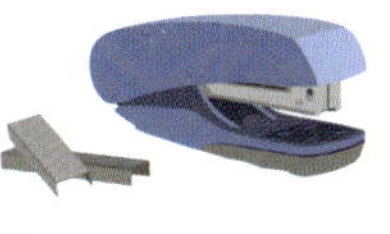

23 ______

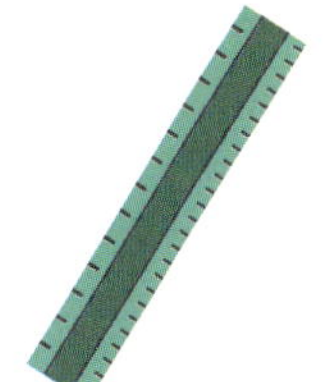

29 ______

30 ______

31 ______

letter adhesive tape

planner (US) / diary (UK) notepad

computer pencil ruler

files / folders stapler

lamp hole punch

pencil sharpener highlighter

laptop pen chair

eraser (US) / rubber (UK)

calendar paper clips headset

rubber bands shredder

~~photocopier~~ clipboard

hard drive scanner

telephone / phone projector

envelope printer tablet

cell phone (US) / mobile phone (UK)

06 Asking questions at work

It is important to use the correct word order and question words in English questions, depending on whether the questions are open-ended.

New language Forming questions
Aa Vocabulary Office equipment
New skill Asking colleagues questions

6.1 REWRITE THE QUESTIONS, PUTTING THE WORDS IN THE CORRECT ORDER

this | Is | cafeteria? | the
Is this the cafeteria?

1. this | working? | printer | Is
2. desk? | this | Is | your
3. closed? | the | windows | Are
4. this | locked? | Is | cupboard
5. messy? | desk | his | Is
6. CEO? | the | she | Is
7. assistant? | Jo's | you | Are

6.2 REWRITE THE STATEMENTS AS QUESTIONS

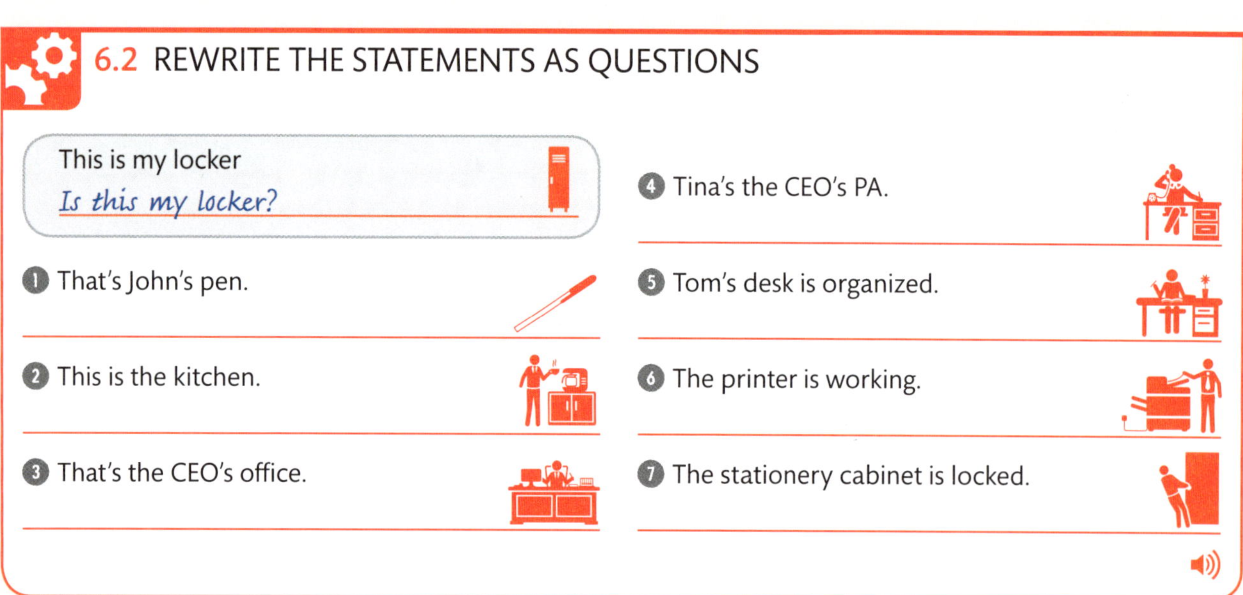

This is my locker
Is this my locker?

1. That's John's pen.
2. This is the kitchen.
3. That's the CEO's office.
4. Tina's the CEO's PA.
5. Tom's desk is organized.
6. The printer is working.
7. The stationery cabinet is locked.

6.3 FILL IN THE GAPS USING "DO" OR "DOES"

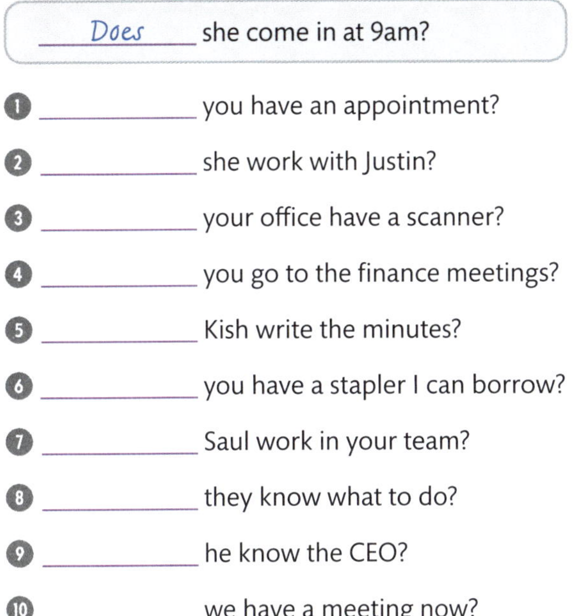

Does she come in at 9am?

1. ______ you have an appointment?
2. ______ she work with Justin?
3. ______ your office have a scanner?
4. ______ you go to the finance meetings?
5. ______ Kish write the minutes?
6. ______ you have a stapler I can borrow?
7. ______ Saul work in your team?
8. ______ they know what to do?
9. ______ he know the CEO?
10. ______ we have a meeting now?

6.4 LISTEN TO THE AUDIO AND ANSWER THE QUESTIONS

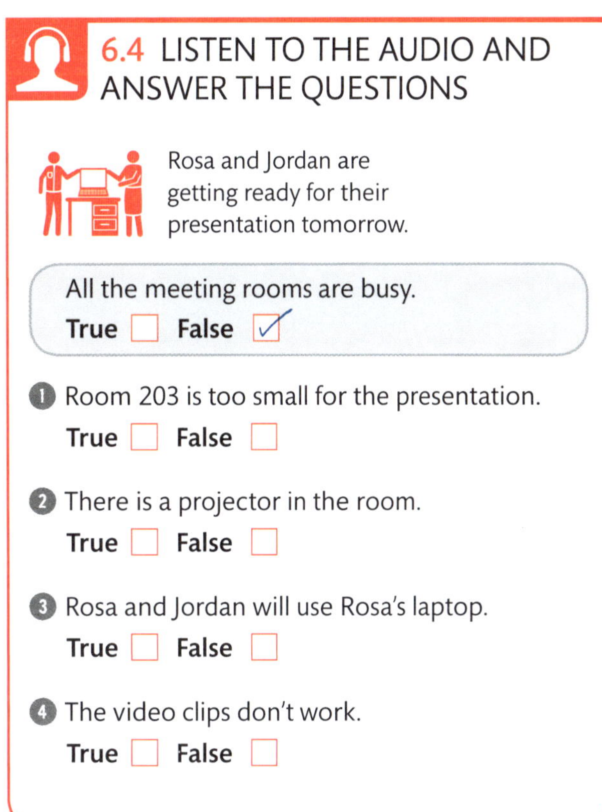

Rosa and Jordan are getting ready for their presentation tomorrow.

All the meeting rooms are busy.
True ☐ False ☑

1. Room 203 is too small for the presentation.
True ☐ False ☐
2. There is a projector in the room.
True ☐ False ☐
3. Rosa and Jordan will use Rosa's laptop.
True ☐ False ☐
4. The video clips don't work.
True ☐ False ☐

6.5 MATCH THE SITUATIONS TO THE CORRECT QUESTIONS

	I need to print this report. → Is the printer working today?	Do you want tea or coffee?
1	We've run out of pens.	Do you know her phone number?
2	I'm going to make some hot drinks.	Is the printer working today?
3	I need to call Paola.	Do you have a laptop I can take home?
4	We should talk to our clients soon.	Is the stationery cabinet open?
5	I want to work from home tomorrow.	Are there any envelopes I can use?
6	You want to see a doctor.	Are they free for a meeting tomorrow?
7	I want to send a letter.	Does he usually arrive late?
8	Henry should be here by now.	Do you have an appointment?

6.6 CROSS OUT THE INCORRECT WORD IN EACH QUESTION

Where / ~~Which~~ are you going on vacation?

1. How / Who does the scanner work?
2. What / When is on the agenda for the meeting?
3. Who / Why is the stationery cabinet locked?
4. Who / When do we have a break for lunch?
5. Where / What is the CEO's office?
6. When / What is the door code?
7. What / Who do I ask for ink for the printer?

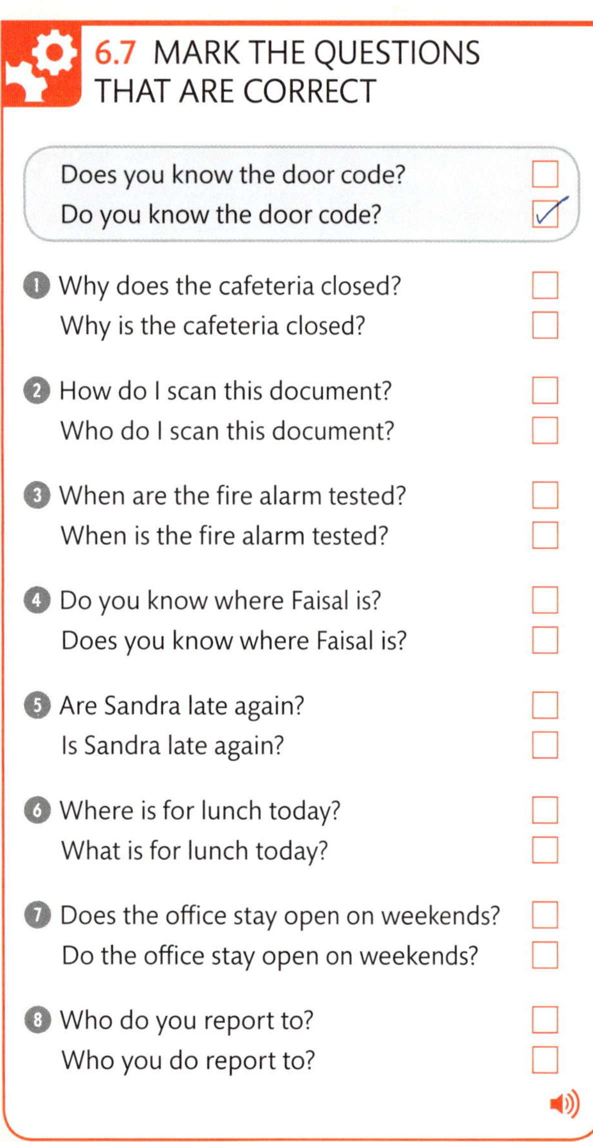

6.7 MARK THE QUESTIONS THAT ARE CORRECT

Does you know the door code? ☐
Do you know the door code? ☑

1. Why does the cafeteria closed? ☐
   Why is the cafeteria closed? ☐
2. How do I scan this document? ☐
   Who do I scan this document? ☐
3. When are the fire alarm tested? ☐
   When is the fire alarm tested? ☐
4. Do you know where Faisal is? ☐
   Does you know where Faisal is? ☐
5. Are Sandra late again? ☐
   Is Sandra late again? ☐
6. Where is for lunch today? ☐
   What is for lunch today? ☐
7. Does the office stay open on weekends? ☐
   Do the office stay open on weekends? ☐
8. Who do you report to? ☐
   Who you do report to? ☐

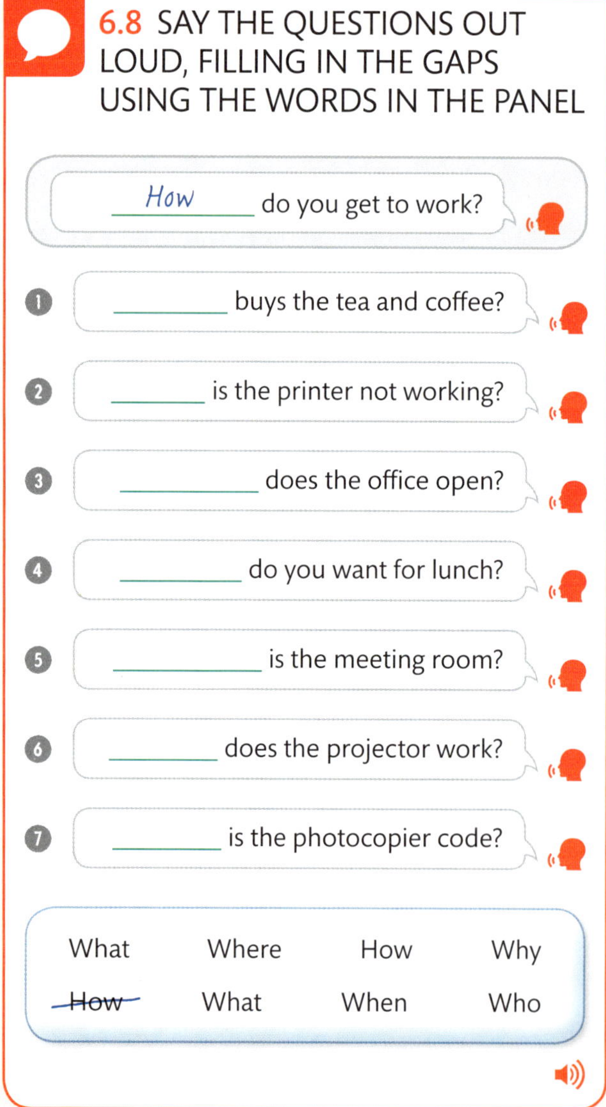

6.8 SAY THE QUESTIONS OUT LOUD, FILLING IN THE GAPS USING THE WORDS IN THE PANEL

How do you get to work?

1. ________ buys the tea and coffee?
2. ________ is the printer not working?
3. ________ does the office open?
4. ________ do you want for lunch?
5. ________ is the meeting room?
6. ________ does the projector work?
7. ________ is the photocopier code?

What	Where	How	Why
~~How~~	What	When	Who

07 Exchanging details

When making new business contacts, there are several phrases you can use to ask for their details and offer yours in return.

New language Short answers
Aa Vocabulary Contact information
New skill Exchanging contact details

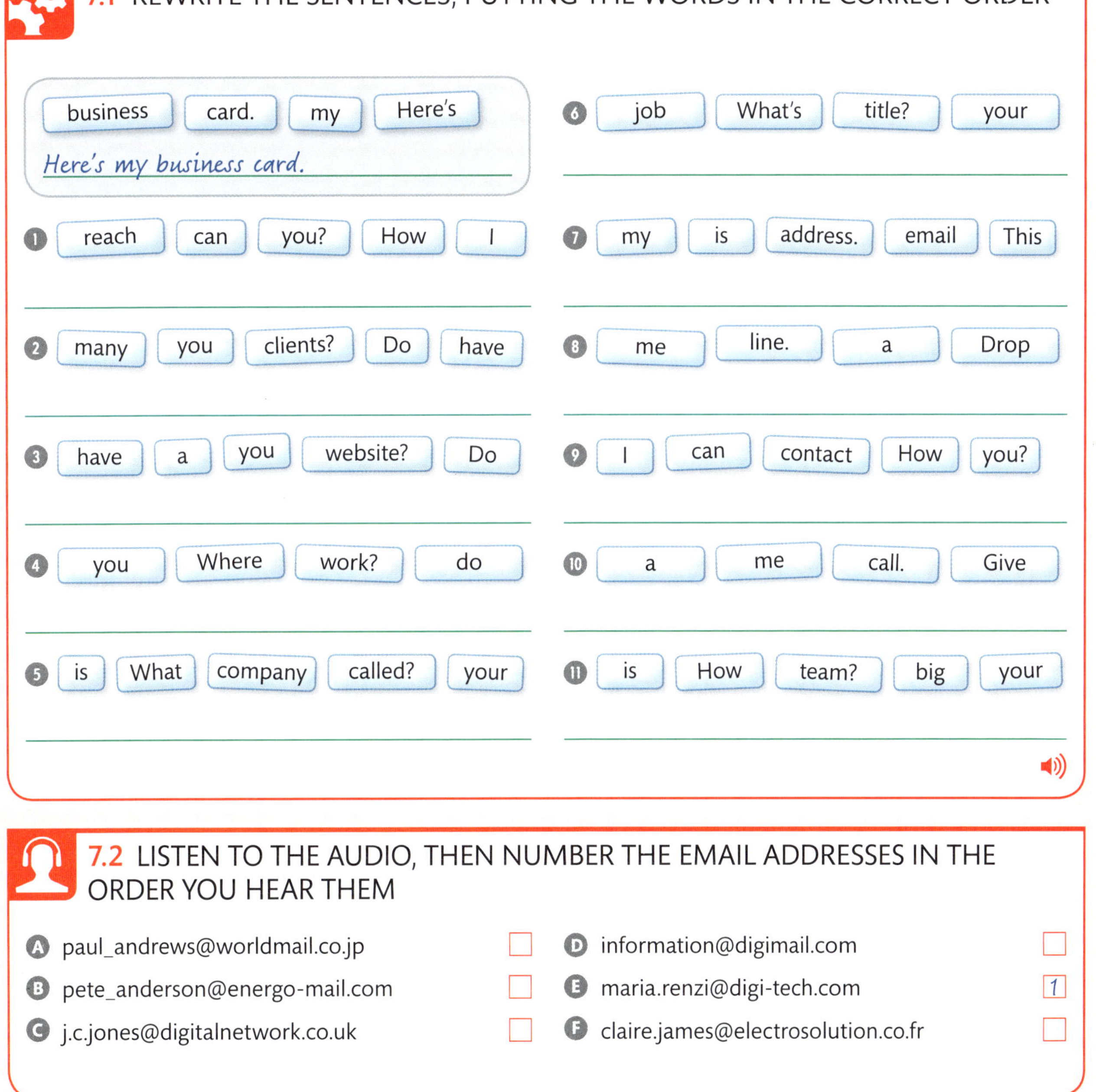

7.1 REWRITE THE SENTENCES, PUTTING THE WORDS IN THE CORRECT ORDER

business | card. | my | Here's

Here's my business card.

1. reach | can | you? | How | I

2. many | you | clients? | Do | have

3. have | a | you | website? | Do

4. you | Where | work? | do

5. is | What | company | called? | your

6. job | What's | title? | your

7. my | is | address. | email | This

8. me | line. | a | Drop

9. I | can | contact | How | you?

10. a | me | call. | Give

11. is | How | team? | big | your

7.2 LISTEN TO THE AUDIO, THEN NUMBER THE EMAIL ADDRESSES IN THE ORDER YOU HEAR THEM

A. paul_andrews@worldmail.co.jp ☐

B. pete_anderson@energo-mail.com ☐

C. j.c.jones@digitalnetwork.co.uk ☐

D. information@digimail.com ☐

E. maria.renzi@digi-tech.com *1*

F. claire.james@electrosolution.co.fr ☐

7.3 CROSS OUT THE INCORRECT WORD IN EACH SENTENCE

Do you have a ~~email~~ / business card?

1. How can I reach / touch you for more information?
2. Drop me a call / line when you're visiting next.
3. Does your company keep / have a website?
4. Please stay in reach / touch.
5. Is this your correct / precise phone number?
6. Line / Call me if you want further details.
7. Is this your present / current email address?
8. My job title / name is on the business card.
9. Do you have / got a portfolio with you?

7.4 LOOK AT THE BUSINESS CARDS AND ANSWER THE QUESTIONS

Stronger Web Solutions is a café.
True ☐ False ☑ Not given ☐

1. Janice Strong is a web designer.
True ☐ False ☐ Not given ☐
2. Stronger Web Solutions has a website.
True ☐ False ☐ Not given ☐
3. Greybridge History Museum is 100 years old.
True ☐ False ☐ Not given ☐
4. Dan has a website.
True ☐ False ☐ Not given ☐
5. Dan works as an archaeologist.
True ☐ False ☐ Not given ☐
6. Dan has an email address.
True ☐ False ☐ Not given ☐
7. Paul is a web designer.
True ☐ False ☐ Not given ☐
8. Consoul is based in Los Angeles.
True ☐ False ☐ Not given ☐

Janice Strong
Web Designer
www.strongerweb.com
STRONGER WEB SOLUTIONS
Tel: 1 (545) 345-2342
info@strongerweb.com

GREYBRIDGE HISTORY MUSEUM
Seal Street, Daltry, Hertfordshire, H23 9NB
Dan Stone – Historian
Email: dstone@greybridge.co.uk
Tel: 0743 235 436

CONSOUL
Managing consultant, ConSoul
CONSOUL
PAUL@CONSOUL.COM
07853453452
23 Garden Walk
Cambridge
C43 7FD

7.5 MATCH THE SENTENCES TO THE CORRECT SHORT ANSWERS

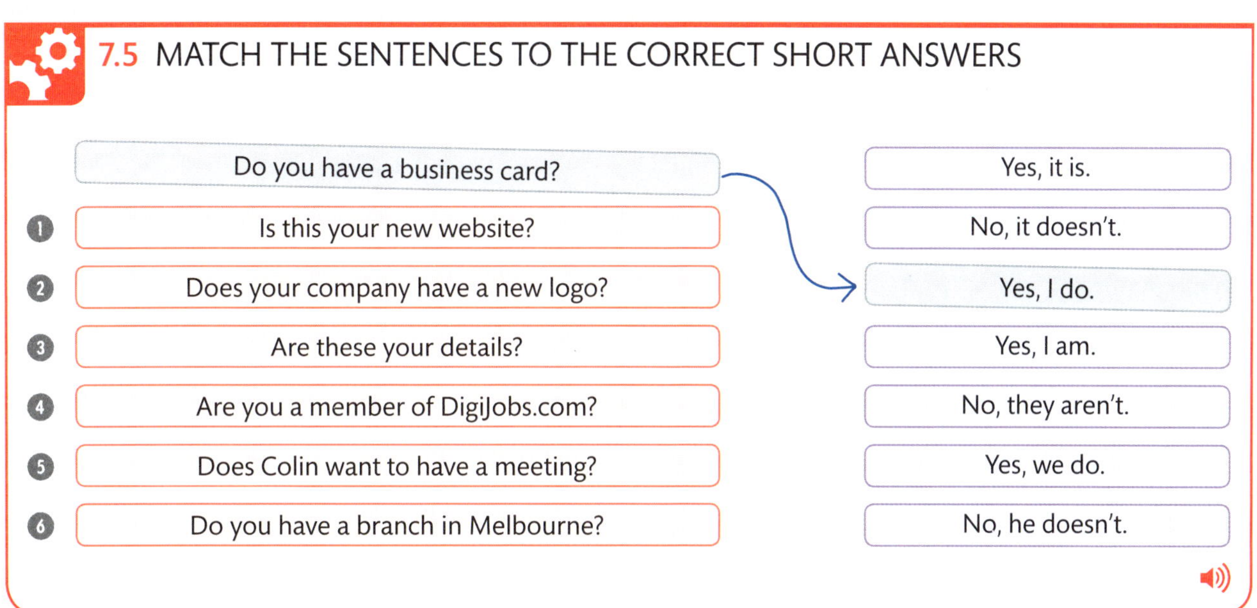

Do you have a business card? → Yes, I do.

1. Is this your new website?
2. Does your company have a new logo?
3. Are these your details?
4. Are you a member of DigiJobs.com?
5. Does Colin want to have a meeting?
6. Do you have a branch in Melbourne?

- Yes, it is.
- No, it doesn't.
- Yes, I do.
- Yes, I am.
- No, they aren't.
- Yes, we do.
- No, he doesn't.

7.6 RESPOND OUT LOUD TO THE AUDIO, FILLING IN THE GAPS

Do you have your portfolio?
No, *I don't*.

1. Is this your correct telephone number?
No, ______.

2. Does your company have a blog?
No, ______.

3. Is this your email address?
Yes, ______.

4. Does your company have a website?
Yes, ______.

5. Do your employees work hard?
No, ______.

6. Are you a member of a trade union?
No, ______.

7. Do they have a branch in Mumbai?
Yes, ______.

8. Does Mrs. Parry have an office?
Yes, ______.

9. Do you want to go for lunch now?
Yes, ______.

08 Skills and experience

English uses the verb "have" to talk about people's skills, experience, and professional attributes. You might also hear "have got" in informal UK English.

New language "Have," "have got," articles
Aa Vocabulary Jobs and skills
New skill Writing a business profile

8.1 CROSS OUT THE INCORRECT WORDS IN EACH SENTENCE

He doesn't **have** / ~~**has**~~ a typing qualification.

1. She **have** / **has** an excellent résumé.
2. I **has** / **have** good people skills.
3. They **don't have** / **don't got** much time.
4. Do you **has** / **have** previous experience?
5. He's **got** / **haves** excellent keyboard skills.
6. I **doesn't have** / **don't have** my own office.
7. Does he **have** / **got** any training?
8. They **having** / **have** a can-do outlook.
9. You don't **have** / **hasn't** his number, do you?

8.2 REWRITE THE SENTENCES, PUTTING THE WORDS IN THE CORRECT ORDER

he | experience | this | Has | for | got | job? | enough

Has he got enough experience for this job?

1. degree | you | in | have | business? | Do | higher | a

2. Business | has | He | the | MBA | School. | from | Boston | an

3. receptionist. | don't | a | full-time | have | They

4. excellent | have | assistant | Does | résumé? | an | your

8.3 READ THE ONLINE PROFILE AND ANSWER THE QUESTIONS

Hamid Syal

SALES AND MARKETING PROFESSIONAL

Experience

I am a creative and proactive marketing professional who has varied experience in the travel industry. I love helping people realize their dreams of visiting new places and devising new ways to market vacations. I started work in the hotel industry as a receptionist before working my way up to deputy manager. I have worked in countries such as Japan, India, and South Africa and for well-known, prestigious hotels such as The Ritz. I have a passion for travel and often visit new countries. My next vacation is to Tanzania, where I hope to go on safari.

Achievements

- Advising Explore the World travel agency on how to grow new markets and existing ones.
- Investigating and taking forward new business ideas, providing strategic recommendations to the SMT (Senior Management Team).
- Acting as the public-facing representative of Safari Travels, giving presentations at industry events.

Skills

I have excellent people skills, learned from my time in the hotel sector.
I enjoy working in teams to market vacations on behalf of a wide range of clients.

Qualifications

- BS Business and Hospitality Management, London South Bank University, 2010
- Diploma in Marketing, CIM (Chartered Institute of Marketing), 2015

What job does Hamid have? **He's a sales rep** ☐ **He's the CEO** ☐ **He works in marketing** ☑

1. What industry does Hamid work in? **Hotels** ☐ **Travel** ☐ **Airlines** ☐
2. Where has Hamid worked before? **A department store** ☐ **A restaurant** ☐ **A hotel** ☐
3. Who has Hamid advised on strategy? **Strategists** ☐ **Management** ☐ **The Chief Executive** ☐
4. How does Hamid describe his people skills? **Average** ☐ **Good** ☐ **Excellent** ☐
5. In what situation does Hamid say he enjoys working? **Alone** ☐ **In teams** ☐ **With clients** ☐
6. What is the subject of Hamid's diploma? **Business** ☐ **Marketing** ☐ **Hospitality Management** ☐

8.4 MARK THE SENTENCES THAT ARE CORRECT

I have excellent interpersonal skills. ☑
I have excellent the interpersonal skills. ☐

1 The new chef is very talented. ☐
A new chef is very talented. ☐

2 Toby is a accountant. ☐
Toby is an accountant. ☐

3 Search engines are invaluable. ☐
The search engines are invaluable. ☐

4 She works for a leading company. ☐
She works for leading company. ☐

5 Have you seen an ad I told you about? ☐
Have you seen the ad I told you about? ☐

6 They are out of office. ☐
They are out of the office. ☐

7 Did you see the new designs? ☐
Did you see a new designs? ☐

8 They hired best candidate. ☐
They hired the best candidate. ☐

9 What skills does the job require? ☐
What a skills does the job require? ☐

10 Is there an office in India? ☐
Is there a office in India? ☐

11 I have the certificate in sales. ☐
I have a certificate in sales. ☐

12 He works for a biggest store. ☐
He works for the biggest store. ☐

13 Interns are only paid expenses. ☐
Interns are only paid the expenses. ☐

8.5 FILL IN THE GAPS USING "A," "AN," OR "THE"

He works in ___a___ phone store.

1 I worked as ______ intern at Beales.

2 I know ______ café you mean.

3 There's ______ printer on the second floor.

4 Jon hasn't got ______ diploma.

5 The CEO is in ______ NY office this week.

6 He's ______ amazing architect.

7 I just started ______ new job.

8 I'd like to put ______ ad in the paper.

9 Have you read ______ job description?

10 I work at ______ theater next door.

11 ______ new café does great coffee.

12 Where is ______ presentation?

13 The Tate is ______ art gallery.

14 I like ______ new CEO.

8.6 LISTEN TO THE AUDIO, THEN NUMBER THE PICTURES IN THE ORDER THEY ARE DESCRIBED

A ☐

B 1

C ☐

D ☐

E ☐

F ☐

G ☐

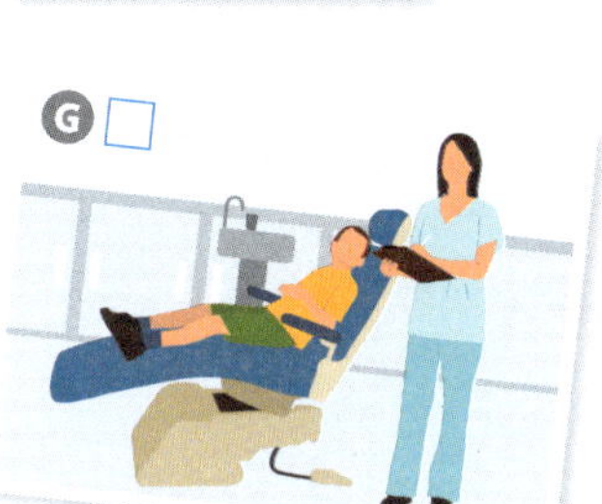

H ☐

8.7 SAY THE SENTENCES OUT LOUD, CORRECTING THE ERRORS

A receptionist here is friendly.

The receptionist here is friendly.

1. I've got a three years' experience.

2. I don't have the degree in business studies.

3. He has an diploma in economics.

4. I saw a ad in The Echo.

5. She has a excellent phone manner.

6. He works in hospital.

7. I don't like the interviews.

8. An agency is in the market place.

9. We are looking for a sales people.

09 Vocabulary

Aa 9.1 **JOBS** WRITE THE WORDS FROM THE PANEL UNDER THE CORRECT PICTURES

gardener

1 ______

2 ______

3 ______

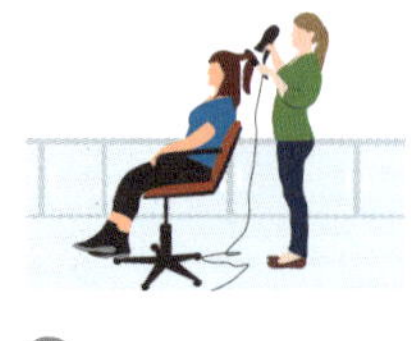

4 ______

7 ______

8 ______

9 ______

10 ______

11 ______

14 ______

15 ______

16 ______

17 ______

18 ______

21 ______

22 ______

23 ______

24 ______

25 ______

tour guide · judge · musician · sales assistant · cleaner / janitor · mechanic

vet · surgeon · ~~gardener~~ · artist · firefighter · librarian · designer

waitress · pilot · travel agent · hairdresser / stylist · electrician · doctor · train driver

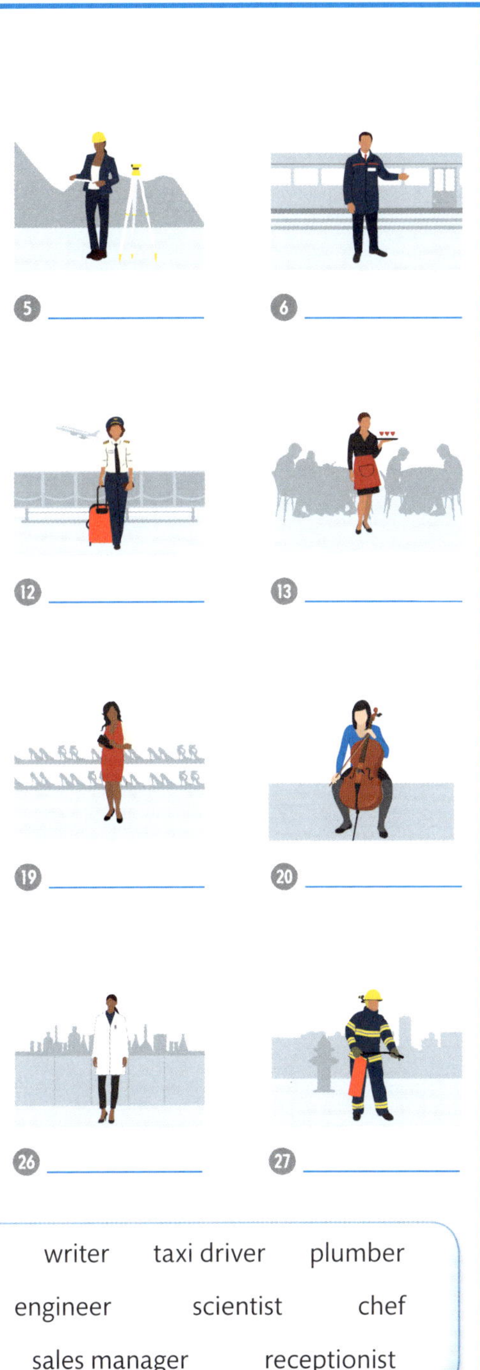

writer taxi driver plumber
engineer scientist chef
sales manager receptionist

Aa 9.2 **EMPLOYMENT** WRITE THE WORDS FROM THE PANEL UNDER THE CORRECT DEFINITIONS

A long-term, salaried position

permanent

1. A period of work with a set number of hours

2. A person who is learning a trade

3. A complete working week

4. A short-term position with a known end date

5. A person you work with in a profession

6. An incomplete working week

part-time (P/T) shift ~~permanent~~ temporary
co-worker / colleague apprentice full-time (F/T)

10 Choosing a job

Verbs such as "like," "enjoy," and "hate" express feelings about things. They are often used to talk about what activities people would like to do in a job.

New language "Like," "enjoy," and "hate"
Vocabulary Workplace activities
New skill Finding the right job

10.1 MATCH THE SENTENCES THAT GO TOGETHER

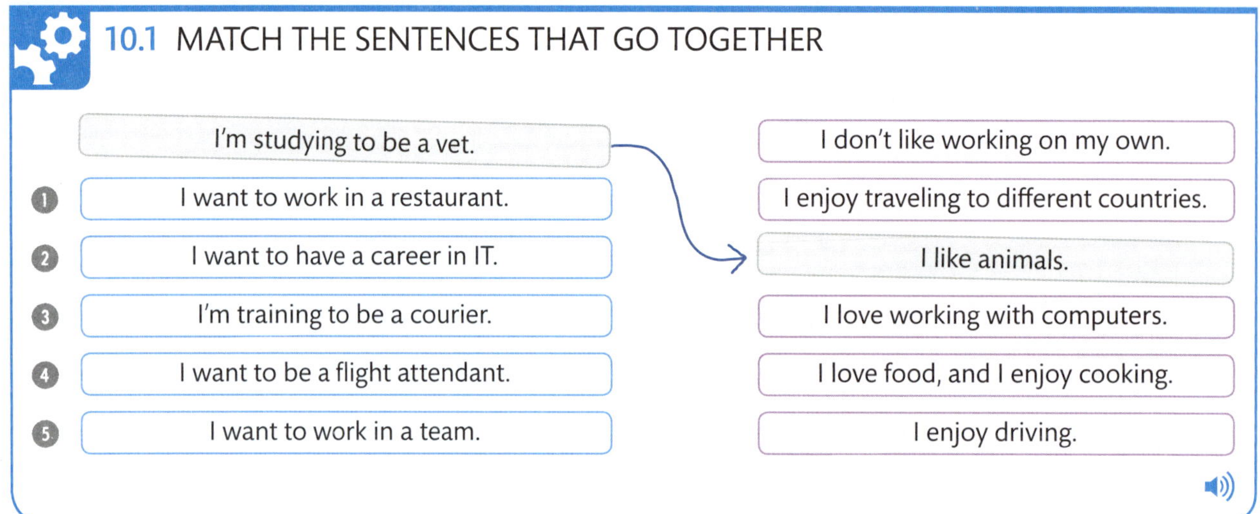

10.2 REWRITE THE SENTENCES, CORRECTING THE ERRORS

I like **work** outdoors.
I like working outdoors.

1. She loves **meet** new clients.
2. He **don't** enjoy giving presentations.
3. I hate **trained** big groups.
4. They like **work** in a team.
5. Jan **enjoy** working with children.
6. Ali doesn't **likes** long meetings.
7. We don't **liked** working weekends.
8. I love **solve** problems.
9. Jim doesn't **enjoying** business trips.

10.3 LISTEN TO THE AUDIO, AND MARK WHETHER THE SPEAKER LIKES OR DISLIKES THE ACTIVITY IN EACH PICTURE

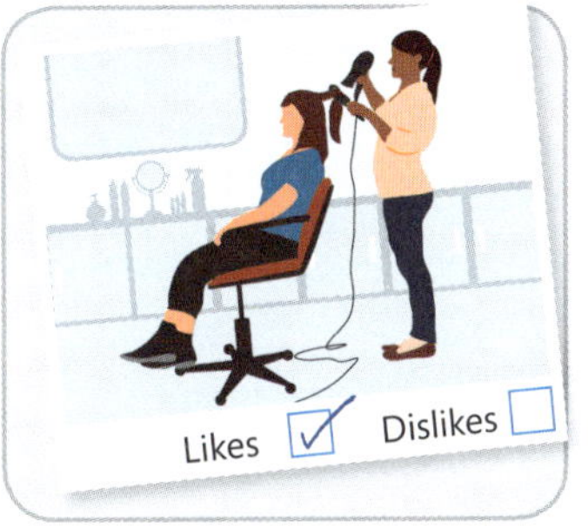

Likes ☑ Dislikes ☐

1 Likes ☐ Dislikes ☐

2 Likes ☐ Dislikes ☐

3 Likes ☐ Dislikes ☐

4 Likes ☐ Dislikes ☐

5 Likes ☐ Dislikes ☐

6 Likes ☐ Dislikes ☐

7 Likes ☐ Dislikes ☐

10.4 CROSS OUT THE INCORRECT WORD IN EACH SENTENCE, THEN SAY THE SENTENCES OUT LOUD

Does he like working / ~~work~~ weekends?

1. I don't / doesn't enjoy work social trips.
2. They like meet / meeting new people.
3. He doesn't like / likes working late.
4. She hates sitting / siting at a desk all day.
5. Do you enjoy work / working in a team?
6. We enjoy give / giving presentations.
7. Angus doesn't like use / using computers.

11 Describing your workplace

One way of telling people about your company is by using "there is" and "there are." Use "Is there...?" or "Are there...?" to ask questions about a workplace.

New language "There is" and "there are"
Aa Vocabulary Office equipment
New skill Describing a workplace

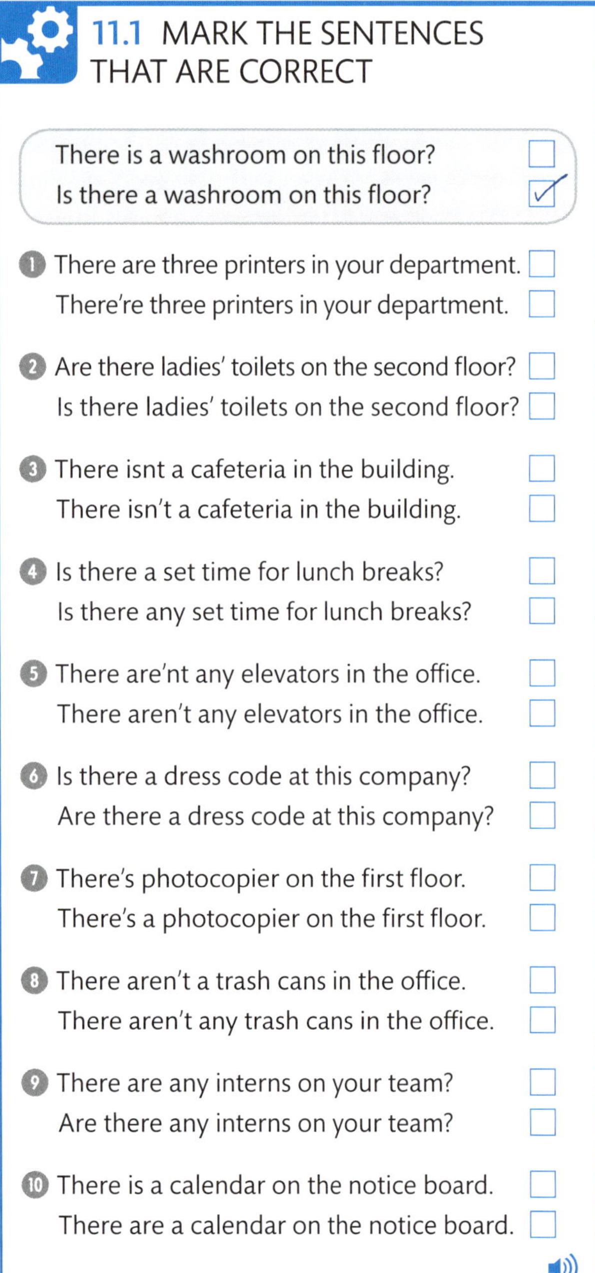

11.1 MARK THE SENTENCES THAT ARE CORRECT

There is a washroom on this floor? ☐
Is there a washroom on this floor? ☑

1. There are three printers in your department. ☐
   There're three printers in your department. ☐
2. Are there ladies' toilets on the second floor? ☐
   Is there ladies' toilets on the second floor? ☐
3. There isnt a cafeteria in the building. ☐
   There isn't a cafeteria in the building. ☐
4. Is there a set time for lunch breaks? ☐
   Is there any set time for lunch breaks? ☐
5. There are'nt any elevators in the office. ☐
   There aren't any elevators in the office. ☐
6. Is there a dress code at this company? ☐
   Are there a dress code at this company? ☐
7. There's photocopier on the first floor. ☐
   There's a photocopier on the first floor. ☐
8. There aren't a trash cans in the office. ☐
   There aren't any trash cans in the office. ☐
9. There are any interns on your team? ☐
   Are there any interns on your team? ☐
10. There is a calendar on the notice board. ☐
    There are a calendar on the notice board. ☐

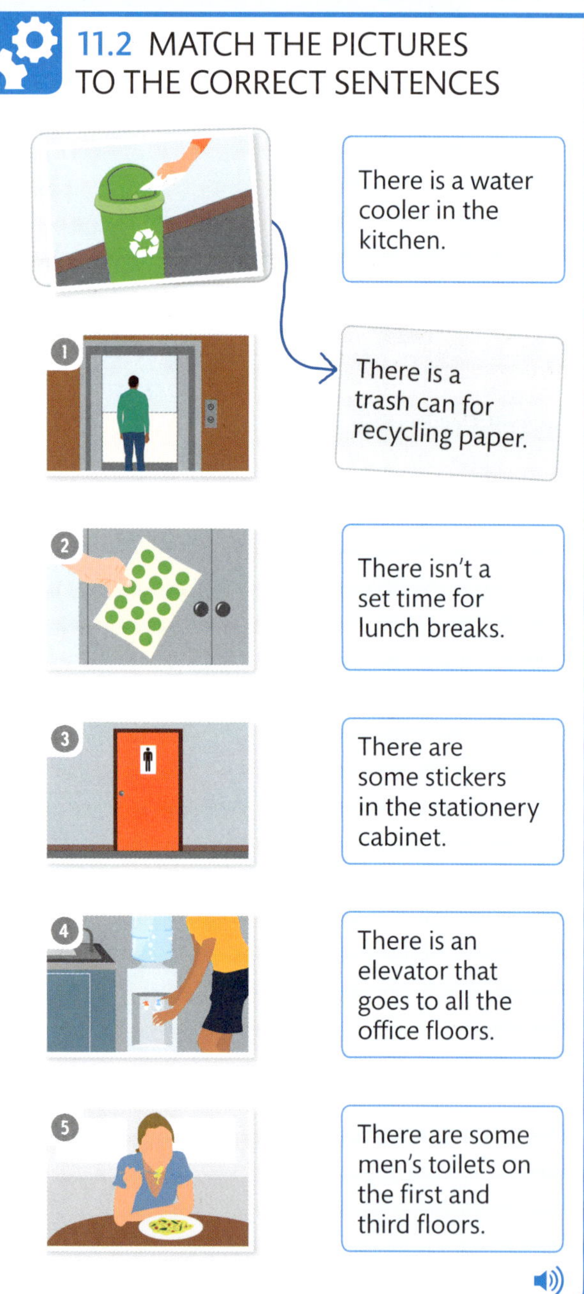

11.2 MATCH THE PICTURES TO THE CORRECT SENTENCES

There is a water cooler in the kitchen.

There is a trash can for recycling paper.

There isn't a set time for lunch breaks.

There are some stickers in the stationery cabinet.

There is an elevator that goes to all the office floors.

There are some men's toilets on the first and third floors.

11.3 LISTEN TO THE AUDIO AND ANSWER THE QUESTIONS

Debbie is telling Boris about her first day at her new job.

There are five people on Debbie's team.
True ☑ **False** ☐ **Not given** ☐

1. There is an elevator in Debbie's office.
True ☐ **False** ☐ **Not given** ☐

2. There isn't a separate office for Debbie's team.
True ☐ **False** ☐ **Not given** ☐

3. Debbie's office is on the third floor.
True ☐ **False** ☐ **Not given** ☐

4. There is a printer in Debbie's office.
True ☐ **False** ☐ **Not given** ☐

5. There is a casual dress code.
True ☐ **False** ☐ **Not given** ☐

6. There's a deli near the office.
True ☐ **False** ☐ **Not given** ☐

11.4 CROSS OUT THE INCORRECT WORD IN EACH SENTENCE, THEN SAY THE SENTENCES OUT LOUD

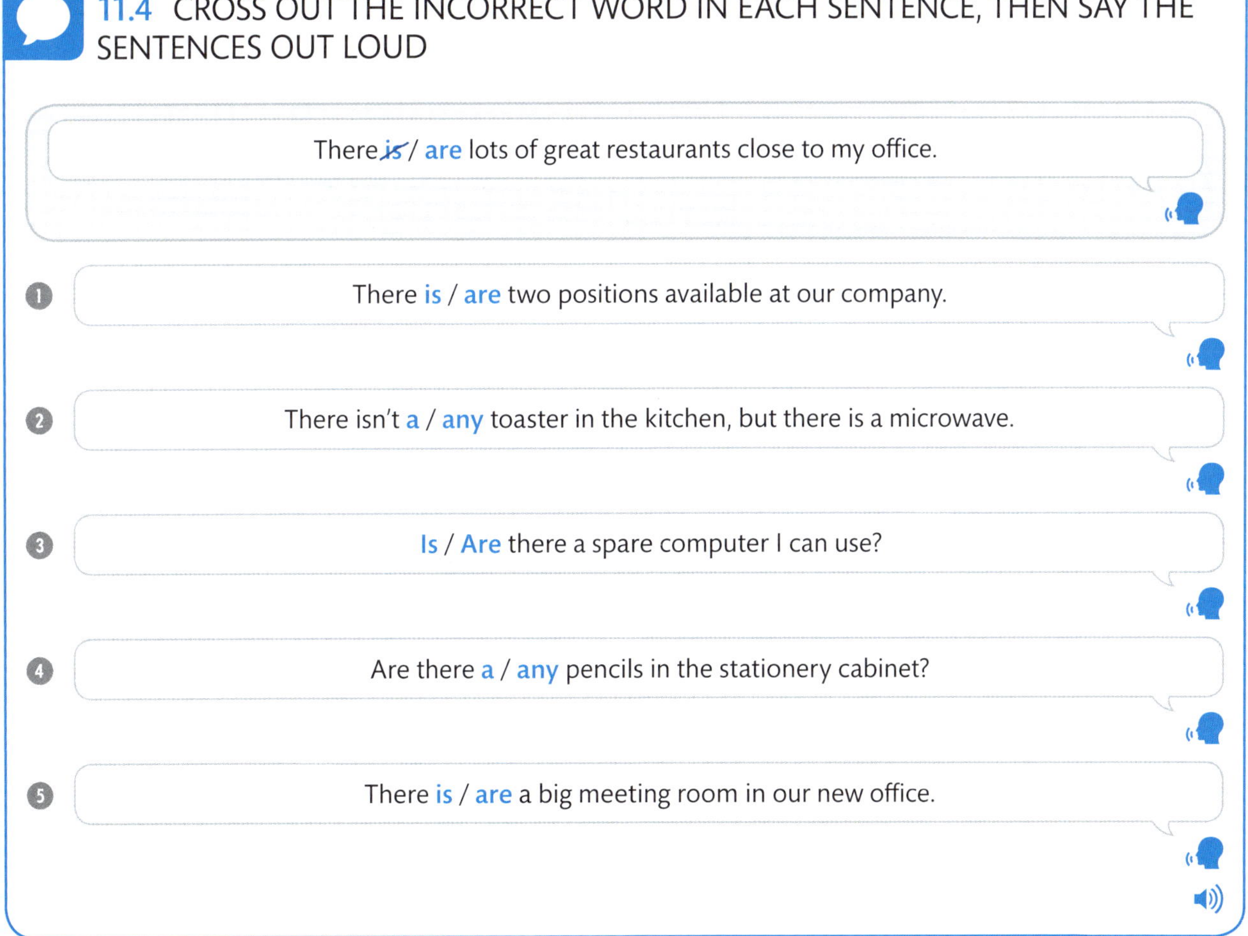

There ~~is~~ / are lots of great restaurants close to my office.

1. There is / are two positions available at our company.

2. There isn't a / any toaster in the kitchen, but there is a microwave.

3. Is / Are there a spare computer I can use?

4. Are there a / any pencils in the stationery cabinet?

5. There is / are a big meeting room in our new office.

12 Vocabulary

Aa 12.1 **MONEY** WRITE THE WORDS FROM THE PANEL UNDER THE CORRECT PICTURES

debit card

1 ______

2 ______

3 ______

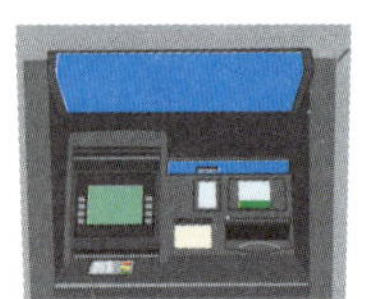

4 ______

5 ______

6 ______

7 ______

8 ______

9 ______

10 ______

11 ______

12 ______

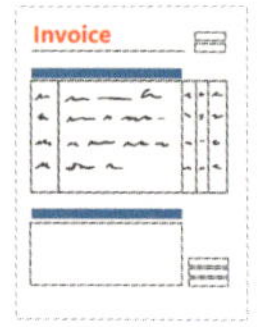

13 ______

14 ______

15 ______

currency	credit card	receipt	cash register (US) / till (UK)	~~debit card~~	bank
bills (US) / notes (UK)	invoice	cash machine / ATM	wallet	withdraw money	
check (US) / cheque (UK)	online banking	safe	mobile banking	transfer money	

Aa 12.2 **PAY AND CONDITIONS** WRITE THE WORDS FROM THE PANEL UNDER THE CORRECT DEFINITIONS

The amount of money paid per week or month

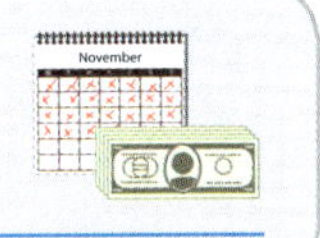

wage

❶ Additional pay for extra hours worked

______

❷ A fixed, regular payment every month, often expressed as an annual sum

______

❸ Extras given to employees in addition to their usual pay

______

❹ An increase in pay

______

❺ To receive money in return for labor or services

______

❻ Money added to a person's wages as a reward for good performance

______

❼ Paid time off work granted by employers

______

❽ The amount of money paid per hour

______

❾ A reduction in pay

______

a bonus | salary | annual vacation (US) / annual leave (UK) | a pay cut | ~~wage~~

to earn | hourly rate | overtime | a raise (US) / a pay rise (UK) | benefits

13 Personal qualities

You will encounter people with different skills and personalities at work. It is useful to be able to describe your co-workers and discuss their strengths and weaknesses.

New language Possessive adjectives
Aa Vocabulary Personality traits
New skill Describing your co-workers

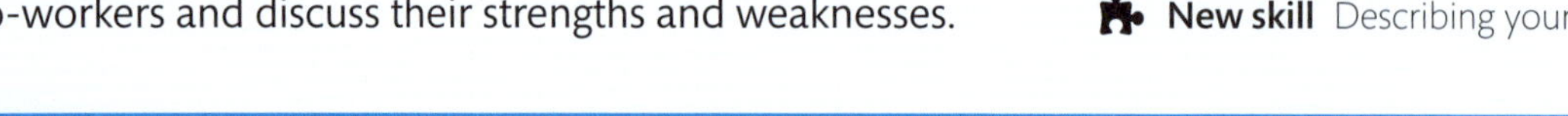

13.1 REWRITE THE SENTENCES, CORRECTING THE ERRORS

I run a team great, but Kezia be really lazy.
I run a great team, but Kezia is really lazy.

1. The new intern seems really bright and she is organized very.

2. My manager doesn't ask employees nervous to give presentations.

3. My director very bossy is and she is also hardworking.

4. Sue and Robin are sometimes rudes to our clients.

5. It's important to stay under pressure calm, even if you're very busy.

6. Mushira is very intelligente, and she will bring a great deal to the team.

7. It's impossible to feel relaxed when you work with people impatient.

8. The people on my team are all very motivateds, and it's great to work with them.

9. We are looking for a designer creative to join our busy production team.

13.2 REWRITE THE SENTENCES, PUTTING THE WORDS IN THE CORRECT ORDER

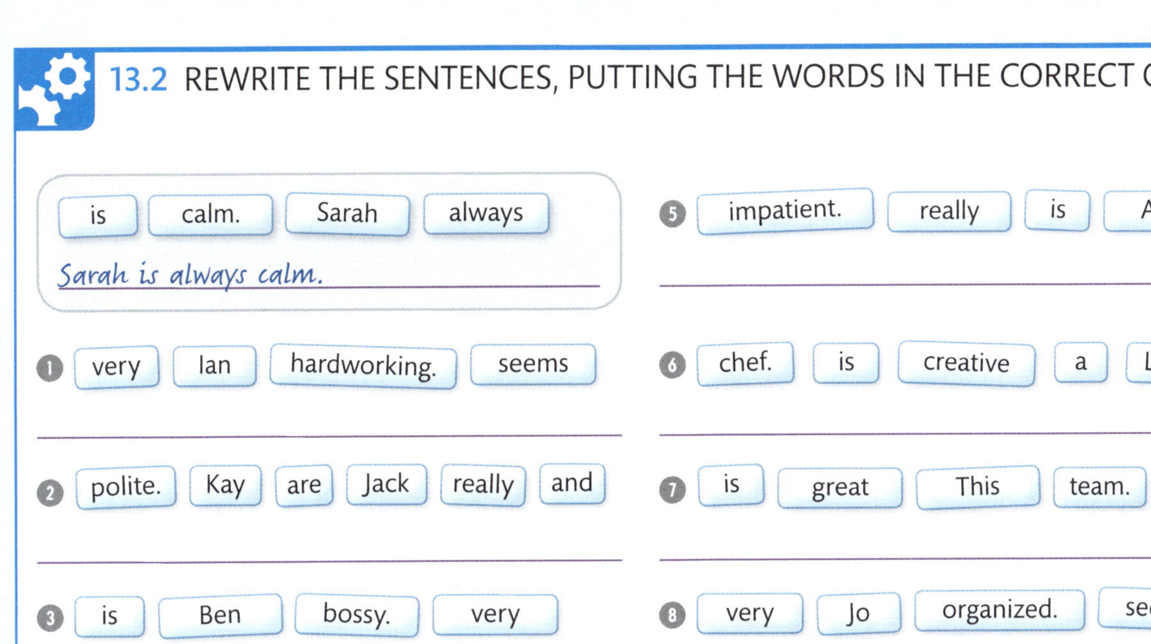

is | calm. | Sarah | always

Sarah is always calm.

1. very | Ian | hardworking. | seems

2. polite. | Kay | are | Jack | really | and

3. is | Ben | bossy. | very

4. always | Diane | dressed. | well | looks

5. impatient. | really | is | Alex

6. chef. | is | creative | a | Lenny

7. is | great | This | team. | a

8. very | Jo | organized. | seems

9. bright. | very | seems | Harry

13.3 LISTEN TO THE AUDIO AND MATCH THE PERSON IN EACH PICTURE WITH THE CORRECT ADJECTIVE

1  2  3  4

organized | polite | calm | well dressed | creative

13.4 FILL IN THE GAPS BY TURNING THE SUBJECT PRONOUNS INTO POSSESSIVE ADJECTIVES

James is very hardworking. *His* (He) list of things to do is very long.

1. ______ (We) team meetings are always interesting.
2. Is this ______ (you) desk? It's very messy!
3. ______ (I) team is very motivated.
4. Is that ______ (they) design? It's great.
5. Kevin is talking to ______ (he) manager.
6. That's Tanya. ______ (She) phone manner is excellent.
7. The company is very proud of ______ (it) reputation.

13.5 CROSS OUT THE INCORRECT WORD IN EACH SENTENCE

This laptop is ~~my~~ / mine.

1. Is this he / his desk?
2. We don't like theirs / their product.
3. My / Mine manager is very smart.
4. This report is your / yours.
5. Jane does her / hers job well.
6. They are proud of their / theirs reputation.
7. Is this tablet her / hers?
8. Their / Theirs manager is never late.
9. Is this your / yours pen?

13.6 MARK THE SENTENCES THAT ARE CORRECT

Toms secretary will take the minutes. ☐
Tom's secretary will take the minutes. ☑

1. The interns have just finished college. ☐
   The intern's have just finished college. ☐
2. Jorges reputation is well deserved. ☐
   Jorge's reputation is well deserved. ☐
3. Nuala's assistant is very helpful. ☐
   Nualas assistant is very helpful. ☐
4. Helens manager often works late. ☐
   Helen's manager often works late. ☐
5. Maria's co-workers are really friendly. ☐
   Marias co-workers are really friendly. ☐
6. The team members' are hardworking. ☐
   The team members are hardworking. ☐
7. Look at this ad. I like it's design. ☐
   Look at this ad. I like its design. ☐
8. Leroy's work is very impressive. ☐
   Leroys' work is very impressive. ☐
9. Are there any file's in the cabinet? ☐
   Are there any files in the cabinet? ☐
10. Johns confidence has grown this year. ☐
    John's confidence has grown this year. ☐
11. Sams' presentation went really well. ☐
    Sam's presentation went really well. ☐
12. The CEO's new assistant is very bright. ☐
    The CEOs' new assistant is very bright. ☐
13. Their products are very popular. ☐
    Their product's are very popular. ☐
14. That's my bosses parking space. ☐
    That's my boss's parking space. ☐
15. Pablo's report is almost finished. ☐
    Pablos report is almost finished. ☐
16. The company is pleased with it's new logo. ☐
    The company is pleased with its new logo. ☐
17. Ethans' team is working on a new project. ☐
    Ethan's team is working on a new project. ☐

13.7 USE THE CHART TO CREATE 14 CORRECT SENTENCES AND SAY THEM OUT LOUD

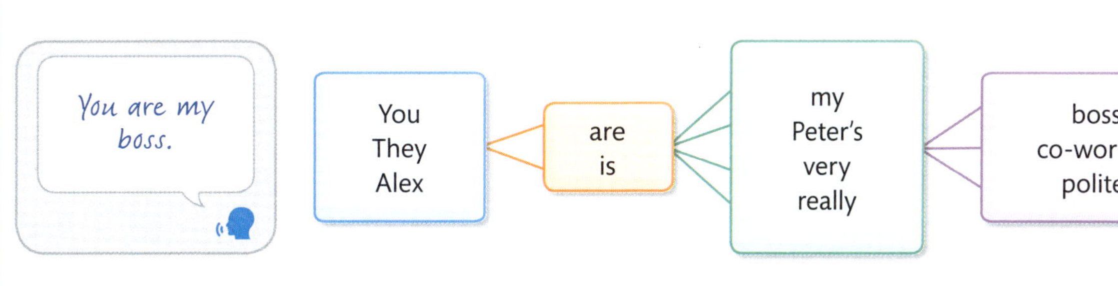

14 Describing your job

One way of telling someone about your job is to use adjectives to describe it. Adjectives can also help you to make comparisons with other roles you have had.

New language Adjectives and comparatives
Aa Vocabulary Money and pay
New skill Describing your job to someone

14.1 CROSS OUT THE INCORRECT WORD IN EACH SENTENCE

Sean has a very ~~interested~~ / interesting proposal.

1. Vihaan is very satisfied / satisfying with his office.
2. The new login system is rather annoyed / annoying.
3. The quarterly results are shocked / shocking.
4. The economic situation is quite worried / worrying.
5. We're excited / exciting about the new office.
6. Simone was tired / tiring after the course.
7. The profits were disappointed / disappointing.
8. John is confused / confusing about the schedule.
9. We were surprised / surprising by the results.
10. We thought the meeting was bored / boring.
11. I'm often exhausted / exhausting by Friday.

Aa 14.2 MATCH THE DEFINITIONS TO THE ADJECTIVES

very tired → exhausted

1. something that is not interesting
2. unable to understand or think clearly
3. something that gives you enthusiasm
4. something that is irritating
5. something that is not expected
6. something you want to know more about
7. sad that something is not as good as expected
8. concerned or anxious about something

- boring
- surprising
- exhausted
- worried
- interesting
- exciting
- annoying
- confused
- disappointed

14.3 FILL IN THE GAPS USING THE ADJECTIVES FROM THE PANEL AND THEIR COMPARATIVE FORMS

Jan is *excited* about the news, but is *more excited* about her promotion.

1. I am very ____________ with the new project, but I'll be even ____________ next week.
2. Our new office is ____________ , but the office in Beijing is ____________ .
3. My job is very ____________ , but being unemployed is ____________ .
4. The meeting was ____________ , but last week's was even ____________ .
5. John's flight ticket was ____________ , but mine was ____________ .
6. Our new photocopier is ____________ , but the HR department's is ____________ .
7. Claire's news was ____________ , but Peter resigning was ____________ .
8. My current job is ____________ , but my old one was ____________ .
9. The new furniture is ____________ , but the furniture at G-Tech is ____________ .
10. This test is ____________ , but the next one will be ____________ .
11. My commute is ____________ ; it's only 10 minutes. Pete's is even ____________ .

comfortable	stressful	interesting	expensive	difficult	large
long	fast	~~excited~~	surprising	short	busy

14.4 REWRITE THE SENTENCES USING THE COMPARATIVE FORM OF THE ADJECTIVE IN BRACKETS

This contract is **(good)** than the old one.

This contract is better than the old one.

1. Your printer is **(quick)** than ours.

2. Today's meeting was **(interesting)** than usual.

3. Growth was **(bad)** than we had expected.

4. Sandra has been **(successful)** than last year.

5. I'm feeling **(good)** after a week off work.

6. There is **(little)** juice left than I thought.

7. My new apartment is **(close)** to the center.

8. The results are **(good)** than in the first quarter.

9. We have an **(early)** start than usual today.

10. Liam has taken a much **(late)** lunch break than everyone else.

11. This restaurant is **(bad)** than the others.

12. The flight was **(expensive)** than I expected.

14.5 MATCH THE BEGINNINGS OF THE SENTENCES TO THE CORRECT ENDINGS

	The new computer system	more helpful than the old one.
1	The new intern is	faster than the old ones.
2	Our hours are longer	is more efficient than the last one.
3	The new computers are	now that I have a new job.
4	I feel better	than those in the German branch.
5	Our new office design	are more expensive than they used to be.
6	The tickets	is more modern than the previous one.
7	My raise was	more interesting than last year.
8	My training this year was	since we merged with our competitors.
9	The office is busier	smaller than last year's.

14.6 LISTEN TO THE AUDIO AND ANSWER THE QUESTIONS

Anne and Patrick are talking about the new office they've just moved to.

Patrick says the new office is more modern.
True ☑ **False** ☐ **Not given** ☐

1. He thinks the old office was more comfortable.
True ☐ **False** ☐ **Not given** ☐

2. He says the new computers are faster.
True ☐ **False** ☐ **Not given** ☐

3. He says the software is more complicated.
True ☐ **False** ☐ **Not given** ☐

4. Patrick likes the new café in the building.
True ☐ **False** ☐ **Not given** ☐

5. He says the building is closer to his apartment.
True ☐ **False** ☐ **Not given** ☐

6. He travels to work on the train.
True ☐ **False** ☐ **Not given** ☐

7. Patrick is going to a Chinese restaurant for lunch.
True ☐ **False** ☐ **Not given** ☐

8. Anne has been to the restaurant before.
True ☐ **False** ☐ **Not given** ☐

15 Workplace routines

Employees have schedules, and workplaces also have their own routines and timetables. It is useful to be able to talk to colleagues about when things usually happen.

New language Prepositions of time
Aa Vocabulary Commuting and transportation
New skill Describing routines

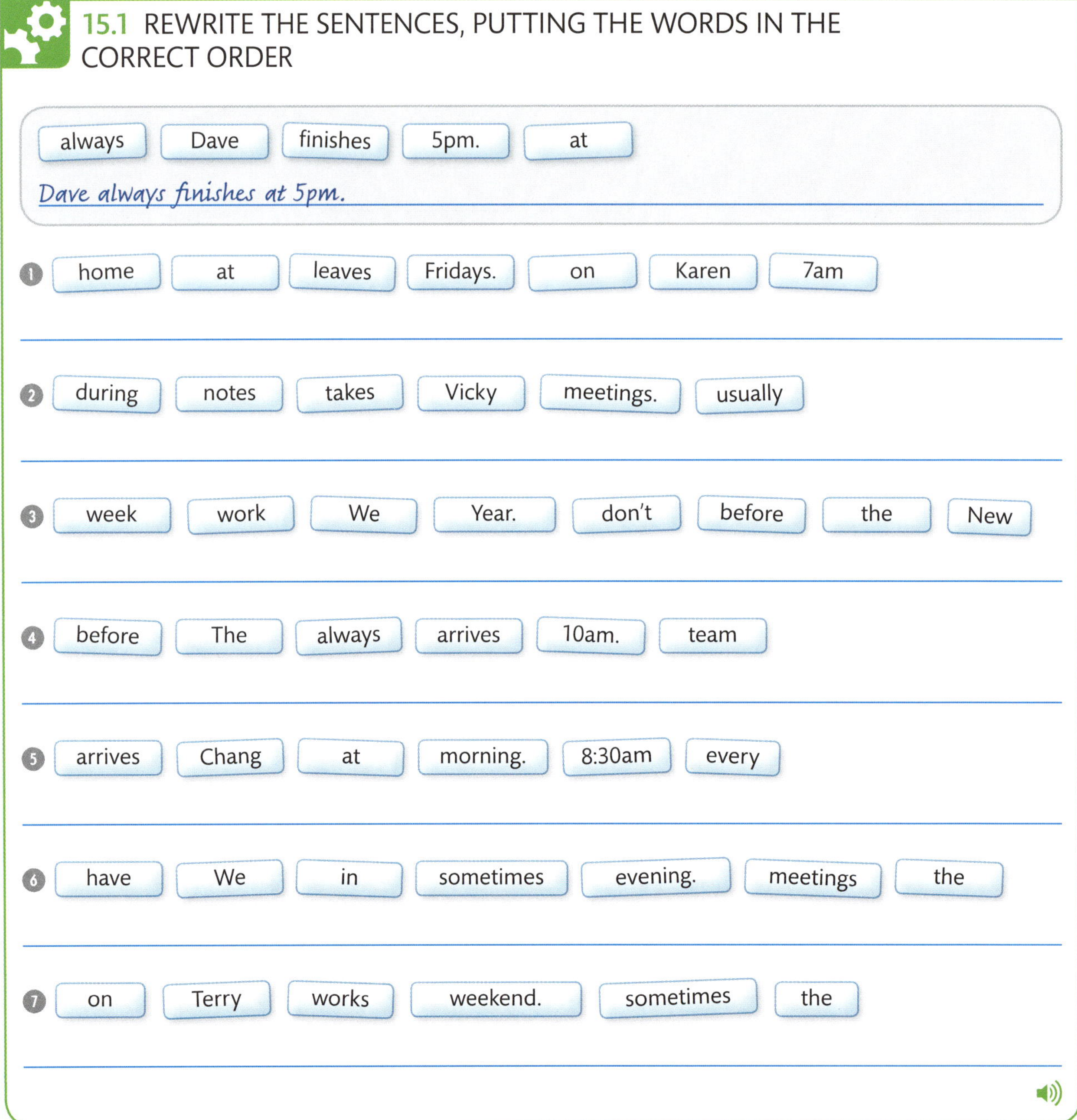

15.1 REWRITE THE SENTENCES, PUTTING THE WORDS IN THE CORRECT ORDER

always | Dave | finishes | 5pm. | at

Dave always finishes at 5pm.

1 home | at | leaves | Fridays. | on | Karen | 7am

2 during | notes | takes | Vicky | meetings. | usually

3 week | work | We | Year. | don't | before | the | New

4 before | The | always | arrives | 10am. | team

5 arrives | Chang | at | morning. | 8:30am | every

6 have | We | in | sometimes | evening. | meetings | the

7 on | Terry | works | weekend. | sometimes | the

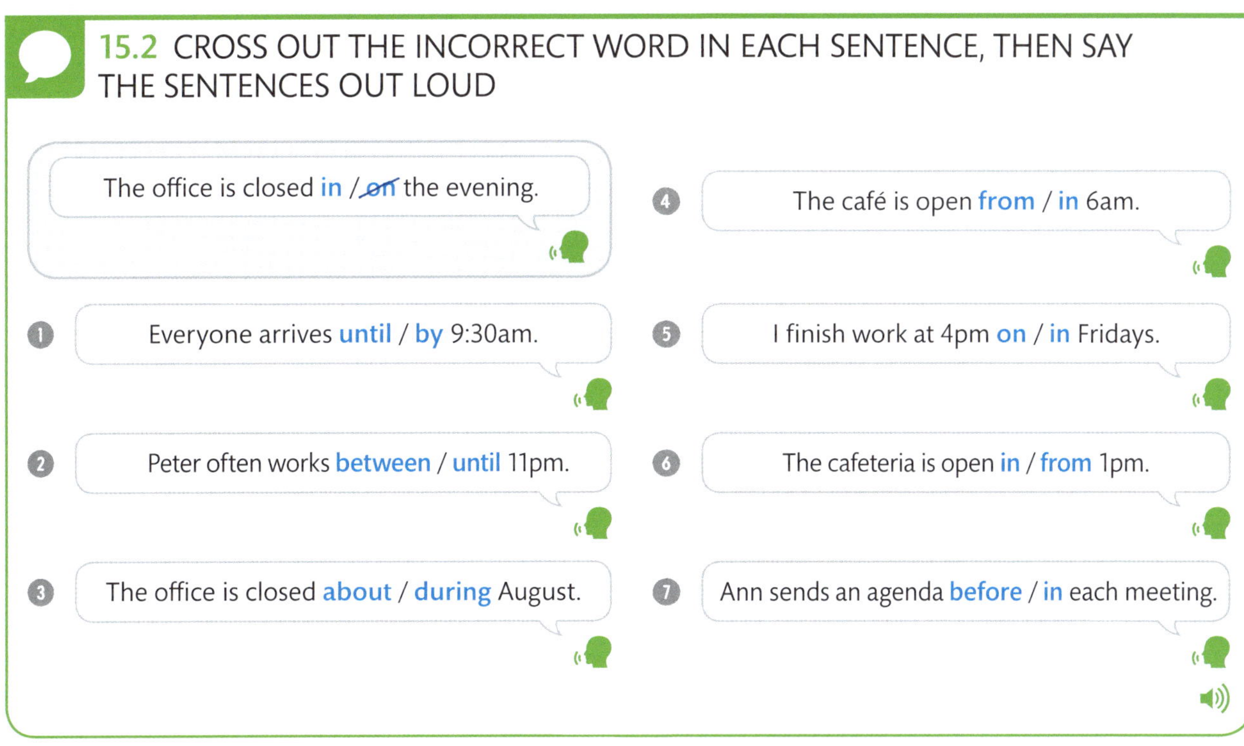

15.2 CROSS OUT THE INCORRECT WORD IN EACH SENTENCE, THEN SAY THE SENTENCES OUT LOUD

The office is closed in / ~~on~~ the evening.

1. Everyone arrives until / by 9:30am.
2. Peter often works between / until 11pm.
3. The office is closed about / during August.
4. The café is open from / in 6am.
5. I finish work at 4pm on / in Fridays.
6. The cafeteria is open in / from 1pm.
7. Ann sends an agenda before / in each meeting.

15.3 READ THE EMAIL AND ANSWER THE QUESTIONS

John lives...
in the city. ☐ **in the suburbs.** ☑ **in a village.** ☐

1. John leaves the house at...
7am. ☐ **8am.** ☐ **9am.** ☐

2. The commute takes...
10 minutes. ☐ **1 hour.** ☐ **30 minutes.** ☐

3. John starts work at...
9am. ☐ **8:30am.** ☐ **9am.** ☐

4. On Fridays, John finishes at...
12am. ☐ **2pm.** ☐ **4pm.** ☐

5. John drives to work...
sometimes. ☐ **every week.** ☐ **never.** ☐

6. There are fewer traffic jams in the...
morning. ☐ **afternoon.** ☐ **evening.** ☐

To: Andrew

Subject: Hello...

Hi Andrew,

It's great to hear from you! I have got quite a lot of news, too. Karen and I have just moved to a new house in the suburbs, so I have to commute to the center of town every day now. I leave the house at 7am, and take the bus at 7:20am. The commute takes about an hour, so it's quite a lot of traveling each day, but I don't mind. I start work at 8:30am and finish at 5pm, but on Friday I finish earlier, at 2pm. Sometimes I drive to work on Fridays because there aren't as many traffic jams in the afternoon.

You should come over and see us soon!

John

15.4 CROSS OUT THE INCORRECT WORD IN EACH SENTENCE

Sarah catches / ~~jumps~~ the bus near the park.

1. I drive because it's so comfortable / convenient.
2. Jim takes / drives the bus every morning.
3. Jack travels on / by bike when he can.
4. The rush / busy hour starts at 7am in my city.
5. Sam takes / makes the metro home each evening.
6. Raymond catches / drives his car to work.
7. I get on / in the bus near the museum.
8. I missed my connection / link.
9. Janet prefers to travel on / by train to work.
10. Karl takes / drives the bus home at night.
11. There are a lot of traffic blocks / jams in the city.
12. You should get off / from the tram at the library.
13. It's much cheaper to cycle / bike than drive.
14. I like to walk / walking to work in the summer.
15. I prefer to cycle / train to my office.

15.5 MARK THE SENTENCES THAT ARE CORRECT

I leave my house before 6am. ☑
I leave my house in front of 6am. ☐

1. I car to work. ☐
   I drive to work. ☐
2. We take the bus. ☐
   We make the bus. ☐
3. Doug catches his bike to work. ☐
   Doug rides his bike to work. ☐
4. I sometimes take a taxi home. ☐
   I sometimes drive a taxi home. ☐
5. The buses run from 5am to 11pm. ☐
   The buses run of 5am to 11pm. ☐
6. I go in train. ☐
   I go by train. ☐
7. The train arrives on 5pm. ☐
   The train arrives at 5pm. ☐
8. Sharon gets off the bus by the station. ☐
   Sharon gets from the bus by the station. ☐
9. I like to go home from work on foot. ☐
   I like to go home from work by foot. ☐
10. My train to work arrives on 7:45am. ☐
    My train to work arrives at 7:45am. ☐
11. Traveling by train is comfortable. ☐
    Traveling on train is comfortable. ☐
12. The train leaves at about 8pm. ☐
    The train leaves at near 8pm. ☐
13. I travel on train every day. ☐
    I travel by train every day. ☐

15.6 LISTEN TO THE AUDIO, THEN NUMBER THE PICTURES IN THE ORDER THEY ARE DESCRIBED

A 1

B

C

D

E

F

G

H

15.7 MATCH THE BEGINNINGS OF THE SENTENCES TO THE CORRECT ENDINGS

All the staff arrives → by 9:30am.

1. There aren't many buses
2. Hank takes the bus because
3. The office stays open
4. I leave for work
5. Sally often walks to work
6. I take the train to work because
7. Ted takes notes
8. I always go to bed

- on the weekend.
- by 9:30am.
- until 10 in the evening.
- during the summer.
- it's cheaper than the train.
- during meetings.
- between 7 and 8am.
- before 11pm.
- it's faster than the bus.

16 Vocabulary

16.1 DAYS OF THE WEEK WRITE THE WORDS FROM THE PANEL UNDER THE CORRECT PICTURES

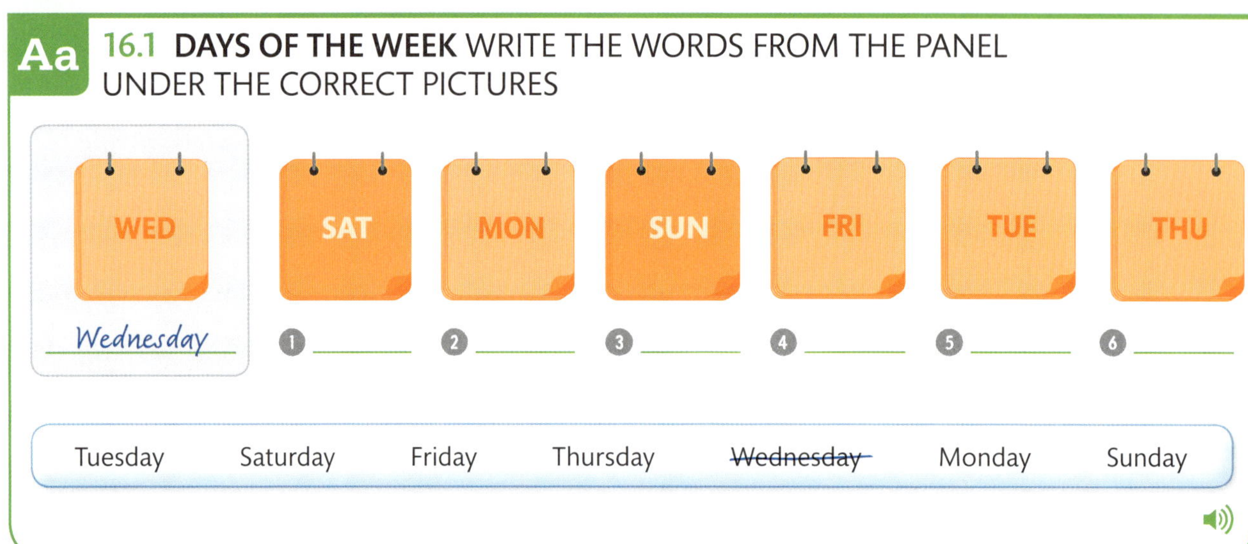

Wednesday

1 ______ 2 ______ 3 ______ 4 ______ 5 ______ 6 ______

Tuesday Saturday Friday Thursday ~~Wednesday~~ Monday Sunday

16.2 FREQUENCY PHRASES WRITE THE PHRASES FROM THE PANEL UNDER THE CORRECT PICTURES

quarterly

1  ______ 2  ______ 3  ______ 4 ______

5  ______ 6  ______ 7  ______ 8  ______ 9 ______

hourly ~~quarterly~~ monthly in the morning before work
in the afternoon in the evening daily three times a week after work

16.3 **FREE TIME** WRITE THE PHRASES FROM THE PANEL UNDER THE CORRECT PICTURES

go running

1 ____________

2 ____________

3 ____________

4 ____________

5 ____________

6 ____________

7 ____________

8 ____________

9 ____________

10 ____________

11 ____________

12 ____________

13 ____________

14 ____________

15 ____________

16 ____________

17 ____________

18 ____________

19 ____________

visit a museum / an art gallery | read | cook | meet friends | write | draw | watch a movie | go camping | take photos | see a play | go out for a meal | go cycling | play board games | do yoga | walk / hike | ~~go running~~ | go shopping | stay (at) home | play sports | play an instrument

17 Hobbies and habits

When talking with colleagues about your hobbies and habits, you may want to use adverbs of frequency to say how often you do the activities.

New language Adverbs of frequency
Aa Vocabulary Hobbies and habits
New skill Talking about free time

17.1 REWRITE THE SENTENCES, PUTTING THE WORDS IN THE CORRECT ORDER

visit | I | a | on | museum | Saturdays. | occasionally

I occasionally visit a museum on Saturdays.

1. often | We | weekend. | camping | the | go | on

2. he | after | meets | work. | Doug | friends | finishes | sometimes

3. running | I | the | in | always | morning. | go

4. My | television. | watches | father | never

5. local | She | a | sees | at | theater. | occasionally | our | play

6. he | Frank | rarely | lazy, | very | does | and | is | exercise. | any

7. sometimes | after | My | video | play | kids | school. | games

17.2 LISTEN TO THE AUDIO AND MATCH THE IMAGES TO THE CORRECT ADVERBS OF FREQUENCY

1

2

3

4

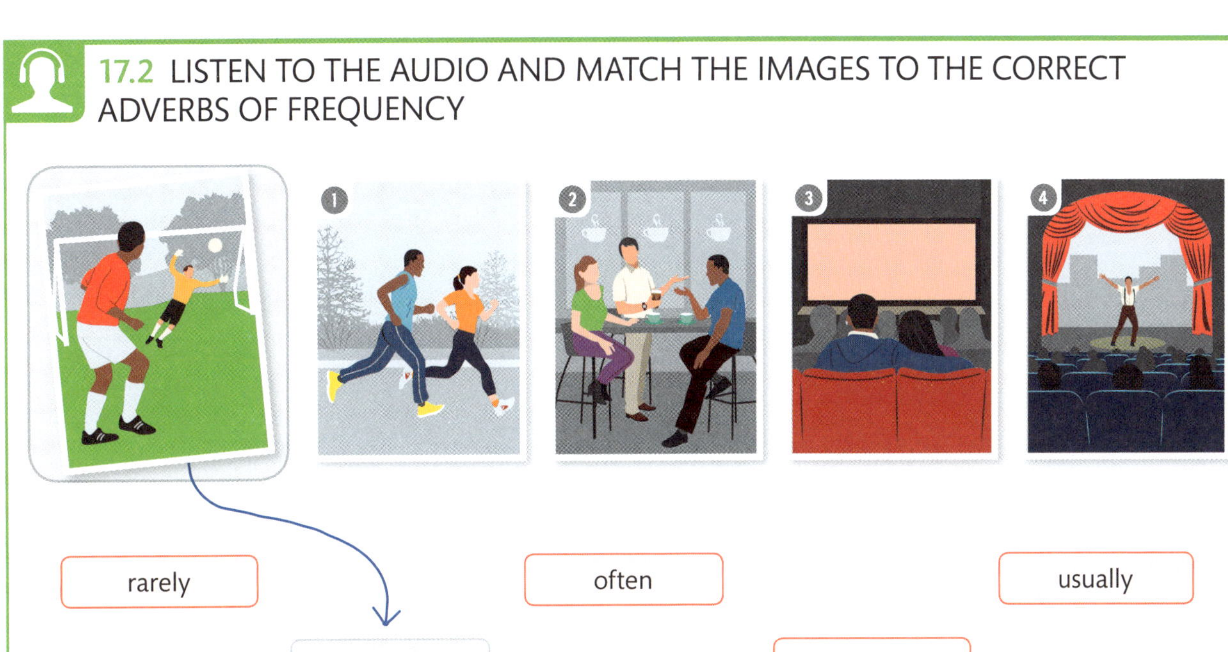

rarely

sometimes

often

never

usually

17.3 MATCH THE BEGINNINGS OF THE SENTENCES TO THE CORRECT ENDINGS

I often go → camping in the forest.

1. Mariam usually stays
2. I sometimes take
3. Dan rarely reads
4. She occasionally sees
5. Marco usually does
6. I sometimes listen to
7. We sometimes go out
8. I often watch

- photos when I go on vacation.
- a play at her local theater.
- camping in the forest.
- at home on weekends.
- a movie when I get home from work.
- a newspaper in the morning.
- for a meal at the Chinese restaurant.
- music while I travel to work.
- some exercises when he gets up.

17.4 MARK THE SENTENCES THAT ARE CORRECT

This is the best way to get home. ☑
This is the most good way to get home. ☐

1. The earliest flight is at 9am. ☐
   The most early flight is at 9am. ☐

2. Sydney is the most largest city in Australia. ☐
   Sydney is the largest city in Australia. ☐

3. Dubai is the hottest place I've visited. ☐
   Dubai is the most hottest place I've visited. ☐

4. This is the most expensive software we sell. ☐
   This is the expensivest software we sell. ☐

5. The most far I've flown is to New Zealand. ☐
   The farthest I've flown is to New Zealand. ☐

6. Spanish is the most easiest language to learn. ☐
   Spanish is the easiest language to learn. ☐

7. Kraków is the most beautiful city in Poland. ☐
   Kraków is the more beautiful city in Poland. ☐

8. The train is the most affordable way to travel. ☐
   The train is the affordablest way to travel. ☐

9. This is the most interesting gallery in town. ☐
   This is the most interestingest gallery in town. ☐

10. Hiroshi is most intelligent person I know. ☐
    Hiroshi is the most intelligent person I know. ☐

11. That was the scariest film I've seen. ☐
    That was the most scary film I've seen. ☐

17.5 SAY THE SENTENCES OUT LOUD, PUTTING THE ADJECTIVES INTO THEIR SUPERLATIVE FORMS

We had our *worst* (bad) results in 10 years.

1. The ________ (long) river in Brazil is the Amazon.

2. We'll have lunch at the ________ (close) café to the office.

3. I just watched the ________ (bad) presentation I've ever seen.

4. I think that snowboarding is the ________ (exciting) sport.

5. Sean lives the ________ (far) from the office.

6. Antonio is our ________ (loyal) employee.

7. This is the ________ (expensive) printer we have.

17.6 READ THE ARTICLE AND ANSWER THE QUESTIONS

LEISURE WEEKLY

How do you spend your free time?

We speak to three different people about what they do in their time away from work.

Chloe Smith, 21

I get up early most days and usually do some exercises. I'm not very sporty, to be honest, but I go jogging twice a week. On the weekend I like to relax; I work in a bank, which is stressful. I go to the theater quite often and I sometimes do yoga on Saturday afternoons. I never watch sports. It's the most boring thing possible!

Pete McManus, 30

I like martial arts. I'm a member of a karate club, and I try to go there as regularly as possible. I think karate is the most exciting sport. It involves a lot of self-discipline. What else? Well, I occasionally go jogging. Oh, and I play tennis with my wife from time to time. You could say that I'm a sporty person!

Dan Stevens, 47

I'm not the most active person. I like to play video games with my friends in the evening. I sometimes watch soccer with my friends on weekends. There's a gym at my workplace, but I go there pretty rarely. My wife thinks I should get more exercise, but I hate working out. I'd much rather relax at home.

Who goes jogging twice a week? Chloe ☑ Pete ☐ Dan ☐

1. Who rarely goes to the gym? Chloe ☐ Pete ☐ Dan ☐
2. Who plays tennis with his wife? Chloe ☐ Pete ☐ Dan ☐
3. Who is the most sporty? Chloe ☐ Pete ☐ Dan ☐
4. Who thinks karate is the most exciting sport? Chloe ☐ Pete ☐ Dan ☐
5. Who sometimes watches soccer? Chloe ☐ Pete ☐ Dan ☐
6. Who does exercise early in the morning? Chloe ☐ Pete ☐ Dan ☐
7. Who is a member of a sports club? Chloe ☐ Pete ☐ Dan ☐
8. Who doesn't go jogging? Chloe ☐ Pete ☐ Dan ☐
9. Who sometimes does yoga? Chloe ☐ Pete ☐ Dan ☐
10. Who likes to play video games? Chloe ☐ Pete ☐ Dan ☐

18 Past events

The past simple is often used when talking with co-workers about events that started and finished at a specific time in the recent or distant past.

New language The past simple
Aa Vocabulary Activities outside work
New skill Talking about past events

18.1 MARK THE SENTENCES THAT ARE CORRECT

Chris played soccer after work. ☑
Chris playd soccer after work. ☐

1. I didn't learn Spanish at school. ☐
   I didn't learned Spanish at school. ☐
2. We walking to the conference center. ☐
   We walked to the conference center. ☐
3. John did lived in New York for 10 years. ☐
   John lived in New York for 10 years. ☐
4. Did the team discussed the merger? ☐
   Did the team discuss the merger? ☐
5. He went to the conference by car. ☐
   He did went to the conference by car. ☐
6. My manager not visited the factory. ☐
   My manager didn't visit the factory. ☐
7. Selma didn't walk to work today. ☐
   Selma didn't walked to work today. ☐
8. Jimish posted the report a week ago. ☐
   Jimish post the report a week ago. ☐
9. Did Tom finish the report? ☐
   Finished Tom the report? ☐

18.2 FILL IN THE GAPS BY PUTTING THE VERBS IN THE PAST SIMPLE

Jenny *studied* (study) hard, but she *did not pass* (not pass) the accounting exam.

1. Akiko ______ (finish) her presentation, then she ______ (watch) some TV.
2. I ______ (not watch) the game because I ______ (need) to prepare for the conference.
3. Derek ______ (want) to work somewhere interesting, so he ______ (move) to New York.
4. We ______ (arrive) late, but we ______ (not miss) the meeting.
5. Sally ______ (pass) her exams, and ______ (decide) to go to college.

18.3 REWRITE THE SENTENCES, PUTTING THE WORDS IN THE CORRECT ORDER

get | explain | Did | Peter | to | how | to | office? | the

Did Peter explain how to get to the office?

1. the | Fred | me | conference | center. | showed | new

2. watched | about | We | documentary | an | Beijing. | interesting

3. company | started | years | at | about | this | ago. | Ramon | five

4. you | Did | presentation | enjoy | the | the | Indian economy? | about

5. play | It | yesterday, | rained | we | soccer. | so | didn't

6. cooked | Arnold | last | me | dinner | a | night. | delicious

7. about | Did | finish | Sam | report | the | product | new | range? | the

8. table | I | in | a | the | center. | in | restaurant | a | booked

9. the | Did Mike | tennis | on | with | CEO | new | Saturday? | play

18.4 REWRITE THE SENTENCES AS QUESTIONS IN THE PAST SIMPLE

Claire finished the presentation on Thursday.
Did Claire finish the presentation on Thursday?

1. Paul started working for us more than five years ago.
2. Sally explained how to use the new photocopier.
3. It rained while they were in Indonesia.
4. Clive picked up the guests from the railway station.
5. Mark joined you for lunch at the Chinese restaurant.
6. The team attended the conference in Paris last year.
7. Philip played golf with the consultants last weekend.
8. Carl and Marie walked to work again today.
9. You watched the game yesterday.
10. Janet showed you the new photocopier.
11. Mo studied economics at Stanford University.
12. The company invested $10 million in R&D.

18.5 LISTEN TO THE AUDIO AND ANSWER THE QUESTIONS

Two co-workers are catching up after the weekend.

Ben visited York with his family.
True ☑ **False** ☐ **Not given** ☐

1. York is a very modern city.
True ☐ **False** ☐ **Not given** ☐

2. The family stayed in a hotel.
True ☐ **False** ☐ **Not given** ☐

3. The castle is over 1,000 years old.
True ☐ **False** ☐ **Not given** ☐

4. Helen visited a shopping mall.
True ☐ **False** ☐ **Not given** ☐

5. They visited the circus.
True ☐ **False** ☐ **Not given** ☐

6. In the evening they went to see a movie.
True ☐ **False** ☐ **Not given** ☐

7. Helen didn't enjoy the food in the restaurant.
True ☐ **False** ☐ **Not given** ☐

18.6 DESCRIBE WHAT EACH PERSON DID, SPEAKING OUT LOUD AND USING THE PAST SIMPLE FORM OF THE PHRASES IN THE PANEL

He played tennis.

1.

2.

3.

4.

5.

walk to work | study for an exam | listen to the radio | ~~play tennis~~ | travel to India | visit a friend

19 Dates and times

When making arrangements or talking about past or future events, it is important to talk about the time correctly. There are a number of ways to do this in English.

New language When things happen
Aa Vocabulary Telling the time
New skill Making appointments

19.1 LISTEN TO THE AUDIO AND MARK THE CORRECT TIMES

A
B
1
A
B
2
A
B
3
A
B
4
A
B
5
A
B

19.2 SAY THE TIMES OUT LOUD

05:15 *It's (a) quarter past five.*

1. 9:17

2.

3.

4. 3:22

5.

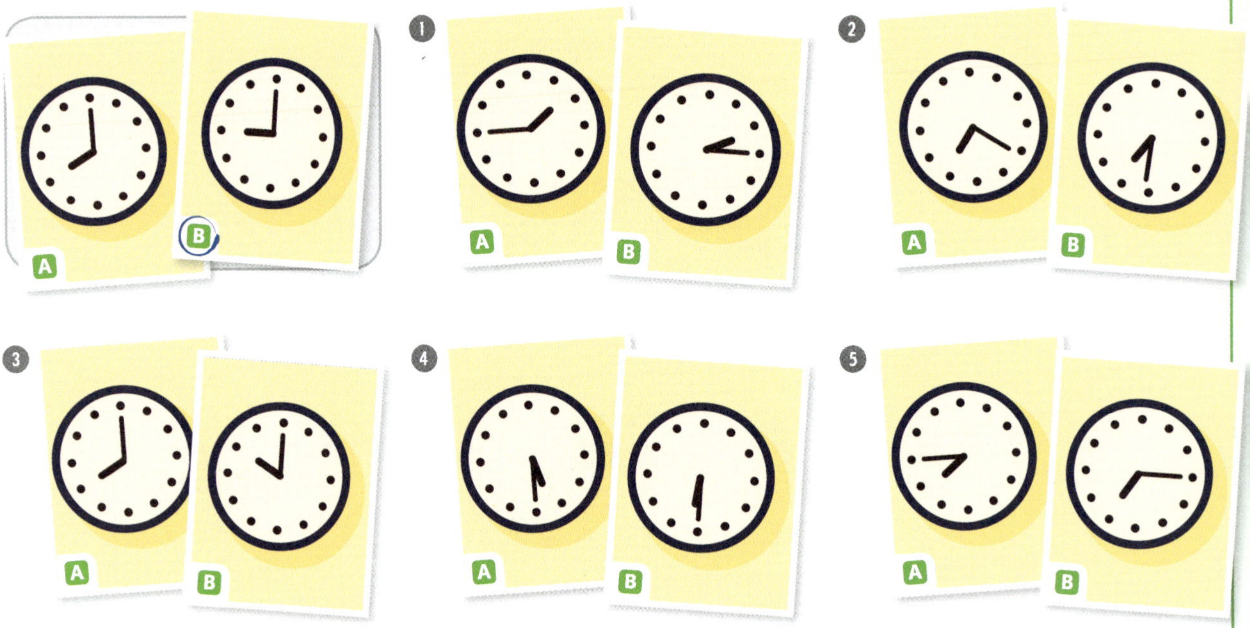

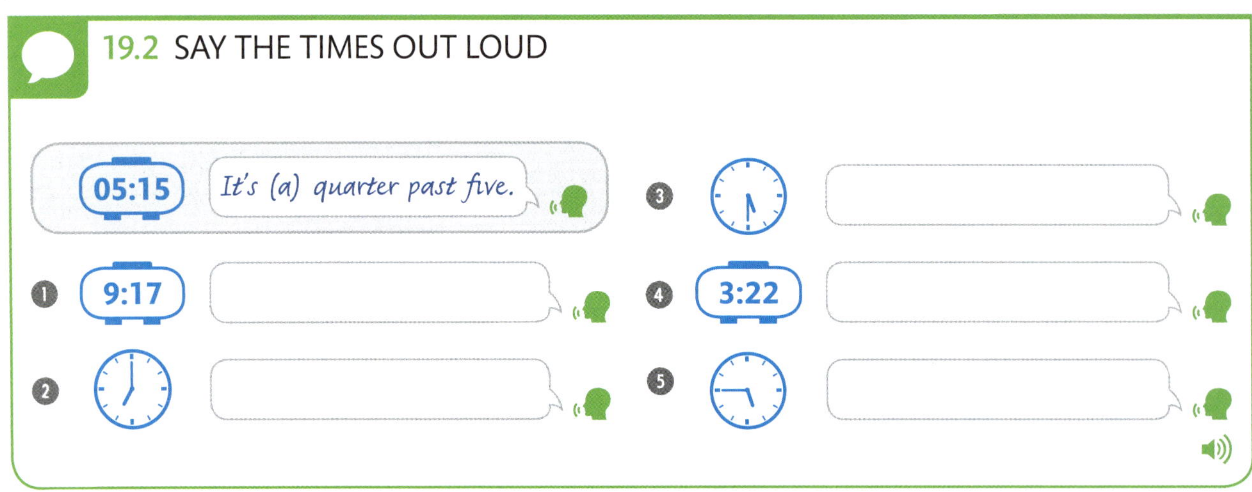

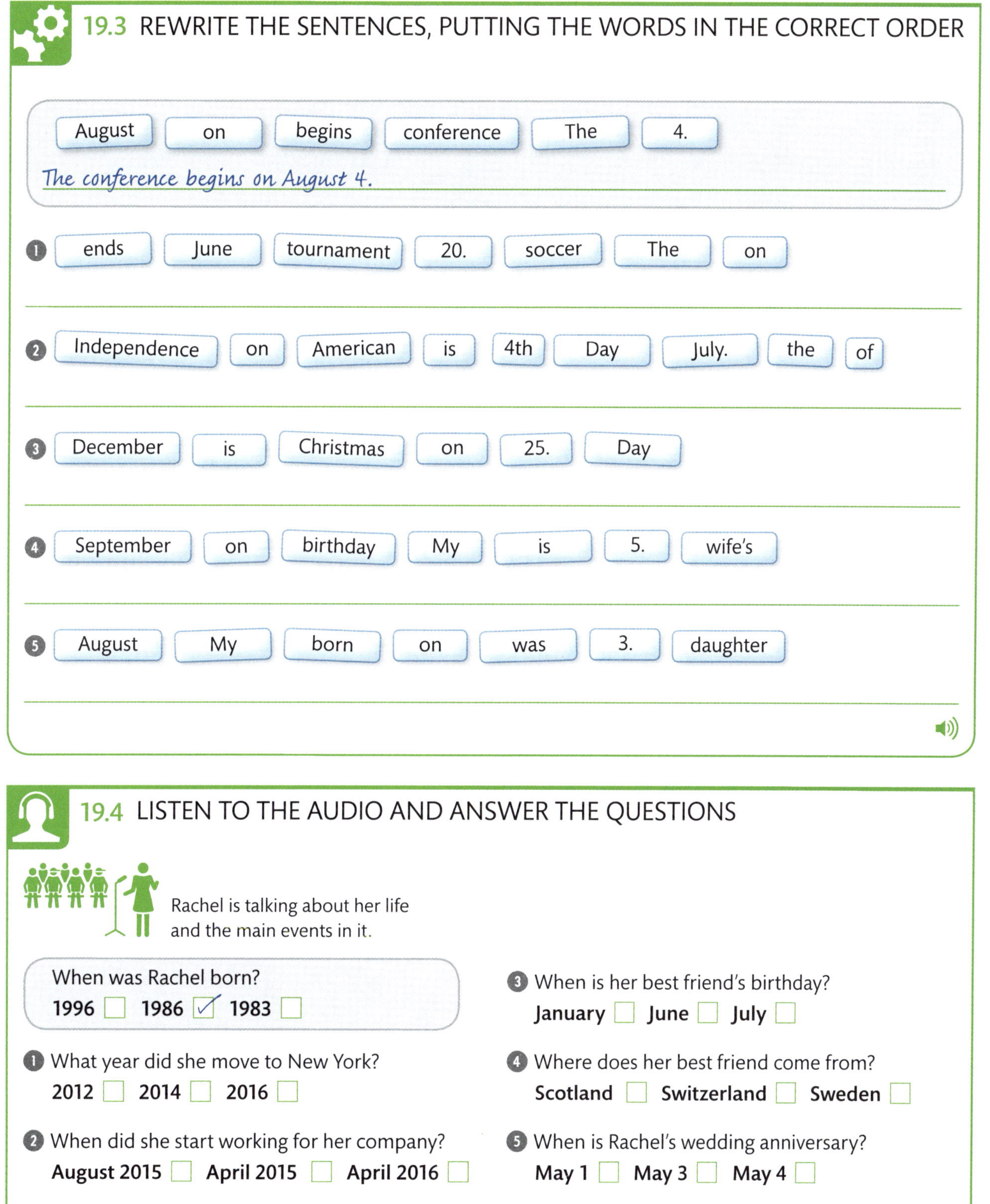

19.3 REWRITE THE SENTENCES, PUTTING THE WORDS IN THE CORRECT ORDER

August | on | begins | conference | The | 4.

The conference begins on August 4.

1. ends | June | tournament | 20. | soccer | The | on

2. Independence | on | American | is | 4th | Day | July. | the | of

3. December | is | Christmas | on | 25. | Day

4. September | on | birthday | My | is | 5. | wife's

5. August | My | born | on | was | 3. | daughter

19.4 LISTEN TO THE AUDIO AND ANSWER THE QUESTIONS

Rachel is talking about her life and the main events in it.

When was Rachel born?
1996 ☐ **1986** ☑ **1983** ☐

1. What year did she move to New York?
   2012 ☐ **2014** ☐ **2016** ☐

2. When did she start working for her company?
   August 2015 ☐ **April 2015** ☐ **April 2016** ☐

3. When is her best friend's birthday?
   January ☐ **June** ☐ **July** ☐

4. Where does her best friend come from?
   Scotland ☐ **Switzerland** ☐ **Sweden** ☐

5. When is Rachel's wedding anniversary?
   May 1 ☐ **May 3** ☐ **May 4** ☐

20 Career history

When you meet new co-workers or attend an interview, people may ask about your previous jobs. It is important to use correct verb forms when talking about the past.

New language Past simple irregular verbs
Aa Vocabulary Jobs and workplaces
New skill Talking about previous jobs

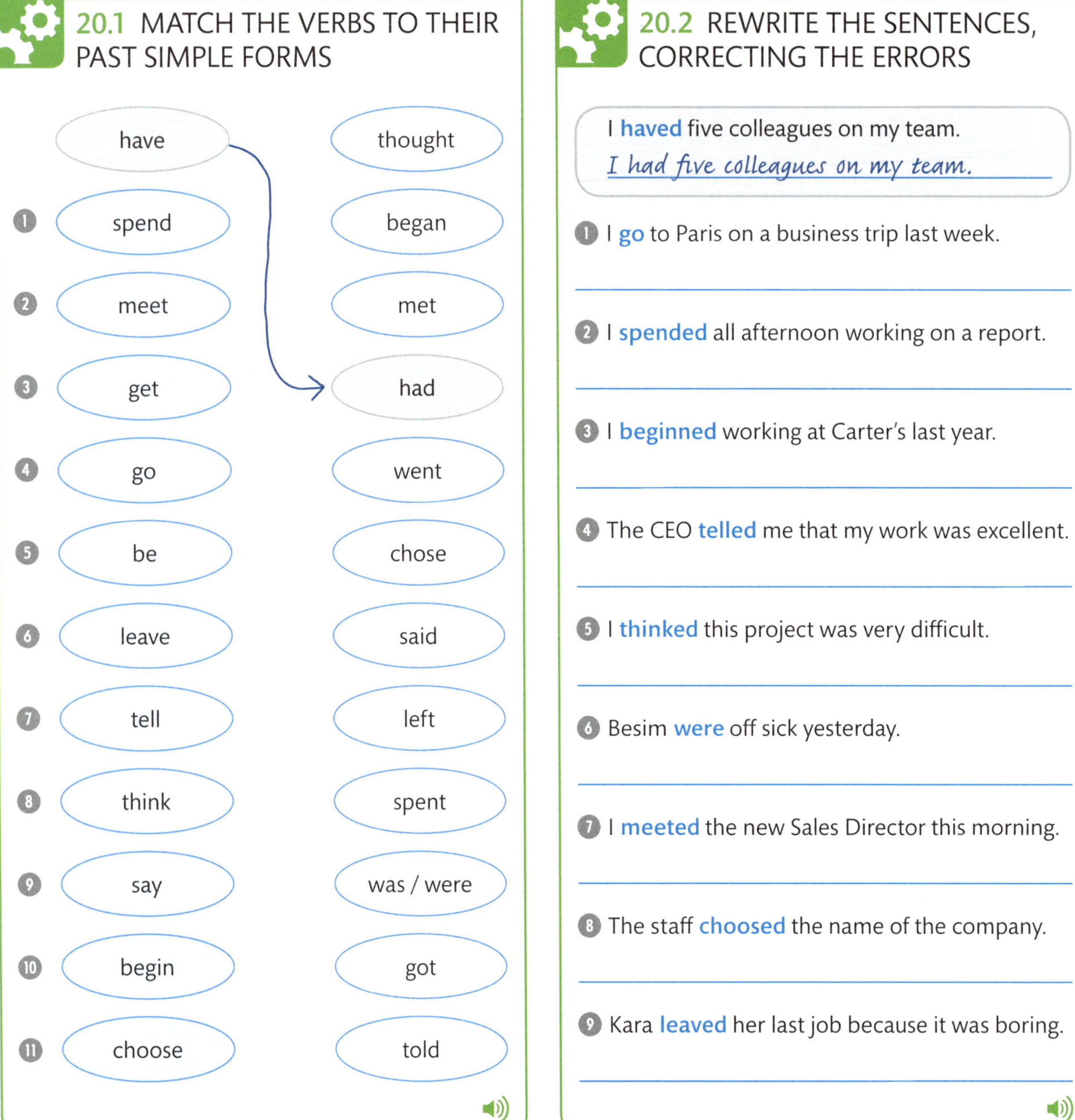

20.1 MATCH THE VERBS TO THEIR PAST SIMPLE FORMS

	have	thought
1	spend	began
2	meet	met
3	get	had
4	go	went
5	be	chose
6	leave	said
7	tell	left
8	think	spent
9	say	was / were
10	begin	got
11	choose	told

20.2 REWRITE THE SENTENCES, CORRECTING THE ERRORS

I **haved** five colleagues on my team.
I had five colleagues on my team.

1. I **go** to Paris on a business trip last week.
2. I **spended** all afternoon working on a report.
3. I **beginned** working at Carter's last year.
4. The CEO **telled** me that my work was excellent.
5. I **thinked** this project was very difficult.
6. Besim **were** off sick yesterday.
7. I **meeted** the new Sales Director this morning.
8. The staff **choosed** the name of the company.
9. Kara **leaved** her last job because it was boring.

20.3 FILL IN THE GAPS BY PUTTING THE VERBS IN THE PAST SIMPLE

My first job ___was___ (be) in a supermarket.

1. I ________________ (meet) the International Marketing Director last week.
2. I ________________ (have) a demanding boss.
3. I ________________ (leave) my last job because it was badly paid.
4. I ________________ (get) to work very early today.
5. They ________________ (go) to the New York office last month.
6. The staff ________________ (choose) new chairs for the office.
7. Sally ________________ (think) that Rohit's presentation went well.

20.4 MATCH THE QUESTIONS TO THE CORRECT ANSWERS

How many people were on your team? → There were five of us.

1. When did you start working at the café?
2. Where did you work on your first job?
3. What did you do as a nanny?
4. Who did you meet as a journalist?
5. How did you get your job as a director?
6. What did you wear on your last job?

- I met many interesting people.
- There were five of us.
- We had a black and white uniform.
- I took the children to school.
- I started work there after I left school.
- I worked in a bank at the start of my career.
- I worked hard and studied for an MBA.

20.5 LISTEN TO THE AUDIO, THEN NUMBER THE PICTURES IN THE ORDER THEY ARE DESCRIBED

A ☐

B 1

C ☐

D ☐

E ☐

F ☐

G ☐

H ☐

20.6 CROSS OUT THE INCORRECT WORD IN EACH SENTENCE, THEN SAY THE SENTENCES OUT LOUD

We had / ~~haved~~ a very demanding boss in the marketing department.

1. I feeled / felt very well respected by my team leader.
2. The Head of Sales taught / teached me to give interesting presentations.
3. My brother made / maked a delicious cake, which I took to work for my birthday.
4. The staff choosed / chose the pictures for the meeting rooms, and they look great.
5. I left / leaved my last job because I didn't get along with the customers.
6. I spended / spent all of yesterday writing a sales report and now I'm very tired.

21 Company history

The past simple can be used to describe repeated or single actions in a company's history. These actions can last for a short or long time.

New language Past simple with time markers
Vocabulary Describing trends
New skill Describing a company's history

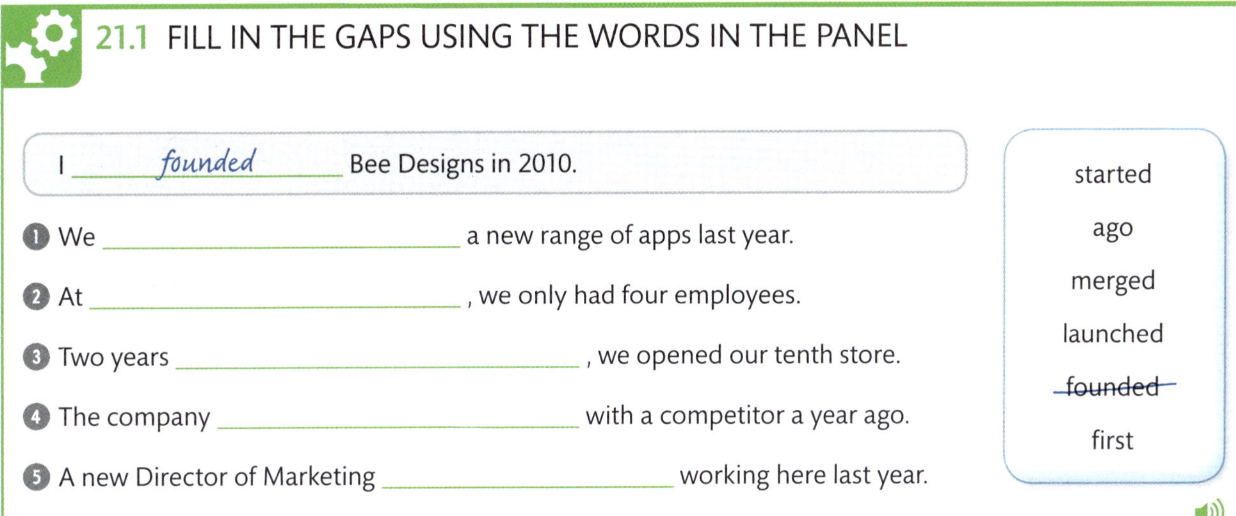

21.1 FILL IN THE GAPS USING THE WORDS IN THE PANEL

I *founded* Bee Designs in 2010.

1. We ______ a new range of apps last year.
2. At ______, we only had four employees.
3. Two years ______, we opened our tenth store.
4. The company ______ with a competitor a year ago.
5. A new Director of Marketing ______ working here last year.

started
ago
merged
launched
~~founded~~
first

21.2 REWRITE THE SENTENCES, CORRECTING THE ERRORS

Maria Hill opened the first Hill Shoe Store past 2015.
Maria Hill opened the first Hill Shoe Store in 2015.

1. At the first, we only had one store. 
2. We open a new flagship store last month. 
3. We launch an exciting new app last year. 
4. A new Director of HR started working here six months before.

21.3 READ THE WEB PAGE AND ANSWER THE QUESTIONS

BUSINESS WORLD

HOME | ENTRIES | ABOUT | CONTACT

POSTED WEDNESDAY SEPTEMBER 16

Market leaders

This week, we look at the history of Bee Designs.

Bee Designs is now a successful company and one of the best-known names in online shopping. Last year, the company made a profit of $500,000 and sold over 10,000 bags.

The company started as a hobby business when Angela Lee couldn't find a bag that she wanted and she made her own. Friends asked her where she had bought it. When they found out that she had made it herself, they asked her to make bags for them. She decided to turn her garage into a workroom and launched Bee Designs in 2010.

The company went from strength to strength and now employs 50 people. Two years ago, Angela moved the operation of her business to a unit in the business park in her town.

Most of the company's business comes from online orders, but Angela started going to craft fairs five years ago. She sold out of bags at the first fair, so she took on 5 extra sewing machinists. The company makes over a hundred bags a week and its turnover for 2015 was more than $1.2 million.

What does Bee Designs make? **Bags** ☑ **Shoes** ☐ **Hats** ☐

1. How many bags did the company sell last year? **Over 1,000** ☐ **Over 10,000** ☐ **Over 100,000** ☐
2. Where did Angela originally make the bags? **In a business unit** ☐ **In a factory** ☐ **In her garage** ☐
3. How many employees does the company currently have? **5** ☐ **50** ☐ **150** ☐
4. When did Angela move the operation of her business? **Two years ago** ☐ **Five years ago** ☐ **2012** ☐
5. Where does Bee Designs sell bags directly? **At wedding fairs** ☐ **At craft fairs** ☐ **At vintage fairs** ☐

21.4 LISTEN TO THE AUDIO AND MATCH THE IMAGES TO THE CORRECT TIME MARKERS

1 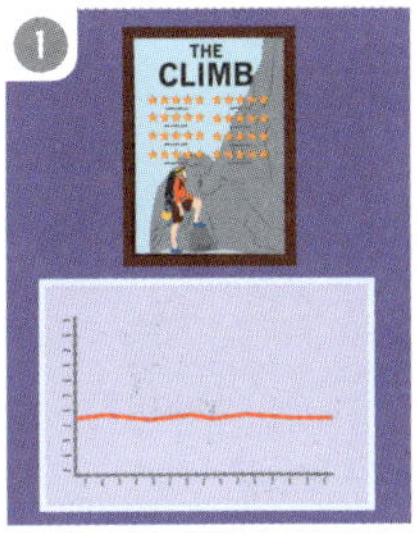 THE CLIMB

2 FOR SALE

3

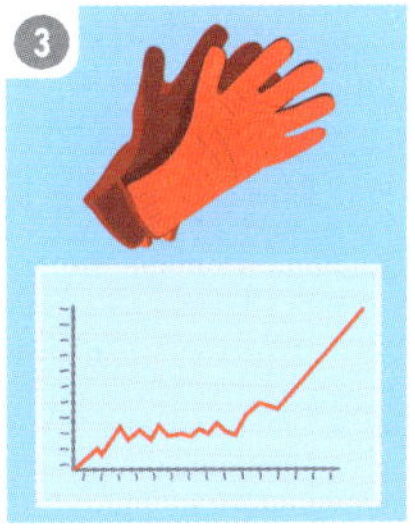

4

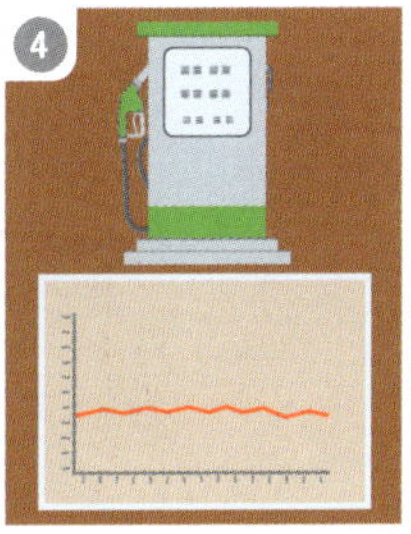

during the first quarter

over the summer

recently

last month

in the winter of 2012

21.5 CROSS OUT THE INCORRECT WORDS IN EACH SENTENCE, THEN SAY THE SENTENCES OUT LOUD

The number of sales decreased / ~~decrease~~, but profits ~~go~~ / went up.

1. Recent / Last spring, sales of umbrellas rising / rose because it was wet.
2. UK sales rose up / went up in 2011, but falled / fell in 2012.
3. At / In first, the value of shares in the company remain / remained steady.
4. Online marketing costs increasing / increased and sales also rose / rised.

22 Vocabulary

Aa 22.1 **MAKING ARRANGEMENTS** WRITE THE PHRASES FROM THE PANEL UNDER THE CORRECT PICTURES

to book a meeting room

1 ______

2 ______

3 ______

8 ______

9 ______

10 ______

11 ______

16 ______

17 ______

18 ______

19 ______

Aa 22.2 **ACCEPTING AND DECLINING** WRITE THE PHRASES FROM THE PANEL UNDER THE CORRECT DEFINITIONS

To be convenient

to suit someone

1 To occur unexpectedly

______

4 Cannot go to

______

5 To be pleased about something that is going to happen

______

4 ______

5 ______

6 ______

7 ______

12 ______

13 ______

14 ______

15 ______

to miss a meeting | refreshments | café | to invite someone | agenda | restaurant | to attend a meeting | evening | ~~to book a meeting room~~ | morning | calendar | to decline an invitation | appointment | running late | reception | boardroom | conference room | to accept an invitation | afternoon | office

2 To decide that a planned event will not happen

______

3 To have lots to do

______

6 To decide on a new time and date for a meeting

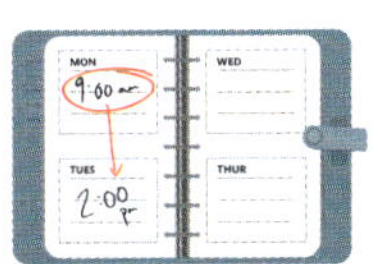

______

to cancel | ~~to suit someone~~ | to come up | to reschedule | to look forward to | to be busy | to be unable to attend

23 Talking about your plans

One way of making plans with a co-worker or client is by using the present continuous to talk about what you are doing at the moment, or plans in the future.

New language The present continuous
Aa Vocabulary Making arrangements
New skill Talking about your plans

23.1 FILL IN THE GAPS BY PUTTING THE VERBS IN THE PRESENT CONTINUOUS

Steve *is working* (work) from home today. He *is writing* (write) the report.

1. The company ______ (lose) money, so we ______ (plan) a restructure.
2. Stacy ______ (not work) in the office today. She ______ (visit) the factory.
3. Dan ______ (meet) a new client. They ______ (chat) in the meeting room.
4. Colin ______ (start) a new project. He ______ (work) with Angela.
5. The head office ______ (relocate) to Delhi. We ______ (move) this week.
6. Profits ______ (fall) this year, and the team ______ (feel) nervous.
7. Anika ______ (work) late tonight. She ______ (prepare) a presentation.
8. Sue and Clive ______ (have) lunch downtown. They ______ (eat) Chinese.
9. I ______ (go) on vacation next week. I ______ (miss) the training day.
10. Our company ______ (sell) a lot to India. We ______ (open) an office in Mumbai.
11. Our secretary ______ (retire). We ______ (recruit) a new one.
12. Sam and Sue are ______ (discuss) the report. They ______ (plan) a meeting about it.
13. Chrissie ______ (choose) a new team. She ______ (consider) Paul for a position.
14. Alex ______ (leave) the company. He ______ (move) to New York.

23.2 REWRITE THE SENTENCES, PUTTING THE WORDS IN THE CORRECT ORDER

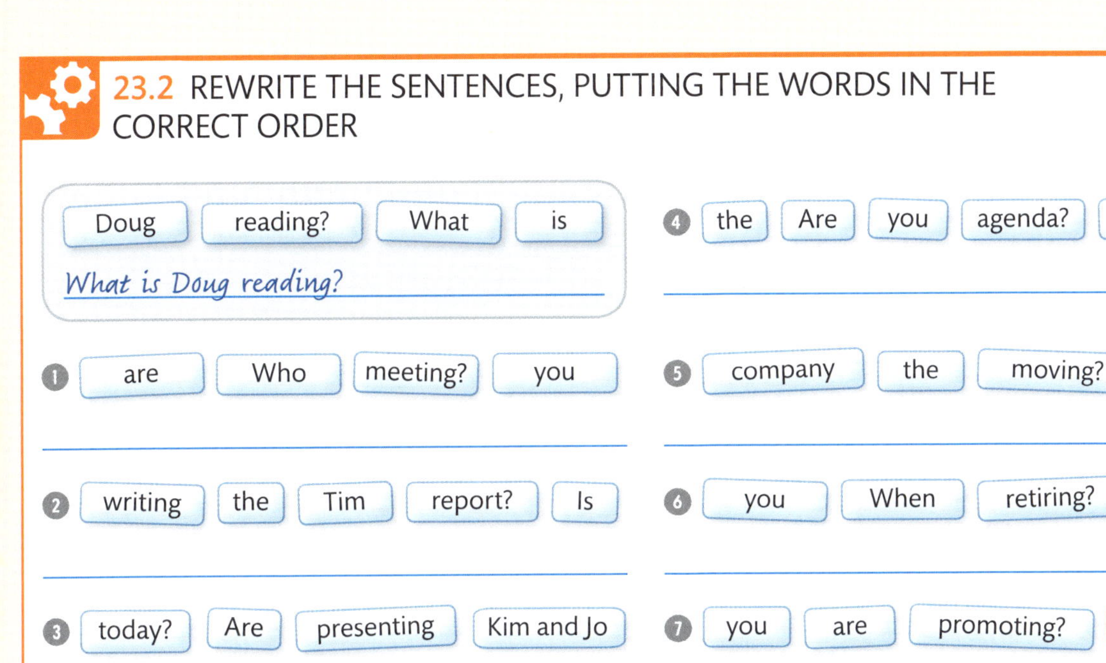

Doug | reading? | What | is

What is Doug reading?

1. are | Who | meeting? | you
2. writing | the | Tim | report? | Is
3. today? | Are | presenting | Kim and Jo
4. the | Are | you | agenda? | printing
5. company | the | moving? | Is
6. you | When | retiring? | are
7. you | are | promoting? | Who

23.3 REWRITE THE STATEMENTS AS QUESTIONS IN THE PRESENT CONTINUOUS

Tom is translating the new contract today.

Is Tom translating the new contract today?

1. The conference is taking place in Venice next April. 
2. Leanne is giving a presentation on the takeover plans. 
3. Our owners are hoping to buy our biggest competitor. 
4. Brendan is programming the software for new machinery. 
5. We're taking time off in August this year.

23.4 MARK THE SENTENCES THAT ARE CORRECT

Where are you working on Friday? ☑
Where does you work on Friday? ☐

1. Are you have lunch at 1pm today? ☐
   Are you having lunch at 1pm today? ☐

2. Tom will going to the conference today. ☐
   Tom is going to the conference today. ☐

3. Is John working until 7pm again? ☐
   Does John working until 7pm again? ☐

4. We are traveling to New York again. ☐
   We are travel to New York again. ☐

5. Is you coming to the meeting on Friday? ☐
   Are you coming to the meeting on Friday? ☐

6. Will you visiting the factory next month? ☐
   Are you visiting the factory next month? ☐

7. I'm not taking time off in August. ☐
   I amn't taking time off in August. ☐

8. The head office will moving in the spring. ☐
   The head office is moving in the spring. ☐

9. Fran aren't coming to the office tomorrow. ☐
   Fran isn't coming to the office tomorrow. ☐

10. What are you doing on Tuesday? ☐
    What you are doing on Tuesday? ☐

11. Sam be meeting the client this afternoon. ☐
    Sam is meeting the client this afternoon. ☐

12. Tim is leaving work at 5pm today. ☐
    Tim leaving work at 5pm today. ☐

23.5 LISTEN TO THE AUDIO AND ANSWER THE QUESTIONS

Clare is calling her colleague, Frank, to arrange a meeting with him.

Clare needs to arrange a meeting about...
the new sales strategy. ☑
the new recruits. ☐
the health and safety presentation. ☐

1. On Monday morning, Frank is...
   attending a course. ☐
   going to the dentist. ☐
   visiting the factory. ☐

2. On Monday afternoon, Clare is...
   free. ☐
   attending a course. ☐
   giving a presentation. ☐

3. On Tuesday, Frank is...
   celebrating his birthday. ☐
   celebrating his wedding anniversary. ☐
   going on vacation. ☐

4. In the evening, he is...
   going to a film. ☐
   going to a restaurant. ☐
   going to the theater. ☐

5. On Thursday at 2pm, Clare is...
   meeting Pete. ☐
   having lunch. ☐
   visiting the factory. ☐

6. They are both available at...
   2:30pm on Thursday. ☐
   3:30pm on Thursday. ☐
   2:30pm on Friday. ☐

23.6 READ THE SCHEDULE, THEN RESPOND TO THE AUDIO, SPEAKING OUT LOUD

July

Monday	Tuesday	Wednesday	Thursday	Friday
10am Give presentation to the interns		12 noon Flight to Edinburgh departs	11:30am Return to London	
2pm Have lunch with the IT team				
	3pm Meet the new clients from Germany		3pm Give report to CEO	
				7pm Sandra's leaving party

What are you doing on Monday morning?

I'm giving a presentation to the interns at 10am.

1. Where are you going on Monday afternoon?

2. What time are you meeting the clients?

3. Where are you going on Wednesday?

4. What time are you returning on Thursday?

5. Where are you going on Friday evening?

24 Giving opinions

English speakers often use set phrases to signal that they want to interrupt without being rude. There are a number of ways to communicate your opinion politely.

New language Interruptions and opinions
Aa Vocabulary Environmental issues
New skill Giving opinions politely

24.1 MARK WHETHER EACH INTERRUPTION IS POLITE OR IMPOLITE

I'm sorry, but I can't agree with you there.
Polite ☑ **Impolite** ☐

1. Excuse me, but I agree with Stacey here.
Polite ☐ **Impolite** ☐

2. What are you talking about? That's wrong.
Polite ☐ **Impolite** ☐

3. I'm afraid I have to disagree with you about that.
Polite ☐ **Impolite** ☐

4. Could I just say that there are other options.
Polite ☐ **Impolite** ☐

5. Sorry to interrupt, but I have different figures.
Polite ☐ **Impolite** ☐

6. That's absolute nonsense.
Polite ☐ **Impolite** ☐

7. If I could just come in here, Robert.
Polite ☐ **Impolite** ☐

24.2 LISTEN TO THE AUDIO AND ANSWER THE QUESTIONS

Dan and Susan are talking at a meeting.

The meeting is about a new policy.
True ☑ **False** ☐ **Not given** ☐

1. Susan wants the company to develop new vehicles.
True ☐ **False** ☐ **Not given** ☐

2. Dan agrees with Susan's suggestion.
True ☐ **False** ☐ **Not given** ☐

3. The company leaves a bad carbon footprint.
True ☐ **False** ☐ **Not given** ☐

4. Dan thinks the workers should use the metro.
True ☐ **False** ☐ **Not given** ☐

5. Agrocorp are developing a motorcycle.
True ☐ **False** ☐ **Not given** ☐

6. The company will develop electric vehicles soon.
True ☐ **False** ☐ **Not given** ☐

7. Agrocorp employees recycle at home.
True ☐ **False** ☐ **Not given** ☐

24.3 RESPOND OUT LOUD TO THE AUDIO, FILLING IN THE GAPS USING THE WORDS IN THE PANEL

This will lead to a fall in profits.

Sorry to disagree, but my figures are different.

1 The company might lose millions of dollars.

I'm sorry. I'm not sure I ________.

2 These clothes won't appeal to people in China.

Sorry, but in my ________ they will sell well.

3 We need to increase our focus on the youth market.

I can see your ________, but I still think senior citizens are more important.

4 We had exactly the same problem last year.

If I could just ________ in here and mention the good news from France.

5 The figures show a dramatic fall this year.

________ me, but my figures tell a different story.

6 We need to employ two new team members.

________ I just say...? The budget won't cover it.

7 India will be our biggest market in 2050.

I'm not ________ I agree. Sales to China are growing faster.

8 And if we sell our new software...

Sorry to ________, but the software is not ready yet.

come | interrupt | agree | excuse | point | ~~disagree~~ | could | sure | opinion

24.4 CROSS OUT THE INCORRECT WORD IN EACH SENTENCE

Claire's ~~timed~~ / scheduled a meeting for later. She'll send the agenda to everyone soon.

1. I'm afraid Sean can't make it to the meeting and has given / sent his apologies.
2. Shall we take / make a vote on the new strategy to see what course of action to take?
3. Ramona will take / recall the minutes and email them to everyone after the meeting.
4. I agree with the motion. How about / for you? What do you think about it?
5. If I could just disturb / interrupt for a moment. I think we need to take a vote on this.
6. That sums up most of the issues we are facing. I just have a few finishing / closing remarks.
7. Claude is the chair, so he has the casting / choosing vote if there is a tie.
8. The chair / seat of our budget meetings likes to keep his closing remarks very short.
9. I read through / up the agenda before the meeting, so I know what we will be talking about.

Aa 24.5 MATCH THE DEFINITIONS TO THE WORDS

	make something usable again → recycle	footprint
1	the mark or effect something leaves behind	reuse
2	environmentally friendly	recycle
3	to use something again	green
4	natural products you can use	environment
5	things we do not need or want	reduce
6	the natural world around us	resources
7	make an amount smaller	waste

25 Agreeing and disagreeing

When you react to someone's opinion, it is important to be polite and respectful. This is especially important when you disagree with someone.

New language Reacting to opinions
Aa Vocabulary Agreeing and disagreeing
New skill Discussing opinions

25.1 MARK THE BEST REPLY TO EACH STATEMENT

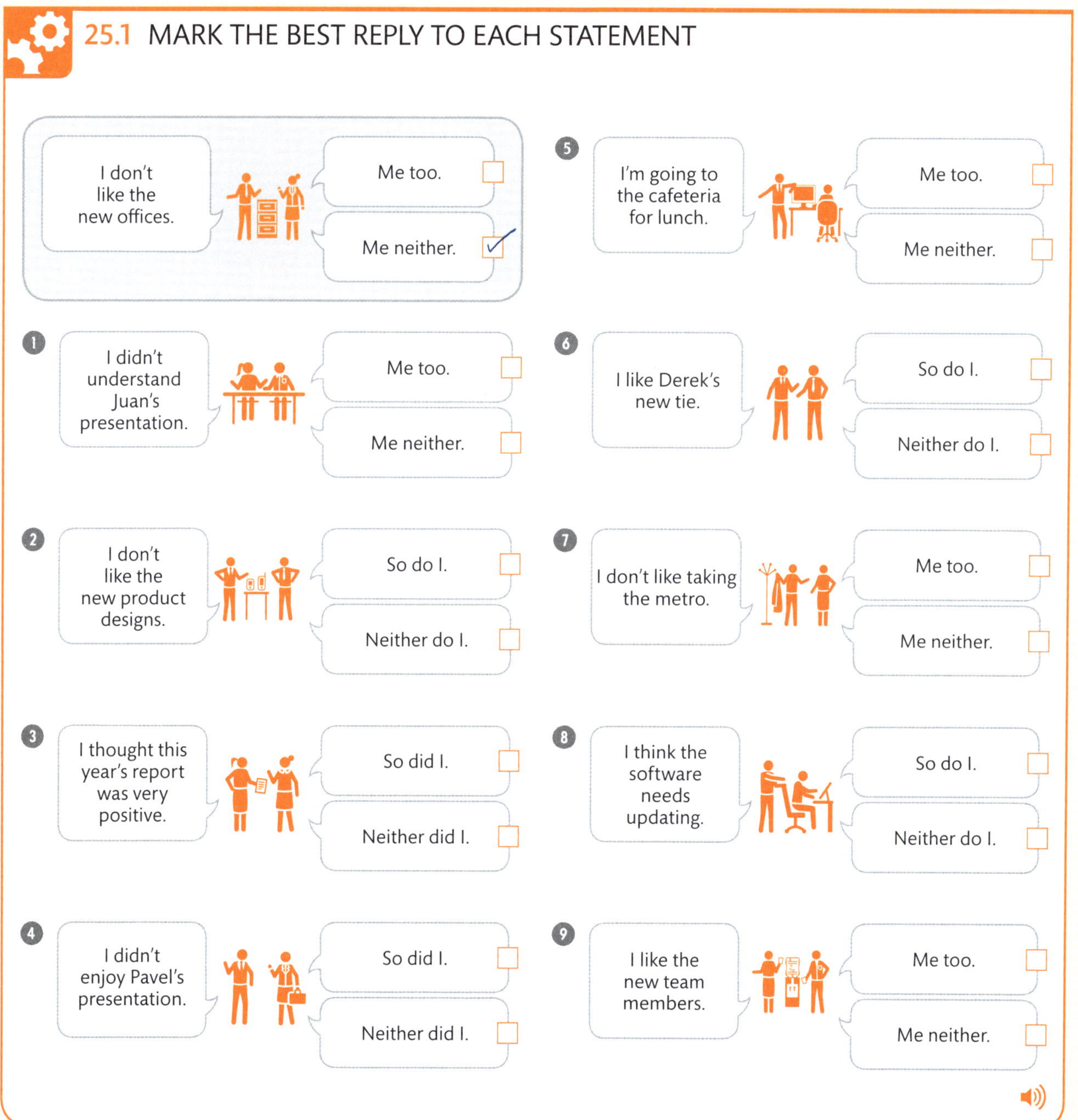

Aa 25.2 MATCH THE STATEMENTS TO THE RESPONSES

	I think the new interns are great.	So did I. He's so entertaining.
1	We should buy a new photocopier.	I'll ask the secretary to send it again.
2	I loved Pablo's presentation.	Me too. They are really helpful.
3	We need to invest more in training.	I suppose so. It will be expensive though.
4	I didn't receive the agenda.	Exactly. I didn't understand it at all.
5	I don't like the cafeteria much.	I agree. The team could improve their skills.
6	I like the new office furniture.	Absolutely. We should promote her.
7	The presentation was really confusing.	I agree. I learned some new skills.
8	The training was useful.	Me neither. The food's very bland.
9	The new HR assistant is really hard working.	So do I. It's very comfortable.

25.3 FILL IN THE GAPS USING THE WORDS IN THE PANEL

I'm sorry, but we disagree *with* the price.

1. I'm ________ we'll have to cancel the meeting.
2. I'm sorry, but I ________ with you.
3. I ________ disagree with you about this.
4. I'm really not ________ about that design.
5. I'm ________ , Pete, but I don't agree with you.
6. I don't agree at ________ . It won't work.
7. I'm not ________ about this. Can we talk later?
8. I'm afraid I ________ agree with you at all.
9. I don't ________ at all with the merger.
10. You ________ be right, but I'm not sure.
11. Sorry, but I disagree ________ this plan.

with, totally, afraid, sorry, don't, sure, could, all, disagree, sure, agree, ~~with~~

25.4 LISTEN TO THE AUDIO AND ANSWER THE QUESTIONS

Two colleagues, Jenny and Greg, are discussing applicants for a job.

How does Jenny feel about the candidates?
She likes all of them. ☑
She likes some of them. ☐
She dislikes all of them. ☐

1 Jenny thinks it's going to be an easy choice.
Greg strongly agrees with her. ☐
Greg agrees with her. ☐
Greg disagrees with her. ☐

2 Jenny thinks John is a strong candidate.
Greg thinks he has lots of enthusiasm. ☐
Greg thinks he doesn't have enough experience. ☐
Greg thinks he has enough qualifications. ☐

3 Greg thinks they need someone with experience.
Jenny strongly agrees. ☐
Jenny disagrees. ☐
Jenny strongly disagrees. ☐

4 Jenny thinks Paula could be a good candidate.
Greg agrees. ☐
Greg strongly agrees. ☐
Greg disagrees. ☐

5 Greg suggests they send Paula on a course.
Jenny agrees. ☐
Jenny strongly agrees. ☐
Jenny strongly disagrees. ☐

25.5 CROSS OUT THE INCORRECT WORD IN EACH SENTENCE, THEN SAY THE SENTENCES OUT LOUD

I agree / ~~argue~~ with you about the new IT system.

1 We totally / perfectly agree about the redesign.

2 I can't agree with you in / at all about the downsizing.

3 We're frightened / afraid we totally disagree.

4 You could / would be right, but I need more evidence.

5 I'm not sure about / with the latest business plan.

26 Health and safety

Many workplaces issue guidelines for how to avoid accidents and stay safe. In English, this topic often uses specialist vocabulary and reflexive pronouns.

New language Reflexive pronouns
Aa Vocabulary Health and safety at work
New skill Talking about safety at work

26.1 MARK THE SENTENCES THAT ARE CORRECT

Anita signed herself up for the course. ☑
Anita signed itself up for the course. ☐

1. Roger hurt him when he slipped. ☐
   Roger hurt himself when he slipped. ☐
2. She burned herself on the coffee maker. ☐
   She burned himself on the coffee maker. ☐
3. Ron blames itself for the accident. ☐
   Ron blames himself for the accident. ☐
4. Jan cut herself on the machinery. ☐
   She cut itself on the machinery. ☐
5. We enjoyed ourselves at the office party. ☐
   We enjoyed ourself at the office party. ☐
6. Juan cut yourself in the kitchen. ☐
   Juan cut himself in the kitchen. ☐
7. We need to protect himself from risks. ☐
   We need to protect ourselves from risks. ☐

26.2 CROSS OUT THE INCORRECT WORD IN EACH SENTENCE, THEN SAY THE SENTENCES OUT LOUD

We locked **ourselves** / ~~themselves~~ in the factory last week.

1. I hurt **yourself** / **myself** when I moved the photocopier.
2. They should prepare **themselves** / **themself** for the course.
3. Claire's cut **herself** / **itself** on the equipment.
4. Have you all signed **yourself** / **yourselves** up for the course?
5. Sam is teaching **himself** / **hisself** Japanese.

26.3 READ THE ARTICLE AND ANSWER THE QUESTIONS

Many employees are afraid of a fire in their building.
True ☑ False ☐ Not given ☐

1 You should leave the building as quickly as possible.
True ☐ False ☐ Not given ☐

2 You should turn off electrical appliances.
True ☐ False ☐ Not given ☐

3 If you smell a fire, activate the fire alarm.
True ☐ False ☐ Not given ☐

4 If you find a large fire, use an extinguisher to fight the fire.
True ☐ False ☐ Not given ☐

5 You should take care to close doors behind you.
True ☐ False ☐ Not given ☐

6 You should make sure you take your belongings with you.
True ☐ False ☐ Not given ☐

7 You should go to the assembly point and wait.
True ☐ False ☐ Not given ☐

8 You can go back to your office when the alarm stops.
True ☐ False ☐ Not given ☐

DAILY NEWS

A Burning Issue

What to do when you hear the fire alarm

A fire in the workplace is what 63% of employees fear the most. But there are some simple steps that you can follow to make sure you stay safe. First of all, don't panic: remember the instructions from your fire drill. If you smell smoke, activate the fire alarm. You should only use a fire extinguisher on a small fire. You should stay calm and leave the building using the stairs. Don't use the elevator, even if you are not fit. You should also leave all your belongings at your desk—don't waste time. Then, go to the nearest assembly point and stay there (even if the alarm has stopped) until the fire officer tells you it is safe to return.

26.4 FILL IN THE GAPS USING THE WORDS IN THE PANEL

If you discover a fire, set off the *fire alarm* .

1 An ______________ is used to stop small fires.

2 If you hear the fire alarm, go to the ______________.

3 Medical equipment is kept in the ______________.

4 Each fire ______________ has a sign above the door.

5 You practice leaving the building during a ______________.

fire drill | extinguisher | escape | ~~fire alarm~~ | first aid kit | assembly area

27 Suggestions and advice

When there are everyday problems in the workplace, it is useful to know how to make suggestions and offer advice. There are several ways to do this in English.

New language Prefixes and suffixes
Aa Vocabulary Everyday workplace problems
New skill Making suggestions

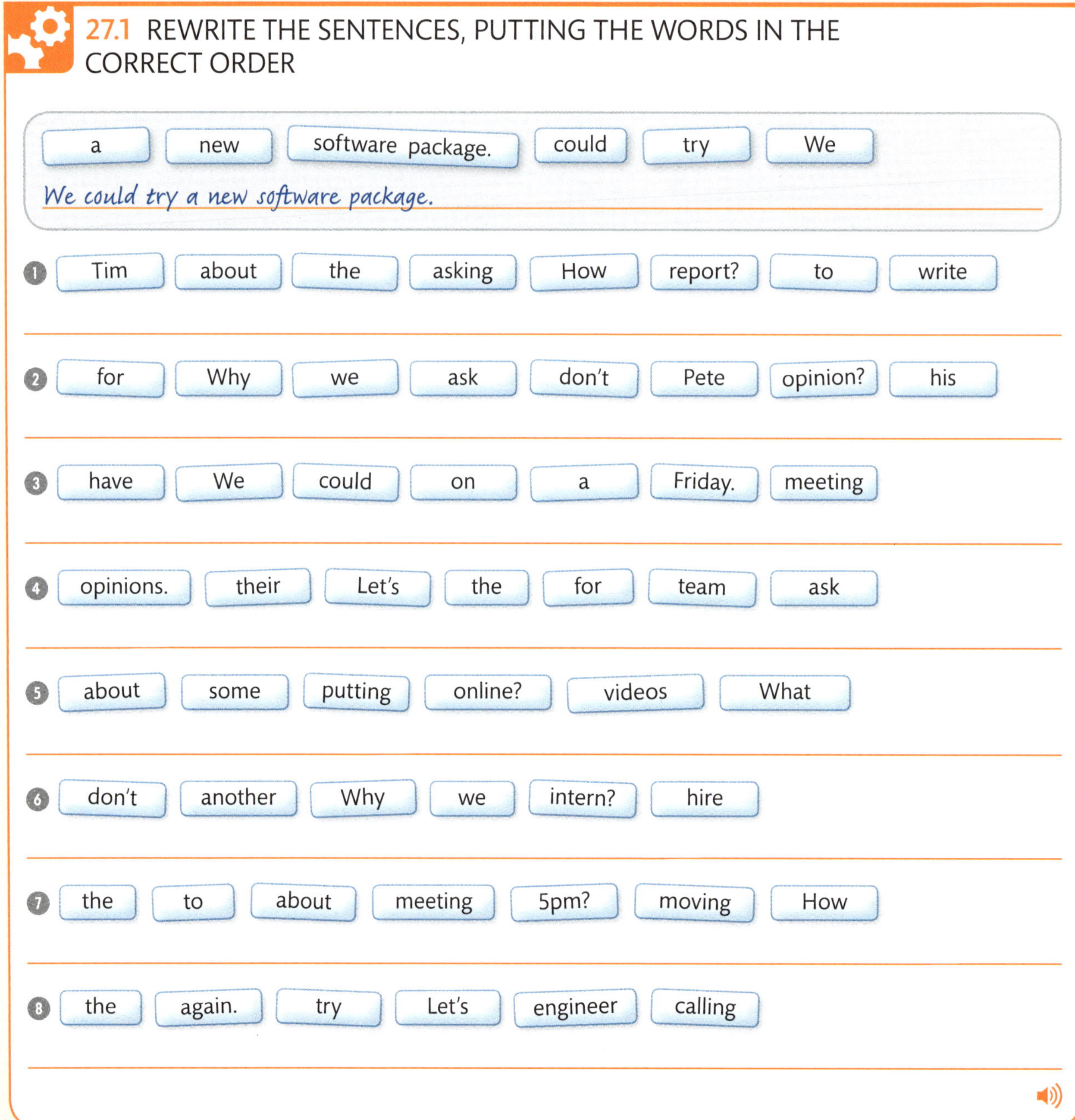

27.1 REWRITE THE SENTENCES, PUTTING THE WORDS IN THE CORRECT ORDER

a | new | software package. | could | try | We

We could try a new software package.

1. Tim | about | the | asking | How | report? | to | write

2. for | Why | we | ask | don't | Pete | opinion? | his

3. have | We | could | on | a | Friday. | meeting

4. opinions. | their | Let's | the | for | team | ask

5. about | some | putting | online? | videos | What

6. don't | another | Why | we | intern? | hire

7. the | to | about | meeting | 5pm? | moving | How

8. the | again. | try | Let's | engineer | calling

27.2 MATCH THE WORKPLACE PROBLEMS TO THE SUGGESTIONS AND ADVICE

I've been at my desk all day. → You should go for a walk.

1. Sally doesn't feel well.
2. I've lost my copy of the agenda.
3. I don't understand the new program.
4. There's no more coffee.
5. Karl's computer keeps crashing.
6. The photocopier's jammed.
7. My deadline is tomorrow.
8. The metro isn't running tomorrow.

- She should go home and rest.
- You should go on a training course.
- You should go for a walk.
- You should order some more.
- You should ask the secretary for another.
- You should call the engineer.
- You should take the bus.
- He should call IT.
- You should ask for an extension.

27.3 FILL IN THE GAPS USING THE WORDS IN THE PANEL

Susan *misspelled* my name. It's Catherine with a "C."

1. Where have the reports gone? They've ________.
2. Pete ________ me. He thought I said 3 o'clock.
3. Cathy isn't coming in today. She's feeling ________.
4. You should be ________ crossing the road.
5. Doug is really ________. He gets angry so easily.
6. I'm ________ to come to the training because I have a meeting.
7. Don't forget to ________ the machine after you've used it.
8. I'm ________ with that program. I don't know it.
9. Jean is so ________. She's always making mistakes.
10. This morning is ________ for me. Can we meet later?

unable
impractical
careful
unfamiliar
~~misspelled~~
misunderstood
impatient
careless
disappeared
unwell
disconnect

27.4 CROSS OUT THE INCORRECT WORD IN EACH SENTENCE, THEN SAY THE SENTENCES OUT LOUD

What about arranging a meeting to discuss some practical / ~~impractical~~ solutions?

1. We should make sure no one understood / misunderstood the instructions.

2. How about organizing training for everyone who is unfamiliar / familiar with the program?

3. Let's make sure no one on the team spells / misspells the name wrongly again.

4. Why don't we ask Pete to help if Laura isn't well / unwell tomorrow?

5. I think we should disconnect / connect the machine since it's not working.

6. I don't think you should be so patient / impatient with the new recruits.

7. Let's send a memo to everyone who isn't able / unable to come to the meeting.

8. Let's explain to Tim that he should be more careful / careless with financial information.

9. Why don't we try to find a time that is convenient / inconvenient for everyone?

28 Giving a presentation

When you are preparing a presentation, make sure it is clear and easy to follow. There are certain phrases you can use to help guide the audience through the talk.

New language Signposting language
Aa Vocabulary Presentation equipment
New skill Structuring a talk

28.1 LISTEN TO THE AUDIO AND ANSWER THE QUESTIONS

The CEO of a clothing company is talking to her employees.

The presentation is about...
marketing. ☑ **TV ads.** ☐ **websites.** ☐

1. The speaker wants to focus on...
retired men. ☐ **young adults.** ☐ **children.** ☐

2. Young adults between 18 and 23 are buying...
sports wear. ☐ **business wear.** ☐ **casual wear.** ☐

3. Young adults between 24 and 30 buy more...
jackets. ☐ **suits.** ☐ **sneakers.** ☐

4. What percentage of Europeans wear sports wear?
50% ☐ **60%** ☐ **65%** ☐

5. What percentage of Americans wear sports wear?
70% ☐ **80%** ☐ **85%** ☐

6. The speaker is disappointed with growth in...
England. ☐ **China.** ☐ **the US.** ☐

7. The speaker hopes that growth will occur in...
South Africa. ☐ **India.** ☐ **New Zealand.** ☐

28.2 REWRITE THE SENTENCES, PUTTING THE WORDS IN THE CORRECT ORDER

we'll | Next, | benefits. | explore | the
Next, we'll explore the benefits.

1. about | Today | going | I'm | talk | profit. | to

2. anyone | questions? | Does | have | any

3. up, | facing | To | we | are | issues. | sum

4. happy | I'm | to | questions. | answer

5. the | Last, | look | let's | future. | at

28.3 MATCH THE BEGINNINGS OF THE SENTENCES TO THE CORRECT ENDINGS

Today, I want to talk → about something really important.

1. I'd like to begin
2. I'm happy to
3. Does anyone have any more
4. Let's move
5. After that, I would
6. To sum up, it's

- by showing you this graph.
- questions or comments?
- about something really important.
- answer any questions.
- been an excellent quarter for the company.
- on to the next topic.
- like to talk about the merger.

Aa 28.4 FILL IN THE GAPS USING THE WORDS IN THE PANEL

Can you please look at the graph on your *handout*?

1. The ______ is black. We can't see the graph.
2. If you use a ______, you can introduce graphs and visuals.
3. I'll write down the company's name on the ______.
4. There are programs to help you make professional-looking ______.
5. If you use a ______, the people at the back will hear you.

projector | slides | ~~handout~~ | flipchart | microphone | screen

28.5 CROSS OUT THE INCORRECT WORD IN EACH SENTENCE, THEN SAY THE SENTENCES OUT LOUD

Feel free to **ask** / ~~answer~~ any questions at the end.

1. I'd **want** / **like** to start with our factory in Vietnam.
2. To sum **up** / **in**, we need to invest more in infrastructure.
3. I'll **explore** / **travel** the benefits of investing in web technology later.
4. Let's begin **in** / **by** looking at the sales figures.
5. In **short** / **small**, we need to develop new products.
6. Let's take a **look** / **view** at the second graph.
7. So we've **completed** / **covered** all the topics I wanted to discuss.
8. Turning **to** / **on** the previous quarter's profits.
9. Then I'm going to **talk** / **discuss** about the situation in China.
10. **For** / **To** start, let's look at this year's performance.
11. Moving **on** / **up**, let's look at our main competitors.
12. First, I'm going to look **at** / **in** last year's results.
13. I'm happy to **ask** / **answer** any questions at the end.
14. I'd like to end **in** / **by** thanking you all for your attention today.

29 Rules and requests

Use "can" and "have to" to talk about rules in the workplace, and verbs such as "could" to politely ask colleagues to help you solve problems.

New language Modal verbs
Aa Vocabulary Polite requests
New skill Talking about rules and regulations

29.1 CROSS OUT THE INCORRECT WORDS IN EACH SENTENCE

There's a formal dress code here. You can't / ~~have to~~ wear shorts to work.

1  You can't / don't have to stay late tonight. It's very quiet.

2  Is your phone broken? You can / have to use mine if you like.

3  We can't / have to wear a jacket and tie when we meet clients.

4  You can't / don't have to park there. It's a space for disabled drivers.

29.2 MATCH THE BEGINNINGS OF THE STATEMENTS TO THE CORRECT ENDINGS

You have to turn off the lights. → It saves energy.

1 You can't leave early tonight.

2 You don't have to pay for lunch.

3 You can make yourself a hot drink.

4 We have to wear business clothes.

5 We have to leave the building now.

There's tea and coffee in the kitchen.

It saves energy.

That's the fire alarm.

There's a formal dress code.

Staff eat for free in the cafeteria.

We have an important meeting at 5pm.

29.3 LISTEN TO THE AUDIO AND ANSWER THE QUESTIONS

Peter is having a difficult conversation with his manager.

Peter can take long lunch breaks.
True ☐ **False** ☑ **Not given** ☐

1. Staff can take their lunch break at 12:00.
True ☐ **False** ☐ **Not given** ☐

2. Peter can wear jeans to work.
True ☐ **False** ☐ **Not given** ☐

3. Women can't wear dresses to work.
True ☐ **False** ☐ **Not given** ☐

4. Men don't always have to wear a tie.
True ☐ **False** ☐ **Not given** ☐

5. Staff don't have to clean up the meeting rooms.
True ☐ **False** ☐ **Not given** ☐

29.4 REWRITE THE SENTENCES, CORRECTING THE ERRORS

I has to stay late tonight. There's so much to do!
I have to stay late tonight. There's so much to do!

1. I can to listen to music at work if I use headphones.

2. He's a pilot. He have to wear a uniform.

3. They doesn't has to go to the training session.

4. He can't taking more than an hour for his lunch break.

5. He doesn't have to leave early. It's too busy.

6. I have back up my files before I turn my computer off.

29.5 MATCH THE PICTURES TO THE CORRECT SENTENCES

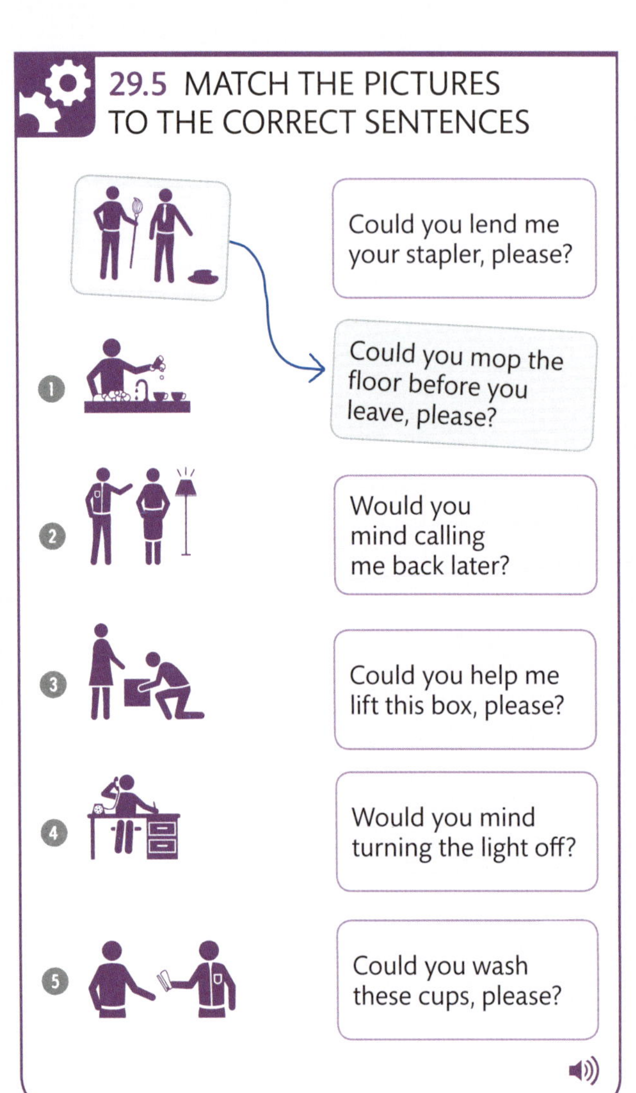

29.6 MARK THE REQUESTS THAT ARE CORRECT

Would you mind call a taxi? ☐
Would you mind calling a taxi? ☑

1. Could you open the window? ☐
   Could you opening the window? ☐
2. Would you mind check this list? ☐
   Would you mind checking this list? ☐
3. Could you forward me Jo's email? ☐
   Could you forwarding me Jo's email? ☐
4. Would you mind print the report? ☐
   Would you mind printing the report? ☐
5. Could you passing around the agenda? ☐
   Could you pass around the agenda? ☐
6. Would you mind ordering more files? ☐
   Would you mind order more files? ☐
7. Could you coming to today's meeting? ☐
   Could you come to today's meeting? ☐

29.7 WRITE EACH SENTENCE IN ITS OTHER FORM

Could you make us tea and coffee? — *Would you mind making us tea and coffee?*

1. ______________ — **Would you mind turning** your music down?
2. **Could you check** my report for me? — ______________
3. ______________ — **Would you mind closing** the window?
4. **Could you invite** Alan to the meeting? — ______________

29.8 REWRITE THE REQUESTS, PUTTING THE WORDS IN THE CORRECT ORDER

you | ordering | more | mind | Would | stationery? | some

Would you mind ordering some more stationery?

1. figures? | you | these | Could | sales | check

____

2. you | now? | deposit | mind | a | Would | paying

____

3. ask | Ian | me | you | back? | to | call | Could

____

4. showing | around? | you | clients | mind | our | Would

____

29.9 SAY THE REQUESTS OUT LOUD, FILLING IN THE GAPS USING THE WORDS IN THE PANEL

Could you *make* tea and coffee for our clients, please?

1. Would you mind _______________ the door? It's really hot in here.
2. Would you mind _______________ John to email me this month's sales figures?
3. Could you _______________ the minutes for this afternoon's meeting?
4. Could you _______________ me who is coming to tomorrow's presentation?

take | asking | ~~make~~ | remind | opening

30 Vocabulary

Aa **30.1 WORK IDIOMS** WRITE THE PHRASES FROM THE PANEL UNDER THE CORRECT DEFINITIONS

To start something

to get the ball rolling

❶ To think about something in an original way

❸ Administration, paperwork, or rules and regulations

❹ To relax or calm down

❻ To gradually relax

❼ The normal daily routine at a company

❾ A situation with no negative outcome

❿ To owe money

⓬ It is your turn to do or say something

⓭ To delay or avoid something

⓯ Wasting money

⓰ To be really busy

2 To start work on something that needs doing

____

5 To be busy doing something else

____

8 To not be working

____

11 To work very long hours

____

14 Not acting or behaving as it should

____

17 To do a fair share of work

____

to work around the clock
going haywire
to be out of order
~~to get the ball rolling~~
to think outside the box
to take it easy
throwing money down the drain
red tape
to pull your weight
to be in the red
a win-win situation
to be swamped
to wind down
the ball is in your court
business as usual
to get down to business
to be tied up with
to put something off

31 Discussing issues

Many common workplace problems arise from an ongoing situation in the past. You can use the past continuous tense to discuss these problems.

New language Past continuous
Aa Vocabulary Work idioms
New skill Describing workplace problems

31.1 MARK THE SENTENCES THAT ARE CORRECT

Chris weren't answering his phone. ☐
Chris wasn't answering his phone. ☑

1. Tanya was feeling very tired. ☐
   Tanya were feeling very tired. ☐
2. I were finishing his report. ☐
   I was finishing his report. ☐
3. Alison was talk to the CEO. ☐
   Alison was talking to the CEO. ☐
4. Was Jamie taking minutes? ☐
   Were Jamie taking minutes? ☐
5. Was you working late yesterday? ☐
   Were you working late yesterday? ☐
6. I trying was to call you. ☐
   I was trying to call you. ☐
7. Claire were playing very loud music. ☐
   Claire was playing very loud music. ☐

31.2 FILL IN THE GAPS BY PUTTING THE VERBS IN THE PAST CONTINUOUS

My computer *wasn't working* (not work) this morning.

1. The train trip here was really bad. All the trains ______ (run) late.
2. The cleaners ______ (complain) that staff left their dirty cups in the sink.
3. Harriet ______ (not listen) to the presentation.
4. Tom's manager was annoyed because Tom ______ (not meet) his deadlines.
5. My email inbox ______ (get) full, so I had to delete some messages.

31.3 LISTEN TO THE AUDIO AND ANSWER THE QUESTIONS

Alina and Howard are talking about a difficult morning at work.

Alina finished her report this morning.
True ☐ **False** ☑

1. Howard's laptop wasn't working.
True ☐ **False** ☐

2. IT solved the problem with Howard's computer.
True ☐ **False** ☐

3. Alina has the sales figures that she needs.
True ☐ **False** ☐

4. Howard thinks the report needs a new approach.
True ☐ **False** ☐

5. They don't have a computer that they can use.
True ☐ **False** ☐

31.4 DESCRIBE THE PICTURES OUT LOUD, USING THE WORDS IN THE PANEL TO FILL IN THE GAPS

The printer _wasn't working_ yesterday.

1. Joshua ______________ a talk about new markets.

2. Fiona ______________ to Bilal's new ideas for products.

3. Lucia ______________ the minutes of the meeting.

4. They ______________ too loudly on the phone.

5. Helen ______________ her lunch at her desk.

wasn't listening | was eating | were speaking | was giving | ~~wasn't working~~ | was taking

31.5 READ THE BLOG AND ANSWER THE QUESTIONS

Louise's Blog

HOME | ENTRIES | ABOUT | CONTACT

Having a bad day at work is something that happens to all of us. Delayed trains, co-workers who annoy you, printers that don't work; it all adds up to stress for the best of us.

Take last week, for example. I missed an important meeting with a new supplier. My boss was sick, so I had to go instead, but my train was running late. I also had a cold because my co-workers were always leaving the windows next to the fire doors and the elevators open. To make matters worse, the people in my pod were talking really loudly and it was hard to concentrate. I knew it was Ben's last day and that they were having drinks and snacks to say goodbye, but I had lots of work to do.

Later that week, I had a long meeting with my boss. I tried to tell him that it didn't help that my assistant was copying me into lots of emails I didn't need to see. My boss said I needed to talk to my assistant and ask him to talk to me first if he was unsure of anything. I felt better after my update meeting, but when I got back to my desk, my USB cable and headphones were missing. Someone was borrowing them without asking. This was always happening. I was fed up.

So what should you do when you have a week like mine? When everything is going haywire, talking to a co-worker for ten minutes can help. It's good to share problems, but don't turn it into a complaining session. Complaining is negative and uses up our energy. Having a quick walk outside should clear your head. Our bodies like to be in the open air and sunlight for half an hour a day, so go for a walk after lunch instead of reading those reports. Then you can tackle a full inbox with a positive perspective.

Why did Louise miss her meeting? **She was sick** ☐ **It was canceled** ☐ **Her train was running late** ☑

1. What were Louise's co-workers always opening? **The windows** ☐ **The doors** ☐ **The elevators** ☐
2. How were Louise's co-workers making it difficult for her to focus? **Talking** ☐ **Eating** ☐ **Drinking** ☐
3. Who was sending Louise too many emails? **Her boss** ☐ **Her assistant** ☐ **Her co-workers** ☐
4. What was missing from Louise's desk? **Her laptop** ☐ **Her files** ☐ **Her USB cable** ☐
5. What should you do if you're stressed? **Complain** ☐ **Talk to a co-worker** ☐ **Use up energy** ☐
6. What does Louise say a walk outside can help us do? **Think clearly** ☐ **Get fit** ☐ **Enjoy nature** ☐

32 Apologies and explanations

English uses a variety of polite phrases to apologize for mistakes. Use the past continuous with the past simple to offer an explanation for a mistake.

New language Past continuous and past simple
Aa Vocabulary Workplace mistakes
New skill Apologizing and giving explanations

32.1 MARK THE SENTENCES THAT ARE CORRECT

I like to apologize for keeping you waiting so long. ☐
I would like to apologize for keeping you waiting so long. ☑

1. I am so sorry I was late for the meeting with our clients today. ☐
   I so sorry I was late for the meeting with our clients today. ☐
2. I would like to apologize for not finish the report yesterday. ☐
   I would like to apologize for not finishing the report yesterday. ☐
3. I'm sorry really. I forgot to charge the office cell phone and it has no power. ☐
   I'm really sorry. I forgot to charge the office cell phone and it has no power. ☐
4. I'm really apologize this line is so bad. I hope we don't get cut off. ☐
   I'm really sorry this line is so bad. I hope we don't get cut off. ☐
5. I'm afraid that's not enough good. I want a full refund on my ticket. ☐
   I'm afraid that's not good enough. I want a full refund on my ticket. ☐

32.2 MATCH THE APOLOGIES WITH THE CORRECT RESPONSES

I'm very sorry if the waiter was rude. → That's all right. I could see he was very busy.

1. I'm so sorry. My presentation isn't ready.
2. I apologize if your food was cold.
3. I'm really sorry, but I have to leave early.
4. I'm very sorry the coffee machine's broken.
5. I'm really sorry. I left the reports at home.

- No problem. I'll help you finish it now.
- That's not good enough. Please heat it up.
- That's all right. I could see he was very busy.
- Don't worry. I'll print off some more.
- Never mind. We're not very busy today.
- No problem. I'll have tea instead.

32.3 LISTEN TO THE AUDIO, THEN NUMBER THE PICTURES IN THE ORDER THEY ARE DESCRIBED

A ☐

B ☐

C 1

D ☐

E ☐

32.4 SAY THE SENTENCES OUT LOUD, FILLING IN THE GAPS USING THE WORDS IN THE PANEL

I really *must* apologize for not calling you back earlier.

1. I'm really ______ . I forgot to send the agenda for the meeting.
2. I would like to ______ for the rudeness of the waitress.
3. I'm ______ that's not good enough. You missed an important meeting.
4. That's all ______ . I'll make you a copy right now.
5. Please ______ sure it doesn't happen again.
6. Never ______ . It's only a cup.
7. I would ______ to apologize for the delay to your train this evening.

~~must~~ like mind apologize sorry afraid make right

32.5 CROSS OUT THE INCORRECT WORDS IN EACH SENTENCE

I ~~wrote~~ / was writing a report when my computer crashed / ~~was crashing~~.

1. Harry practiced / was practicing his presentation when I called / was calling him.
2. Sam's cell phone rang / was ringing when Tom described / was describing the sales for this quarter.
3. The elevator got / was getting stuck while they waited / were waiting for it.
4. Tina didn't listen / wasn't listening when the CEO said / was saying all staff would get a raise.
5. The fire alarm went / was going off when we had / were having our update meeting.
6. I worked / was working late when I heard / was hearing a strange noise.
7. I edited / was editing the report when the fire alarm went / was going off.

32.6 FILL IN THE GAPS BY PUTTING THE VERBS IN THE PAST CONTINUOUS OR PAST SIMPLE

I was driving (drive) to a meeting when someone crashed (crash) into me.

1. The photocopier ______________ (break) while I ______________ (copy) your sales report.
2. We ______________ (listen) to Janet's presentation when the power ______________ (go) off.
3. John ______________ (sign) the contract when the lawyer ______________ (call) him.
4. Anna ______________ (be) furious when she found out George ______________ (copy) her ideas.
5. Simon ______________ (edit) the report when his computer ______________ (crash).
6. We ______________ (wait) for the bus when two buses ______________ (arrive).

33 Tasks and targets

When you are dealing with deadlines and pressure at work, you can use the present perfect to let your co-workers know how your work is progressing.

New language Present perfect and past simple
Aa Vocabulary Workplace tasks
New skill Discussing achievements at work

33.1 FILL IN THE GAPS BY PUTTING THE VERBS IN THE PRESENT PERFECT

I *have written* (write) the report you wanted.

1.  I ______________ (call) eight customers this morning.
2.  Gareth ______________ (make) coffee for the visitors.
3.  Piotr ______________ (cut) the hair of many famous people.
4.  I ______________ (not finish) checking my emails.
5.  Carl ______________ (not email) me the sales data.

33.2 CROSS OUT THE INCORRECT WORD IN EACH SENTENCE

I've just / ~~yet~~ sent him the files.

1. She hasn't sent the invoice just / yet.
2. We have yet / just heard the CEO is leaving.
3. I haven't met the new director yet / just.
4. Has Tom finished fixing my laptop just / yet?
5. George has just / yet called me.
6. The painters haven't finished yet / just.
7. Have you had a meeting with Ann yet / just?
8. The trainer has just / yet arrived.
9. Have you just / yet finished the report?

33.3 REWRITE THE SENTENCES, PUTTING THE WORDS IN THE CORRECT ORDER

just | preparing | have | my | I | presentation. | finished

I have just finished preparing my presentation.

1. the | haven't | stationery | yet. | I | ordered

2. the | They | packaging. | just | new | introduced | have

3. answered | you | emails | yet? | those | Have

4. our | minutes | has | written | from | Derinda | the | meeting. | just

33.4 READ LAILA'S TO DO LIST AND ANSWER THE QUESTIONS

Laila has emailed the CEO.
True ☐ **False** ☐ **Not given** ☑

1. Laila has organized the team meeting.
True ☐ **False** ☐ **Not given** ☐

2. Laila has photocopied the expenses claims.
True ☐ **False** ☐ **Not given** ☐

3. Laila hasn't updated the database.
True ☐ **False** ☐ **Not given** ☐

4. Accounts has found the missing invoice.
True ☐ **False** ☐ **Not given** ☐

To do list

- ~~Organize team meeting~~
- ~~Write FAQs for new staff~~
- Photocopy boss's expenses claims
- Update the database
- ~~Call Accounts about missing invoice~~
- Get bus timetables for visitors

33.5 REWRITE THE SENTENCES, CORRECTING THE ERRORS

Tim **has given** a great presentation yesterday afternoon.
Tim gave a great presentation yesterday afternoon.

1. Daniel **has sent** your package last Friday.

2. Jenny **has shown** me the new designs yesterday.

3. Babu and Zack **hasn't finished** their research yet.

4. Kate **has spoken** to the HR manager last week.

33.6 LISTEN TO THE AUDIO AND MARK WHICH THINGS ACTUALLY HAPPENED

1.
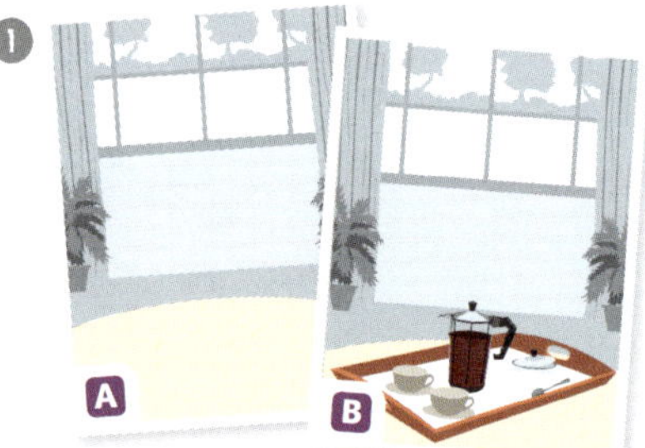

2.
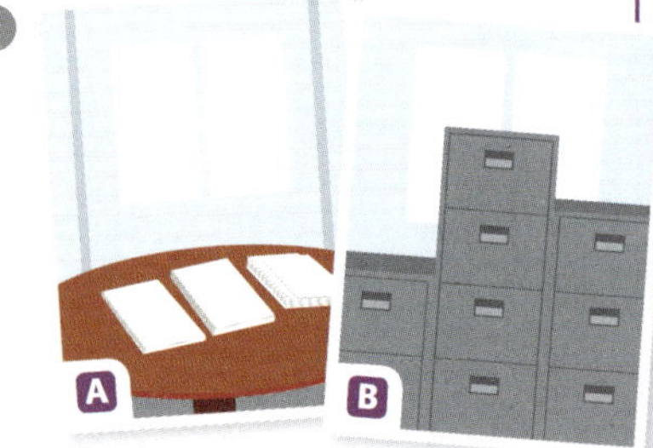

3.

4.

5.
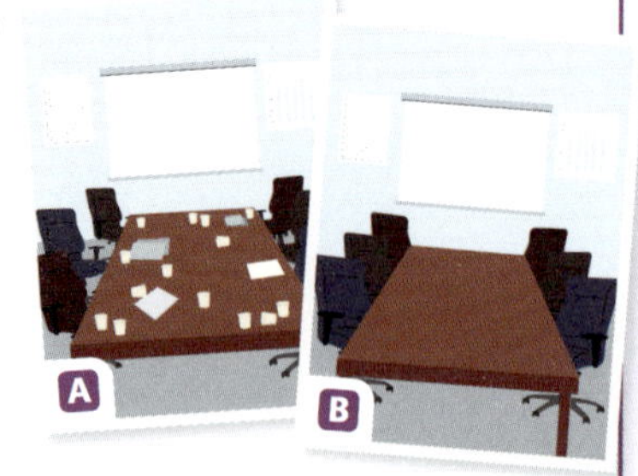

33.7 MARK THE SENTENCES THAT AREN'T CORRECT

I've finished the reports last week. ☐
I finished the reports last week. ☑

1. I has done all the invoices for June. ☐
   I have done all the invoices for June. ☐

2. He met the Chinese partners last month. ☐
   He has met the Chinese partners last month. ☐

3. He hasn't sent the salaries to payroll yet. ☐
   He hasn't sended the salaries to payroll yet. ☐

4. They not started the audit yet. ☐
   They have not started the audit yet. ☐

5. He has left this morning. ☐
   He left this morning. ☐

6. I have yet heard about your promotion. ☐
   I have just heard about your promotion. ☐

7. She have sold the most products. ☐
   She has sold the most products. ☐

8. Have you designed that box yet? ☐
   You have designed that box yet? ☐

9. They have given him a verbal warning. ☐
   They have gived him a verbal warning. ☐

10. Mark hasn't scanned it just. ☐
    Mark hasn't scanned it yet. ☐

11. I have speaked to your team. ☐
    I have spoken to your team. ☐

33.8 RESPOND OUT LOUD TO THE AUDIO, FILLING IN THE GAPS USING THE WORDS IN THE PANEL

Have you finished the reports?
No, I haven't finished them _yet._

1. Have you scanned the photos?
   Yes, I've ______ scanned them.

2. Has Philip audited the books?
   No, he ______ done them yet.

3. Where are the contracts?
   ______ filed them all in the cabinet.

4. Why are there no newspapers?
   We've ______ the delivery.

I've just stopped hasn't ~~yet~~

34 Dealing with complaints

If a customer complains about a problem, one way to offer a solution, and to make predictions or promises, is to use the future with "will."

New language The future with "will"
Aa Vocabulary Complaints and apologies
New skill Dealing with complaints

34.1 MARK THE SENTENCES THAT ARE CORRECT

The company wills offer you a discount. ☐
The company will offer you a discount. ☑

1. We will replace your tablet free of charge. ☐
   We will to replace your tablet free of charge. ☐
2. The chef will cooks you another pizza. ☐
   The chef will cook you another pizza. ☐
3. I'll talk to the boss about it. ☐
   I'll talking to the boss about it. ☐
4. The manager be will with you soon. ☐
   The manager will be with you soon. ☐
5. I contact our courier immediately. ☐
   I'll contact our courier immediately. ☐
6. We will give you a full refund. ☐
   We will to give you a full refund. ☐
7. I promise that your order arrive today. ☐
   I promise that your order will arrive today. ☐
8. I'm afraid we won't finish the project on time. ☐
   I'm afraid we willn't finish the project on time. ☐
9. I'm sorry, but we don't will cancel your order. ☐
   I'm sorry, but we won't cancel your order. ☐

34.2 MATCH THE COMPLAINTS TO THE CORRECT RESPONSES

My bus was three hours late. → We'll refund you the price of your ticket.

1. My luggage didn't arrive.
2. This food is cold.
3. You have charged me twice.
4. I've been waiting for a taxi for 40 minutes.
5. There is no hot water in our bathroom.

- We'll move you to another room.
- I will call the driver immediately.
- We'll refund you the price of your ticket.
- We'll send it to your hotel when it gets here.
- I'll ask the chef to cook it properly.
- I'll refund the money to your credit card.

34.3 READ THE LETTER AND ANSWER THE QUESTIONS

Dear Mr. Vance,

Thank you for your letter of March 3. I am sorry to hear you were not happy with the service provided by our hotel during your two-day business trip to Rome last month. First of all, I sincerely apologize that there was no receptionist when you arrived at midnight. We will ask our receptionists to work late when travelers are delayed so that there is always someone to welcome our guests in the future. I am also sorry to hear that the bathroom in your hotel suite had not been cleaned. I agree that this was unacceptable, and I will speak to the cleaning services manager. Regarding breakfast, I am sorry that there was no bread and that you had to ask for hot coffee. I will speak to the catering staff to ensure this does not happen again. With reference to the hotel's policy on guaranteeing residents a good night's sleep, I am so sorry to hear that you were kept awake by guests in the adjoining room. Given all the above, I would like to offer a full refund of what you paid for your two-night hotel stay.

I hope this is satisfactory.

Yours sincerely,

Mr. J Silvano

Why did Mr. Vance write to the hotel?

To complain about the food in Rome ☐

To thank them for a pleasant stay ☐

To complain about his stay there ☑

1 What was the problem when Mr. Vance checked in?

The security guard arrived after midnight ☐

The security guard was rude ☐

There was no receptionist ☐

2 What will the hotel do in the future?

They will ask receptionists to work late ☐

Receptionists will go to the airport ☐

Receptionists will not work late ☐

3 What was wrong with Mr. Vance's hotel suite?

It was noisy at night ☐

The light didn't work ☐

The bathroom was dirty ☐

4 How will this complaint be addressed?

Mr. Silvano will clean the bathrooms ☐

Mr. Silvano will apologize to the cleaner. ☐

He will speak to the cleaners' manager ☐

5 What was wrong with the breakfast?

There wasn't any hot coffee ☐

There wasn't any juice ☐

There wasn't any cereal ☐

6 What was the problem that evening?

Mr. Vance had to work late ☐

Mr. Vance went to a party ☐

Mr. Vance was kept awake ☐

7 What does Mr. Silvano offer Mr. Vance?

A discount off his next stay ☐

A full refund ☐

A refund for one night's stay in the hotel ☐

34.4 REWRITE THE SENTENCES, PUTTING THE WORDS IN THE CORRECT ORDER

in | arrive | minutes? | next | Will | the | ten | train | the

Will the train arrive in the next ten minutes?

1 next | you | stay. | a | hotel | discount | offer | We'll | your | off

____

2 to | refunded | the | card? | money | Will | credit | be | my

____

3 your | chase | The | order | you. | will | up | for | company

____

4 with | will | very | The | you | manager | soon. | be | store

____

5 the | washing | Will | machine? | broken | on | part | my | replace | you

____

34.5 LISTEN TO THE AUDIO AND MARK WHETHER EACH SCENARIO WILL OR WON'T HAPPEN TODAY

Will ☑
Won't ☐

1 Will ☐
Won't ☐

2 Will ☐
Won't ☐

3 Will ☐
Won't ☐

4 Will ☐
Won't ☐

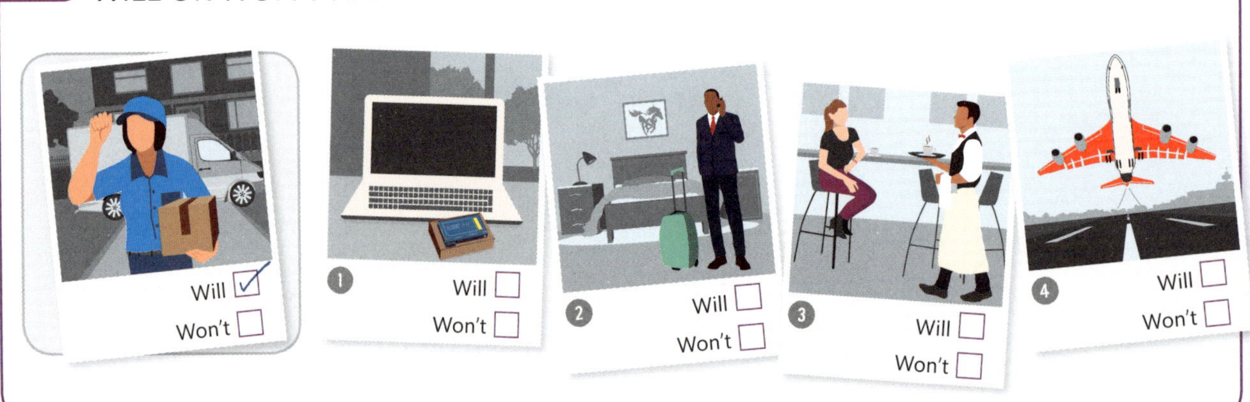

34.6 RESPOND OUT LOUD TO THE AUDIO, FILLING IN THE GAPS USING THE PHRASES IN THE PANEL

My train was an hour late.

I do apologize. We *'ll refund* the fare to your credit card.

1. The concert was canceled when we got to the venue last night.

   I'm very sorry about that. ________________ you a refund.

2. My pasta is cold.

   I really must apologize. I ________________ it back to the kitchen.

3. Where is the sales assistant? I want to try these shoes on.

   She ________________ with you in a minute.

4. The receptionist was rude.

   I ________________ to her about this.

5. Your assistant didn't finish that report I asked him to prepare.

   It ________________ again.

6. There aren't any vegetarian options on this menu.

   I ________________ the chef to make you something vegetarian.

won't happen | 'll take | ~~'ll refund~~ | 'll ask | We'll offer | 'll be | 'll talk

35 Vocabulary

Aa 35.1 **TRANSPORTATION** WRITE THE WORDS FROM THE PANEL UNDER THE CORRECT PICTURES

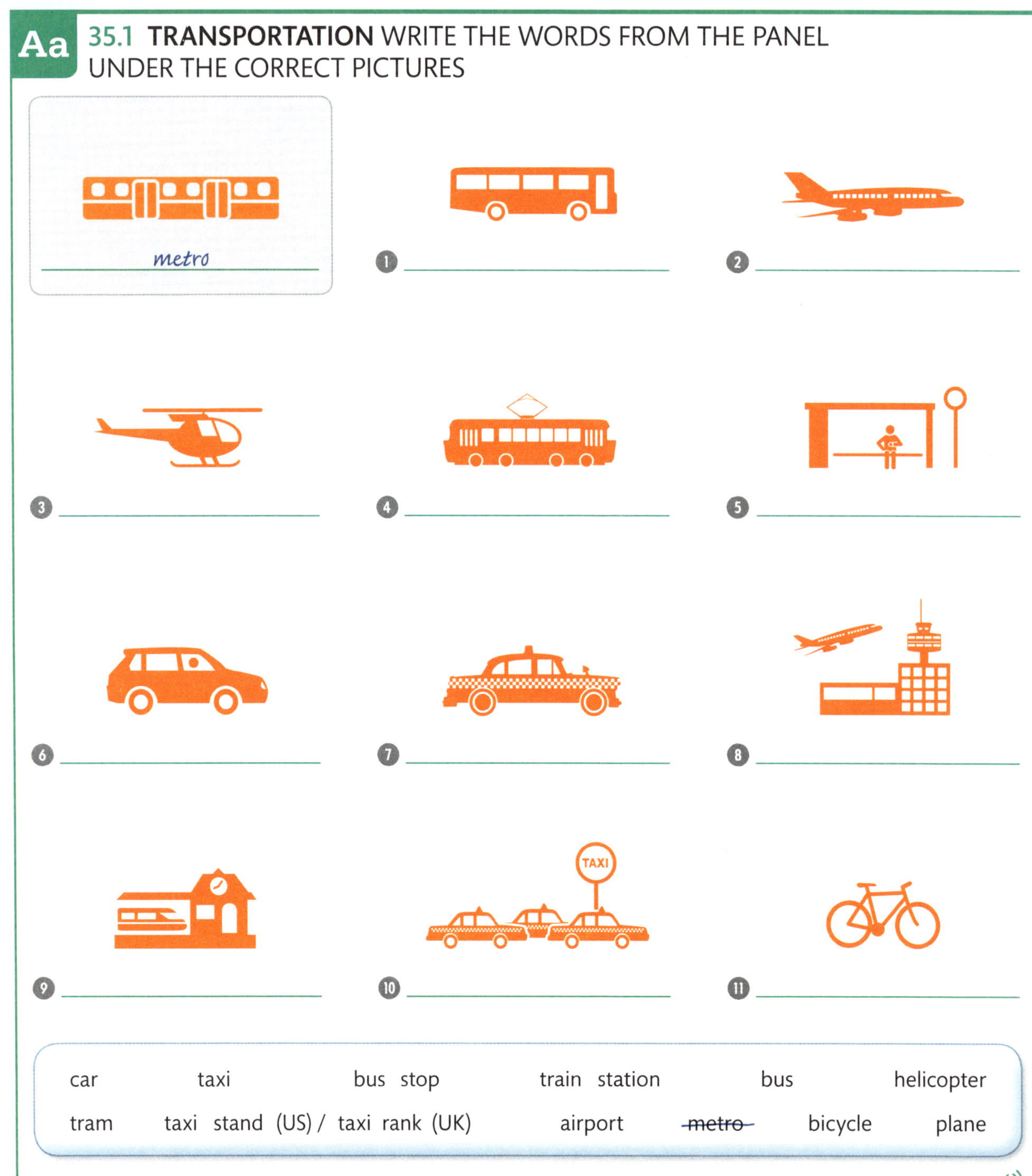

Aa 35.2 **TRAVEL** WRITE THE WORDS FROM THE PANEL UNDER THE CORRECT PICTURES

one-way ticket

1 ______

2 ______

3 ______

4 ______

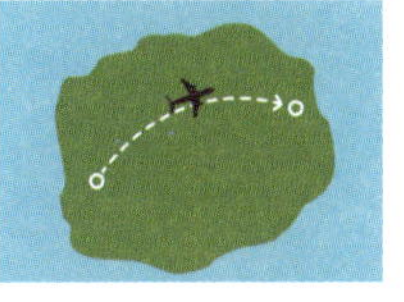

5 ______

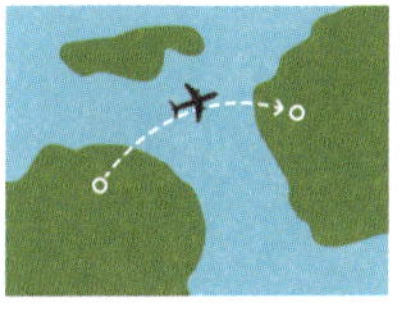

6 ______

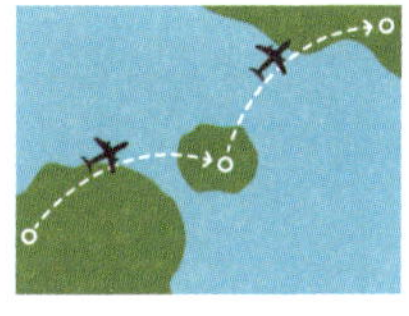

7 ______

8 ______

9 ______

10 ______

11 ______

12 ______

13 ______

14 ______

15 ______

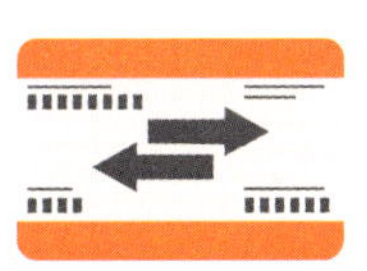

16 ______

17 ______

18 ______

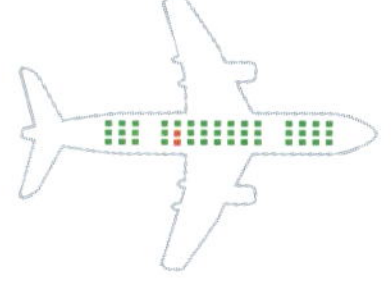

19 ______

passport aisle seat terminal passport control board a plane check-in ~~one-way ticket~~
international flight round-trip ticket (US) / return ticket (UK) window seat late boarding pass
on time domestic flight delay luggage connecting flight seat reservation security hotel

36 Making travel arrangements

When you have travel plans or want to discuss the arrangements for a trip, it is useful to be able to talk about the possible results of actions and choices.

New language Zero and first conditional
Aa Vocabulary Travel
New skill Talking about actions and results

36.1 FILL IN THE GAPS BY PUTTING THE VERBS IN THE CORRECT TENSES TO MAKE SENTENCES IN THE FIRST CONDITIONAL

If you *book* (book) in advance, you *will get* (get) a discount.

1. If we ______ (not hurry) , we ______ (miss) the flight.
2. If we ______ (meet) in Berlin, it ______ (save) us some time.
3. We ______ (take) on a new intern if we ______ (win) the contract.
4. If the train ______ (be) late, we ______ (miss) the meeting.
5. If the bank ______ (be) closed, we ______ (not have) any money.
6. We ______ (pay) for your flight if you ______ (fly) to Denver.
7. If you ______ (work) hard, you ______ (pass) the exam.
8. The firm ______ (pay) expenses if you ______ (be) delayed.
9. If I ______ (go) to Rome, I ______ (visit) the Colosseum.
10. If I ______ (lose) my job, I don't know what I ______ (do).

36.2 MATCH THE BEGINNINGS OF THE SENTENCES TO THE CORRECT ENDINGS

We will win the contract → if we negotiate effectively.

1. If we don't hurry up,
2. We will get a discount
3. Will you pay expenses
4. What will Samantha do if
5. If we lose the contract,
6. Will you visit the factory

- we'll miss our connecting flight.
- if we book early.
- if we negotiate effectively.
- we will have to lay Sean off.
- if you go to China?
- if we attend the conference?
- she loses her job next month?

36.3 MARK THE SENTENCES THAT ARE CORRECT

If the flight is delayed, we will definitely miss the meeting. ☑
If the flight will be delayed, we definitely miss the meeting. ☐

1. Will you have a celebration if you get the job? ☐
   Do you have a celebration if you get the job? ☐
2. If you'll buy the ticket online, it will be cheaper. ☐
   If you buy the ticket online, it will be cheaper. ☐
3. If we visit Paris, we probably go sightseeing. ☐
   If we visit Paris, we will probably go sightseeing. ☐
4. What will we do if we don't win the contract? ☐
   What do we do if we won't win the contract? ☐
5. If we'll take on a new intern, where do they sit? ☐
   If we take on a new intern, where will they sit? ☐
6. How will you travel to Berlin if the flight is canceled? ☐
   How do you travel to Berlin if the flight will be canceled? ☐

36.4 LISTEN TO THE AUDIO AND ANSWER THE QUESTIONS

Clara is speaking to Jane on the phone in order to sort out the details of an upcoming trip.

Clara has already booked the flights.
True ☐ **False** ☑ **Not given** ☐

1. If they book the flights online, they will be cheaper.
True ☐ **False** ☐ **Not given** ☐

2. They both agree to take a taxi.
True ☐ **False** ☐ **Not given** ☐

3. The Hotel Ritz is more expensive.
True ☐ **False** ☐ **Not given** ☐

4. The Hotel Grande is closer to the convention hall.
True ☐ **False** ☐ **Not given** ☐

5. The Hotel Ritz includes breakfast.
True ☐ **False** ☐ **Not given** ☐

6. The company will pay for all meals.
True ☐ **False** ☐ **Not given** ☐

36.5 REWRITE THE SENTENCES, PUTTING THE WORDS IN THE CORRECT ORDER

pay | travel | to | class, | you | more. | If | you | first | have

If you travel first class, you have to pay more.

1. If | to | nice | work. | walk | it's | a | day, | I

2. water, | If | heat | it | boils. | you

3. for | late | boss | isn't | work, | you're | If | unhappy? | your

4. that | press | If | machine | button, | the | you | stops.

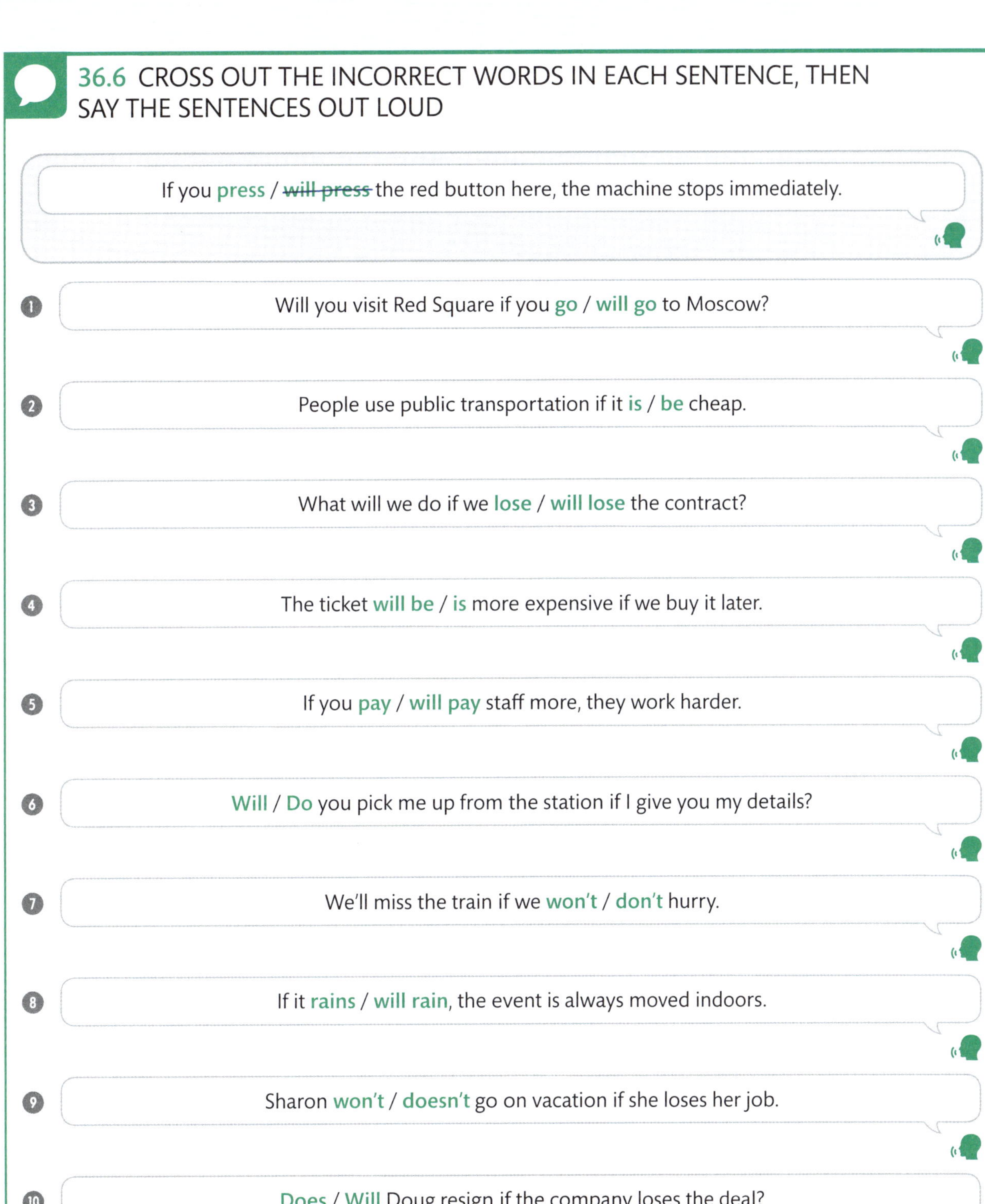

36.6 CROSS OUT THE INCORRECT WORDS IN EACH SENTENCE, THEN SAY THE SENTENCES OUT LOUD

If you press / ~~will press~~ the red button here, the machine stops immediately.

1. Will you visit Red Square if you go / will go to Moscow?
2. People use public transportation if it is / be cheap.
3. What will we do if we lose / will lose the contract?
4. The ticket will be / is more expensive if we buy it later.
5. If you pay / will pay staff more, they work harder.
6. Will / Do you pick me up from the station if I give you my details?
7. We'll miss the train if we won't / don't hurry.
8. If it rains / will rain, the event is always moved indoors.
9. Sharon won't / doesn't go on vacation if she loses her job.
10. Does / Will Doug resign if the company loses the deal?

37 Asking for directions

When traveling to conferences and meetings, you may need to ask for directions. Knowing how to be polite but clear is essential.

New language Imperatives, prepositions of place
Aa Vocabulary Directions
New skill Asking for and giving directions

37.1 CROSS OUT THE INCORRECT WORD IN EACH SENTENCE

Go past the café and ~~turning~~ / turn left.

1.  Do you know the where / way to the station?
2.  The bank is in / on the corner.
3.  Do you know how to go / get to the hotel?
4.  The museum is on / in front of the park.
5.  You should take / make the second left.
6.  The library is straight ahead on the / a right.
7.  Our house is just ahead on / in the left.
8.  Sorry, did you tell / say it is near the school?
9.  Turn right on / at the sign.

37.2 MARK THE SENTENCES THAT ARE CORRECT

The office is 30 yards ahead on the right. ☑
The office is 30 yards ahead by the right. ☐

1. The entrance is in front of the factory. ☐
   The entrance is on front of the factory. ☐
2. Turn right in the sign. ☐
   Turn right at the sign. ☐
3. The bank is opposite the school. ☐
   The bank is between the school. ☐
4. Take the first road in the left. ☐
   Take the first road on the left. ☐
5. Go past the movie theater. ☐
   Go after the movie theater. ☐
6. The bank is on the corner. ☐
   The bank is at the corner. ☐
7. The station is next in the police station. ☐
   The station is next to the police station. ☐

37.3 REWRITE THE SENTENCES, PUTTING THE WORDS IN THE CORRECT ORDER

conference | the | of | The | city | is | in | hall. | front | center

The conference center is in front of the city hall.

1. do | to | Excuse | you | the | know | way | the | hotel? | me,

2. it's | the | and | train | station. | straight | Go | opposite | on

3. next | post | Sorry, | you | the | say | it's | office? | did | to

4. the | yards | corner. | The | on | 40 | ahead | bank | is

37.4 LISTEN TO THE AUDIO AND MARK THE DIRECTIONS GIVEN

1 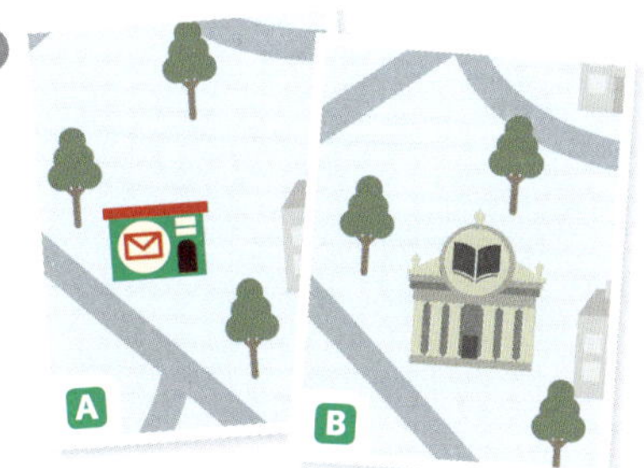

2 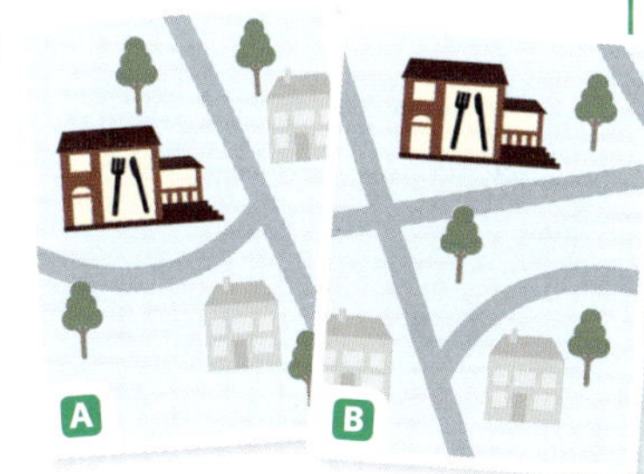

3 

4 

5 

37.5 LOOK AT THE MAP THEN ANSWER THE QUESTIONS, SPEAKING OUT LOUD

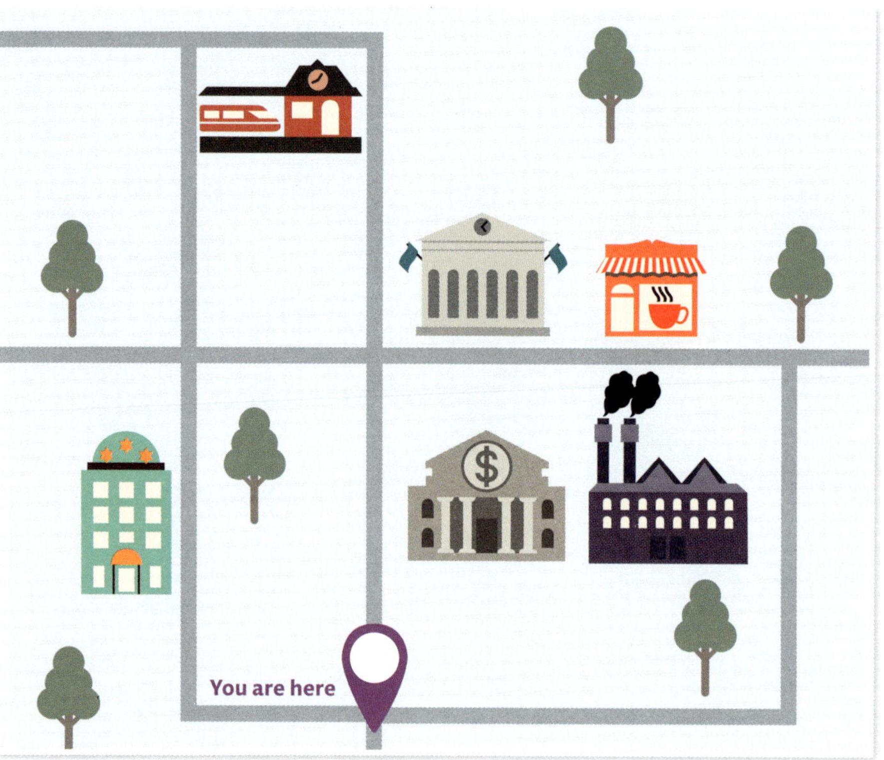

Do you know the way to the town hall?

Yes, turn right after the bank.

1. How do I get to the café?

2. Could you tell me the way to the train station?

3. Do you know where I can find a bank?

4. Do you know where the factory is?

5. Where is the closest hotel to here?

38 Describing your stay

You can describe events using either active or passive sentences. The focus in a passive sentence is on the action itself rather than the thing that caused it.

New language The passive voice
Aa Vocabulary Hotels and accommodation
New skill Using the passive voice

38.1 REWRITE THE PASSIVE SENTENCES, PUTTING THE WORDS IN THE CORRECT ORDER

and | between | Breakfast | 9am. | served | be | will | 6:30am

Breakfast will be served between 6:30am and 9am.

1. opened | in | hotel | 1932. | The | was

2. new | by | was | factory | president. | the | opened | The

3. was | our | company | 2013. | in | employed | by | Simon

4. of | be | released | next | new | month. | Our | will | products | range

5. head | moved | four | office | Shanghai | about | ago. | was | Our | to | years

6. introduced | new | management | was | to | the | team. | Peter

7. during | break. | the | served | and | tea | will | be | Coffee

8. The | to | will | the | be | new | team | package. | software | shown | how | use

38.2 REWRITE THE ACTIVE SENTENCES AS PASSIVE SENTENCES

Someone moved the photocopier last night. = *The photocopier was moved last night.*

1. Someone met the CEO at the airport. = ______
2. Danny has redecorated the meeting room. = ______
3. My assistant booked a double room yesterday. = ______
4. Julia taught the team some Mandarin. = ______
5. Someone left the files on the train again. = ______
6. John booked the rooms on Monday. = ______
7. The hotel serves breakfast at 7:30am. = ______
8. Someone has organized the office. = ______

38.3 LISTEN TO THE AUDIO, THEN NUMBER THE PICTURES IN THE ORDER THEY ARE DESCRIBED

A ☐

B *1*

C ☐

D ☐

E ☐

F ☐

G ☐

H ☐

38.4 READ THE REVIEWS AND ANSWER THE QUESTIONS

The reviewer thinks Hotel Destiny is expensive.
True ☐ False ☑ Not given ☐

1. The reviewer took a taxi to Hotel Destiny.
True ☐ False ☐ Not given ☐

2. There are conference facilities at Hotel Destiny.
True ☐ False ☐ Not given ☐

3. The television at Hotel Belvedere did not work.
True ☐ False ☐ Not given ☐

4. The receptionist was helpful at Hotel Belvedere.
True ☐ False ☐ Not given ☐

Hotels etc

Hotel Destiny ★★★★

This hotel is comfortable and affordable. It's perfect if you're staying in Shanghai for work or a short break. My colleague and I were picked up by the hotel minibus from the airport. After checking in, we looked around the hotel: there is a small restaurant, a gym in the basement, and a karaoke bar. Great fun!

Hotel Belvedere ★

We had been told that this is one of the best hotels in the area, but what we found proved shocking. The TV didn't turn on, and the bed fell apart on the second night. When I went downstairs to complain, I was ignored by the receptionist, and finally my wife and I were forced to check out three days early.

38.5 RESPOND OUT LOUD TO THE AUDIO, FILLING IN THE GAPS USING THE PHRASES IN THE PANEL

How was your flight?
The flight *was delayed* by eight hours.

1. How did you get to the hotel?
We __________ at the airport by the driver.

2. How was the breakfast?
Great. It __________ at 7am each morning.

3. Was there a TV in the room?
Yes. But unfortunately it __________.

was broken | were picked up | ~~was delayed~~ | was served

39 Vocabulary

39.1 **EATING OUT** WRITE THE WORDS FROM THE PANEL UNDER THE CORRECT PICTURES

1 ______

2 ______

3 ______

4 ______

5 ______

6 ______

7 ______

8 ______

9 ______

10 ______

11 ______

12 ______

13 ______

14 ______

15 ______

16 ______

17 ______

18 ______

19 ______

menu vegan vegetarian boil waitress ~~restaurant~~ roast fry
lunch café food allergy / intolerance tip waiter receipt
bar chef dessert breakfast make a reservation / booking dinner

Aa 39.2 **FOOD AND DRINK** WRITE THE WORDS FROM THE PANEL UNDER THE CORRECT PICTURES

soup

1 ______

2 ______

3 ______

4 ______

5 ______

6 ______

7 ______

8 ______

9 ______

10 ______

11 ______

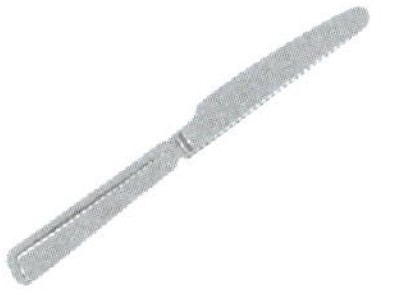

12 ______

13 ______

14 ______

15 ______

16 ______

17 ______

18 ______

19 ______

fruit napkin fork tea bread ~~soup~~ coffee
pasta seafood vegetables salad fish milk cake
meat water sandwich knife butter potatoes

40 Conferences and visitors

Whether you are welcoming visitors, or visiting somewhere on business yourself, it is important to know how to interact politely in English.

New language "A," "some," "any"
Vocabulary Hospitality
New skill Welcoming visitors

40.1 MARK THE SENTENCES THAT ARE CORRECT

Welcome to China, Mr. Arnold. ☑
Welcome in China, Mr. Arnold. ☐

1. Did you have any trouble getting here? ☐
   Did you have any trouble arriving here? ☐
2. Can I serve you anything? ☐
   Can I get you anything? ☐
3. It's great to meet you on person. ☐
   It's great to meet you in person. ☐
4. Have you been to Toronto before? ☐
   Have you been in Toronto before? ☐
5. Did you have a good flight? ☐
   Had you a good flight? ☐
6. Would you like something to drink? ☐
   Would you want something to drink? ☐
7. I've been looking forward to meet you. ☐
   I've been looking forward to meeting you. ☐
8. We've heard so much about you. ☐
   We're hearing so much about you. ☐
9. I'll let Mr. Song know that you arrived. ☐
   I'll inform Mr. Song know you arrived. ☐
10. Is this your first visit in India? ☐
    Is this your first visit to India? ☐

40.2 REWRITE THE SENTENCES, CORRECTING THE ERRORS

I'm eating a pasta for lunch today.
I'm eating some pasta for lunch today.

1. Is there some information about flights?
2. I need to buy any food.
3. Are there some good hotels nearby?
4. Can I get you some cup of coffee?
5. Are there some interesting talks today?
6. Do you have some luggage?
7. There is some presentation later.
8. Do you have some tea?
9. Please take some seat at the front.

40.3 MATCH THE BEGINNINGS OF THE SENTENCES TO THE CORRECT ENDINGS

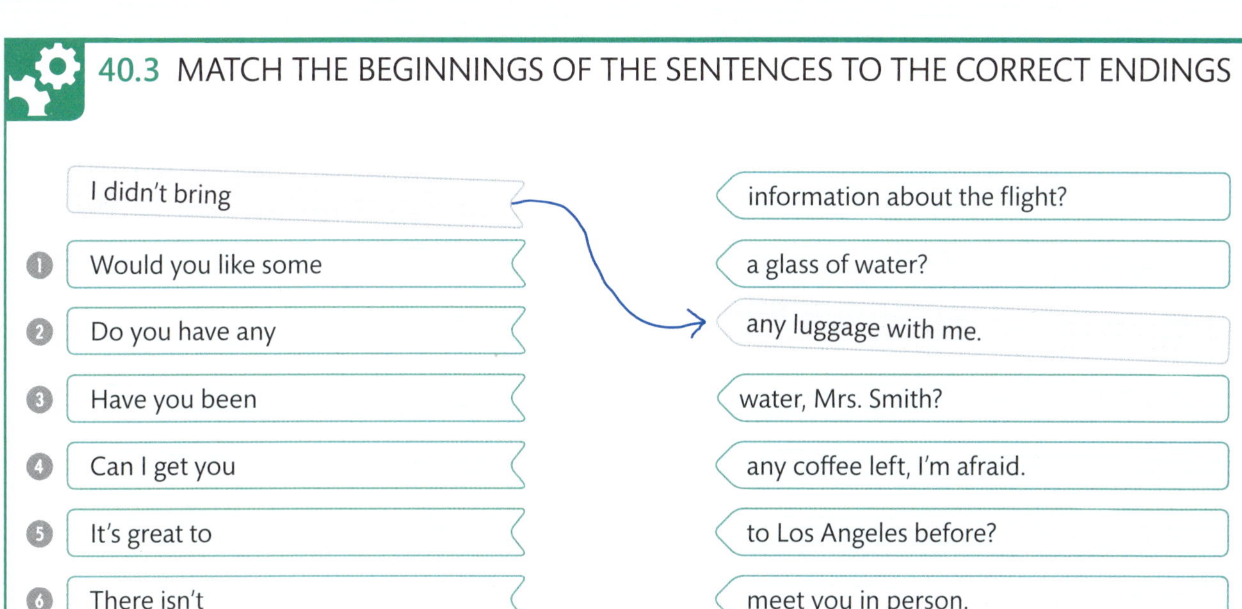

I didn't bring [→ any luggage with me.]

1. Would you like some
2. Do you have any
3. Have you been
4. Can I get you
5. It's great to
6. There isn't

- information about the flight?
- a glass of water?
- any luggage with me.
- water, Mrs. Smith?
- any coffee left, I'm afraid.
- to Los Angeles before?
- meet you in person.

40.4 CROSS OUT THE INCORRECT WORD IN EACH SENTENCE, THEN SAY THE SENTENCES OUT LOUD

There is a / ~~some~~ workshop at noon in the main hall.

1. Are you going to some / any talks later?
2. James is giving any / a presentation later today.
3. There isn't any / some coffee or tea, I'm sorry.
4. Are any / an of your colleagues staying here?
5. Would you like some / a cup of tea, Jen?
6. They don't have a / any workshops this afternoon.
7. Have any / some of the attendees arrived yet?
8. Is there any / an information about the conference?
9. There's any / some food and drink in the main hall.

40.5 READ THE LEAFLET AND ANSWER THE QUESTIONS

iTech99

Where the future is discussed today...

Welcome to our 15th annual iTech99 conference!
Guests should report to reception at the Lions Hotel, where they can collect their name badges and conference pack. The opening plenary will be in the main hall from 3pm to 5pm, during which our keynote speaker, Doctor Arnold Smith, CEO of AstroPlus, will discuss how to develop an effective app. In the evening, there will be a reception at the Westerton Hotel. A choice of snacks and drinks will be served.

On Tuesday, AstroPlus will launch their new phone, the GH34. This will be an excellent chance for networking, during which delegates can meet some of the big stars from the world of technology.

Wednesday will see a question-and-answer session, during which attendees will have the chance to ask the some of the CEOs from the tech giants questions.

Finally on Friday, there will be talks about new developments in marketing and changes in the Asian market.

Guests should collect their conference packs from...
their hotel. ☐ **reception.** ☑ **the main hall.** ☐

1. The opening plenary will take place in...
the main hall. ☐ **the Westerton Hotel.** ☐ **the reception area.** ☐

2. The keynote speaker will discuss...
his company's future. ☐ **developing an app.** ☐ **building an IT team.** ☐

3. At the reception there will be...
live music. ☐ **a choice of food and drink.** ☐ **team-building exercises.** ☐

4. On Tuesday, there will be...
a product launch. ☐ **a question-and-answer session.** ☐ **a final plenary.** ☐

5. During the question-and-answer session, attendees will meet...
consumer focus groups. ☐ **leading CEOs.** ☐ **journalists.** ☐

6. The talks on Friday will discuss...
the Asian market. ☐ **networking.** ☐ **the European market.** ☐

41 Dining and hospitality

It is important to learn local customs for dining and entertaining. At business lunches and conferences, follow these customs and use polite language.

New language "Much / many," "too / enough"
Aa Vocabulary Restaurants
New skill Offering and accepting hospitality

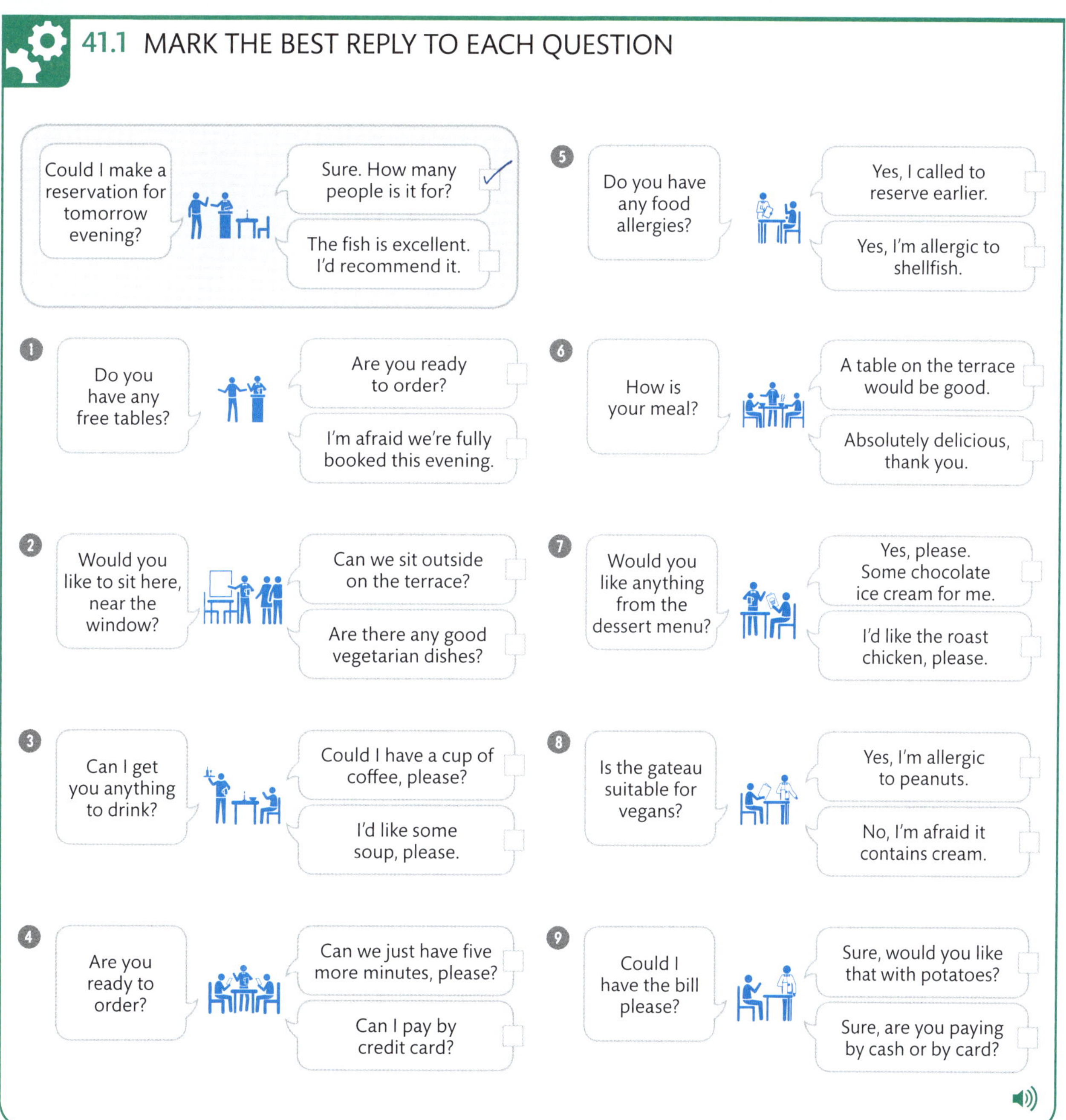

41.1 MARK THE BEST REPLY TO EACH QUESTION

Could I make a reservation for tomorrow evening?
- Sure. How many people is it for? ✓
- The fish is excellent. I'd recommend it.

1. Do you have any free tables?
   - Are you ready to order?
   - I'm afraid we're fully booked this evening.

2. Would you like to sit here, near the window?
   - Can we sit outside on the terrace?
   - Are there any good vegetarian dishes?

3. Can I get you anything to drink?
   - Could I have a cup of coffee, please?
   - I'd like some soup, please.

4. Are you ready to order?
   - Can we just have five more minutes, please?
   - Can I pay by credit card?

5. Do you have any food allergies?
   - Yes, I called to reserve earlier.
   - Yes, I'm allergic to shellfish.

6. How is your meal?
   - A table on the terrace would be good.
   - Absolutely delicious, thank you.

7. Would you like anything from the dessert menu?
   - Yes, please. Some chocolate ice cream for me.
   - I'd like the roast chicken, please.

8. Is the gateau suitable for vegans?
   - Yes, I'm allergic to peanuts.
   - No, I'm afraid it contains cream.

9. Could I have the bill please?
   - Sure, would you like that with potatoes?
   - Sure, are you paying by cash or by card?

41.2 REWRITE THE SENTENCES, PUTTING THE WORDS IN THE CORRECT ORDER

a | I'm | wait. | 15-minute | there's | afraid

I'm afraid there's a 15-minute wait.

1. you | to | Are | order? | ready

2. reserve | for | like | to | please. | I'd | table | two, | a

3. reserved | madam? | Have | you | table, | a

4. people | many | there | in | party? | How | are | your

5. at | please? | dessert | I | a | the | have | menu, | Could | look

6. the | you | would | What | for | like | entree?

7. or | you | Do | any | allergies | intolerances? | have

8. many | are | How | there | today? | options | vegetarian

9. the | we | bill, | have | please? | Could

10. you | to | cash | like | card? | or | by | Would | pay

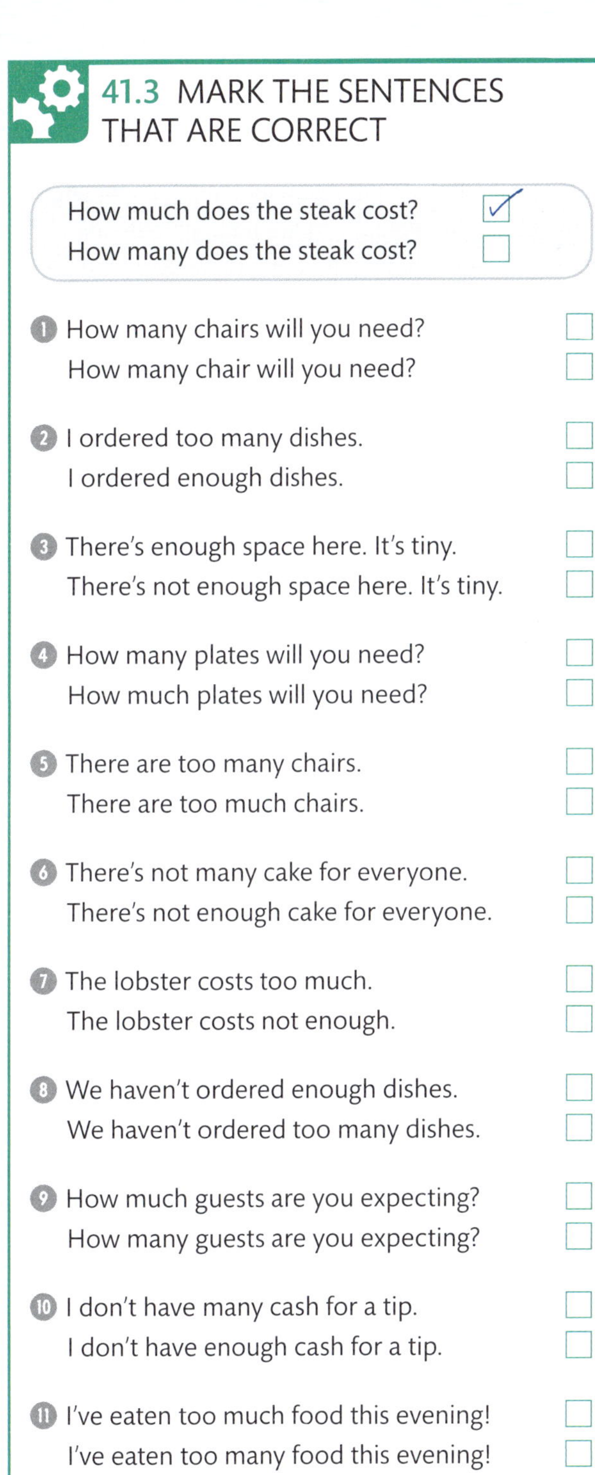

41.3 MARK THE SENTENCES THAT ARE CORRECT

How much does the steak cost? ☑
How many does the steak cost? ☐

1. How many chairs will you need? ☐
   How many chair will you need? ☐
2. I ordered too many dishes. ☐
   I ordered enough dishes. ☐
3. There's enough space here. It's tiny. ☐
   There's not enough space here. It's tiny. ☐
4. How many plates will you need? ☐
   How much plates will you need? ☐
5. There are too many chairs. ☐
   There are too much chairs. ☐
6. There's not many cake for everyone. ☐
   There's not enough cake for everyone. ☐
7. The lobster costs too much. ☐
   The lobster costs not enough. ☐
8. We haven't ordered enough dishes. ☐
   We haven't ordered too many dishes. ☐
9. How much guests are you expecting? ☐
   How many guests are you expecting? ☐
10. I don't have many cash for a tip. ☐
    I don't have enough cash for a tip. ☐
11. I've eaten too much food this evening! ☐
    I've eaten too many food this evening! ☐
12. There's enough tea for everyone. ☐
    There's much tea for everyone. ☐

41.4 SAY THE SENTENCES OUT LOUD, FILLING IN THE GAPS USING THE WORDS IN THE PANEL

Tell me how ___much___ rice you'd like.

1. How ________ people are coming tonight?
2. Is there ________ space at the table for everyone?
3. How ________ does the meal usually cost?
4. I've eaten too ________ cake.
5. There's ________ much salt in my soup.
6. There are not ________ chairs for all of us!
7. ________ many glasses will we need this evening?

How	~~much~~	too	much
enough	much	many	enough

42 Informal phone calls

In most workplaces, you can use polite but informal language to call your co-workers. English often uses two- or three-part verbs in informal telephone language.

New language Telephone language
Aa Vocabulary Phone numbers and etiquette
New skill Calling your co-workers

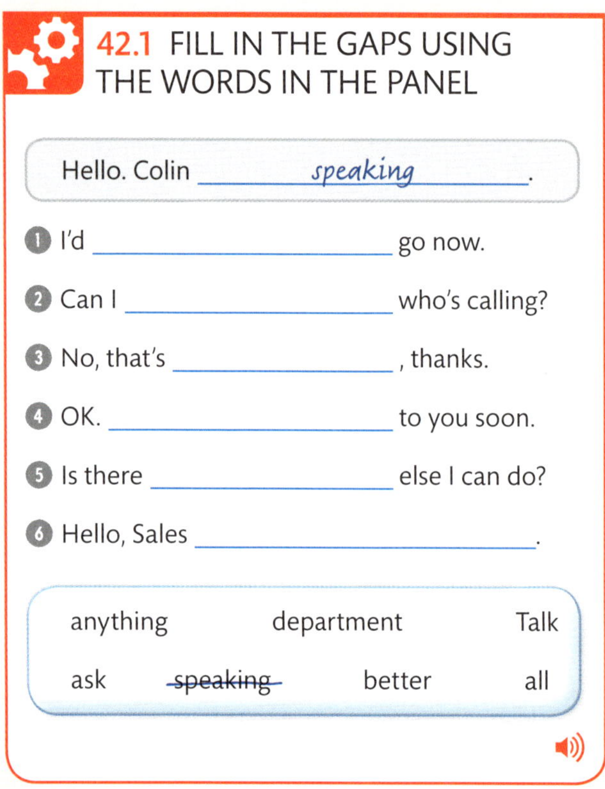

42.1 FILL IN THE GAPS USING THE WORDS IN THE PANEL

Hello. Colin *speaking*.

1. I'd ______ go now.
2. Can I ______ who's calling?
3. No, that's ______, thanks.
4. OK. ______ to you soon.
5. Is there ______ else I can do?
6. Hello, Sales ______.

anything | department | Talk | ask | ~~speaking~~ | better | all

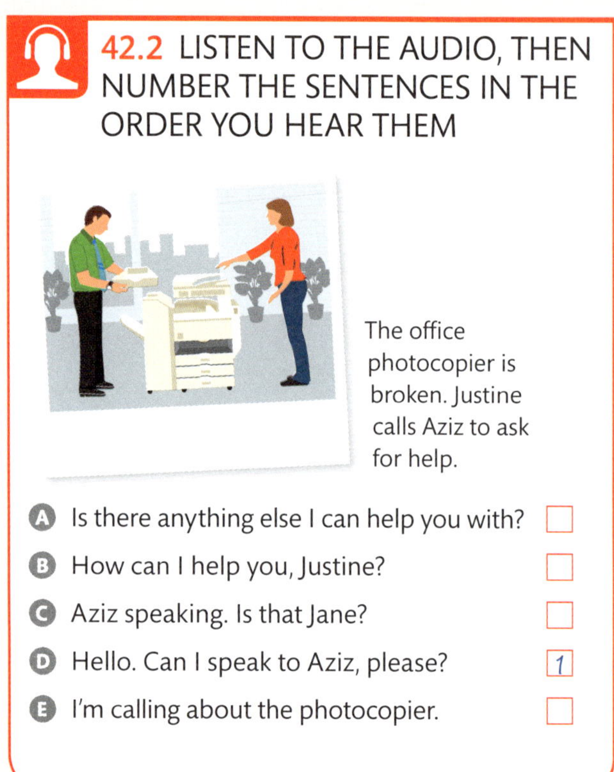

42.2 LISTEN TO THE AUDIO, THEN NUMBER THE SENTENCES IN THE ORDER YOU HEAR THEM

The office photocopier is broken. Justine calls Aziz to ask for help.

A. Is there anything else I can help you with? ☐
B. How can I help you, Justine? ☐
C. Aziz speaking. Is that Jane? ☐
D. Hello. Can I speak to Aziz, please? 1
E. I'm calling about the photocopier. ☐

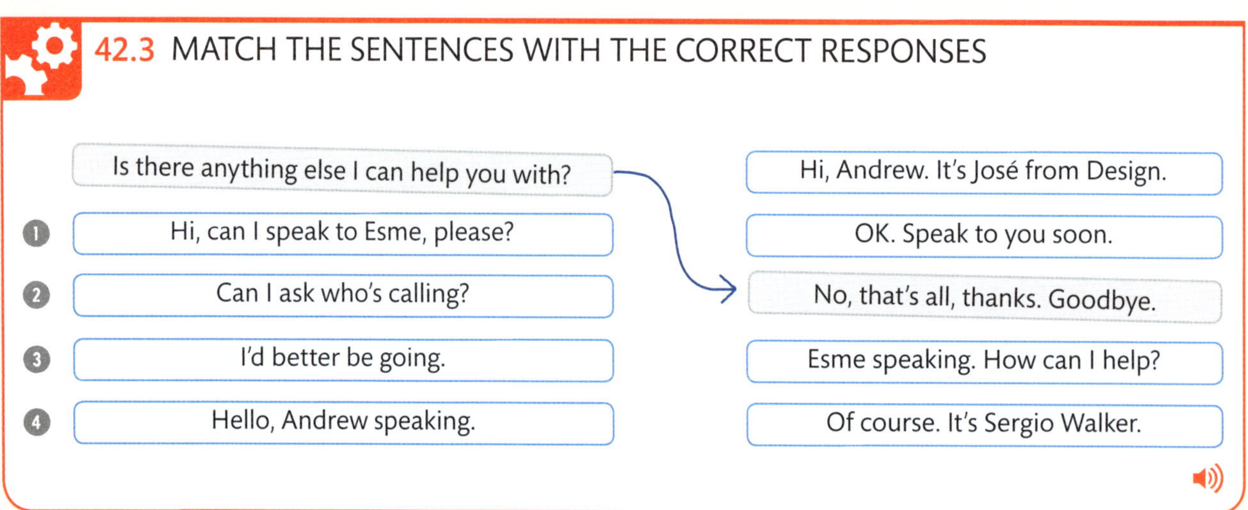

42.3 MATCH THE SENTENCES WITH THE CORRECT RESPONSES

Is there anything else I can help you with? → No, that's all, thanks. Goodbye.

1. Hi, can I speak to Esme, please?
2. Can I ask who's calling?
3. I'd better be going.
4. Hello, Andrew speaking.

Hi, Andrew. It's José from Design.
OK. Speak to you soon.
No, that's all, thanks. Goodbye.
Esme speaking. How can I help?
Of course. It's Sergio Walker.

42.4 LISTEN TO THE AUDIO AND WRITE DOWN THE TELEPHONE NUMBERS THAT YOU HEAR

07358135288

1 ______

2 ______

3 ______

4 ______

5 ______

6 ______

7 ______

42.5 LOOK AT THE BUSINESS CARDS, THEN RESPOND TO THE AUDIO, SPEAKING OUT LOUD

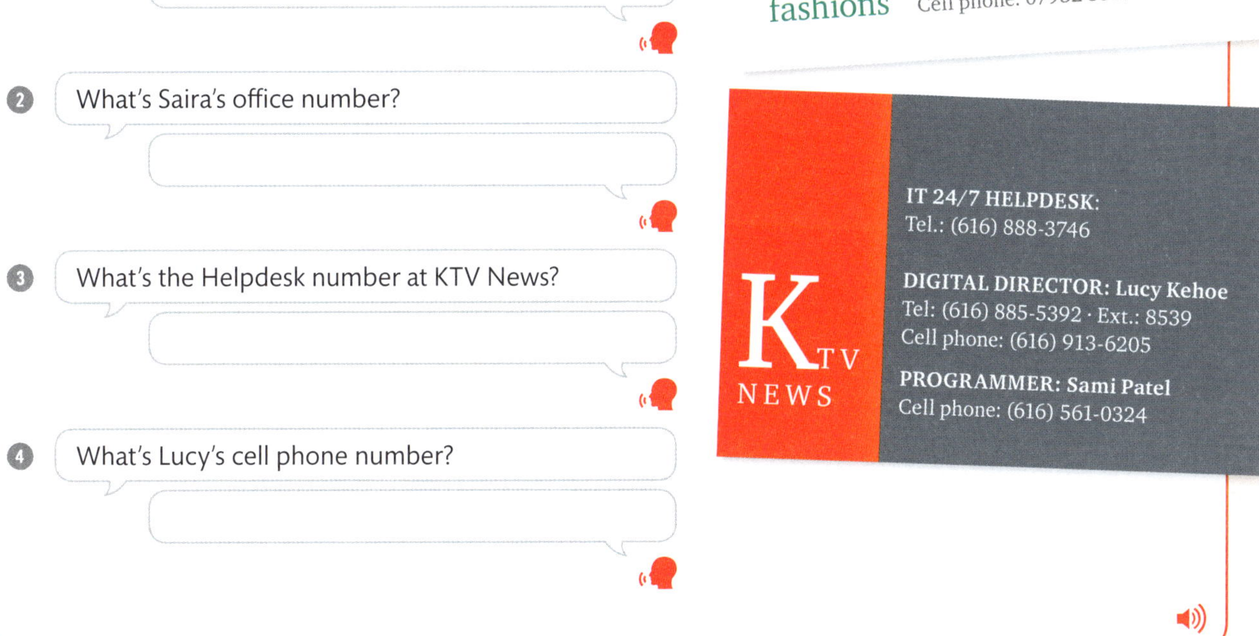

42.6 FILL IN THE GAPS USING THE PHRASES IN THE PANEL

I've got a meeting in five minutes, so I have to __hang up__ now.

1. I don't know why Hal's not ______________ the phone.
2. I'll ______________ to customer services now.
3. Can you ______________, please? I can't hear you.
4. Sorry, I'm busy now. I'll ______________ to you later.
5. I'm sorry I ______________. This line is very bad.
6. You're ______________. Can I call you back?

cut you off
~~hang up~~
speak up
get back
picking up
put you through
breaking up

42.7 CROSS OUT THE INCORRECT WORDS IN EACH SENTENCE

Don't hang ~~on~~ / ~~down~~ / up. I need to talk to you about the China sales.

1. Could you possibly speak on / off / up, please? The line is very faint.
2. I'll call they / you / us back in ten minutes. Is that OK? I have to finish writing an email.
3. If I get cut of / on / off, call me back on the office phone. I'm back at my desk now.
4. Can I get back to / with / from you about the design later today? We're still working on it.
5. I've called Fatima three times, but she didn't pick on / up / over. Is she at work today?
6. Marc kept breaking for / up / down when I called him. The signal here is awful!
7. Katie is back at her desk now. I'll just put you through / over / up to her.
8. Mateo got back for / to / of me about the new manual. He has a few comments on it.

42.8 REWRITE THE SENTENCES, PUTTING THE WORDS IN THE CORRECT ORDER

hang | rude | can | on | You | customer. | up | a

You can hang up on a rude customer.

1. you | please? | speak | Can | up,

2. get | hope | off | cut | I | again. | don't | I

3. me | Let | Finance. | through | put | to | you

4. you | I | pick | up | didn't | called. | Sorry | when

5. back | him | you | afternoon? | to | get | this | Can

6. the | breaking | keeps | Sorry, | up. | line

7. five | I'll | you | minutes. | call | back | in

8. yesterday. | He | back | to | didn't | get | me

9. up | Don't | Dan | pick | the | calls. | phone | if

43 Formal phone calls

When you talk to clients or receptionists, you may need to use formal language on the phone. You may also need to take or leave a phone message.

New language Adjective order
Aa Vocabulary Formal telephone language
New skill Leaving phone messages

43.1 MARK THE BEST REPLY TO EACH STATEMENT

43.2 CROSS OUT THE INCORRECT WORD IN EACH SENTENCE, THEN SAY THE SENTENCES OUT LOUD

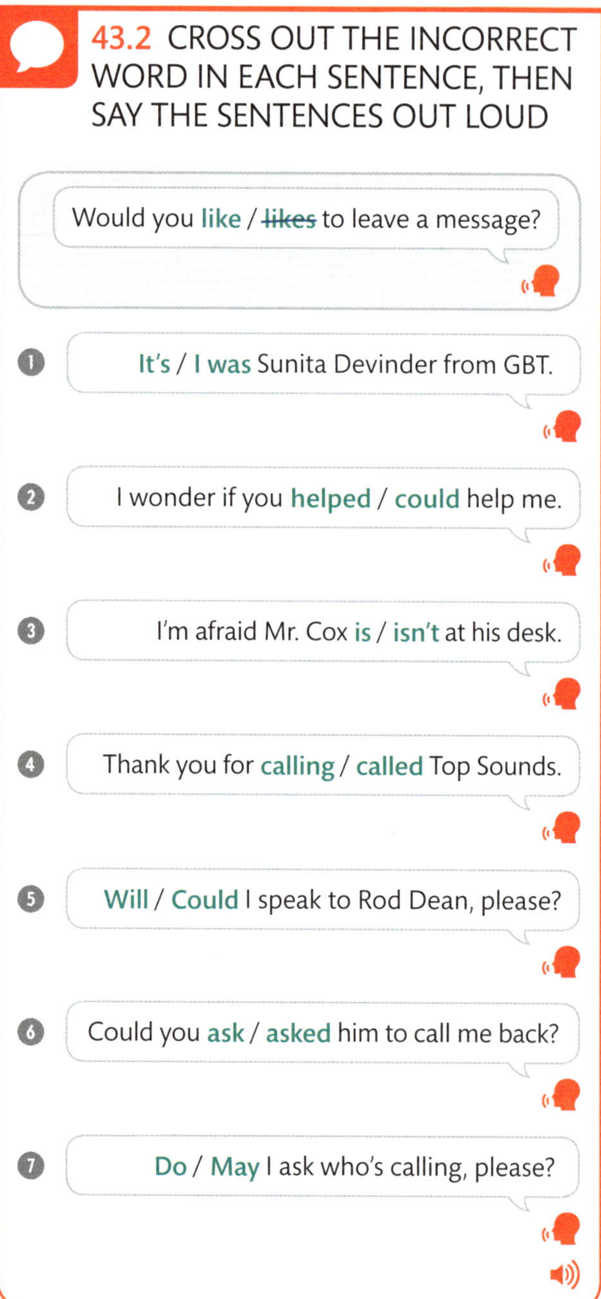

43.3 MARK THE SENTENCES THAT ARE CORRECT

I'm afraid my manager isn't here. ☑
I'm apologize my manager isn't here. ☐

1. How can I helps you? ☐
   How can I help you? ☐

2. May I ask who's calling? ☐
   May I ask who calls? ☐

3. I'll yet put you through. ☐
   I'll just put you through. ☐

4. Will you like to leave a message? ☐
   Would you like to leave a message? ☐

5. Could you ask him to call me back, please? ☐
   Could you ask him call me back, please? ☐

6. How can I help you? IT department. ☐
   IT department. How can I help you? ☐

7. I'll put you over to HR now. ☐
   I'll put you through to HR now. ☐

8. I'm afraid he's not on his desk. ☐
   I'm afraid he's not at his desk. ☐

9. Thank you for calling Quadfax. ☐
   Thank you to call Quadfax. ☐

43.4 FILL IN THE GAPS USING THE PHRASES IN THE PANEL

Yes, of course. *May I ask* who's calling?

1. Savino's. How ______ you?
2. Thank you ______ Ready Solutions.
3. Hello. ______ you can help me.
4. I'm calling ______ I placed last month.
5. ______ to Becky Bradley, please?
6. I'm afraid the Accounts Manager is away ______.
7. Yes, please. ______ 20 desks?
8. ______ to leave a message?
9. Thank you. ______ you through.

I'll just put
Could I speak
can I help
~~May I ask~~
Would you like
about an order
Could I order
at the moment
for calling
I wonder if

Aa 43.5 WRITE THE WORDS FROM THE PANEL IN THE CORRECT GROUPS

OPINION	SIZE	AGE	COLOR	MATERIAL
nice				

ancient, blue, leather, awful, tiny, ~~nice~~, metal, modern, purple, stylish, pink, large, plastic, antique, huge

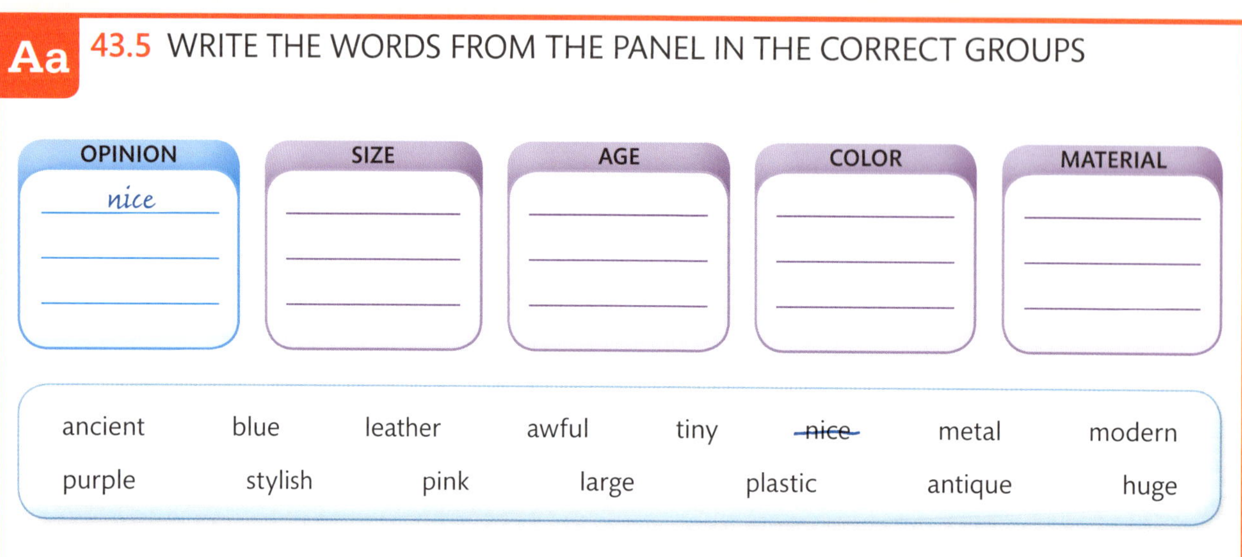

43.6 REWRITE THE SENTENCES, PUTTING THE WORDS IN THE CORRECT ORDER

beautiful | laptop | new | is | model. | a | My | silver

My laptop is a beautiful new silver model.

1. little | gold | lamp. | We're | a | stylish | developing

2. amazing | new | has | Tom | tiny | an | smartphone. | got

3. a | has | cat. | black and white | pet store | big | The | nice

4. in | is | large | There | an | painting | awful | cafeteria. | modern | the

5. exciting | seen | the | marketing | Have | posters? | new | you | colorful

43.7 MATCH THE PICTURES TO THE CORRECT SENTENCES

1 

2 

3 

4 

5 

6 

7 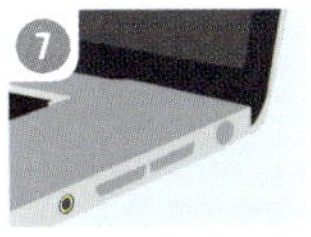

8 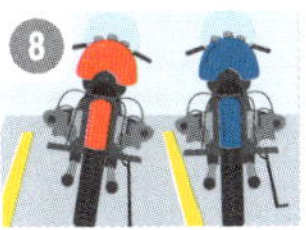

That's a stylish new design for the company logo.

Let's have lunch at that nice big café in the square.

There's a big yellow and red truck outside.

There's a nice big green and white plant in my office.

There's a huge round hole in the wall where the truck hit it.

Have you seen the fabulous new office chairs?

Have you tasted the awful new coffee?

There's a large rectangular parking space for motorbikes.

The headphones for my laptop go in a tiny round hole.

43.8 LISTEN TO THE AUDIO AND ANSWER THE QUESTIONS

Shaun calls a hotel to make arrangements for a conference.

Who does Shaun want to speak to?
- **The receptionist** ☐
- **The hotel manager** ☑
- **The customer services department** ☐

1 What does Shaun's company produce?
- **Sports cars** ☐
- **Printed materials** ☐
- **Cakes and cookies** ☐

2 When is the conference?
- **Next Monday** ☐
- **Next Thursday** ☐
- **Next Tuesday** ☐

3 What time will the conference start?
- **9:00** ☐
- **9:30** ☐
- **9:00–9:30** ☐

4 How many attendees will there be?
- **50** ☐
- **56** ☐
- **60** ☐

5 What else does Shaun ask to book?
- **Six taxis** ☐
- **A minibus** ☐
- **An extra meeting room** ☐

6 What extra dietary requests does Shaun make?
- **Vegetarian and vegan food** ☐
- **Vegan and gluten-free food** ☐
- **Vegetarian and gluten-free food** ☐

44 Writing a résumé

A résumé (or CV in UK English) is a clear summary of your skills and career history. Past simple action verbs are particularly useful for describing past achievements.

New language Action verbs for achievements
Aa Vocabulary Résumé vocabulary
New skill Writing a résumé

Aa 44.1 MATCH THE DEFINITIONS TO THE CORRECT RÉSUMÉ HEADINGS

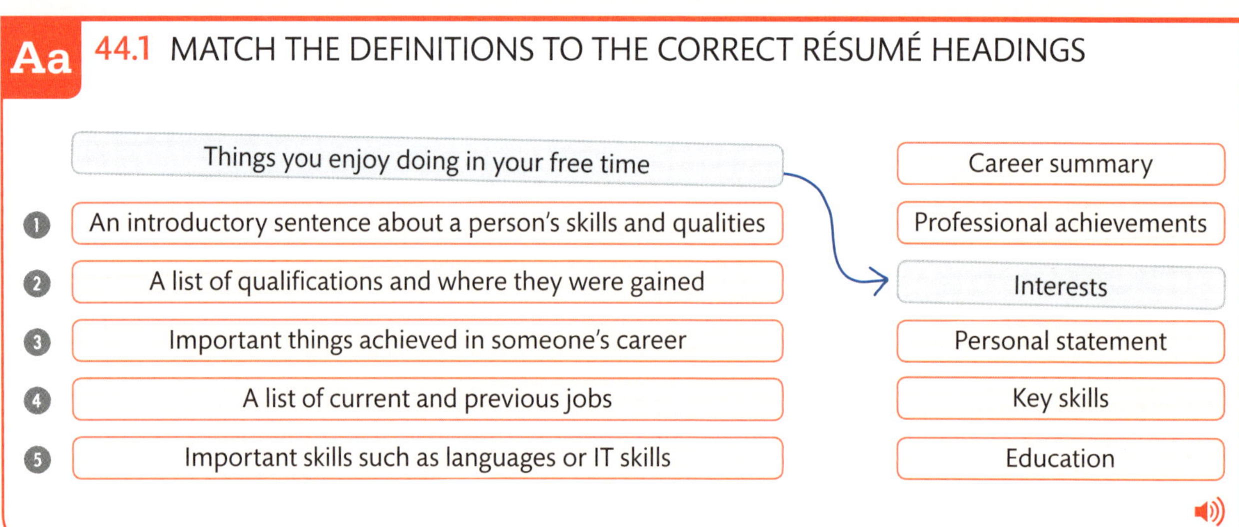

44.2 REWRITE THE SENTENCES, CORRECTING THE ERRORS

I am fluent on French, German, and Spanish.
I am fluent in French, German, and Spanish.

1. I have a proved track record in the tourism industry.

2. I am proficient on using a wide range of software.

3. I have hands-on experiences of customer service.

4. I have experience working in a serving-oriented environment.

44.3 REWRITE THE SENTENCES, PUTTING THE WORDS IN THE CORRECT ORDER

and | in | French, | I | am | German, | English. | fluent

I am fluent in French, German, and English.

1. in | individual | working | am | motivated | and | highly | love | I | tourism. | a

2. construction | I | knowledge | the | gained | of | industry. | in-depth

3. in | experience | catering | I | a | of | the | great | deal | industry. | have

4. software. | am | in | most | types | I | accounting | of | proficient

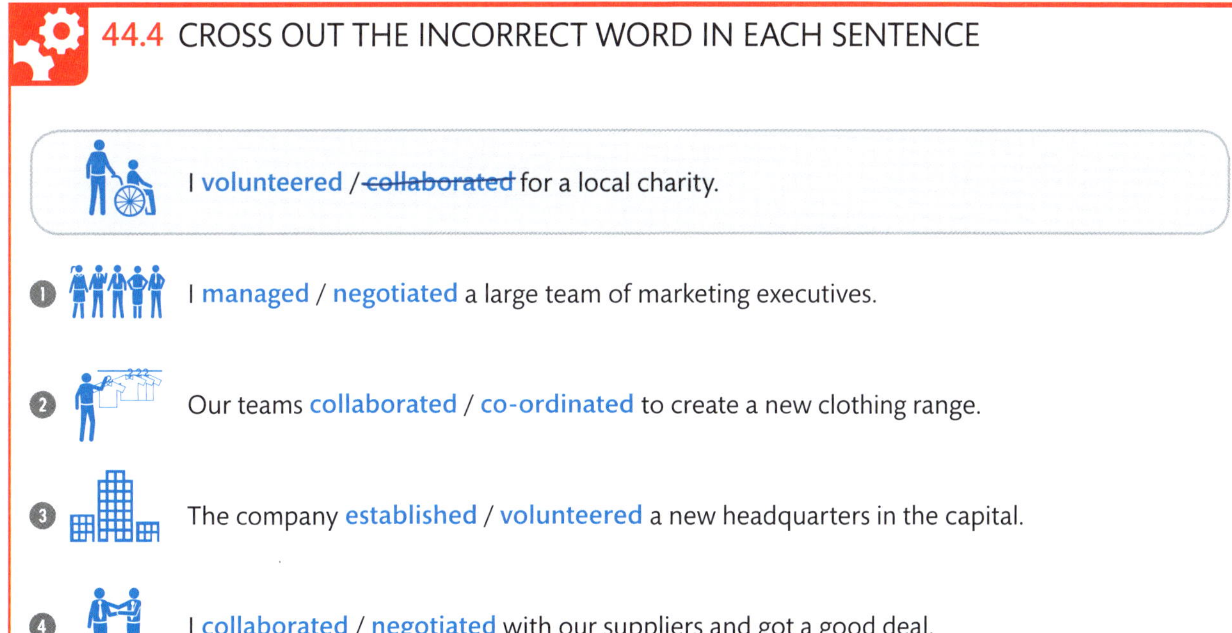

44.4 CROSS OUT THE INCORRECT WORD IN EACH SENTENCE

I volunteered / ~~collaborated~~ for a local charity.

1. I managed / negotiated a large team of marketing executives.

2. Our teams collaborated / co-ordinated to create a new clothing range.

3. The company established / volunteered a new headquarters in the capital.

4. I collaborated / negotiated with our suppliers and got a good deal.

44.5 READ THE RÉSUMÉ AND WRITE ANSWERS TO THE QUESTIONS AS FULL SENTENCES

AYIDA LAMIA

123 Hills Road
Cambridge, MA 02138
ayida@lamia.com (617) 548-81313

PERSONAL STATEMENT

I am a highly motivated individual who enjoys working with others to creatively problem solve. I have a proven track record in the field of accounting.

PROFESSIONAL ACHIEVEMENTS

I oversaw the introduction of new accounting software and co-ordinated a training program for all staff in Accounts last year.

WORK EXPERIENCE

Tomkins Travel

Deputy Director of Accounts April 2013 – present

- I oversee the processing and auditing of the company's accounts
- I train staff to use a range of software packages

Kelsey Homes

Accountant September 2010 – April 2013

- I was responsible for the accounts of a construction company building new homes.

EDUCATION

- Diploma in Accounting June 2010
- BA in Business June 2009

KEY SKILLS

- Proficient in IT use, including all major accountancy software
- Fluent in Spanish and English, intermediate level Polish
- First aid qualified; I am a named first aider in the workplace

INTERESTS

Acting in the local drama group, traveling, and reading contemporary fiction

References available upon request.

How does Ayida describe herself in her personal statement?

She says she is highly motivated.

1. What does Ayida count as a notable professional achievement?

   ____

2. What is Ayida's current job?

   ____

3. What industry did Ayida work in before her current role?

   ____

4. When did Ayida gain her diploma in Accounting?

   ____

5. What languages can Ayida speak fluently?

   ____

45 Making plans

English uses the future with "going to" to talk about plans and decisions that have already been made. It is useful for informing co-workers about your plans.

New language The future with "going to"
Aa Vocabulary Polite requests
New skill Making arrangements and plans

45.1 FILL IN THE GAPS USING THE FUTURE WITH "GOING TO"

I *am going to call* (call) the Miami office this afternoon.

1. He ______________ (travel) to the conference by plane.
2. She ______________ (not make) it to the meeting.
3. They ______________ (meet) the staff from the Paris office.
4. He ______________ (write) a letter to the suppliers.
5. They ______________ (not sell) their shares in the company just now.
6. ________ she ________ (order) business cards with the new company logo?
7. Sergio ______________ (give) a presentation about the new training course.
8. ________ you ________ (make) tea and coffee for the visitors?
9. Diana ______________ (design) the new company logo.
10. They ______________ (join) us for our team meeting today.
11. ________ you ________ (review) the sales data this afternoon?

45.2 MARK THE MOST POLITE SENTENCE OF EACH PAIR

Please could you call a taxi? ☑
You have to call a taxi now. ☐

1. Why don't we ask what Marketing think? ☐
   I want to ask Marketing what they think. ☐
2. Load the printer with paper. ☐
   Could you load the printer with paper? ☐
3. Can you help me with these files, please? ☐
   I need help with these files. ☐
4. You should send the files to production. ☐
   Could you send the files to production? ☐
5. Could we meet at 4 instead of 5? ☐
   I want to meet at 4 instead of 5. ☐
6. Can you finish the report today? ☐
   Why haven't you finished the report? ☐
7. We need to invite Jeff to the meeting. ☐
   Couldn't we invite Jeff to the meeting? ☐
8. Could you call me back later, please? ☐
   I'm too busy to talk to you now. ☐
9. Could you make coffee for the CEO? ☐
   You have to make coffee for the CEO. ☐
10. We need to cancel the meeting. ☐
    Could we possibly cancel the meeting? ☐
11. You must check this report. ☐
    Can you check this report, please? ☐
12. Could you pass round the agenda? ☐
    Pass round the agenda. ☐
13. Can we try a different approach? ☐
    Your approach to this isn't working. ☐
14. You must call the Delhi office now. ☐
    Please could you call the Delhi office? ☐
15. Could you lock up before you leave? ☐
    Why haven't you locked the door? ☐
16. Could you possibly stay late tonight? ☐
    You have to stay late tonight. ☐
17. Have you printed out these designs? ☐
    Please can you print out these designs? ☐

45.3 USE THE CHART TO CREATE 18 CORRECT SENTENCES AND SAY THEM OUT LOUD

I am going to email the director.

I You Kelly	am going to are going to is going to	email speak to	the director. the IT help desk. the sales department

45.4 LISTEN TO THE AUDIO AND ANSWER THE QUESTIONS

Diego and Janet are organizing a conference.

Diego is going to call the hotel.
True ☑ **False** ☐ **Not given** ☐

1. The Boston office will attend the conference.
True ☐ **False** ☐ **Not given** ☐

2. Diego doesn't like the company logo designs.
True ☐ **False** ☐ **Not given** ☐

3. Janet is going to make the name badges.
True ☐ **False** ☐ **Not given** ☐

4. Diego is going to check that the rooms have Wi-Fi.
True ☐ **False** ☐ **Not given** ☐

5. The interns won't be involved in the conference.
True ☐ **False** ☐ **Not given** ☐

45.5 READ THE EMAIL AND WRITE ANSWERS TO THE QUESTIONS AS FULL SENTENCES

When did Jack meet Omar?
Jack met Omar on Monday.

1. Who is going to contact the presenters?

2. What is Paul going to ask the printers for?

3. What else are the printers going to supply?

4. Who is going to meet the presenters?

5. How will the presenters get to the venue?

6. Why is Omar going to go to the venue?

To: Jack Brown

Subject: Training day preparations

Hi Jack,

Following our meeting on Monday, I have an update on the preparations for the training day. I spoke to Paul and he is going to contact the presenters. He's also going to call the printers and ask if they can print ten extra copies of the training booklets. We have asked the printers to supply name badges in the form of lanyards. They are going to assemble the name badges to save us time.

Marie is going to meet the presenters at the station and bring them to the conference center by taxi. I am going to the venue later today to talk to the catering manager. We have quite a few delegates with special dietary requirements so I want to check they will be catered for. I'll email you later with a further update.

Best wishes,

Omar

46 Vocabulary

Aa 46.1 **FORMS OF COMMUNICATION** WRITE THE WORDS FROM THE PANEL UNDER THE CORRECT PICTURES

switchboard

1 ______

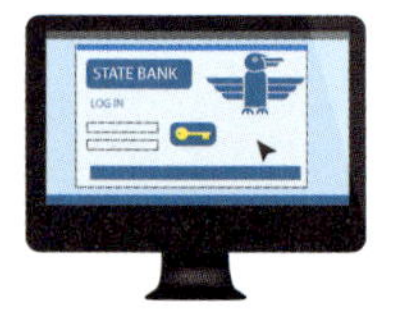

2 ______

3 ______

4 ______

5 ______

6 ______

7 ______

8 ______

9 ______

10 ______

11 ______

12 ______

13 ______

14 ______

15 ______

envelope | text message | social networking | voicemail | ~~switchboard~~ | stamp | bulletin board (US) / notice board (UK) | transfer a call | conference call | internal mail | web conference | mail (US) / post (UK) | presentation | letter | website | email

Aa 46.2 **SENDING EMAILS** WRITE THE WORDS FROM THE PANEL UNDER THE CORRECT PICTURES

contact

1 ______

2 ______

3 ______

4 ______

5 ______

6 ______

7 ______

8 ______

9 ______

outbox · trash · reply all · attachment · forward · subject · ~~contact~~ · signature · print · inbox

Aa 46.3 **ABBREVIATIONS** WRITE THE ABBREVIATIONS FROM THE PANEL UNDER THE CORRECT DEFINITIONS

respond
RSVP

1 to be confirmed ______

2 blind copy ______

3 regarding ______

4 copy ______

5 for your information ______

6 estimated time of arrival ______

7 note ______

8 as soon as possible ______

CC · TBC · FYI · ~~RSVP~~ · NB · ASAP · RE · BCC · ETA

47 Emailing a client

Emails to clients should be polite and clearly state your future plans and intentions. Use the present continuous or "going to" to discuss plans and arrangements.

New language Future tenses for plans
Aa Vocabulary Polite email language
New skill Emailing a client

47.1 REWRITE THE SENTENCES, CORRECTING THE ERRORS

I am writing with regarding to your order.
I am writing with regard to your order.

1. I work at the finance department at Forrester's.
2. Please confirm your availability APAS.
3. Please find your attached receipt to this email.
4. Please hesitate not to contact me.
5. I am writing reference with invoice number 146.
6. Please see the agenda attach here.
7. I work in the IT department in Transtech.
8. I writing to invite you to a meeting next week.
9. Please hesitate to contact me.
10. Please return ASAP your signed contract.
11. I be grateful if you could get back to me soon.
12. I am writing regard to your complaint.
13. Please find the minutes attachment here.
14. I would grateful if we could arrange a meeting.
15. I work at the company's catering department.
16. I am the new Head of Sales in Codequote.
17. I am writing with regard our schedule.
18. Please let me know if you any questions.
19. Please finding the new designs attached here.

47.2 REWRITE THE SENTENCES, PUTTING THE WORDS IN THE CORRECT ORDER

would | if | ASAP. | grateful | could | you | I | be | me | contact

I would be grateful if you could contact me ASAP.

1. to | your | writing | latest | regard | I | feedback. | am | with

2. invoice | here. | the | Please | attached | find

3. grateful | would | invoice. | if | pay | could | the | I | outstanding | be | you

4. do | questions, | If | contact | any | me. | please | not | you | to | have | hesitate

47.3 MATCH THE BEGINNINGS OF THE SENTENCES TO THE CORRECT ENDINGS

If you have any questions, → please do not hesitate to contact me.

1. I am writing with
2. I work in
3. I would be grateful if you
4. I deal with
5. It has come to our attention
6. I wonder if
7. I am writing to

- could let us know when you have been paid.
- that invoice DY895 has not been paid.
- please do not hesitate to contact me.
- the supply and payment of invoices.
- you are aware that we have not been paid.
- the accounts department at Shuberg's.
- inform you that we are going to use a new supplier.
- regard to our invoice number AB3168.

47.4 FILL IN THE GAPS USING THE PHRASES IN THE PANEL

We're going to send you the package you ordered ASAP.

1. He ______________ all the candidates a task to do before their interview.
2. We ______________ other suppliers on Tuesday.
3. Sam ______________ coffee for the CEO's visitors.
4. Carlos ______________ the sales figures tomorrow.
5. We ______________ sales figures for the last quarter.
6. They ______________ all their clients a voucher.
7. He ______________ to Italy to meet the new CEO.
8. Greg ______________ all the boxes into the delivery van.
9. A famous hairdresser ______________ the new salon.
10. We ______________ the new company logo at the sales conference.
11. The company ______________ all the stationery with the old logo.

is going to pack, is giving, is going to make, is going to recycle, are going to discuss, are meeting, ~~going to send~~, are launching, is going to travel, is presenting, are giving, is going to open

47.5 MARK THE SENTENCES THAT ARE CORRECT

I am writing to inform you that we paying your invoice ASAP. ☐
I am writing to inform you that we are going to pay your invoice ASAP. ☑

1. I am writing with regard to the shareholders' meeting on Thursday. ☐
   I am writing with regarding the shareholders' meeting on Thursday. ☐

2. We are going to meeting new clients at the Radcliffe Hotel. ☐
   We are meeting new clients at the Radcliffe Hotel. ☐

3. The meeting is taking place in the hotel's conference center. ☐
   The meeting is going take place in the hotel's conference center. ☐

4. We is going to discuss the last quarter's sales figures. ☐
   We are going to discuss the last quarter's sales figures. ☐

5. The new CEO is go to take questions after his presentation. ☐
   The new CEO is taking questions after his presentation. ☐

6. He is going to discuss the company's future marketing strategy. ☐
   He is going to discussing the company's future marketing strategy. ☐

47.6 READ THE EMAIL AND MARK THE CORRECT SUMMARY

1. Bruno wants to meet the Head of Marketing but cannot find a suitable time. ☐

2. Bruno suggests that Ms. Moran should contact the Head of Marketing directly. ☐

3. Bruno wants to arrange a meeting. His client has not yet confirmed a suitable time for it. ☐

4. Bruno wants to arrange a conference for Mr. Jefferies. ☐

To: Laila Moran

Subject: Date for meeting

Dear Ms. Moran,

I work in the marketing department of Hailey's. I am writing with regard to the meeting you wish to have with our Head of Marketing about the launch of your new products. As you will recall, I wrote to you a week ago asking when you would be available to meet at our premises. Mr. Jefferies has availability next Wednesday afternoon and also on the morning of Friday, July 14. If you could confirm which of those slots works for you, I would be most grateful. I will then send you all the documentation ahead of your meeting with Mr. Jefferies.

Kind regards,

Bruno Martell

Answers

01

1.1

1. My name's Ali Patel.
2. Hi, I'm Jeff.
3. It's good to meet you, Jane.
4. Pleased to meet you.
5. My name is Deepak Kaur.
6. Great to meet you, Tanya.
7. It's nice to meet you, too.
8. Good morning. My name is Ben Lewis.
9. It's great to meet you, Gill.
10. Good evening. My name is Karen.

1.2

1. Hello, my name's Fiona Hill.
2. Nice to meet you, too.
3. It's good to meet you, Jim.
4. Pleased to meet you.
5. It's a pleasure to meet you.
6. Good evening. My name is Roy.

1.3

1. A
2. B
3. B
4. A
5. A

1.4

1. A-L-E-X H-A-N-N
2. D-E-V S-I-N-G-H
3. F-R-A-N-C-I-S P-A-L-M-E-R
4. H-A-N-S-A S-Y-A
5. Z-A-N-D-R-A F-E-L-L-I-N-I
6. R-A-J D-H-A-B-I
7. K-A-T-Y A-D-E-N-O-V-A

1.5

1. This **is** our new designer.
2. Raj and I **work** together.
3. I **would** like you to meet our CEO. / **I'd** like you to meet our CEO.
4. Hi, **my** name's Lola. / Hi, **I'm Lola**.
5. It's great to **meet you**, Emily.
6. **May I** introduce Ewan Carlton?
7. Farah, this **is** my colleague, Leon.

1.6

1. Good morning. **My** name's Saira Khan.
2. **I'm** Harry.
3. **I'm** Andrew Shaw.
4. **It's** good to meet you.
5. Pleased **to** meet you.
6. It's a **pleasure** to meet you.
7. **May** I introduce our new HR assistant?
8. Keira, **meet** John.
9. **Great** to meet you.
10. I **would** like you to meet Dan.
11. Colin and I **work** together.

1.7

- A 5
- B 6
- C 7
- D 4
- E 1
- F 3
- G 2

02

2.1

1. I start work at 9 o'clock.
2. She has an update with her boss.
3. Mrs. Reece is a fantastic teacher.
4. I'm a firefighter.
5. Elena works late on Thursdays.
6. He drinks coffee every afternoon.
7. She leaves work at 5:30pm.

2.2

1. The IT Helpdesk **is** really good.
2. She **works** in a car factory.
3. I **eat** my lunch in the park.
4. We **take** a break at 11am.
5. John **writes** the minutes of our meetings.
6. Mrs. Rae **cleans** the meeting rooms.
7. The CEO **brings** cake on his birthday.
8. I **prepare** presentations.
9. Jomir **stops** for tea at 3pm.

2.3

1. The CEO arrives at work early.
2. We have a hot-desking policy.
3. My assistant opens my mail.
4. Shazia is an engineer.
5. Hal works for his uncle.
6. I start work at 8:30am.
7. They finish at 5pm.
8. They eat lunch in the cafeteria.
9. Kate only drinks coffee.
10. I call the US office every Monday.
11. Andrew helps me with my PC.
12. I reply to emails at 11am and 3pm.

2.4

1. The manager's PA
2. After the break
3. An hour
4. 12:30pm
5. They analyze sales
6. Twice a week

2.5

1. The director **has** an open door policy.
2. I **deal** with all his emails.
3. Gavin **leaves** work at 7pm.
4. They **work** evenings and weekends.
5. She **rides** her bike to work.
6. Tim and Pat **bring** their own lunch.
7. Deepak **turns** off his phone after work.
8. Sobek and Kurt **play** tennis after work.
9. My boss **plans** my work for the week.

2.6

1. Lulu always **gets** to work early.
2. Our reps **meet** clients at their office.
3. The CEO **talks** to all new staff.
4. He's a nurse and he **works** weekends.
5. Imran **deals** with all the contracts.
6. The printer **stops** working late in the day.
7. The staff **go** to a nearby café for lunch.
8. Raj **takes** a break at 11am.
9. Sophie **is** a travel agent.

03

3.1

1. Argentina
2. Australia
3. South America
4. China
5. Canada
6. Egypt
7. South Korea
8. France
9. Australasia
10. Japan
11. India
12. United States of America (US / USA)
13. Netherlands
14. Asia
15. Mongolia
16. Pakistan
17. New Zealand
18. Russia
19. South Africa
20. North America
21. Thailand
22. United Arab Emirates (UAE)
23. United Kingdom (UK)
24. Turkey
25. Spain
26. Africa
27. Singapore
28. Republic of Ireland (ROI)
29. Europe
30. Mexico
31. Brazil
32. Germany
33. Austria
34. Switzerland

04

4.1

1 Russia 2 India 3 Japan 4 Chile 5 Greece

4.2

COUNTRIES:
South Africa, **France**, **Italy**, **Vietnam**, **Switzerland**, **China**
NATIONALITIES:
Brazilian, **British**, **Greek**, **Canadian**, **Japanese**, **Spanish**

4.3

1. The new CEO is **from Australia**.
2. These new robots are **Japanese**.
3. We sell leather bags **from Portugal**.
4. I'm **from Argentina**, but I work in the US.
5. The designer is **British**.
6. Our sales director is **from South Korea**.
7. Our best-selling rugs are **Indian**.
8. These beautiful clothes are **from Africa**.

4.4

1. Our CEO is from America.
2. I've got a flight to Italy next Monday.
3. These sports cars are from France.
4. Most of our fabrics are from Africa.
5. My PA is from Spain.

4.5

1. We sell smartphones from **Japan**.
2. The HR manager is from **America**.
3. My team follows the **Chinese** markets.
4. Travel to the **Greek** islands with us.
5. Our products are from **Vietnam**.
6. Our CEO is **Canadian**.
7. Most of the sales team is from **Spain**.
8. I'm British, but I work in **Italy**.
9. I have a lot of **Mexican** co-workers.
10. My new assistant is from **France**.

4.6

1. **I'm not** very tall.
2. He **doesn't work** in an office.
3. We **don't sell** French cars.
4. **They're not** from Italy. / They **aren't** from Italy.
5. The fruit in the supermarket **isn't** local.
6. I **don't work** for an Asian company.
7. **You're** not happy. / You **aren't** happy.
8. She **isn't** from China. / **She's not** from China.
9. We **don't produce** robots.
10. You **don't** have any meetings today.
11. It **isn't** a steel factory. / **It's not** a steel factory.

4.7

1. These dresses **aren't** made in India.
2. She **doesn't** come from Russia.
3. The workers in this factory **aren't** American.
4. They **don't** sell energy to South Korea.
5. He **isn't** from Chile. / **He's not** from Chile.

4.8

1. IT
2. Carlos
3. Marketing
4. Tim
5. China

4.9

1. True
2. Not given
3. False
4. True
5. Not given
6. False
7. False

05

5.1

1. adhesive tape
2. calendar
3. clipboard
4. computer
5. planner (US) / diary (UK)
6. rubber bands
7. envelope
8. hole punch
9. hard drive
10. pen
11. laptop
12. pencil
13. files / folders
14. paper clips
15. eraser (US) / rubber (UK)
16. letter
17. shredder
18. cell phone (US) / mobile phone (UK)
19. printer
20. headset
21. highlighter
22. pencil sharpener
23. stapler
24. telephone / phone
25. tablet
26. notepad
27. projector
28. chair
29. ruler
30. scanner
31. lamp

06

6.1

1. Is this printer working?
2. Is this your desk?
3. Are the windows closed?
4. Is this cupboard locked?
5. Is his desk messy?
6. Is she the CEO?
7. Are you Jo's assistant?

6.2

1. Is that John's pen?
2. Is this the kitchen?
3. Is that the CEO's office?
4. Is Tina the CEO's PA?
5. Is Tom's desk organized?
6. Is the printer working?
7. Is the stationery cabinet locked?

6.3

1. **Do** you have an appointment?
2. **Does** she work with Justin?
3. **Does** your office have a scanner?
4. **Do** you go to the finance meetings?
5. **Does** Kish write the minutes?
6. **Do** you have a stapler I can borrow?
7. **Does** Saul work in your team?
8. **Do** they know what to do?
9. **Does** he know the CEO?
10. **Do** we have a meeting now?

6.4

1. False
2. True
3. False
4. False

6.5

1. Is the stationery cabinet open?
2. Do you want tea or coffee?
3. Do you know her phone number?
4. Are they free for a meeting tomorrow?
5. Do you have a laptop I can take home?
6. Do you have an appointment?
7. Are there any envelopes I can use?
8. Does he usually arrive late?

6.6

1. **How** does the scanner work?
2. **What** is on the agenda for the meeting?
3. **Why** is the stationery cabinet locked?
4. **When** do we have a break for lunch?
5. **Where** is the CEO's office?
6. **What** is the door code?
7. **Who** do I ask for ink for the printer?

6.7

1. Why is the cafeteria closed?
2. How do I scan this document?
3. When is the fire alarm tested?
4. Do you know where Faisal is?
5. Is Sandra late again?
6. What is for lunch today?
7. Does the office stay open on weekends?
8. Who do you report to?

6.8

1. **Who** buys the tea and coffee?
2. **Why** is the printer not working?
3. **When** does the office open?
4. **What** do you want for lunch?
5. **Where** is the meeting room?
6. **How** does the projector work?
7. **What** is the photocopier code?

07

7.1

1. How can I reach you?
2. Do you have many clients?
3. Do you have a website?
4. Where do you work?
5. What is your company called?

6 What's your job title?
7 This is my email address.
8 Drop me a line.
9 How can I contact you?
10 Give me a call.
11 How big is your team?

7.2

A 6
B 2
C 3
D 5
E 1
F 4

7.3

1 How can I **reach** you for more infomation?
2 Drop me a **line** when you're visiting next.
3 Does your company **have** a website?
4 Please stay in **touch**.
5 Is this your **correct** phone number?
6 **Call** me if you want further details.
7 Is this your **current** email address?
8 My job **title** is on the business card.
9 Do you **have** a portfolio with you?

7.4

1 True
2 True
3 Not given
4 Not given
5 False
6 True
7 False
8 False

7.5

1 Yes, it is.
2 No, it doesn't.
3 No, they aren't.
4 Yes, I am.
5 No, he doesn't.
6 Yes, we do.

7.6

1 No, **it isn't**.
2 No, **it doesn't**.
3 Yes, **it is**.
4 Yes, **it does**.
5 No, **they don't**.
6 No, **I'm not**.
7 Yes, **they do**.
8 Yes, **she does**.
9 Yes, **I do**.

08

8.1

1 She **has** an excellent résumé.
2 I **have** good people skills.
3 They **don't have** much time.
4 Do you **have** previous experience?
5 He's **got** excellent keyboard skills.
6 I **don't have** my own office.
7 Does he **have** any training?
8 They **have** a can-do outlook.
9 You don't **have** his number, do you?

8.2

1 Do you have a higher degree in business?
2 He has an MBA from the Boston Business School.
3 They don't have a full-time receptionist.
4 Does your assistant have an excellent résumé?

8.3

1 Travel
2 A hotel
3 Management
4 Excellent
5 In teams
6 Marketing

8.4

1 The new chef is very talented.
2 Toby is an accountant.
3 Search engines are invaluable.
4 She works for a leading company.
5 Have you seen the ad I told you about?
6 They are out of the office.
7 Did you see the new designs?
8 They hired the best candidate.
9 What skills does the job require?
10 Is there an office in India?
11 I have a certificate in sales.
12 He works for the biggest store.
13 Interns are only paid expenses.

8.5

1 I worked as **an** intern at Beales.
2 I know **the** café you mean.
3 There's **a** printer on the second floor.
4 Jon hasn't got **a** diploma.
5 The CEO is in **the** NY office this week.
6 He's **an** amazing architect.
7 I just started **a** new job.
8 I'd like to put **an** ad in the paper.
9 Have you read **the** job description?
10 I work at **the** theater next door.
11 **The** new café does great coffee.
12 Where is **the** presentation?
13 The Tate is **an** art gallery.
14 I like **the** new CEO.

8.6

A 7
B 1
C 4
D 2
E 6
F 3
G 8
H 5

8.7

1. I've **got three** years' experience.
2. I don't have **a** degree in business studies.
3. He has **a** diploma in economics.
4. I saw **an** ad in The Echo.
5. She has **an** excellent phone manner.
6. He works in **a** hospital.
7. I don't **like interviews**.
8. **The** agency is in the market place.
9. We are looking **for sales people**.

09

9.1

1. sales manager
2. librarian
3. doctor
4. hairdresser / stylist
5. engineer
6. train driver
7. writer
8. cleaner / janitor
9. chef
10. electrician
11. mechanic
12. pilot
13. waitress
14. vet
15. travel agent
16. plumber
17. artist
18. judge
19. sales assistant
20. musician
21. surgeon
22. receptionist
23. tour guide
24. taxi driver
25. designer
26. scientist
27. firefighter

9.2

1. shift
2. apprentice
3. full-time (F/T)
4. temporary
5. co-worker / colleague
6. part-time (P/T)

10

10.1

1. I love food, and I enjoy cooking.
2. I love working with computers.
3. I enjoy driving.
4. I enjoy traveling to different countries.
5. I don't like working on my own.

10.2

1. She loves **meeting** new clients.
2. He **doesn't** enjoy giving presentations.
3. I hate **training** big groups.
4. They like **working** in a team.
5. Jan **enjoys** working with children.
6. Ali doesn't **like** long meetings.
7. We don't **like** working weekends.
8. I love **solving** problems.
9. Jim doesn't **enjoy** business trips.

10.3

1. Dislikes
2. Likes
3. Likes
4. Dislikes
5. Likes
6. Dislikes
7. Likes

10.4

1. I **don't** enjoy work social trips.
2. They like **meeting** new people.
3. He doesn't **like** working late.
4. She hates **sitting** at a desk all day.
5. Do you enjoy **working** in a team?
6. We enjoy **giving** presentations.
7. Angus doesn't like **using** computers.

11

11.1

1. There are three printers in your department.
2. Are there ladies' toilets on the second floor?
3. There isn't a cafeteria in the building.
4. Is there a set time for lunch breaks?
5. There aren't any elevators in the office.
6. Is there a dress code at this company?
7. There's a photocopier on the first floor.
8. There aren't any trash cans in the office.
9. Are there any interns on your team?
10. There is a calendar on the notice board.

11.2

1. There is an elevator that goes to all the office floors.
2. There are some stickers in the stationery cabinet.
3. There are some men's toilets on the first and third floors.
4. There is a water cooler in the kitchen.
5. There isn't a set time for lunch breaks.

11.3

1. False
2. True
3. False
4. True
5. False
6. Not given

11.4

1. There **are** two positions available at our company.
2. There isn't **a** toaster in the kitchen, but there is a microwave.
3. **Is** there a spare computer I can use?
4. Are there **any** pencils in the stationery cabinet?
5. There **is** a big meeting room in our new office.

12

12.1

1. safe
2. transfer money
3. receipt
4. cash machine / ATM
5. bank
6. currency
7. wallet
8. mobile banking
9. bills (US) / notes (UK)
10. check (US) / cheque (UK)
11. cash register (US) / till (UK)
12. withdraw money
13. invoice
14. online banking
15. credit card

12.2

1. overtime
2. salary
3. benefits
4. a raise (US) / a pay rise (UK)
5. to earn
6. a bonus
7. annual vacation (US) / annual leave (UK)
8. hourly rate
9. a pay cut

13

13.1

1. The new intern seems really bright and she is **very organized.**
2. My manager doesn't ask **nervous employees** to give presentations.
3. My director **is very bossy** and she is also hardworking.
4. Sue and Robin are sometimes **rude** to our clients.
5. It's important to stay **calm under pressure**, even if you're very busy.
6. Mushira is very **intelligent**, and she will bring a great deal to the team.
7. It's impossible to feel relaxed when you work with **impatient people**.
8. The people on my team are all very **motivated**, and it's great to work with them.
9. We are looking for a **creative designer** to join our busy production team.

13.2

1. Ian seems very hardworking.
2. Kay and Jack are really polite.
3. Ben is very bossy.
4. Diane always looks well dressed.
5. Alex is really impatient.
6. Lenny is a creative chef.
7. This is a great team.
8. Jo seems very organized.
9. Harry seems very bright.

13.3

1. creative
2. organized
3. calm
4. well dressed

13.4

1. **Our** team meetings are always interesting.
2. Is this **your** desk? It's very messy!
3. **My** team is very motivated.
4. Is that **their** design? It's great.
5. Kevin is talking to **his** manager.
6. That's Tanya. **Her** phone manner is excellent.
7. The company is very proud of **its** reputation.

13.5

1. Is this **his** desk?
2. We don't like **their** product.
3. **My** manager is very smart.
4. This report is **yours**.
5. Jane does **her** job well.
6. They are proud of **their** reputation.
7. Is this tablet **hers**?
8. **Their** manager is never late.
9. Is this **your** pen?

13.6

1. The interns have just finished college.
2. Jorge's reputation is well deserved.
3. Nuala's assistant is very helpful.
4. Helen's manager often works late.
5. Maria's co-workers are really friendly.
6. The team members are hardworking.
7. Look at this ad. I like its design.
8. Leroy's work is very impressive.
9. Are there any files in the cabinet?
10. John's confidence has grown this year.
11. Sam's presentation went really well.
12. The CEO's new assistant is very bright.
13. Their products are very popular.
14. That's my boss's parking space.
15. Pablo's report is almost finished.
16. The company is pleased with its new logo.
17. Ethan's team is working on a new project.

13.7

1. You are my boss.
2. You are my co-worker.
3. You are Peter's boss.
4. You are Peter's co-worker.
5. You are very polite.
6. You are really polite.
7. They are very polite.
8. They are really polite.
9. Alex is my boss.
10. Alex is my co-worker.
11. Alex is Peter's boss.
12. Alex is Peter's co-worker.
13. Alex is very polite.
14. Alex is really polite.

14

14.1

1 Vihaan is very **satisfied** with his office.
2 The new login system is rather **annoying**.
3 The quarterly results are **shocking**.
4 The economic situation is quite **worrying**.
5 We're **excited** about the new office.
6 Simone was **tired** after the course.
7 The profits were **disappointing**.
8 John is **confused** about the schedule.
9 We were **surprised** by the results.
10 We thought the meeting was **boring**.
11 I'm often **exhausted** by Friday.

14.2

1 boring
2 confused
3 exciting
4 annoying
5 surprising
6 interesting
7 disappointed
8 worried

14.3

1 I am very **busy** with the new project, but I'll be even **busier** next week.
2 Our new office is **large**, but the office in Beijing is **larger**.
3 My job is very **stressful**, but being unemployed is **more stressful**.
4 The meeting was **long**, but last week's was even **longer**.
5 John's flight ticket was **expensive**, but mine was **more expensive**.
6 Our new photocopier is **fast**, but the HR department's is **faster**.
7 Claire's news was **surprising**, but Peter resigning was **more surprising**.
8 My current job is **interesting**, but my old one was **more interesting**.
9 The new furniture is **comfortable**, but the furniture at G-Tech is **more comfortable**.
10 This test is **difficult**, but the next one will be **more difficult**.
11 My commute is **short**; it's only 10 minutes. Pete's is even **shorter**.

14.4

1 Your printer is **quicker** than ours.
2 Today's meeting was **more interesting** than usual.
3 Growth was **worse** than we had expected.
4 Sandra has been **more successful** than last year.
5 I'm feeling **better** after a week off work.
6 There is **less** juice left than I thought.
7 My new apartment is **closer** to the center.
8 The results are **better** than in the first quarter.
9 We have an **earlier** start than usual today.
10 Liam has taken a much **later** lunch break than everyone else.
11 This restaurant is **worse** than the others.
12 The flight was **more expensive** than I expected.

14.5

1 The new intern is **more helpful than the old one**.
2 Our hours are longer **than those in the German branch**.
3 The new computers are **faster than the old ones**.
4 I feel better **now that I have a new job**.
5 Our new office design **is more modern than the previous one**.
6 The tickets **are more expensive than they used to be**.
7 My raise was **smaller than last year's**.
8 My training this year was **more interesting than last year**.
9 The office is busier **since we merged with our competitors**.

14.6

1 False 2 True 3 False
4 Not given 5 True 6 True
7 False 8 Not given

15

15.1

1 Karen leaves home at 7am on Fridays.
2 Vicky usually takes notes during meetings.
3 We don't work the week before New Year.
4 The team always arrives before 10am.
5 Chang arrives at 8:30am every morning.
6 We sometimes have meetings in the evening.
7 Terry sometimes works on the weekend.

15.2

1. Everyone arrives **by** 9:30am.
2. Peter often works **until** 11pm.
3. The office is closed **during** August.
4. The café is open **from** 6am.
5. I finish work at 4pm **on** Fridays.
6. The cafeteria is open **from** 1pm.
7. Ann sends an agenda **before** each meeting.

15.3

1. 7am
2. 1 hour
3. 8:30am
4. 2pm
5. sometimes
6. afternoon

15.4

1. I drive because it's so **convenient**.
2. Jim **takes** the bus every morning.
3. Jack travels **by** bike when he can.
4. The **rush** hour starts at 7am in my city.
5. Sam **takes** the metro home each evening.
6. Raymond **drives** his car to work.
7. I get **on** the bus near the museum.
8. I missed my **connection**.
9. Janet prefers to travel **by** train to work.
10. Karl **takes** the bus home at night.
11. There are a lot of traffic **jams** in the city.
12. You should get **off** the tram at the library.
13. It's much cheaper to **cycle** than drive.
14. I like to **walk** to work in the summer.
15. I prefer to **cycle** to my office.

15.5

1. I drive to work.
2. We take the bus.
3. Doug rides his bike to work.
4. I sometimes take a taxi home.
5. The buses run from 5am to 11pm.
6. I go by train.
7. The train arrives at 5pm.
8. Sharon gets off the bus by the station.
9. I like to go home from work on foot.
10. My train to work arrives at 7:45am.
11. Traveling by train is comfortable.
12. The train leaves at about 8pm.
13. I travel by train every day.

15.6

A. 1
B. 7
C. 2
D. 4
E. 3
F. 6
G. 5
H. 8

15.7

1. There aren't many buses **on the weekend**.
2. Hank takes the bus because **it's cheaper than the train**.
3. The office stays open **until 10 in the evening**.
4. I leave for work **between 7 and 8am**.
5. Sally often walks to work **during the summer**.
6. I take the train to work because **it's faster than the bus**.
7. Ted takes notes **during meetings**.
8. I always go to bed **before 11pm**.

16

16.1

1. Saturday
2. Monday
3. Sunday
4. Friday
5. Tuesday
6. Thursday

16.2

1. three times a week
2. hourly
3. monthly
4. daily
5. in the morning
6. in the afternoon
7. in the evening
8. before work
9. after work

16.3

1. see a play
2. do yoga
3. draw
4. meet friends
5. walk / hike
6. go out for a meal
7. play an instrument
8. watch a movie
9. stay (at) home
10. visit a museum / an art gallery
11. read
12. cook
13. play sports
14. take photos
15. go shopping
16. go camping
17. write
18. go cycling
19. play board games

17

17.1

1. We often go camping on the weekend.
2. Doug sometimes meets friends after he finishes work.
3. I always go running in the morning.
4. My father never watches television.
5. She occasionally sees a play at our local theater.

6 Frank is very lazy, and he rarely does any exercise.
7 My kids sometimes play video games after school.

17.2

1 rarely 2 usually
3 often 4 never

17.3

1 Mariam usually stays **at home on weekends**.
2 I sometimes take **photos when I go on vacation**.
3 Dan rarely reads **a newspaper in the morning**.
4 She occasionally sees **a play at her local theater**.
5 Marco usually does **some exercises when he gets up**.
6 I sometimes listen to **music while I travel to work**.
7 We sometimes go out **for a meal at the Chinese restaurant**.
8 I often watch **a movie when I get home from work**.

17.4

1 The earliest flight is at 9am.
2 Sydney is the largest city in Australia.
3 Dubai is the hottest place I've visited.
4 This is the most expensive software we sell.
5 The farthest I've flown is to New Zealand.
6 Spanish is the easiest language to learn.
7 Kraków is the most beautiful city in Poland.
8 The train is the most affordable way to travel.
9 This is the most interesting gallery in town.
10 Hiroshi is the most intelligent person I know.
11 That was the scariest film I've seen.

17.5

1 The **longest** river in Brazil is the Amazon.
2 We'll have lunch at the **closest** café to the office.
3 I just watched the **worst** presentation I've ever seen.
4 I think that snowboarding is the **most exciting** sport.
5 Sean lives the **farthest** / **furthest** from the office.
6 Antonio is our **most loyal** employee.
7 This is the **most expensive** printer we have.

17.6

1 Dan
2 Pete
3 Pete
4 Pete
5 Dan
6 Chloe
7 Pete
8 Dan
9 Chloe
10 Dan

18

18.1

1 I didn't learn Spanish at school.
2 We walked to the conference center.
3 John lived in New York for 10 years.
4 Did the team discuss the merger?
5 He went to the conference by car.
6 My manager didn't visit the factory.
7 Selma didn't walk to work today.
8 Jimish posted the report a week ago.
9 Did Tom finish the report?

18.2

Note: "did not" can also be written in contracted form.
1 Akiko **finished** her presentation, then she **watched** some TV.
2 I **did not watch** the game because I **needed** to prepare for the conference.
3 Derek **wanted** to work somewhere interesting, so he **moved** to New York.
4 We **arrived** late, but we **did not miss** the meeting.
5 Sally **passed** her exams, and **decided** to go to college.

18.3

1 Fred showed me the new conference center.
2 We watched an interesting documentary about Beijing.
3 Ramon started at this company about five years ago.
4 Did you enjoy the presentation about the Indian economy?
5 It rained yesterday, so we didn't play soccer.
6 Arnold cooked me a delicious dinner last night.
7 Did Sam finish the report about the new product range?
8 I booked a table in a restaurant in the center.
9 Did Mike play tennis with the new CEO on Saturday?

18.4

1 Did Paul start working for us more than five years ago?
2 Did Sally explain how to use the new photocopier?
3 Did it rain while they were in Indonesia?
4 Did Clive pick up the guests from the railway station?
5 Did Mark join you for lunch at the Chinese restaurant?
6 Did the team attend the conference in Paris last year?
7 Did Philip play golf with the consultants last weekend?
8 Did Carl and Marie walk to work again today?
9 Did you watch the game yesterday?

10 Did Janet show you the new photocopier?
11 Did Mo study economics at Stanford University?
12 Did the company invest $10 million in R&D?

18.5

1 False
2 True
3 Not given
4 Not given
5 False
6 True
7 False

18.6

1 He studied for an exam.
2 She visited a friend.
3 She walked to work.
4 He traveled to India.
5 He listened to the radio.

19

19.1

1 A
2 A
3 B
4 A
5 B

19.2

1 It's nine seventeen. / It's seventeen minutes past nine.
2 It's seven o'clock. / It's seven.
3 It's half past five. / It's five thirty.
4 It's three twenty-two. / It's twenty-two minutes past three.
5 It's a quarter to six. / It's five forty-five.

19.3

1 The soccer tournament ends on June 20.
2 American Independence Day is on the 4th of July.
3 Christmas Day is on December 25.
4 My wife's birthday is on September 5.
5 My daughter was born on August 3.

19.4

1 2014
2 August 2015
3 July
4 Scotland
5 May 3

20

20.1

1 spent
2 met
3 got
4 went
5 was / were
6 left
7 told
8 thought
9 said
10 began
11 chose

20.2

1 I **went** to Paris on a business trip last week.
2 I **spent** all afternoon working on a report.
3 I **began** working at Carter's last year.
4 The CEO **told** me that my work was excellent.
5 I **thought** this project was very difficult.
6 Besim **was** off sick yesterday.
7 I **met** the new Sales Director this morning.
8 The staff **chose** the name of the company.
9 Kara **left** her last job because it was boring.

20.3

1 I **met** the International Marketing Director last week.
2 I **had** a demanding boss.
3 I **left** my last job because it was badly paid.
4 I **got** to work very early today.
5 They **went** to the New York office last month.
6 The staff **chose** new chairs for the office.
7 Sally **thought** that Rohit's presentation went well.

20.4

1 I started work there after I left school.
2 I worked in a bank at the start of my career.
3 I took the children to school.
4 I met many interesting people.
5 I worked hard and studied for an MBA.
6 We had a black and white uniform.

20.5

A 7
B 1
C 2
D 8
E 3
F 5
G 4
H 6

20.6

1 I **felt** very well respected by my team leader.
2 The Head of Sales **taught** me to give interesting presentations.
3 My brother **made** a delicious cake, which I took to work for my birthday.

4 The staff **chose** the pictures for the meeting rooms, and they look great.
5 I **left** my last job because I didn't get along with the customers.
6 I **spent** all of yesterday writing a sales report and now I'm very tired.

21

21.1

1 We **launched** a new range of apps last year.
2 At **first**, we only had four employees.
3 Two years **ago**, we opened our tenth store.
4 The company **merged** with a competitor a year ago.
5 A new Director of Marketing **started** working here last year.

21.2

1 **At first**, we only had one store.
2 We **opened** a new flagship store last month.
3 We **launched** an exciting new app last year.
4 A new Director of HR started working six months **ago**.

21.3

1 Over 10,000
2 In her garage
3 50
4 Two years ago
5 At craft fairs

21.4

1 last month
2 during the first quarter
3 in the winter of 2012
4 recently

21.5

1 **Last** spring, sales of umbrellas **rose** because it was wet.
2 UK sales **went up** in 2011, but **fell** in 2012.
3 **At** first, the value of shares in the company **remained** steady.
4 Online marketing costs **increased** and sales also **rose**.

22

22.1

1 to accept an invitation
2 to attend a meeting
3 calendar
4 boardroom
5 to invite someone
6 office
7 conference room
8 running late
9 restaurant
10 reception
11 café
12 morning
13 afternoon
14 evening
15 appointment
16 refreshments
17 to decline an invitation
18 to miss a meeting
19 agenda

22.2

1 to come up
2 to cancel
3 to be busy
4 to be unable to attend
5 to look forward to
6 to reschedule

23

23.1

1 The company **is losing** money, so we **are planning** a restructure.
2 Stacy **is not working** in the office today. She **is visiting** the factory.
3 Dan **is meeting** a new client. They **are chatting** in the meeting room.
4 Colin **is starting** a new project. He **is working** with Angela.
5 The head office **is relocating** to Delhi. We **are moving** this week.
6 Profits **are falling** this year, and the team **is feeling** nervous.
7 Anika **is working** late tonight. She **is preparing** a presentation.
8 Sue and Clive **are having** lunch downtown. They **are eating** Chinese.
9 I **am going** on vacation next week. I **am missing** the training day.
10 Our company **is selling** a lot to India. We **are opening** an office in Mumbai.
11 Our secretary **is retiring**. We **are recruiting** a new one.
12 Sam and Sue **are discussing** the report. They **are planning** a meeting about it.
13 Chrissie **is choosing** a new team. She **is considering** Paul for a position.
14 Alex **is leaving** the company. He **is moving** to New York.

23.2

1 Who are you meeting?
2 Is Tim writing the report?
3 Are Kim and Jo presenting today?
4 Are you printing the agenda?
5 Is the company moving?
6 When are you retiring?
7 Who are you promoting?

23.3

1. Is the conference taking place in Venice next April?
2. Is Leanne giving a presentation on the takeover plans?
3. Are our owners hoping to buy our biggest competitor?
4. Is Brendan programming the software for new machinery?
5. Are we taking time off in August this year?

23.4

1. Are you having lunch at 1pm today?
2. Tom is going to the conference today.
3. Is John working until 7pm again?
4. We are traveling to New York again.
5. Are you coming to the meeting on Friday?
6. Are you visiting the factory next month?
7. I'm not taking time off in August.
8. The head office is moving in the spring.
9. Fran isn't coming to the office tomorrow.
10. What are you doing on Tuesday?
11. Sam is meeting the client this afternoon.
12. Tim is leaving work at 5pm today.

23.5

1. On Monday morning, Frank is **visiting the factory**.
2. On Monday afternoon, Clare is **attending a course**.
3. On Tuesday, Frank is **celebrating his wedding anniversary**.
4. In the evening, he is **going to the theater**.
5. On Thursday at 2pm, Clare is **meeting Pete**.
6. They are both free at **2:30pm on Thursday**.

23.6

1. I'm having lunch with the IT team.
2. I'm meeting them at 3pm.
3. I'm flying to Edinburgh.
4. I'm returning to London at 11:30am.
5. I'm going to Sandra's leaving party.

24

24.1

1. Polite
2. Impolite
3. Polite
4. Polite
5. Polite
6. Impolite
7. Polite

24.2

1. True
2. False
3. True
4. False
5. Not given
6. False
7. Not given

24.3

1. I'm sorry. I'm not sure I **agree**.
2. Sorry, but in my **opinion** they will sell well.
3. I can see your **point**, but I still think senior citizens are more important.
4. If I could just **come** in here and mention the good news from France.
5. **Excuse** me, but my figures tell a different story.
6. **Could** I just say...? The budget won't cover it.
7. I'm not **sure** I agree. Sales to China are growing faster.
8. Sorry to **interrupt**, but the software is not ready yet.

24.4

1. I'm afraid Sean can't make it to the meeting and has **sent** his apologies.
2. Shall we **take** a vote on the new strategy to see what course of action to take?
3. Ramona will **take** the minutes and email them to everyone after the meeting.
4. I agree with the motion. How **about** you? What do you think about it?
5. If I could just **interrupt** for a moment. I think we need to take a vote on this.
6. That sums up most of the issues we are facing. I just have a few **closing** remarks.
7. Claude is the chair, so he has the **casting** vote if there is a tie.
8. The **chair** of our budget meetings likes to keep his closing remarks very short.
9. I read **through** the agenda before the meeting, so I know what we will be talking about.

24.5

1. footprint
2. green
3. reuse
4. resources
5. waste
6. environment
7. reduce

25

25.1

1. Me neither.
2. Neither do I.
3. So did I.
4. Neither did I.
5. Me too.
6. So do I.
7. Me neither.
8. So do I.
9. Me too.

25.2

1. I suppose so. It will be expensive though.
2. So did I. He's so entertaining.
3. I agree. The team could improve their skills.
4. I'll ask the secretary to send it again.
5. Me neither. The food's very bland.
6. So do I. It's very comfortable.
7. Exactly. I didn't understand it at all.
8. I agree. I learned some new skills.
9. Absolutely. We should promote her.

25.3

1. I'm **afraid** we'll have to cancel the meeting.
2. I'm sorry, but I **disagree** with you.
3. I **totally** disagree with you about this.
4. I'm really not **sure** about that design.
5. I'm **sorry**, Pete, but I don't agree with you.
6. I don't agree at **all**. It won't work.
7. I'm not **sure** about this. Can we talk later?
8. I'm afraid I **don't** agree with you at all.
9. I don't **agree** at all with the merger.
10. You **could** be right, but I'm not sure.
11. Sorry, but I disagree **with** this plan.

25.4

1. Greg disagrees with her.
2. Greg thinks he doesn't have enough experience.
3. Jenny strongly disagrees.
4. Greg agrees.
5. Jenny strongly agrees.

25.5

1. We **totally** agree about the redesign.
2. I can't agree with you **at** all about the downsizing.
3. We're **afraid** we totally disagree.
4. You **could** be right, but I need more evidence.
5. I'm not sure **about** the latest business plan.

26

26.1

1. Roger hurt himself when he slipped.
2. She burned herself on the coffee maker.
3. Ron blames himself for the accident.
4. Jan cut herself on the machinery.
5. We enjoyed ourselves at the office party.
6. Juan cut himself in the kitchen.
7. We need to protect ourselves from risks.

26.2

1. I hurt **myself** when I moved the photocopier.
2. They should prepare **themselves** for the course.
3. Claire's cut **herself** on the equipment.
4. Have you all signed **yourselves** up for the course?
5. Sam is teaching **himself** Japanese.

26.3

1. Not given
2. Not given
3. True
4. False
5. Not given
6. False
7. True
8. False

26.4

1. An **extinguisher** is used to stop small fires.
2. If you hear the fire alarm, go to the **assembly area**.
3. Medical equipment is kept in the **first aid kit**.
4. Each fire **escape** has a sign above the door.
5. You practice leaving the building during a **fire drill**.

27

27.1

1. How about asking Tim to write the report?
2. Why don't we ask Pete for his opinion?
3. We could have a meeting on Friday.
4. Let's ask the team for their opinions.
5. What about putting some videos online?
6. Why don't we hire another intern?
7. How about moving the meeting to 5pm?
8. Let's try calling the engineer again.

27.2

1. She should go home and rest.
2. You should ask the secretary for another.
3. You should go on a training course.
4. You should order some more.
5. He should call IT.
6. You should call the engineer.
7. You should ask for an extension.
8. You should take the bus.

27.3

1. Where have the reports gone? They've **disappeared**.
2. Pete **misunderstood** me. He thought I said 3 o'clock.
3. Cathy isn't coming in today. She's feeling **unwell**.
4. You should be **careful** crossing the road.
5. Doug is really **impatient**. He gets angry so easily.
6. I'm **unable** to come to the training because I have a meeting.
7. Don't forget to **disconnect** the machine after you've used it.
8. I'm **unfamiliar** with that program. I don't know it.
9. Jean is so **careless**. She's always making mistakes.

10. This morning is **impractical** for me. Can we meet later?

27.4

1. We should make sure no one **misunderstood** the instructions.
2. How about organizing training for everyone who is **unfamiliar** with the program?
3. Let's make sure no one on the team **spells** the name wrongly again.
4. Why don't we ask Pete to help if Laura isn't **well** tomorrow?
5. I think we should **disconnect** the machine since it's not working.
6. I don't think you should be so **impatient** with the new recruits.
7. Let's send a memo to everyone who isn't **able** to come to the meeting.
8. Let's explain to Tim that he should be more **careful** with financial information.
9. Why don't we try to find a time that is **convenient** for everyone?

28

28.1

1. young adults
2. sports wear
3. jackets
4. 65%
5. 80%
6. China
7. India

28.2

1. Today I'm going to talk about profit.
2. Does anyone have any questions?
3. To sum up, we are facing issues.
4. I'm happy to answer questions.
5. Last, let's look at the future.

28.3

1. I'd like to begin **by showing you this graph**.
2. I'm happy to **answer any questions**.
3. Does anyone have any more **questions or comments**?
4. Let's move **on to the next topic**.
5. After that, I would **like to talk about the merger**.
6. To sum up, it's **been an excellent quarter for the company**.

28.4

1. The **screen** is black. We can't see the graph.
2. If you use a **projector**, you can introduce graphs and visuals.
3. I'll write down the company's name on the **flipchart**.
4. There are programs to help you make professional-looking **slides**.
5. If you use a **microphone**, the people at the back will hear you.

28.5

1. I'd **like** to start with our factory in Vietnam.
2. To sum **up**, we need to invest more in infrastructure.
3. I'll **explore** the benefits of investing in web technology later.
4. Let's begin by looking at the sales figures.
5. In **short**, we need to develop new products.
6. Let's take a **look** at the second graph.
7. So we've **covered** all the topics I wanted to discuss.
8. Turning to the previous quarter's profits.
9. Then I'm going to **talk** about the situation in China.
10. **To** start, let's look at this year's performance.
11. Moving **on**, let's look at our main competitors.
12. First, I'm going to look **at** last year's results.
13. I'm happy to **answer** any questions at the end.
14. I'd like to end **by** thanking you all for your attention today.

29

29.1

1. You **don't have to** stay late tonight. It's very quiet.
2. Is your phone broken? You **can** use mine if you like.
3. We **have to** wear a jacket and tie when we meet clients.
4. You **can't** park there. It's a space for disabled drivers.

29.2

1. You can't leave early tonight. **We have an important meeting at 5pm.**
2. You don't have to pay for lunch. **Staff eat for free in the cafeteria.**
3. You can make yourself a hot drink. **There's tea and coffee in the kitchen.**
4. We have to wear business clothes. **There's a formal dress code.**
5. We have to leave the building now. **That's the fire alarm.**

29.3

1. True
2. False
3. Not given
4. True
5. False

29.4

1. I **can listen** to music at work if I use headphones.
2. He's a pilot. He **has** to wear a uniform.
3. They **don't have** to go to the training session.
4. He can't **take** more than an hour for his lunch break.
5. He **can't** leave early. It's too busy.
6. I have **to** back up my files before I turn my computer off.

29.5

1. Could you wash these cups, please?
2. Would you mind turning the light off?
3. Could you help me lift this box, please?
4. Would you mind calling me back later?
5. Could you lend me your stapler, please?

29.6

1. Could you open the window?
2. Would you mind checking this list?
3. Could you forward me Jo's email?
4. Would you mind printing the report?
5. Could you pass around the agenda?
6. Would you mind ordering more files?
7. Could you come to today's meeting?

29.7

1. Could you turn your music down?
2. Would you mind checking my report for me?
3. Could you close the window?
4. Would you mind inviting Alan to the meeting?

29.8

1. Could you check these sales figures?
2. Would you mind paying a deposit now?
3. Could you ask Ian to call me back?
4. Would you mind showing our clients around?

29.9

1. Would you mind **opening** the door? It's really hot in here.
2. Would you mind **asking** John to email me this month's sales figures?
3. Could you **take** the minutes for this afternoon's meeting?
4. Could you **remind** me who is coming to tomorrow's presentation?

30

30.1

1. to think outside the box
2. to get down to business
3. red tape
4. to take it easy
5. to be tied up with
6. to wind down
7. business as usual
8. to be out of order
9. a win-win situation
10. to be in the red
11. to work around the clock
12. the ball is in your court
13. to put something off
14. going haywire
15. throwing money down the drain
16. to be swamped
17. to pull your weight

31

31.1

1. Tanya was feeling very tired.
2. I was finishing his report.
3. Alison was talking to the CEO.
4. Was Jamie taking minutes?
5. Were you working late yesterday?
6. I was trying to call you.
7. Claire was playing very loud music.

31.2

Note: Negative answers can also use long forms.

1. The train trip here was really bad. All the trains **were running** late.
2. The cleaners **were complaining** that staff left their dirty cups in the sink.
3. Harriet **wasn't listening** to the presentation.
4. Tom's manager was annoyed because Tom **wasn't meeting** his deadlines.
5. My email inbox **was getting** full, so I had to delete some messages.

31.3

1. True
2. False
3. True
4. True
5. False

31.4

1. Joshua **was giving** a talk about new markets.
2. Fiona **wasn't listening** to Bilal's new ideas for products.
3. Lucia **was taking** the minutes of the meeting.
4. They **were speaking** too loudly on the phone.
5. Helen **was eating** her lunch at her desk.

31.5

1. The windows
2. Talking
3. Her assistant
4. Her USB cable
5. Talk to a co-worker
6. Think clearly

32

32.1

1. I am so sorry I was late for the meeting with our clients today.
2. I would like to apologize for not finishing the report yesterday.
3. I'm really sorry. I forgot to charge the office cell phone and it has no power.
4. I'm really sorry this line is so bad. I hope we don't get cut off.
5. I'm afraid that's not good enough. I want a full refund on my ticket.

32.2

1. No problem. I'll help you finish it now.
2. That's not good enough. Please heat it up.
3. Never mind. We're not very busy today.
4. No problem. I'll have tea instead.
5. Don't worry. I'll print off some more.

32.3

- A 4
- B 3
- C 1
- D 5
- E 2

32.4

1. I'm really **sorry**. I forgot to send the agenda for the meeting.
2. I would like to **apologize** for the rudeness of the waitress.
3. I'm **afraid** that's not good enough. You missed an important meeting.
4. That's all **right**. I'll make you a copy right now.
5. Please **make** sure it doesn't happen again.
6. Never **mind**. It's only a cup.
7. I would **like** to apologize for the delay to your train this evening.

32.5

1. Harry **was practicing** his presentation when I **called** him.
2. Sam's cell phone **rang** when Tom **was describing** the sales for this quarter.
3. The elevator **got** stuck while they **were waiting** for it.
4. Tina **wasn't listening** when the CEO **said** all staff would get a raise.
5. The fire alarm **went** off when we **were having** our update meeting.
6. I **was working** late when I **heard** a strange noise.
7. I **was editing** the report when the fire alarm **went** off.

32.6

1. The photocopier **broke** while I **was copying** your sales report.
2. We **were listening** to Janet's presentation when the power **went** off.
3. John **was signing** the contract when the lawyer **called** him.
4. Anna **was** furious when she found out George **was copying** her ideas.
5. Simon **was editing** the report when his computer **crashed**.
6. We **were waiting** for the bus when two buses **arrived**.

33

33.1

Note: All answers can also be written in contracted form.

1. I **have called** eight customers this morning.
2. Gareth **has made** coffee for the visitors.
3. Piotr **has cut** the hair of many famous people.
4. I **have not finished** checking my emails.
5. Carl **has not emailed** me the sales data.

33.2

1. She hasn't sent the invoice **yet**.
2. We have **just** heard the CEO is leaving.
3. I haven't met the new director **yet**.
4. Has Tom finished fixing my laptop **yet**?
5. George has **just** called me.
6. The painters haven't finished **yet**.
7. Have you had a meeting with Ann **yet**?
8. The trainer has **just** arrived.
9. Have you **just** finished the report?

33.3

1. I haven't ordered the stationery yet.
2. They have just introduced the new packaging.
3. Have you answered those emails yet?
4. Derinda has just written the minutes from our meeting.

33.4

1. True
2. False
3. True
4. Not given

33.5

1. Daniel **sent** your package last Friday.
2. Jenny **showed** me the new designs yesterday.
3. Babu and Zack **haven't finished** their research yet.
4. Kate **spoke** to the HR manager last week.

33.6

1. B
2. A
3. B
4. A
5. A

33.7

1. I have done all the invoices for June.
2. He met the Chinese partners last month.
3. He hasn't sent the salaries to payroll yet.
4. They have not started the audit yet.
5. He left this morning.
6. I have just heard about your promotion.
7. She has sold the most products.
8. Have you designed that box yet?
9. They have given him a verbal warning.
10. Mark hasn't scanned it yet.
11. I have spoken to your team.

33.8

1. Yes, I've **just** scanned them.
2. No, he **hasn't** done them yet.
3. **I've** filed them all in the cabinet.
4. We've **stopped** the delivery.

34

34.1

1. We will replace your tablet free of charge.
2. The chef will cook you another pizza.
3. I'll talk to the boss about it.
4. The manager will be with you soon.
5. I'll contact our courier immediately.
6. We will give you a full refund.
7. I promise that your order will arrive today.
8. I'm afraid we won't finish the project on time.
9. I'm sorry, but we won't cancel your order.

34.2

1. We'll send it to your hotel when it gets here.
2. I'll ask the chef to cook it properly.
3. I'll refund the money to your credit card.
4. I will call the driver immediately.
5. We'll move you to another room.

34.3

1. There was no receptionist
2. They will ask receptionists to work late
3. The bathroom was dirty
4. He will speak to the cleaners' manager
5. There wasn't any hot coffee
6. Mr. Vance was kept awake
7. A full refund

34.4

1. We'll offer you a discount off your next hotel stay.
2. Will the money be refunded to my credit card?
3. The company will chase your order up for you.
4. The store manager will be with you very soon.
5. Will you replace the part on my broken washing machine?

34.5

1. Won't
2. Will
3. Will
4. Won't

34.6

1. I'm very sorry about that. **We'll offer** you a refund.
2. I really must apologize. I'**ll take** it back to the kitchen.
3. She'**ll be** with you in a minute.
4. I'**ll talk** to her about this.
5. It **won't happen** again.
6. I'**ll ask** the chef to make you something vegetarian.

35

35.1

1. bus
2. plane
3. helicopter
4. tram
5. bus stop
6. car
7. taxi
8. airport
9. train station
10. taxi stand (US) / taxi rank (UK)
11. bicycle

35.2

1. terminal
2. security
3. boarding pass
4. on time
5. domestic flight
6. international flight
7. connecting flight
8. delay
9. passport control
10. late
11. hotel
12. board a plane
13. check-in
14. passport
15. luggage
16. round-trip ticket (US) / return ticket (UK)
17. window seat
18. aisle seat
19. seat reservation

36

36.1

Note: All answers can be written in contracted form.

1. If we **don't hurry**, we **will miss** the flight.
2. If we **meet** in Berlin, it **will save** us some time.
3. We **will take** on a new intern if we **win** the contract.
4. If the train **is** late, we **will miss** the meeting.
5. If the bank **is** closed, we **will not have** any money.
6. We **will pay** for your flight if you **fly** to Denver.
7. If you **work** hard, you **will pass** the exam.
8. The firm **will pay** expenses if you **are** delayed.
9. If I **go** to Rome, I **will visit** the Colosseum.
10. If I **lose** my job, I don't know what I **will do**.

36.2

1. If we don't hurry up, **we'll miss our connecting flight**.
2. We will get a discount **if we book early**.
3. Will you pay expenses **if we attend the conference**?
4. What will Samantha do if **she loses her job next month**?
5. If we lose the contract, **we will have to lay Sean off**.
6. Will you visit the factory **if you go to China**?

36.3

1. Will you have a celebration if you get the job?
2. If you buy the ticket online, it will be cheaper.
3. If we visit Paris, we will probably go sightseeing.
4. What will we do if we don't win the contract?
5. If we take on a new intern, where will they sit?
6. How will you travel to Berlin if the flight is canceled?

36.4

1. True
2. False
3. True
4. False
5. Not given
6. True

36.5

1. If it's a nice day, I walk to work.
2. If you heat water, it boils.
3. If you're late for work, isn't your boss unhappy?
4. If you press that button, the machine stops.

36.6

1. Will you visit Red Square if you **go** to Moscow?
2. People use public transportation if it **is** cheap.
3. What will we do if we **lose** the contract?
4. The ticket **will be** more expensive if we buy it later.
5. If you **pay** staff more, they work harder.
6. **Will** you pick me up from the station if I give you my details?
7. We'll miss the train if we **don't** hurry.
8. If it **rains**, the event is always moved indoors.
9. Sharon **won't** go on vacation if she loses her job.
10. **Will** Doug resign if the company loses the deal?

37

37.1

1. Do you know the **way** to the station?
2. The bank is **on** the corner.
3. Do you know how to **get** to the hotel?
4. The museum is **in** front of the park.
5. You should **take** the second left.
6. The library is straight ahead on **the** right.
7. Our house is just ahead **on** the left.
8. Sorry, did you **say** it is near the school?
9. Turn right **at** the sign.

37.2

1. The entrance is in front of the factory.
2. Turn right at the sign.
3. The bank is opposite the school.
4. Take the first road on the left.
5. Go past the movie theater.
6. The bank is on the corner.
7. The station is next to the police station.

37.3

1. Excuse me, do you know the way to the hotel?
2. Go straight on and it's opposite the train station.
3. Sorry, did you say it's next to the post office?
4. The bank is 40 yards ahead on the corner.

37.4

1. A
2. B
3. A
4. A
5. B

37.5 Model Answers

1. Take the first right, and it's on the left after the town hall.
2. Sure, go straight ahead, and it's on the left.
3. Yes, go straight ahead, and it's on the right.
4. Yes, take the first right, and then it's on the right.
5. Turn left, then turn right, and it's on the left.

38

38.1

1. The hotel was opened in 1932.
2. The new factory was opened by the president.
3. Simon was employed by our company in 2013.
4. Our new range of products will be released next month.
5. Our head office was moved to Shanghai about four years ago.
6. Peter was introduced to the new management team.
7. Coffee and tea will be served during the break.
8. The team will be shown how to use the new software package.

38.2

Model Answers

1. The CEO was met at the airport.
2. The meeting room has been redecorated.
3. A double room was booked yesterday.
4. The team was taught some Mandarin.
5. The files were left on the train again.
6. The rooms were booked on Monday.
7. Breakfast is served at 7:30am.
8. The office has been organized.

38.3

A 5
B 1
C 4
D 3
E 2
F 7
G 6
H 8

38.4

1 False 2 Not given
3 True 4 False

38.5

1. We **were picked up** at the airport by the driver.
2. Great. It **was served** at 7am each morning.
3. Yes. But unfortunately it **was broken**.

39

39.1

1. fry
2. waiter
3. vegetarian
4. chef
5. waitress
6. menu
7. make a reservation / booking
8. boil
9. receipt
10. breakfast
11. lunch
12. dinner
13. café
14. vegan
15. dessert
16. food allergy / intolerance
17. bar
18. tip
19. roast

39.2

1. fruit
2. bread
3. water
4. napkin
5. milk
6. fish
7. coffee
8. pasta
9. tea
10. meat
11. fork
12. knife
13. vegetables
14. seafood
15. salad
16. sandwich
17. potatoes
18. butter
19. cake

40

40.1

1. Did you have any trouble getting here?
2. Can I get you anything?
3. It's great to meet you in person.
4. Have you been to Toronto before?
5. Did you have a good flight?
6. Would you like something to drink?
7. I've been looking forward to meeting you.
8. We've heard so much about you.
9. I'll let Mr. Song know that you arrived.
10. Is this your first visit to India?

40.2

1. Is there **any** information about flights?
2. I need to buy **some** food.
3. Are there **any** good hotels nearby?
4. Can I get you **a** cup of coffee?
5. Are there **any** interesting talks today?
6. Do you have **any** luggage?

7. There is **a** presentation later.
8. Do you have **any** tea?
9. Please take **a** seat at the front.

40.3

1. Would you like some **water, Mrs. Smith**?
2. Do you have any **information about the flight**?
3. Have you been **to Los Angeles before**?
4. Can I get you **a glass of water**?
5. It's great to **meet you in person**.
6. There isn't **any coffee left, I'm afraid**.

40.4

1. Are you going to **any** talks later?
2. James is giving **a** presentation later today.
3. There isn't **any** coffee or tea, I'm sorry.
4. Are **any** of your colleagues staying here?
5. Would you like **a** cup of tea, Jen?
6. They don't have **any** workshops this afternoon.
7. Have **any** of the attendees arrived yet?
8. Is there **any** information about the conference?
9. There's **some** food and drink in the main hall.

40.5

1. the main hall
2. developing an app
3. a choice of food and drink
4. a product launch
5. leading CEOs
6. the Asian market

41

41.1

1. I'm afraid we're fully booked this evening.
2. Can we sit outside on the terrace?
3. Could I have a cup of coffee, please?
4. Can we just have five more minutes, please?
5. Yes, I'm allergic to shellfish.
6. Absolutely delicious, thank you.
7. Yes, please. Some chocolate ice cream for me.
8. No, I'm afraid it contains cream.
9. Sure, are you paying by cash or by card?

41.2

1. Are you ready to order?
2. I'd like to reserve a table for two, please.
3. Have you reserved a table, madam?
4. How many people are there in your party?
5. Could I have a look at the dessert menu, please?
6. What would you like for the entree?
7. Do you have any allergies or intolerances?
8. How many vegetarian options are there today?
9. Could we have the bill, please?
10. Would you like to pay by cash or card?

41.3

1. How many chairs will you need?
2. I ordered too many dishes.
3. There's not enough space here. It's tiny.
4. How many plates will you need?
5. There are too many chairs.
6. There's not enough cake for everyone.
7. The lobster costs too much.
8. We haven't ordered enough dishes.
9. How many guests are you expecting?
10. I don't have enough cash for a tip.
11. I've eaten too much food this evening!
12. There's enough tea for everyone.

41.4

1. How **many** people are coming tonight?
2. Is there **enough** space at the table for everyone?
3. How **much** does the meal usually cost?
4. I've eaten too **much** cake.
5. There's **too** much salt in my soup.
6. There are not **enough** chairs for all of us!
7. **How** many glasses will we need this evening?

42

42.1

1. I'd **better** go now.
2. Can I **ask** who's calling?
3. No, that's **all**, thanks.
4. OK. **Talk** to you soon.
5. Is there **anything** else I can do?
6. Hello, Sales **department**.

42.2

- A 5
- B 3
- C 2
- D 1
- E 4

42.3

1. Esme speaking. How can I help?
2. Of course. It's Sergio Walker.
3. OK. Speak to you soon.
4. Hi, Andrew. It's José from Design.

42.4

1. 57336
2. 0114342190
3. 031297778
4. 0092736430
5. 2074440016
6. 00340621485
7. 8694472165

42.5

Model Answers

1. Liz's extension is 3864.
2. Saira's office number is 01928 335178.
3. The Helpdesk number at KTV News is 616 888 3746.
4. Lucy's cell phone number is 616 913 6205.

42.6

1. I don't know why Hal's not **picking up** the phone.
2. I'll **put you through** to customer services now.
3. Can you **speak up**, please? I can't hear you.
4. Sorry, I'm busy now. I'll **get back** to you later.
5. I'm sorry I **cut you off**. This line is very bad.
6. You're **breaking up**. Can I call you back?

42.7

1. Could you possibly speak **up**, please? The line is very faint.
2. I'll call **you** back in ten minutes. Is that OK? I have to finish writing an email.
3. If I get cut **off**, call me back on the office phone. I'm back at my desk now.
4. Can I get back **to** you about the design later today? We're still working on it.
5. I've called Fatima three times, but she didn't pick **up**. Is she at work today?
6. Marc kept breaking **up** when I called him. The signal here is awful!
7. Katie is back at her desk now. I'll just put you **through** to her.
8. Mateo got back **to** me about the new manual. He has a few comments on it.

42.8

1. Can you speak up, please?
2. I hope I don't get cut off again.
3. Let me put you through to Finance.
4. Sorry I didn't pick up when you called.
5. Can you get back to him this afternoon?
6. Sorry, the line keeps breaking up.
7. I'll call you back in five minutes.
8. He didn't get back to me yesterday.
9. Don't pick up the phone if Dan calls.

43

43.1

1. Yes, of course. May I ask who's calling?
2. I'm calling because my laptop is broken.
3. Yes. Can you ask her to call me back?
4. Could you ask her to call me back today?

43.2

1. **It's** Sunita Devinder from GBT.
2. I wonder if you **could** help me.
3. I'm afraid Mr. Cox **isn't** at his desk.
4. Thank you for **calling** Top Sounds.
5. **Could** I speak to Rod Dean, please?
6. Could you **ask** him to call me back?
7. **May** I ask who's calling, please?

43.3

1. How can I help you?
2. May I ask who's calling?
3. I'll just put you through.
4. Would you like to leave a message?
5. Could you ask him to call me back, please?
6. IT department. How can I help you?
7. I'll put you through to HR now.
8. I'm afraid he's not at his desk.
9. Thank you for calling Quadfax.

43.4

1. Savino's. How **can I help** you?
2. Thank you **for calling** Ready Solutions.
3. Hello. **I wonder if** you can help me.
4. I'm calling **about an order** I placed last month.
5. **Could I speak** to Becky Bradley, please?
6. I'm afraid the Accounts Manager is away **at the moment**.
7. Yes, please. **Could I order** 20 desks?
8. **Would you like** to leave a message?
9. Thank you. **I'll just put** you through.

43.5

OPINION:
nice, **awful**, **stylish**
SIZE:
tiny, **large**, **huge**
AGE:
ancient, **modern**, **antique**
COLOR:
blue, **purple**, **pink**
MATERIAL:
leather, **metal**, **plastic**

43.6

1. We're developing a stylish little gold lamp.
2. Tom has got an amazing tiny new smartphone.
3. The pet store has a nice big black and white cat.
4. There is an awful large modern painting in the cafeteria.
5. Have you seen the exciting new colorful marketing posters?

43.7

1. That's a stylish new design for the company logo.
2. There's a huge round hole in the wall where the truck hit it.
3. Have you seen the fabulous new office chairs?
4. There's a big yellow and red truck outside.
5. There's a nice big green and white plant in my office.
6. Have you tasted the awful new coffee?
7. The headphones for my laptop go in a tiny round hole.
8. There's a large rectangular parking space for motorbikes.

43.8

1. Printed materials
2. Next Tuesday
3. 9:00
4. 60
5. Six taxis
6. Vegetarian and gluten-free food

44

44.1

1. Personal statement
2. Education
3. Professional achievements
4. Career summary
5. Key skills

44.2

1. I have a **proven** track record in the tourism industry.
2. I am proficient **in** using a wide range of software.
3. I have hands-on **experience** of customer service.
4. I have experience working in a **service-oriented** environment.

44.3

1. I am a highly motivated individual and love working in tourism.
2. I gained in-depth knowledge of the construction industry.
3. I have a great deal of experience in the catering industry.
4. I am proficient in most types of accounting software.

44.4

1. I **managed** a large team of marketing executives.
2. Our teams **collaborated** to create a new clothing range.
3. The company **established** a new headquarters in the capital.
4. I **negotiated** with our suppliers and got a good deal.

44.5 Model Answers

1. She oversaw the introduction of new accounting software and co-ordinated a training program.
2. She is the Deputy Director of Accounts at Tomkins Travel.
3. She worked in the construction industry.
4. She gained her diploma in Accounting in June 2010.
5. She can speak Spanish and English fluently.

45

45.1

Note: All answers except 6, 8, and 11 can also be written in contracted form.

1. He **is going to travel** to the conference by plane.
2. She **is not going to make** it to the meeting.
3. They **are going to meet** the staff from the Paris office.
4. He **is going to write** a letter to the suppliers.
5. They **are not going to sell** their shares in the company just now.
6. **Is** she **going to order** business cards with the new company logo?
7. Sergio **is going to give** a presentation about the new training course.
8. **Are** you **going to make** tea and coffee for the visitors?
9. Diana **is going to design** the new company logo.
10. They **are going to join** us for our team meeting today.
11. **Are** you **going to review** the sales data this afternoon?

45.2

1. Why don't we ask what Marketing think?
2. Could you load the printer with paper?
3. Can you help me with these files, please?
4. Could you send the files to production?
5. Could we meet at 4 instead of 5?
6. Can you finish the report today?
7. Couldn't we invite Jeff to the meeting?
8. Could you call me back later, please?
9. Could you make coffee for the CEO?
10. Could we possibly cancel the meeting?
11. Can you check this report, please?
12. Could you pass round the agenda?

13 Can we try a different approach?
14 Please could you call the Delhi office?
15 Could you lock up before you leave?
16 Could you possibly stay late tonight?
17 Please can you print out these designs?

45.3

1. I am going to email the director.
2. I am going to email the IT help desk.
3. I am going to email the sales department.
4. I am going to speak to the director.
5. I am going to speak to the IT help desk.
6. I am going to speak to the sales department.
7. You are going to email the director.
8. You are going to email the IT help desk.
9. You are going to email the sales department.
10. You are going to speak to the director.
11. You are going to speak to the IT help desk.
12. You are going to speak to the sales department.
13. Kelly is going to email the director.
14. Kelly is going to email the IT help desk.
15. Kelly is going to email the sales department.
16. Kelly is going to speak to the director.
17. Kelly is going to speak to the IT help desk.
18. Kelly is going to speak to the sales department.

45.4

1 False
2 Not given
3 False
4 True
5 False

45.5

Model Answers

1 Paul is going to contact the presenters.
2 Paul is going to ask the printers for ten extra copies of the training booklets.
3 The printers are going to supply name badges in the form of lanyards.
4 Marie is going to meet the presenters.
5 The presenters will get to the venue by taxi.
6 Omar is going to check that the venue will cater for people with special dietary requirements.

46

46.1

1 text message
2 website
3 stamp
4 voicemail
5 conference call
6 email
7 bulletin board (US) / notice board (UK)
8 letter
9 internal mail
10 mail (US) / post (UK)
11 web conference
12 presentation
13 transfer a call
14 envelope
15 social networking

46.2

1 attachment
2 forward
3 trash
4 signature
5 outbox
6 print
7 reply all
8 inbox
9 subject

46.3

1 TBC
2 BCC
3 RE
4 CC
5 FYI
6 ETA
7 NB
8 ASAP

47

47.1

1 I work **in** the finance department at Forrester's.
2 Please confirm your availability **ASAP**.
3 Please find your **receipt attached** to this email.
4 Please **don't hesitate** to contact me.
5 I am writing **with reference to** invoice number 146.
6 Please see the agenda **attached** here.
7 I work in the IT department **at** Transtech.
8 I **am** writing to invite you to a meeting next week.
9 Please **don't** hesitate to contact me.
10 Please return your signed contract **ASAP**.
11 I **would** be grateful if you could get back to me soon.
12 I am writing **with** regard to your complaint.
13 Please find the minutes **attached** here.
14 I would **be** grateful if we could arrange a meeting.
15 I work **in** the company's catering department.
16 I am the new Head of Sales **at** Codequote.
17 I am writing with regard **to** our schedule.
18 Please let me know if you **have** any questions.

19 Please **find** the new designs attached here.

7 I am writing to **inform you that we are going to use a new supplier**.

47.2

1 I am writing with regard to your latest feedback.
2 Please find the invoice attached here.
3 I would be grateful if you could pay the outstanding invoice.
4 If you have any questions, please do not hesitate to contact me.

47.3

1 I am writing with **regard to our invoice number AB3168**.
2 I work in **the accounts department at Shuberg's**.
3 I would be grateful if you **could let us know when you have been paid**.
4 I deal with **the supply and payment of invoices**.
5 It has come to our attention **that invoice DY895 has not been paid**.
6 I wonder if **you are aware that we have not been paid**.

47.4

1 He **is giving** all the candidates a task to do before their interview.
2 We **are meeting** other suppliers on Tuesday.
3 Sam **is going to make** coffee for the CEO's visitors.
4 Carlos **is presenting** the sales figures tomorrow.
5 We **are going to discuss** sales figures for the last quarter.
6 They **are giving** all their clients a voucher.
7 He **is going to travel** to Italy to meet the new CEO.
8 Greg **is going to pack** all the boxes into the delivery van.
9 A famous hairdresser **is going to open** the new salon.
10 We **are launching** the new company logo at the sales conference.
11 The company **is going to recycle** all the stationery with the old logo.

47.5

1 I am writing with regard to the shareholders' meeting on Thursday.
2 We are meeting new clients at the Radcliffe Hotel.
3 The meeting is taking place in the hotel's conference center.
4 We are going to discuss the last quarter's sales figures.
5 The new CEO is taking questions after his presentation.
6 He is going to discuss the company's future marketing strategy.

47.6

ENGLISH
FOR EVERYONE

PRACTICE BOOK **LEVEL** 

BUSINESS ENGLISH

Level 2 Contents

01 Introductions

When you first join a company, there are many phrases that you can use to introduce yourself. Other people may also use a variety of phrases to introduce you.

New language Present simple and continuous
Aa Vocabulary Etiquette for introductions
New skill Introducing yourself and others

1.1 FILL IN THE GAPS USING THE WORDS IN THE PANEL

How do you ___do___ ? I'm Christophe from BlueTech.

1. I'd like to ______ you to Marco from IT.
2. You ______ be Paola from Madrid.
3. Gloria, ______ Julia, our new secretary.
4. Have you two ______ each other before?
5. Great to ______ you again!
6. ______ to meet you, Antonio.
7. Sanjay has ______ me all about you.
8. I don't ______ we've met before, have we?
9. It's a ______ to meet you.

pleasure | see | ~~do~~ | told | met | must | think | meet | introduce | Nice

1.2 MATCH THE BEGINNINGS OF THE INTRODUCTIONS TO THE CORRECT ENDINGS

Peter, Philippe, I'm not sure → if you have met each other.

1. Simone, I'd like to introduce you to
2. Hello. I don't think we've
3. You must be Selma from the
4. Hi, Omar. I think we
5. My boss has told me
6. This is Colin from IT.

- Gerald, our new sales manager.
- met. My name's Jana.
- if you have met each other.
- so much about your work.
- Colin, meet Liam. He's joining our team soon.
- Chicago branch. Great to meet you.
- met at the conference in Dubai last year.

1.3 READ THE ARTICLE AND ANSWER THE QUESTIONS

The author says that meeting people is easy.
True ☐ **False** ☑ **Not given** ☐

1. Meeting people will always make you successful.
True ☐ **False** ☐ **Not given** ☐

2. You should talk about your recent experiences.
True ☐ **False** ☐ **Not given** ☐

3. The author thinks food is a good topic of conversation.
True ☐ **False** ☐ **Not given** ☐

4. You shouldn't ask how much someone earns.
True ☐ **False** ☐ **Not given** ☐

5. The author suggests talking about your education.
True ☐ **False** ☐ **Not given** ☐

6. The author says that you shouldn't talk about clients.
True ☐ **False** ☐ **Not given** ☐

ESSENTIAL SKILLS

Meeting and greeting

Meeting new people isn't always easy, but it's an essential skill for a young business professional.

Whether you're looking for a new job, hope to grow your business, or just want to find new clients, you need to talk to the right people. It doesn't always lead to success, but it can provide a great first step. So, what's the best way to start talking?

Talk about your recent experience: "I'm working with some great software engineers at the moment" is a great way to start. You can tell them about your personal life and interests: "I play golf with my friend on the weekend" might be a good starter. But you shouldn't talk about things that are too personal. If you ask someone how much money they earn, they might be offended! Another good idea is to talk about one of your clients: "I often work with ElectroSan, an exciting new Japanese start-up." You will soon find that the person you're talking to wants to know more...

1.4 REWRITE THE SENTENCES, CORRECTING THE ERRORS

I staying at the hotel on Park Lane all this week.
I'm staying at the hotel on Park Lane all this week.

1. I am catching the train to work at 8:15am each morning.

2. We are having a new printer that is difficult to use.

3. I working at the Guangdong branch all this August.

4. Sanchez is knowing Katie because they worked together.

5. Do you enjoying this presentation? I think it's great.

6. Tim isn't knowing Anna from the Montevideo branch.

7. Marek is liking the new furniture we bought for the office.

8. How are you spelling your name?

9. The meeting usually is take only half an hour.

10. Doug is really enjoy the conference this year.

11. I'd like introduce you to my manager, José Rodriguez.

12. Clara working from 8:30 to 4:30 on Thursdays and Fridays.

1.5 CROSS OUT THE INCORRECT WORDS IN EACH SENTENCE, THEN SAY THE SENTENCES OUT LOUD

Raul ~~presents~~ / is presenting at the moment.

1. Our company is having / have some difficulties at the moment.
2. Pablo, I'd like you to meet / meeting my wife, Elvira.
3. I usually hate conferences, but I enjoy / am enjoying this one a lot.
4. I have / am having two children, a son and a daughter.
5. Michael, I like / I'd like to introduce you to Michelle.
6. I don't think / am not thinking we've met before, have we?
7. It's so great to see / see you again after such a long time.
8. How do you pronounce / are you pronouncing your last name?
9. You must be / being Harold from Copenhagen. Nice to meet you.
10. Hi, I think we met in Oslo, aren't we / didn't we?

02 Getting to know colleagues

Talking about your past work experience is a good way to get to know your colleagues. Past simple and past continuous tenses are often used to do this.

New language Past simple and past continuous
Aa Vocabulary Sharing past experiences
New skill Talking about past experiences

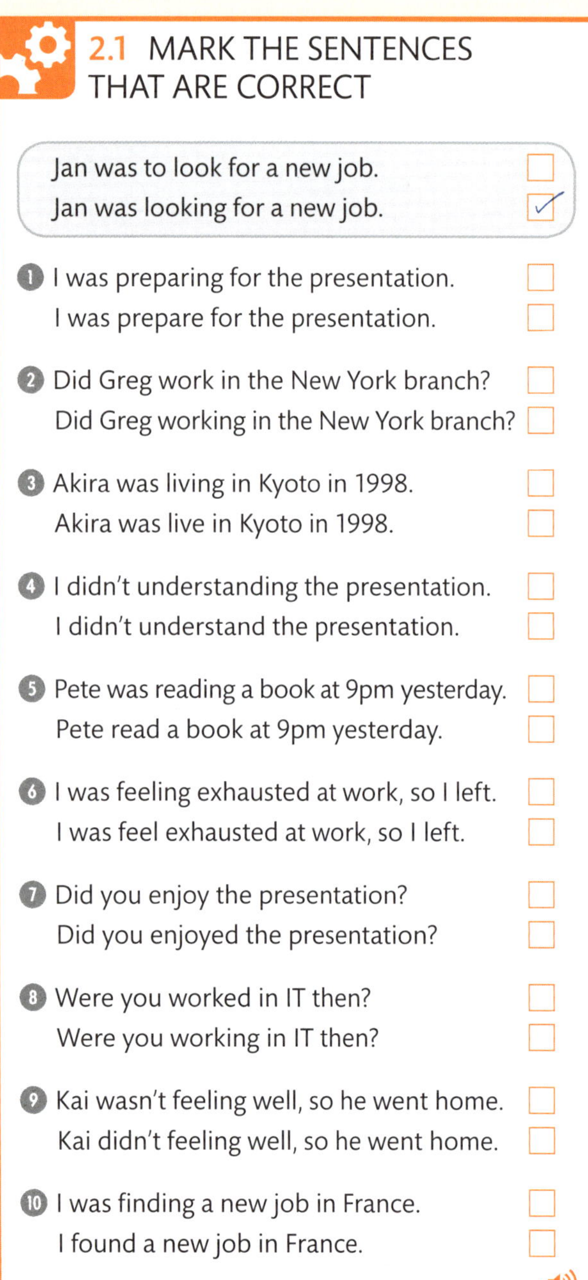

2.1 MARK THE SENTENCES THAT ARE CORRECT

Jan was to look for a new job. ☐
Jan was looking for a new job. ☑

1. I was preparing for the presentation. ☐
   I was prepare for the presentation. ☐
2. Did Greg work in the New York branch? ☐
   Did Greg working in the New York branch? ☐
3. Akira was living in Kyoto in 1998. ☐
   Akira was live in Kyoto in 1998. ☐
4. I didn't understanding the presentation. ☐
   I didn't understand the presentation. ☐
5. Pete was reading a book at 9pm yesterday. ☐
   Pete read a book at 9pm yesterday. ☐
6. I was feeling exhausted at work, so I left. ☐
   I was feel exhausted at work, so I left. ☐
7. Did you enjoy the presentation? ☐
   Did you enjoyed the presentation? ☐
8. Were you worked in IT then? ☐
   Were you working in IT then? ☐
9. Kai wasn't feeling well, so he went home. ☐
   Kai didn't feeling well, so he went home. ☐
10. I was finding a new job in France. ☐
    I found a new job in France. ☐

2.2 LISTEN TO THE AUDIO, THEN NUMBER THE PICTURES IN THE ORDER THEY ARE DESCRIBED

2.3 FILL IN THE GAPS BY PUTTING THE VERBS IN THE PRESENT PERFECT SIMPLE

Chloe *has bought* (buy) a new apartment in Paris.

1. Daniel ______________ (work) for more than five different law firms.
2. I ______________ (take) the bus to work all my working life.
3. The company ______________ (employ) five new people since September.
4. Peter is a terrible waiter. He ______________ (start) looking for a different job.
5. Andrea ______________ (work) here since she graduated in 1999.
6. The factory ______________ (produce) 15,000 machines this year.
7. Tim's really happy. He ______________ (finish) his presentation for tomorrow.
8. We ______________ (sell) our products in more than 25 countries.
9. I ______________ (walk) to work since my car broke down.
10. I ______________ (decide) that I'm going to retire next year.
11. Dave ______________ (take) more time than we expected.
12. I ______________ (work) at this office for more than 25 years now.
13. Chris ______________ (visit) more than 50 countries so far.

2.4 MATCH THE BEGINNINGS OF THE SENTENCES TO THE CORRECT ENDINGS

Claire was working for a bank	for more than ten years.
1 Jim was preparing a presentation	more than an hour.
2 I've worked at this company	when she received a new job offer.
3 Chris had to wait for a taxi for	before I started working here.
4 Tim moved to New York	when his boss entered the room.
5 I ran my own software company	bought a smaller Canadian software firm.
6 In 2013, our company	when he was transferred to the US office.

(Example: Claire was working for a bank → when she received a new job offer.)

2.5 READ THE ARTICLE AND ANSWER THE QUESTIONS

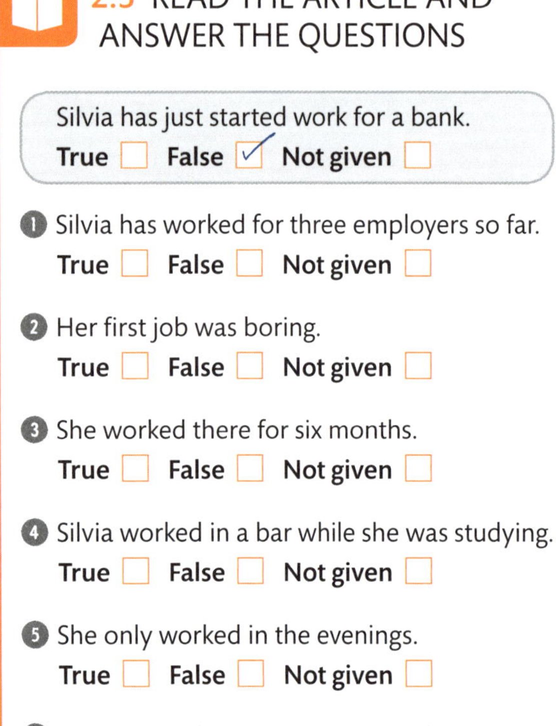

Silvia has just started work for a bank.
True ☐ False ☑ Not given ☐

1 Silvia has worked for three employers so far.
True ☐ False ☐ Not given ☐

2 Her first job was boring.
True ☐ False ☐ Not given ☐

3 She worked there for six months.
True ☐ False ☐ Not given ☐

4 Silvia worked in a bar while she was studying.
True ☐ False ☐ Not given ☐

5 She only worked in the evenings.
True ☐ False ☐ Not given ☐

6 She was working as an intern until recently.
True ☐ False ☐ Not given ☐

Silvia's Blog

HOME | ENTRIES | ABOUT | CONTACT

POSTED FRIDAY, 7:30AM

On the up!

I've just started my new job at Moda Fashions in Edinburgh. I've worked for three different employers so far, and I'm hoping that this job will be the best I've had.

My first job was in a local supermarket. I hated it. I was bored, I had no responsibilities, and the customers were often rude to me. I left after only three months.

After that, I worked in a bar. It was more interesting and I met some interesting people. I was studying for my business diploma while I worked there, so I had something to dream about.

Then I started to become interested in fashion. I was working as an intern for a small fashion agency when I received my job offer. I'm so excited.

2.6 CROSS OUT THE INCORRECT WORDS IN EACH SENTENCE, THEN SAY THE SENTENCES OUT LOUD

My doctor **told** / ~~was telling~~ me that I should take a vacation.

1. At 3pm yesterday, I **discussed** / **was discussing** the new software with our IT team.
2. While Susan **has eaten** / **was eating** lunch, her team was working hard.
3. Karl moved to Berlin when he **lost** / **has lost** his job in Paris.
4. Alan **traveled** / **was traveling** to work when he received a call from his wife.
5. In 2007, I **was working** / **have worked** in the company headquarters in Geneva.
6. I **have lived** / **was living** in San Francisco since 2003.
7. Peter **is sleeping** / **was sleeping** at his desk when his phone rang.
8. They **was** / **have been** based in Frankfurt since 1994.
9. While I **was living** / **have living** in France, I worked as a waiter.
10. Derek **was buying** / **bought** his first house in 2009.
11. What **were you doing** / **have you done** at 4pm this afternoon?
12. I **was studying** / **studied** in college when I decided to work as a lawyer.
13. Who was in the meeting room when you **entered** / **have entered**?
14. We **were selling** / **sold** our first machine in China in 2003.

03 Vocabulary

Aa 3.1 **DEPARTMENTS** WRITE THE DEPARTMENTS FROM THE PANEL UNDER THE CORRECT DEFINITIONS

Deals with buying goods and raw materials

Purchasing

1 Deals with employee relations and matters such as hiring staff

2 Ensures that all technological systems are working and maintained

3 Deals with selling a finished product to outside markets

4 Deals with maintaining a positive public image for a company

5 Ensures that all contracts and company activities are legal

6 Ensures the smooth day-to-day running of the practical aspects of a company

7 Deals with organization and internal and external communication

8 Deals with researching and developing future products for a company

9 Deals with money matters, from paying bills to projecting sales

10 Deals with promoting products

11 Ensures all manufacturing stages run smoothly

Public Relations (PR) | Administration | Research and Development (R&D) | Production | Facilities / Office Services | Accounts / Finance | Information Technology (IT) | Human Resources (HR) | Sales | ~~Purchasing~~ | Legal | Marketing

Aa 3.2 **ROLES** WRITE THE WORDS FROM THE PANEL UNDER THE CORRECT PICTURES

employer

1 ______

2 ______

3 ______

4 ______

5 ______

manager

Chief Executive Officer (CEO)

~~employer~~

Chief Financial Officer (CFO)

employee

assistant

Aa 3.3 **DESCRIBING ROLES** WRITE THE PHRASES FROM THE PANEL UNDER THE CORRECT DEFINITIONS

To ensure something runs smoothly

to look after

1 To be employed by a company

______

2 To have a particular job or role

______

3 To have the duty of ensuring something is done effectively

______

4 To have control and authority over something

______

5 To be employed in a department or area of an industry

______

to work as ~~to look after~~ to be in charge of to be responsible for to work in to work for

04 Talking about changes

There are many ways to talk about changes at work in the past and present. Many of the phrases include "used to," which can have several different meanings.

New language "Used to," "be / get used to"
Aa Vocabulary Small talk
New skill Talking about changes at work

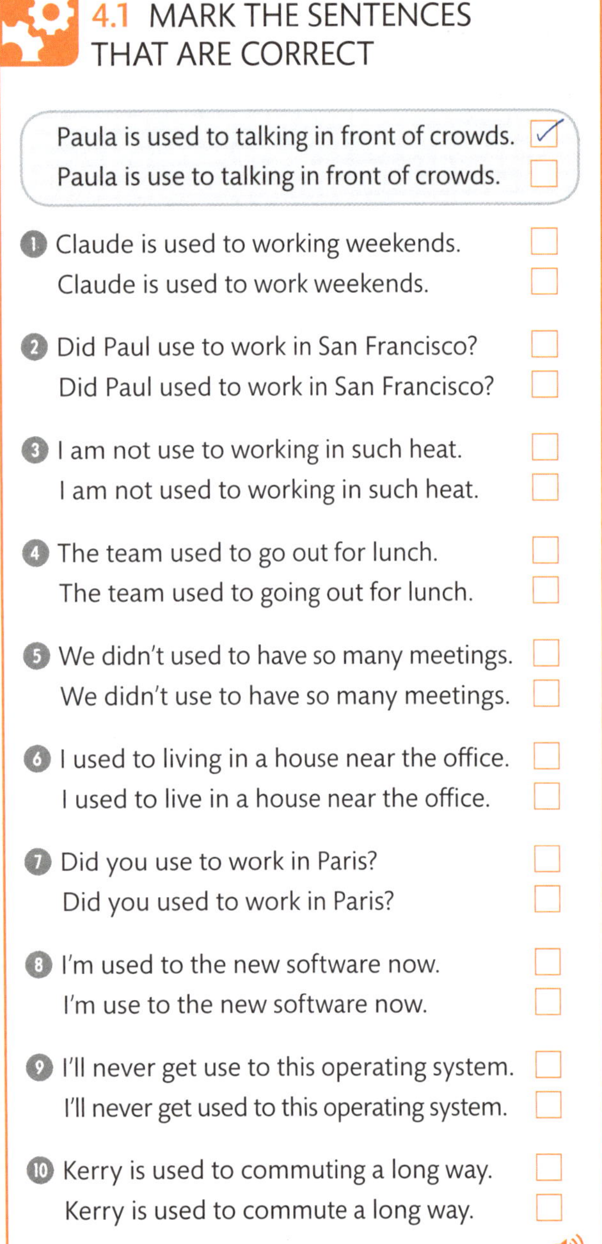

4.1 MARK THE SENTENCES THAT ARE CORRECT

Paula is used to talking in front of crowds. ☑
Paula is use to talking in front of crowds. ☐

1. Claude is used to working weekends. ☐
   Claude is used to work weekends. ☐
2. Did Paul use to work in San Francisco? ☐
   Did Paul used to work in San Francisco? ☐
3. I am not use to working in such heat. ☐
   I am not used to working in such heat. ☐
4. The team used to go out for lunch. ☐
   The team used to going out for lunch. ☐
5. We didn't used to have so many meetings. ☐
   We didn't use to have so many meetings. ☐
6. I used to living in a house near the office. ☐
   I used to live in a house near the office. ☐
7. Did you use to work in Paris? ☐
   Did you used to work in Paris? ☐
8. I'm used to the new software now. ☐
   I'm use to the new software now. ☐
9. I'll never get use to this operating system. ☐
   I'll never get used to this operating system. ☐
10. Kerry is used to commuting a long way. ☐
    Kerry is used to commute a long way. ☐

4.2 LISTEN TO THE AUDIO, THEN NUMBER THE PICTURES IN THE ORDER THEY ARE DESCRIBED

A ☐ B 1  C  ☐ D  ☐ E  ☐ F  ☐ G ☐

4.3 REWRITE THE SENTENCES, PUTTING THE WORDS IN THE CORRECT ORDER

working | Peter | used | from | to | home. | is

Peter is used to working from home.

1. to | time. | We | use | didn't | so | have | free | much

2. get | the | used | on | to | never | I'll | left. | driving

3. to | branch? | use | Anthony | work | Did | in | the | Frankfurt

4. get up | to | I | to | am | having | 6am. | used | at

5. used | Derek | to | isn't | so | work. | commuting | far | to

6. got | new | The | hasn't | to | the | team | system. | used | operating

7. lunch | near | used | the | We | to | in | café | park. | have | the

8. giving | Danielle | isn't | presentations. | to | used

9. to | Pam | in | branch | used | work | the | Cologne. | in

10. uniform | Phil | used | a | to | isn't | work. | wearing | for

4.4 MATCH THE PAIRS OF PHRASES THAT MEAN THE SAME THING

I worked in a bank in the past.	She's not used to working long hours.
1 She doesn't usually work long hours.	I used to work as a doctor.
2 In the past I was a doctor.	I used to work in a bank.
3 Dan's driven on the left for years.	She's used to getting up early.
4 She began getting up early 10 years ago.	I'm not used to spicy food.
5 I tried Indian food once. It's spicy!	Dan's used to driving on the left.
6 I still hate the weather in England after 20 years.	I'm not used to working so late.
7 I don't usually work this late.	We're getting used to the new boss.
8 We've had our new boss for three months.	I'll never get used to English weather.

4.5 MARK THE BEST REPLY TO EACH STATEMENT

1 Would you like some coffee?

No, thanks. I'm fine. ☐

I'm used to drinking tea. ☐

2 You look exhausted, Jenny.

I'm not used to this hot weather! ☐

I will sleep later. ☐

3 Would you like to go for lunch?

I'm not used to invitations. ☐

That would be great! ☐

4 Have you seen that new movie?

I haven't yet. Is it any good? ☐

Thanks. Tomorrow would be good. ☐

5 How was your commute?

I hate public transportation. ☐

I'm getting used to the traffic. ☐

4.6 CROSS OUT THE INCORRECT WORDS IN EACH SENTENCE, THEN SAY THE SENTENCES OUT LOUD

I took a while to get used to / ~~am used to~~ the weather here.

1. Are you used to / got used to living in a tropical country yet?
2. I was used to / used to travel to work on foot before they built the metro.
3. When I lived in Berlin, we used to / get used to live in an apartment downtown.
4. Were you used to / Did you use to work in the Edinburgh branch?
5. I grew up in Japan, so I'm used to / got used to driving on the left.
6. Arnold's used to / use to waking up at 5am every morning.
7. I used to / am used to working for a demanding boss.
8. When I was a child, I didn't get used to / use to like going to school.
9. We are used to / used to go to Florida each year on vacation.
10. My father used to / getting used to work in a factory until it closed down.

05 Delegating tasks

When things get busy, you may want to delegate tasks to colleagues. To do this, different modal verbs are used in English to show the level of obligation.

New language Modal verbs for obligation
Aa Vocabulary Delegation and politeness
New skill Delegating tasks to colleagues

5.1 MARK THE SENTENCES THAT ARE CORRECT

Peter has to stop working during lunch. ☑
Peter has stop working during lunch. ☐

1. Staff must not smoking in the building. ☐
   Staff must not smoke in the building. ☐
2. We don't have to go to work tomorrow. ☐
   We not have to go to work tomorrow. ☐
3. I have to go home early on Thursday. ☐
   I have going home early on Thursday. ☐
4. You have to do this assignment today. ☐
   You has to do this assignment today. ☐
5. We need increase sales this year. ☐
   We need to increase sales this year. ☐
6. Jim doesn't have to attend the meeting. ☐
   Jim don't have to attend the meeting. ☐
7. The team must not forget their timesheets. ☐
   The team must forget not their timesheets. ☐
8. Paolo has got to signing up for the course. ☐
   Paolo has got to sign up for the course. ☐
9. We will need to hire new staff this fall. ☐
   We will need hiring new staff this fall. ☐
10. We must improve our productivity. ☐
    We must to improve our productivity. ☐

5.2 LISTEN TO THE AUDIO AND ANSWER THE QUESTIONS

A manager, Janice, is giving tasks to her assistant, James.

Janice is giving a presentation on Wednesday.
True ☐ False ☑ Not given ☐

1. Janice's presentation is about marketing.
   True ☐ False ☐ Not given ☐
2. She hasn't reserved a meeting room yet.
   True ☐ False ☐ Not given ☐
3. Janice wants James to reserve a small room.
   True ☐ False ☐ Not given ☐
4. She doesn't need a projector or sound system.
   True ☐ False ☐ Not given ☐
5. Janice needs the room from 2:30 to 5pm.
   True ☐ False ☐ Not given ☐
6. Janice wants James to email the team.
   True ☐ False ☐ Not given ☐
7. James should order refreshments for the break.
   True ☐ False ☐ Not given ☐
8. Janice wants James to check the visuals.
   True ☐ False ☐ Not given ☐
9. Janice invites James for lunch to say thank you.
   True ☐ False ☐ Not given ☐

5.3 REWRITE THE SENTENCES, PUTTING THE WORDS IN THE CORRECT ORDER

have | before | to | the | We | presentation | 5pm. | finish

We have to finish the presentation before 5pm.

1. copy | you | minutes, | of | please? | give | the | Would | Peter | a

2. at | leave | reception. | passes | All | their | must | visitors

3. the | post | to | office, | please? | this | take | Could | letter | you

4. harder | Ramon | to | if | work | he | a promotion. | needs | wants

5. needs | the | Sharon | sign up | training | for | course. | to

6. copy | you | of | Could | on | leave a | agenda | the | please? | my desk,

7. enrolment | before | You | complete | must | the | on | Friday. | form | 5pm

8. inside | smoke | Staff | the | must | building. | not

9. everyone | Would | you | an email | to | the | send | meeting? | about

10. the | by | finish | You | project | must | evening. | Wednesday

5.4 MATCH THE BEGINNINGS OF THE SENTENCES TO THE CORRECT ENDINGS

	Staff must wear	if it wants to survive.
1	The company must change	record of everything you spend this week?
2	I need you to finish	identity cards at all times in the building.
3	Could you keep a	the team about the recent changes, please?
4	Would you inform	the presentation by Friday.
5	The company has got to	about closing some of our branches.
6	You don't have	invest more in training.
7	We need to think	to finish the assignment today.

5.5 READ THE ARTICLE AND ANSWER THE QUESTIONS

The author says delegating is always effective.
True ☐ False ☑ Not given ☐

1. You should think about who to delegate to.
True ☐ False ☐ Not given ☐

2. You should follow your team's every step.
True ☐ False ☐ Not given ☐

3. You should organize team-building activities.
True ☐ False ☐ Not given ☐

4. Deadlines should always be flexible.
True ☐ False ☐ Not given ☐

5. Your team won't appreciate negative feedback.
True ☐ False ☐ Not given ☐

DAILY OFFICE TIPS

A problem shared… can be a problem halved

Getting your fellow team members involved in your daily tasks makes life easier for everyone, surely? But only when you know how to delegate effectively. In my experience, I've found it helps if you think about these four simple steps:

1 You need to think about who you're delegating to. Are they the best person for the job? What will they give, and what will they learn?

2 You don't have to follow your team's every step or decision. But you should be communicative and offer advice. A supported team is an effective team.

3 You must set a clear deadline. Everyone needs to know when the project should end. Otherwise your project will lose its momentum.

4 You have to offer your team feedback. Everyone appreciates credit for success, but they also want to know what went wrong.

5.6 RESPOND OUT LOUD TO THE AUDIO, FILLING IN THE GAPS USING THE WORDS IN THE PANEL

I just received Eric's memo about the conference.

Great. Would you print me a copy, please?

1. Is this presentation high priority?

   No, I ______ you to finish it today.

2. Is it OK if I hand in the report next week?

   I'm sorry, Mike. We really ______ have it by Friday.

3. Can we look around the factory?

   I'm sorry, but members of the public ______ enter the building.

4. The new uniforms still haven't arrived.

   We need them tomorrow. ______ you call the supplier, please?

5. Do you want me to stay late tonight?

   No, you ______ to. The deadline is next week.

6. I'm afraid I still haven't finished the report.

   Well, I ______ it by 1pm today.

don't have	need	~~Would~~	must	don't need	Could	must not

06 Vocabulary

Aa 6.1 **MONEY AND FINANCE** WRITE THE PHRASES FROM THE PANEL UNDER THE CORRECT DEFINITIONS

The amount of money that is available to spend on something

a budget

❶ To lose money by spending more than you earn

❸ Extra money the bank allows you to spend

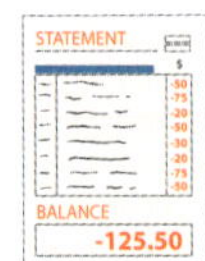

❹ The regular costs of running a business, such as wages

❻ To get into a situation where you owe people money

❼ To earn just enough to cover the costs of producing a product

❾ Money coming into a business

❿ An amount of money spent

⓬ Records of money paid into and out of a business

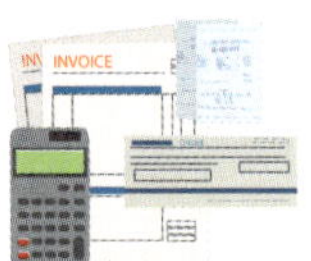

⓭ To fall, especially in worth or value

⓯ To reach the highest point

⓰ The amount of one currency that you get when you change it for another

2 To charge less than others who sell the same goods or services as you

____

5 The amount or value of total sales over a particular period

____

8 A major decline in economic activity

____

11 A change to more positive business conditions

____

14 The rate at which money comes into and goes out of a business

____

17 To no longer be able to exist as a business

____

to make a loss　an upturn in the market

sales figures　income

an economic downturn　overheads

the exchange rate　cash flow

an overdraft　to get into debt

to go out of business　to peak

expenditure / outlay　~~a budget~~

to undercut competitors　to drop

accounts　to break even

07 Writing a report

When writing a report, you may need to use different past tenses to show sequences of events. You may also need to use more formal phrasing.

New language Past perfect and past simple
Aa Vocabulary Formal business English
New skill Writing reports

7.1 FILL IN THE GAPS BY PUTTING THE VERBS IN THE PAST PERFECT OR PAST SIMPLE

We *stayed* (stay) in the hotel that our client *had recommended* (recommend) to us.

1. Sales ________ (be) good because we ______________ (organize) a good marketing campaign. 
2. Sales ________ (fall) sharply, so we ______________ (decide) to withdraw the product. 
3. Aditya ________ (want) to try a program that the team ______________ (not use) before. 
4. After Peter ________ (finish) the report, he ______________ (want) to go on vacation.

7.2 CROSS OUT THE INCORRECT WORDS IN EACH SENTENCE

Sandra gave / ~~had given~~ a presentation that she ~~prepared~~ / had prepared two years ago.

1. Ramon wrote / had written ten pages of the report when his computer crashed / had crashed.
2. Many of our employees did not / had not visited the factory before and were / had been very impressed.
3. Bob's speech was / had been disappointing because he didn't prepare / hadn't prepared well.
4. Nobody told / had told the conference delegates where their hotel was / had been.
5. I didn't delegate / hadn't delegated tasks to Kai before, but I thought / had thought he did a good job.

7.3 REWRITE THE SENTENCES, CORRECTING THE ERRORS

The purpose of this report is review our advertising campaign for next year.
The purpose of this report is to review our advertising campaign for next year.

1. The followed report will explore our new sales strategy.
2. As can be seeing in the table, we have invested $4 million this year.
3. Some of our customers have stating that they are not satisfied with the result.
4. Our initial investigation suggestion that this is not true.
5. Our beginning recommendation is to reduce the budget by 50 percent.
6. We consulting a number of focus groups for this report.

Aa 7.4 MATCH THE BEGINNINGS OF THE SENTENCES TO THE CORRECT ENDINGS

	We consulted a number	is to review our current sales strategy.
1	The purpose of our report	we should invest more in R&D.
2	The following report presents	of focus groups for this report.
3	Our clients stated that	proceed with the sale of the subsidiary.
4	Based on the initial research,	a summary of our findings.
5	Our principal recommendation is to	they were unhappy with the changes.

7.5 READ THE REPORT AND ANSWER THE QUESTIONS

LOCATION REPORT

The aim of this report is to assess the advantages and disadvantages of moving the company headquarters to Alchester. The following report will look at location, transportation, housing, and the available tax breaks.

Location The site in Alchester is 20 miles from downtown. The town has two large colleges and a number of other IT companies. However, it is more than 200 miles to the nearest major city.

Transportation There is an airport and the rail connections to other cities are good. However, the airport is far (30 miles away) and the station can only be reached by taxi.

Housing Based on the initial research, we concluded that housing is much more affordable than in major cities. The proposed site is near an attractive suburb.

Tax subsidies The local government offers large grants to companies that want to move to the area. However, these are only available if the company is willing to stay in the area for more than ten years.

Conclusion Many of our employees stated that they would not be happy living so far from a city. Others stated that they found the affordable accommodation very attractive. The grants offered are attractive, but the company will need to make a big commitment.

What does the report aim to assess?

- **The company's profits for the year** ☐
- **A potential new location for the company** ☑
- **The company's current location** ☐

1 Where is the site in Alchester?

- **20 miles from downtown** ☐
- **200 miles from downtown** ☐
- **Downtown** ☐

2 What is good about the transportation links?

- **The location of the station** ☐
- **The location of the airport** ☐
- **Rail connections to other cities** ☐

3 What are the findings about housing?

- **It is affordable in Alchester** ☐
- **The company is still researching it** ☐
- **The suburbs are not attractive** ☐

4 What must companies do to get a tax subsidy?

- **Move to Alchester** ☐
- **Stay in Alchester for over ten years** ☐
- **Work with the local government** ☐

5 What is the conclusion of the report?

- **The company will move to Alchester** ☐
- **The company won't move to Alchester** ☐
- **A decision has not yet been made** ☐

7.6 MARK THE SENTENCES THAT ARE CORRECT

As can be see in the table, our profits have declined by 9 percent this year. ☐
As can be seen in the table, our profits have declined by 9 percent this year. ☑

1. The purpose of this report is to compare the two factories. ☐
   The purpose of this report is compare the two factories. ☐

2. Focus groups had been consulted before we implemented the policy. ☐
   Focus groups had be consulted before we implemented the policy. ☐

3. Sales of our products are fallen in comparison with the previous quarter. ☐
   Sales of our products had fallen in comparison with the previous quarter. ☐

4. Our principal recommendation is to increase investment in R&D. ☐
   Our principal recommendation is increase investment in R&D. ☐

5. Profits had risen by more than 20 percent in the first half of 2015. ☐
   Profits had risen with more than 20 percent in the first half of 2015. ☐

7.7 FILL IN THE GAPS USING THE WORDS IN THE PANEL

CLOSED We closed the branch after our costs had ___risen___ by more than 20 percent.

1. In this report we will ____________ the findings of our research.

2. The ____________ of this report is to investigate the pros and cons of the new software.

3. This bar chart ____________ the sales figures for the last two years.

4. Our customers ____________ that they had been disappointed with the product.

purpose | stated | compares | ~~risen~~ | present

08 Making apologies

The present perfect continuous describes ongoing situations in the past that may affect the present. It can be used in apologies and to give reasons for problems.

New language Present perfect continuous
Aa Vocabulary Apologies
New skill Apologizing on the telephone

8.1 MARK THE BEST REPLY TO EACH STATEMENT

My new laptop hasn't arrived yet. 
- I'm very sorry about that. ☑
- Of course not. ☐

1. Can you look into the problem for me? 
   - Sorry. That's not possible. ☐
   - Of course. Let me see what I can do. ☐

2. Could you tell me your order number, please? 
   - Yes, I want a full refund please. ☐
   - Certainly. It's ZX42 9JL. ☐

3. What caused the delay? 
   - We've been having difficulties with our software. ☐
   - I don't know. Can you call later? ☐

4. Will you be able to offer our company any compensation? 
   - I'm really sorry to hear that. ☐
   - We'll offer you a discount on your next order. ☐

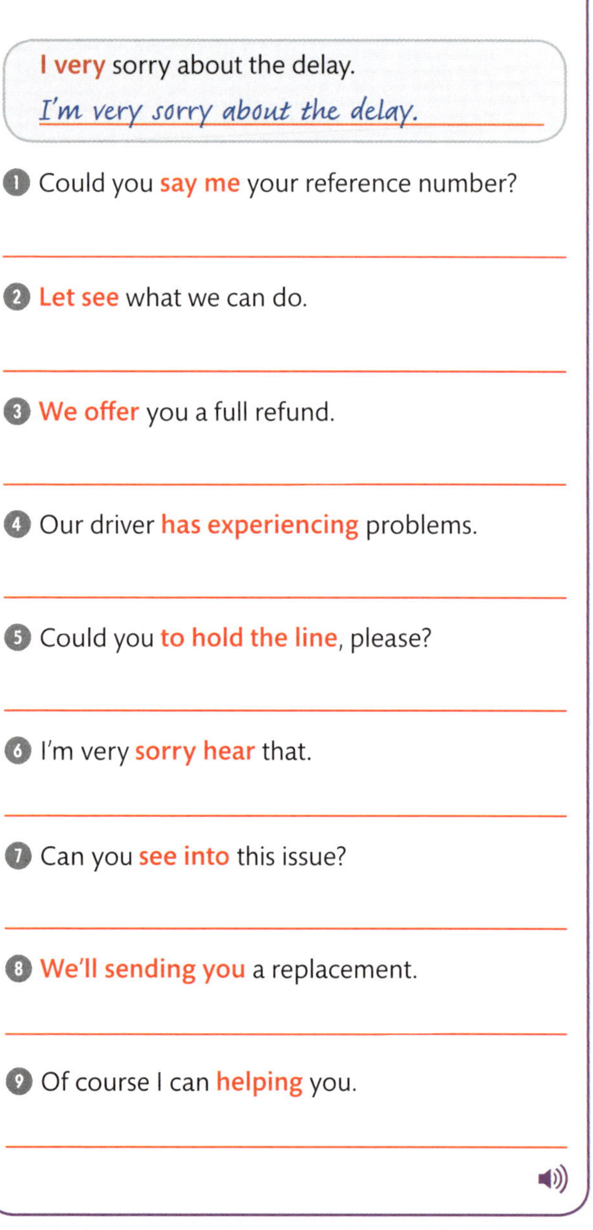

8.2 REWRITE THE SENTENCES, CORRECTING THE ERRORS

I very sorry about the delay.
I'm very sorry about the delay.

1. Could you **say me** your reference number?

2. **Let see** what we can do.

3. **We offer** you a full refund.

4. Our driver **has experiencing** problems.

5. Could you **to hold the line**, please?

6. I'm very **sorry hear** that.

7. Can you **see into** this issue?

8. **We'll sending you** a replacement.

9. Of course I can **helping** you.

8.3 FILL IN THE GAPS USING THE PHRASES IN THE PANEL

Can you *look into* the problem for me?

1. I'm very ______________ to hear that, sir.
2. Certainly. Let's ______________ what I can do.
3. Could you tell me your ______________ number, please?
4. Could you please ______________ the line?
5. I'm sorry. Our IT system's been ______________ difficulties.
6. My order ______________ dirty and broken.
7. Can you ______________ any compensation?
8. Of course. We'll give you a ______________ on your next order.

reference
hold
sorry
~~look into~~
offer
experiencing
discount
see
arrived

8.4 CROSS OUT THE INCORRECT WORD IN EACH SENTENCE, THEN SAY THE SENTENCES OUT LOUD

I'm very **sorry** / ~~sad~~ about the delay. Let's see what we can do.

1. Could you look **through** / **into** the problem for me?
2. The company **has** / **is** been experiencing difficulties recently.
3. Please **keep** / **hold** the line for a moment.
4. I've been **wait** / **waiting** all day for my order to arrive.

8.5 FILL IN THE GAPS BY PUTTING THE VERBS IN THE PRESENT PERFECT CONTINUOUS

Katherine *has been waiting* **(wait)** for her feedback from the interview.

1. We __________________ **(prepare)** a proposal all evening.
2. Our website __________________ **(experience)** difficulties this morning.
3. Chris __________________ **(work)** on that project for three months now.
4. Our products __________________ **(not sell)** well so far this year.

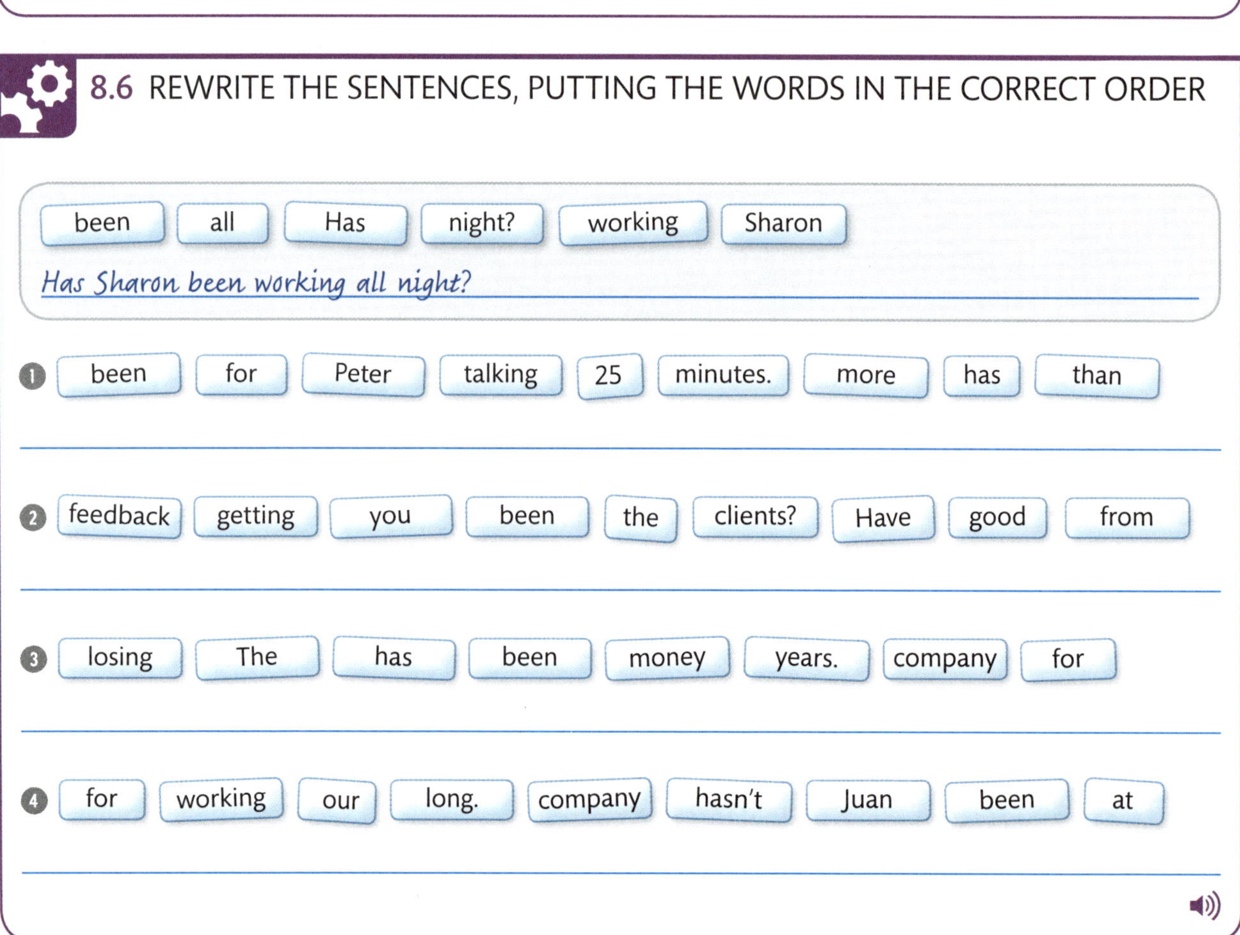

8.6 REWRITE THE SENTENCES, PUTTING THE WORDS IN THE CORRECT ORDER

been | all | Has | night? | working | Sharon

Has Sharon been working all night?

1. been | for | Peter | talking | 25 | minutes. | more | has | than

____

2. feedback | getting | you | been | the | clients? | Have | good | from

____

3. losing | The | has | been | money | years. | company | for

____

4. for | working | our | long. | company | hasn't | Juan | been | at

____

8.7 LISTEN TO THE AUDIO, THEN NUMBER THE SENTENCES IN THE ORDER YOU HEAR THEM

Jock Douglas calls his suppliers to ask about an order that he's expecting.

A I've been waiting for three weeks now, so I'm not at all happy. ☐

B Could you tell me your order reference number? ☐

C We would like to offer you a gift voucher worth $100. ☐

D Could you please hold the line one moment? ☐

E I'm really sorry to hear that, Mr. Douglas. 1

F Your order was dispatched yesterday. ☐

8.8 READ THE EMAIL AND MARK THE CORRECT SUMMARY

1 The wrong model of laptop arrived. This happened because of a software problem at the warehouse. The company has offered a 10 percent discount on the next order. ☐

2 The wrong model of printer arrived. This happened because of a software problem at the warehouse. The company has offered a 40 percent discount on the next order. ☐

3 The wrong model of software arrived. This happened because of a flood at the warehouse. The company has offered a 25 percent discount on the next order. ☐

4 The wrong model of laptop arrived. This happened because of a software upgrade at the warehouse. The company has offered a 25 percent discount on the next order. ☐

To: Mario Grando

Subject: Your order

Dear Mario Grando,

Thank you for your email regarding your order dated August 4th. I am very sorry to hear that the wrong model of laptop arrived, and we apologize for the inconvenience this caused. I've been looking into the problem and see that you received model A147 instead of A149. We've been upgrading the software in our warehouse recently, and, unfortunately, last week we were unable to fulfill all our orders correctly. As an apology, however, we'd like to offer you a refund of 25 percent off your next order with our company. I've attached the voucher to this email.

Best regards,

Mohammed Ahmed

09 Vocabulary

Aa 9.1 **COMMUNICATION TECHNOLOGY** WRITE THE PHRASES FROM THE PANEL UNDER THE CORRECT DEFINITIONS

Computer programs

1 Internet-based tools for communicating with friends and communities

3 Computerized; not operated by a human

4 To enter or connect to something

6 Current and modern

7 Easy for the operator to use

9 A group conversation held by phone

10 Losing a phone or internet connection

12 A small computing device, such as a smartphone or tablet, that is easily carried

13 To work without an internet connection

15 To connect a mobile device to electricity to give it more power

16 A name and code used to access an account on a computing device

2 A collection of linked pages accessed through the internet

5 To work with an internet connection

8 To save an extra copy of a document in case the original is lost

11 To get an application from the internet onto a device or computer

14 An email has been automatically returned without reaching the intended recipient

17 A system of interconnected technology

social media

to download an app

a username and password

to work offline

to charge

a website

to access

automated

to back up

an email has bounced

up to date

a mobile device

user-friendly

~~software~~

a network

to work online

breaking up

a conference call

10 Making plans by email

English uses a variety of phrases to make and check plans with co-workers by email. It is important to ensure that even informal messages are polite.

New language Email language
Vocabulary Meetings and workshops
New skill Making plans

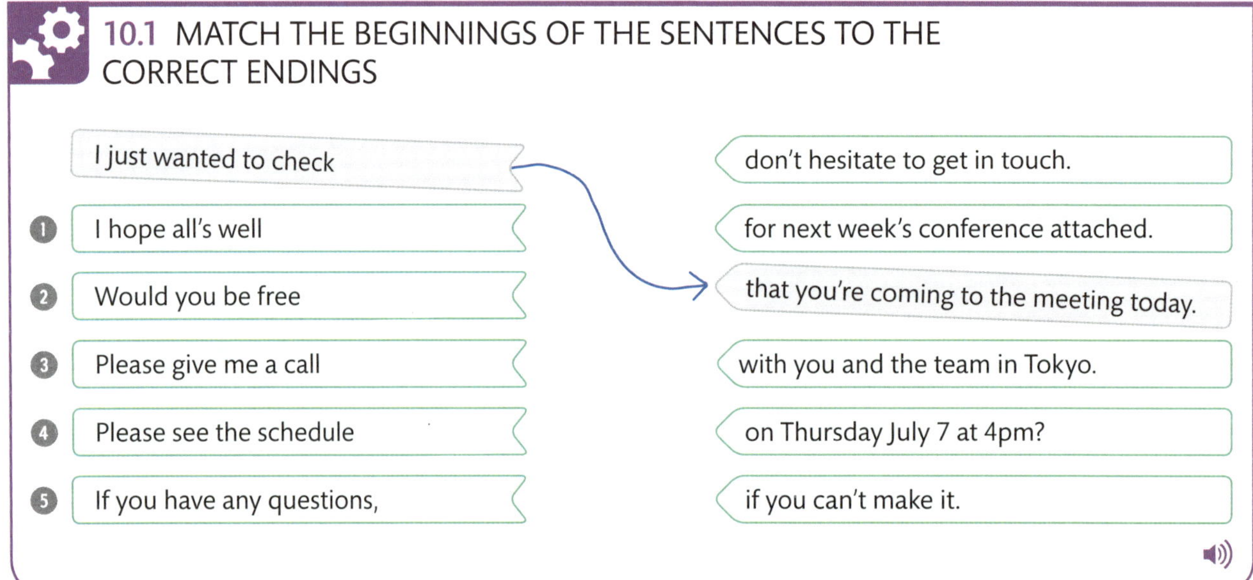

10.1 MATCH THE BEGINNINGS OF THE SENTENCES TO THE CORRECT ENDINGS

I just wanted to check → that you're coming to the meeting today.

1. I hope all's well
2. Would you be free
3. Please give me a call
4. Please see the schedule
5. If you have any questions,

- don't hesitate to get in touch.
- for next week's conference attached.
- that you're coming to the meeting today.
- with you and the team in Tokyo.
- on Thursday July 7 at 4pm?
- if you can't make it.

10.2 FILL IN THE GAPS USING THE WORDS IN THE PANEL

I just wanted to *check* that you're attending this week's meeting.

1. I was ______ if you could help me prepare my presentation.
2. Would you be free to ______ on Thursday evening?
3. I'm ______ Sanjay and Anita in on this email.
4. I ______ all's well with you and the team in Delhi.
5. Please see the minutes of yesterday's meeting ______ .
6. If you have any ______ , please let me know.
7. How ______ joining us at the pizza place later this evening?

about
hope
meet
questions
~~check~~
copying
wondering
attached

10.3 REWRITE THE SENTENCES, CORRECTING THE ERRORS

I hope all well with you and the team.
I hope all's well with you and the team.

1. I just wanted check that you're coming to the presentation.

2. Would you free next Wednesday morning at 11:30?

3. Please find a copy of the report attach.

4. If you any questions, please let me know.

5. I'm copy Ricardo in on this.

10.4 READ THE EMAIL AND MARK THE CORRECT SUMMARY

1. Jerome wants to meet tomorrow to discuss the new software package. He has asked Claude to send him the timetable. ☐

2. Jerome is inviting Françoise and Claude to come to software training in Room 3. ☐

3. Jerome is emailing to check that Claude is coming to the IT meeting. Françoise has sent the agenda and a memo. ☐

4. Jerome is inviting Françoise to a meeting with the IT team. He has sent Françoise and Claude a copy of the agenda. ☐

To: Françoise Thomas

Subject: Software package

Hi Françoise,

I hope all's well with you and the team. I just wanted to check that you got the email I sent yesterday about the new software package that goes live on Thursday. Claude and I want to meet the IT department tomorrow morning to discuss it. Would you be free to join us in meeting room 3 at 9:30am? Please find attached an agenda and memo about the software specifications. I've copied Claude in on this message. If you have any questions, please let me know.

Best regards,

Jerome

11 Keeping clients informed

Use the present continuous to inform clients about current situations and future arrangements. Continuous tenses can also soften questions and requests.

New language Continuous tenses
Aa Vocabulary Arrangements and schedules
New skill Keeping clients informed

11.1 REWRITE THE PRESENT CONTINUOUS SENTENCES, CORRECTING THE ERRORS

I **are hoping** to finish my report on July's sales later today.
I am hoping to finish my report on July's sales later today.

1. Mohammed **is meet** the new supplier to discuss a new deal.

2. Jola **is talk** to Sales this afternoon to agree new discounts.

3. They **is aiming** to have the presentation ready by 5:00pm.

4. I **am writeing** to inform you that there is a delay with the part you need.

5. We **still are waiting** to hear from the Chinese partners.

11.2 LISTEN TO THE AUDIO AND MARK WHETHER THE ACTIVITY IN EACH PICTURE TAKES PLACE IN THE PRESENT OR THE FUTURE

Present ☑ Future ☐

1 Present ☐ Future ☐

2 Present ☐ Future ☐

3 Present ☐ Future ☐

4 Present ☐ Future ☐

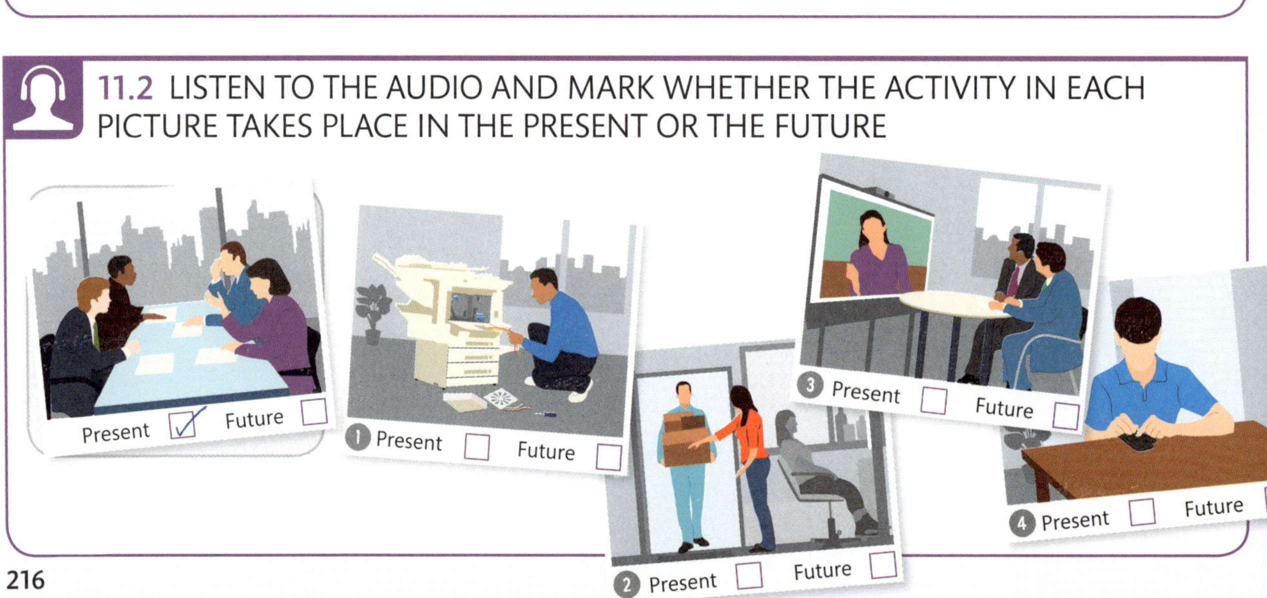

Aa 11.3 READ THE CLUES AND WRITE THE WORDS FROM THE PANEL IN THE CORRECT PLACES ON THE GRID

1 h e s i t a t e

ACROSS

1 To pause

2 To get

3 To make something definite

DOWN

4 To tell

5 To like more

6 To promise

assure | obtain | confirm | ~~hesitate~~ | prefer | inform

11.4 MARK THE MOST POLITE SENTENCE IN EACH PAIR

You need to extend the deadline. ☐
I was wondering if you would consider extending the deadline. ☑

1. Are you going to the new product launch? ☐
   Will you be attending the launch of the new products? ☐

2. I was wondering if we could put our meeting back to tomorrow. ☐
   Can we put our meeting back to tomorrow? ☐

3. We want to send new designs by Friday. ☐
   We are aiming to send the new designs by Friday. ☐

4. Will you be paying for the order in cash or by card? ☐
   Will you pay in cash or by card? ☐

5. I was wondering if you would take the clients out for dinner. ☐
   Will you take the clients out for dinner? ☐

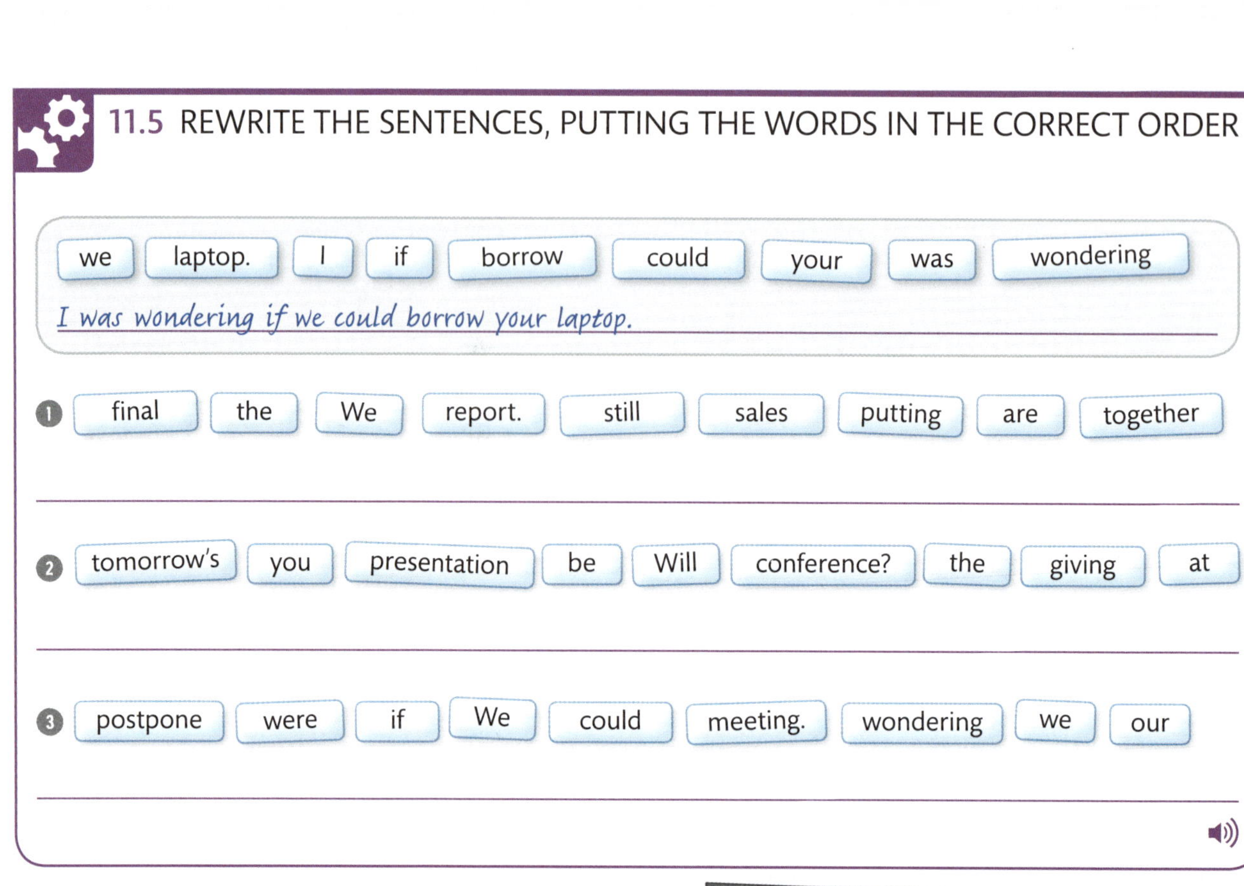

11.5 REWRITE THE SENTENCES, PUTTING THE WORDS IN THE CORRECT ORDER

we | laptop. | I | if | borrow | could | your | was | wondering

I was wondering if we could borrow your laptop.

1. final | the | We | report. | still | sales | putting | are | together

2. tomorrow's | you | presentation | be | Will | conference? | the | giving | at

3. postpone | were | if | We | could | meeting. | wondering | we | our

11.6 READ THE EMAIL AND ANSWER THE QUESTIONS

Sanjay's project is running on time.
True ☐ **False** ☑ **Not given** ☐

1. Sanjay wants to meet the suppliers.
True ☐ **False** ☐ **Not given** ☐

2. The new designs for the fabric are complex.
True ☐ **False** ☐ **Not given** ☐

3. The fabrics will be delivered in two weeks' time.
True ☐ **False** ☐ **Not given** ☐

4. Sanjay offers Fiona compensation.
True ☐ **False** ☐ **Not given** ☐

To: Fiona McRae

Subject: Project update

Dear Fiona,

I was wondering if we could have a brief project update meeting as the project is running late. Unfortunately, the new designs for the fabric that we plan to launch have proved more complicated to print than we initially thought. The suppliers in Bangladesh have informed us that the final printed materials will be with us at the end of this month, not in two weeks as per our order.

The suppliers have told us they will work around the clock to minimize the delay, and they apologize for any inconvenience this may cause us.

Yours truly,
Sanjay

12 Informal communication

Phrasal verbs have two or more parts. They are often used in informal spoken and written English, in things such as messages and requests to co-workers.

New language Phrasal verbs
Aa Vocabulary Arrangements and plans
New skill Keeping co-workers informed

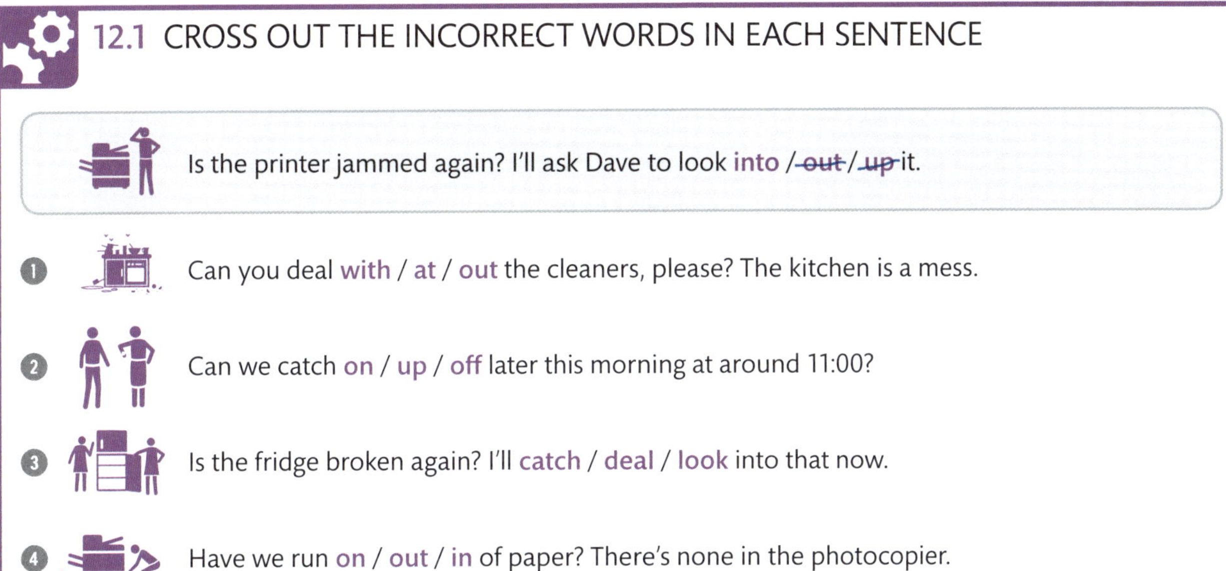

12.1 CROSS OUT THE INCORRECT WORDS IN EACH SENTENCE

Is the printer jammed again? I'll ask Dave to look **into** / ~~**out**~~ / ~~**up**~~ it.

1. Can you deal **with** / **at** / **out** the cleaners, please? The kitchen is a mess.
2. Can we catch **on** / **up** / **off** later this morning at around 11:00?
3. Is the fridge broken again? I'll **catch** / **deal** / **look** into that now.
4. Have we run **on** / **out** / **in** of paper? There's none in the photocopier.

12.2 FILL IN THE GAPS USING THE PHRASAL VERBS IN THE PANEL

Let's *catch up* now you're back from your vacation.

1. Can we ______________ a meeting with Marketing and Sales?
2. Have you asked Surina to ______________ all the paperwork?
3. The printer has ______________ of ink again.
4. I can't ______________ what Dave wants me to do.
5. I need to ______________ the topic of punctuality with you.

figure out | bring up | fix up | ~~catch up~~ | fill out | run out

12.3 REWRITE THE SENTENCES BY CHANGING THE POSITION OF THE PARTICLE

Can you **fill out** that form?
Can you fill that form out?

1. I need to **back up** my files.
____

2. Can you **give out** the agenda?
____

3. Can we **call off** tomorrow's meeting?
____

4. Can you **pass on** my message to her?
____

5. Let me **hand out** the minutes.
____

6. I want to **put on** my tie.
____

7. Can you **fix up** another meeting?
____

8. I need to **send out** an email.
____

9. We are **taking on** new staff.
____

10. Can you **set up** the projector?
____

11. I'd like to **talk over** the sales plan.
____

12.4 LISTEN TO THE AUDIO AND ANSWER THE QUESTIONS

It is Jack's first day back at work after his vacation. His co-worker Amanda calls him.

Why is Amanda calling Jack?
- **To arrange a meeting** ☐
- **To cancel a meeting** ☑
- **To place some orders** ☐

1. What is the problem with Amanda's files?
   - **She hasn't backed them up** ☐
   - **She has deleted them** ☐
   - **Some of them are missing** ☐

2. When does Jack set up a meeting with Amanda?
   - **Thursday morning** ☐
   - **Thursday afternoon** ☐
   - **Friday morning** ☐

3. What does Amanda want Jack to do?
   - **Call customers about their feedback** ☐
   - **Deal with new customers** ☐
   - **Write a report about feedback** ☐

4. What does Jack offer to do?
   - **Delegate some of Amanda's emails** ☐
   - **Delete some of Amanda's emails** ☐
   - **Deal with some of Amanda's emails** ☐

5. What does Amanda ask Jack to pass on?
   - **A message** ☐
   - **A package** ☐
   - **A sales report** ☐

6. What will Jack wear for his site visit?
   - **His best suit** ☐
   - **His best tie** ☐
   - **His best suit and tie** ☐

12.5 CROSS OUT THE INCORRECT WORDS IN EACH SENTENCE, THEN SAY THE SENTENCES OUT LOUD

Can you pass a message on / ~~up~~ / ~~off~~ to Syed? I can't make this afternoon's meeting. 

1. Jamil's flight is delayed. I think we'll have to call our meeting with him in / off / out. 

2. All employees have to put an apron in / up / on before entering the kitchen. 

3. We're hoping to give off / out / in samples of our work at the exhibition. 

4. It's really important to back your files over / on / up every night or you could lose work. 

12.6 FILL IN THE GAPS USING THE PHRASES IN THE PANEL

The paper in the printer has ___run out___ .

1. Khalil has ______________ out.
2. She has just ______________ on me without saying goodbye!
3. He ______________ because he had an important meeting.
4. He gave ______________ to everyone at the meeting.
5. They ______________ up for later in the week.

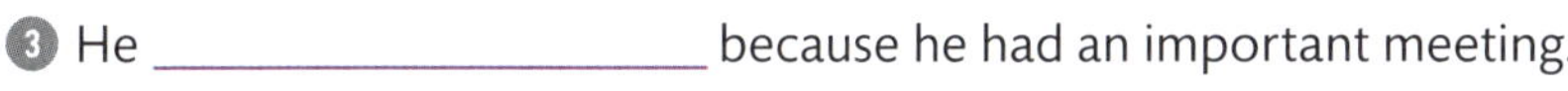

his report out	~~run out~~	set a meeting
hung up	put his tie on	filled the form

13 Vocabulary

Aa 13.1 **PRODUCTION** WRITE THE PHRASES FROM THE PANEL UNDER THE CORRECT DEFINITIONS

Systems that ensure that products are of a high standard

quality control

❶ The external wrapping of goods before they are sold

❸ Made by a person without the use of a machine

❹ Something that is made or produced only once

❻ Goods that a company has made but not yet sold

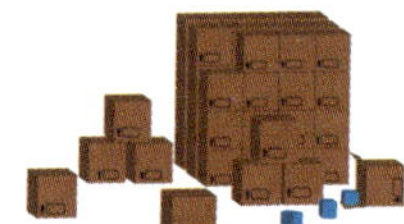

❼ A declaration that a product meets certain standards and is suitable for sale

❾ The first form of a design that can be changed, copied, or developed

❿ A line of people or machinery in a factory, each making a specific part of a product

⓬ Moving goods from one place to another

⓭ Found or bought in a morally acceptable way

⓯ A building or group of buildings where goods are made

⓰ The process of making large numbers of goods, usually in a factory

2 A process to check that goods meet certain standards

5 Requiring a lot of human effort to make something

8 The basic substances that are used to make a product

11 A place where goods are stored before being shipped to customers or sellers

14 Manufacturing too much of something in relation to demand

17 A company that provides or supplies another company with goods and services

packaging
labor-intensive
mass production
shipping
ethically sourced
handmade
raw materials
a one-off production
~~quality control~~
overproduction
stock
product approval
a factory
a prototype
a warehouse
product testing
a supplier
a production line

14 Describing a process

The passive voice can be useful when you need to describe how a process works. It places emphasis on the action rather than the person or thing doing it.

New language The passive voice
Aa Vocabulary Processes and manufacturing
New skill Discussing how things are done

14.1 CROSS OUT THE INCORRECT WORDS IN EACH SENTENCE

Our soaps **are made** / ~~maked~~ using the finest French lavender.

1. The media **had been** / **have** told about the press launch and were out in force.
2. New models **are been** / **are being** created to coincide with the premiere of the movie.
3. The design has been **patent** / **patented** so nobody can copy it.
4. Our coffee is **producing** / **produced** using the finest coffee beans from Kenya.
5. It is thought that the sandwich **was** / **were** invented in 1762.

14.2 LISTEN TO THE AUDIO AND NUMBER THE PICTURES IN THE ORDER THEY ARE DESCRIBED

A ☐
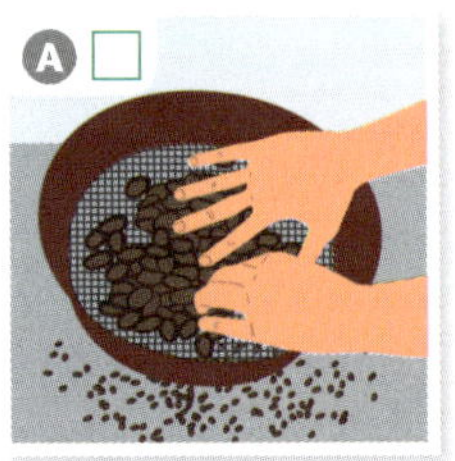

B 1

C ☐
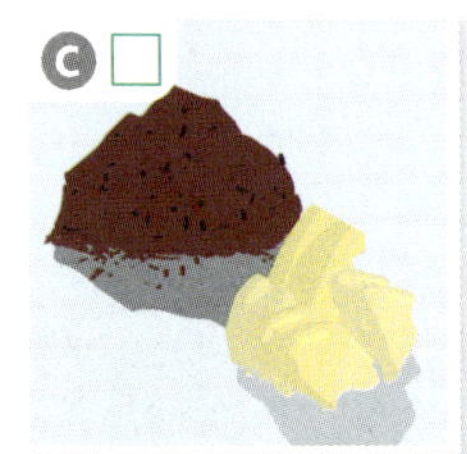

D ☐
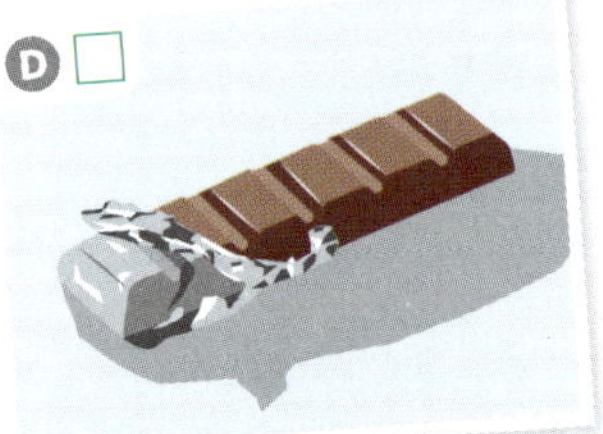

E ☐

F ☐

G ☐

H ☐

14.3 REWRITE THE SENTENCES USING THE PASSIVE VOICE

Our distribution team sends out our products from our warehouse in Michigan.
Our products are sent out from our warehouse in Michigan by our distribution team.

1. A separate department audits our accounts every May.

2. Our professional coffee tasters approve the coffee blends we produce.

3. Security staff scan all passengers' luggage when they go through Departures.

4. Jane designs all our marketing material for the Asia office.

5. Our packing department checks all the orders before delivery.

6. Stephen updates the database with customers' details.

7. Our cosmetics buyer buys all our ingredients from Fair Trade suppliers.

8. Nicola adds new lines to our women's fashion range on a regular basis.

9. Jason invented the new product tracking app for customers.

10. Our marketing team launched our new website in January.

14.4 READ THE ARTICLE AND ANSWER THE QUESTIONS

Bread was invented in modern times.
True ☐ False ☑ Not given ☐

1. Bread is not eaten in many cultures.
True ☐ False ☐ Not given ☐

2. Yeast is added to the dough after kneading.
True ☐ False ☐ Not given ☐

3. The dough is kneaded for about 10 minutes.
True ☐ False ☐ Not given ☐

4. Different countries have different shapes of bread.
True ☐ False ☐ Not given ☐

5. The dough is left to rise two times before it is baked.
True ☐ False ☐ Not given ☐

FOOD TODAY

The stuff of life

This week we look at how bread is made throughout the world.

Bread has been made since prehistoric times and is eaten by most cultures today. But how is it made? A raising agent like yeast is added to flour with warm water. A dough is made and the gluten in the flour is activated by a process called kneading, which is when the dough is massaged for about 10 minutes. The dough is then left in a warm place to rise. Then the air is knocked out of it and it is kneaded a second time. The dough is then shaped into a loaf or rolls. Some of these are very decorative, and individual bakers often have their own special design. Finally, the dough is left to rise again and then baked in a hot oven. The result is delicious warm bread!

14.5 MATCH THE ACTIVE SENTENCES TO THE PASSIVE SENTENCES WITH THE SAME MEANING

We must beat our competitors' prices. → Our competitors' prices must be beaten.

1. They can't have checked these toys.
2. She should have given them a discount.
3. Freya can't have taken the order.
4. We can give every customer a free bag.
5. We shouldn't ignore faults in the products.
6. You can't beat our prices.
7. He must have placed his order late.

- The order can't have been taken by her.
- Our prices can't be beaten.
- Our competitors' prices must be beaten.
- These toys can't have been checked.
- Faults in the products shouldn't be ignored.
- A free bag can be given to every customer.
- His order must have been placed late.
- A discount should have been given.

14.6 LOOK AT THE DIAGRAM AND SAY THE SENTENCES OUT LOUD, FILLING IN THE GAPS USING THE WORDS IN THE PANEL

How It's Made

Learn how our cakes are baked.

First, a cake recipe ___is chosen___ by the cake-maker.

1. Next, the ingredients ______________ together to make a cake mixture.
2. Then the cake mixture ______________ into cake pans.
3. Next, the cakes ______________ in a hot oven.
4. When the cakes are cooked, they ______________ out of the oven.
5. The cakes ______________ to cool on a wire cooling rack.
6. Finally, the cakes ______________ and decorated with icing.

are taken | are mixed | ~~is chosen~~ | is poured | are assembled | are left | are put

15 Describing a product

When describing a product, you will usually use adjectives. You can use more than one adjective, but they must be in a particular order.

New language Adjective order
Aa Vocabulary Opinion and fact adjectives
New skill Describing a product

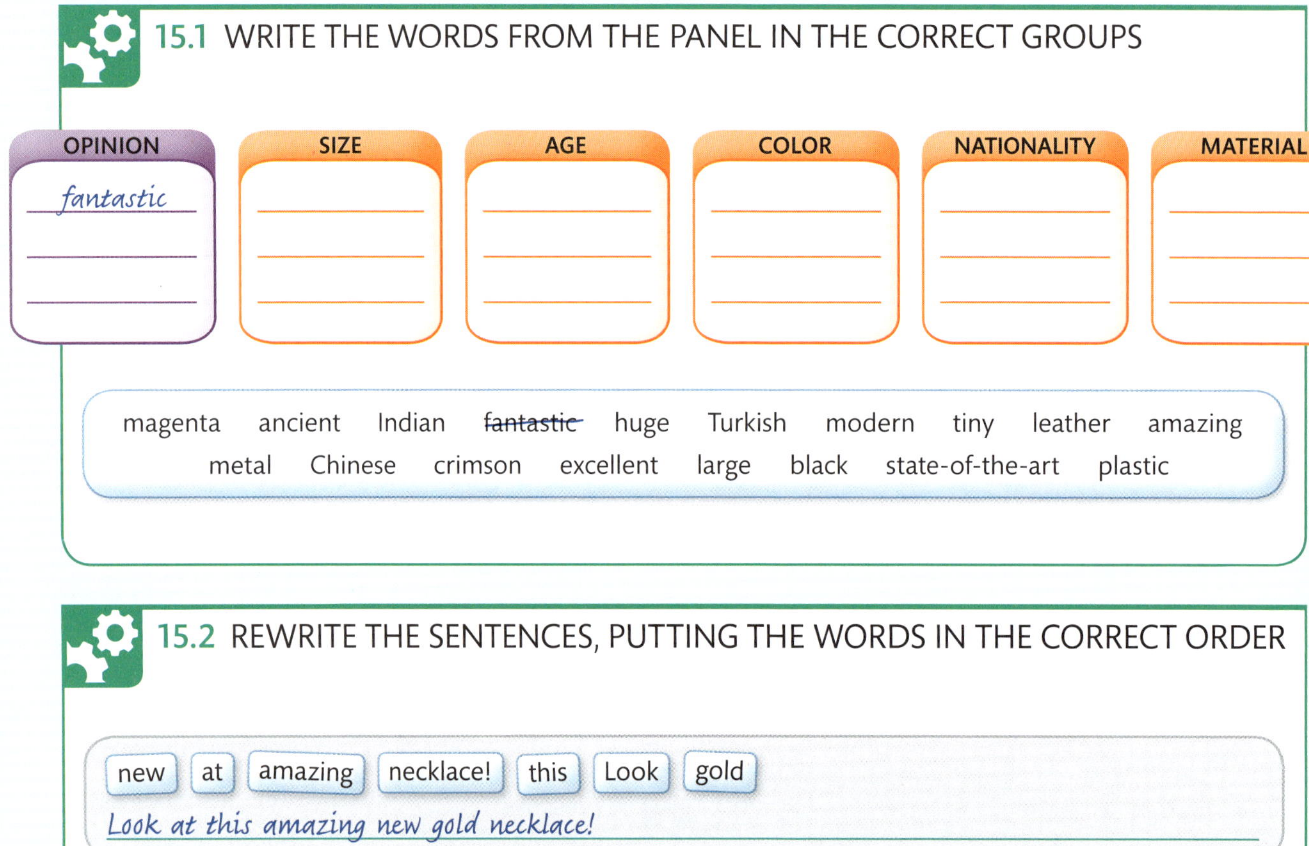

15.1 WRITE THE WORDS FROM THE PANEL IN THE CORRECT GROUPS

OPINION	SIZE	AGE	COLOR	NATIONALITY	MATERIAL
fantastic					

magenta ancient Indian ~~fantastic~~ huge Turkish modern tiny leather amazing metal Chinese crimson excellent large black state-of-the-art plastic

15.2 REWRITE THE SENTENCES, PUTTING THE WORDS IN THE CORRECT ORDER

new | at | amazing | necklace! | this | Look | gold

Look at this amazing new gold necklace!

1. Indian | It's | by | designer. | fabulous, | young | made | a

____

2. I | bowls. | these | small, | china | blue | fantastic, | love

____

3. outstanding | launching | an | new | clothes. | We're | of | range

____

15.3 CROSS OUT THE INCORRECT WORD IN EACH SENTENCE

I really like the new **red** / ~~**diamond**~~ velvet sofas around the office.

1. What a lovely **plastic** / **stylish** desk you have!

2. Sam asked me to design a **silver** / **classic** brown chair.

3. I brought back some delicious **china** / **Turkish** candy from my trip.

4. Do you like this **pretty** / **paper** crimson watch for ladies?

5. Do you like our cute **green** / **ugly** teddy bear for our new children's range?

6. Our competitors are selling **unfashionable** / **intelligent** black suits.

7. Our team is developing an innovative **leather** / **popular** interior for our executive car.

8. I love buying large **awesome** / **yellow** flowers for the office.

9. Jane has bought an **expensive** / **friendly** classic car at an auction.

10. We have an amazing **cotton** / **Italian** coffee machine in our office.

11. I have ordered some of those fabulous **leather** / **double-sided** business cards.

12. We have an amazing **awful** / **gray** oven in our staff kitchen.

13. This is our new **lightweight** / **comfortable** digital camera.

15.4 LISTEN TO THE AUDIO AND MARK WHICH THINGS ARE DESCRIBED

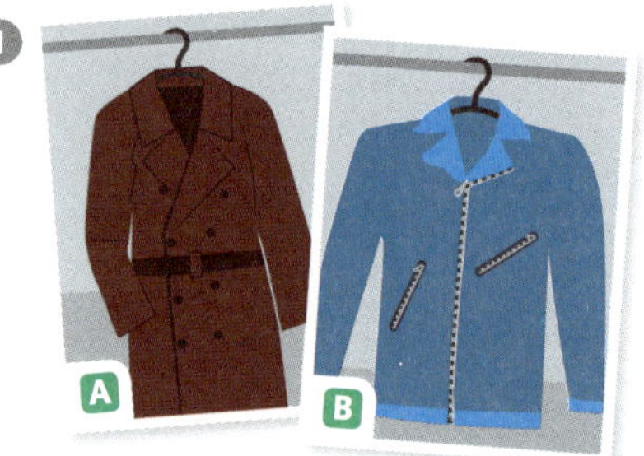

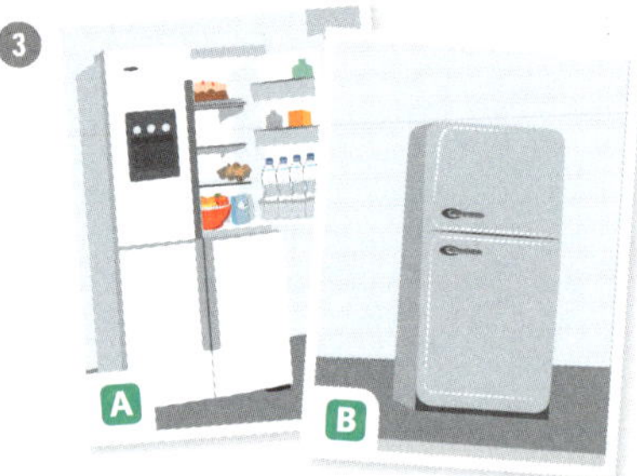

15.5 READ THE ARTICLE AND ANSWER THE QUESTIONS

Dress Right only sells clothes for men and women.
True ☐ False ☑ Not given ☐

1. The new range of clothing is mainly beige.
True ☐ False ☐ Not given ☐

2. Dress Right sells fashionable clothes.
True ☐ False ☐ Not given ☐

3. The new denim range is ground-breaking.
True ☐ False ☐ Not given ☐

4. Dress Right only sells uniforms in one set of colors.
True ☐ False ☐ Not given ☐

5. Dress Right is having fashion shows in all its stores.
True ☐ False ☐ Not given ☐

FASHION AND STYLE

Dress Right for all occasions

We have everything you need to dress the family in style, whether it is for school, work, a trip or a special event. Want to know what is new? We have kept our trademark stylish, modern, and colorful style in our new range of clothing. You'll find the usual brown and red clothes as well as fashionable, new bags and shoes. In the Directions collection, there are fabulous, trend-setting styles for both men and women. In addition to this, we are also launching an innovative, modern, denim range of casual wear.

This year also sees the launch of practical, hard-wearing school clothes in a range of colors. So come and see what Dress Right can do for you in a store near you or online.

15.6 SAY THE SENTENCES OUT LOUD, FILLING IN THE GAPS USING THE WORDS IN THE PANEL

We offer good, cheap food that people can afford.

1. Their website is easy to use because it has a ______, effective style.
2. Zander's Pizzeria makes ______, oven-baked pizzas.
3. I love this ______, leather armchair.
4. The new, ______ brochure is very bright and attractive.
5. I like the ______, new rooms in that hotel.
6. Those small, ______ earrings are beautiful.
7. My dad drives a ______, black truck.
8. Ella makes high-quality, ______ curtains.
9. We aim to give ______ customer service.
10. We offer a ______, personal experience.
11. I don't like those ugly, ______ desks. They're hideous!
12. This modern, ______ car is much faster than my old one.
13. What a ______, big photo of all the team!

huge	cotton	full-color	clean	delicious	~~cheap~~	Japanese
unique	simple	gorgeous	comfortable	diamond	excellent	wooden

16 Vocabulary

Aa **16.1 MARKETING AND ADVERTISING** WRITE THE WORDS FROM THE PANEL UNDER THE CORRECT PICTURES

direct mail

1 ______

2 ______

3 ______

6 ______

7 ______

8 ______

9 ______

12 ______

13 ______

14 ______

15 ______

18 ______

19 ______

20 ______

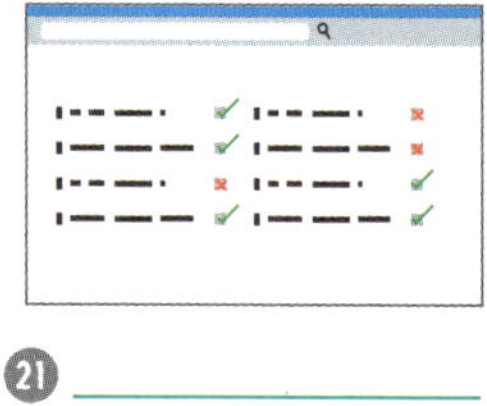
21 ______

4 ______

5 ______

10 ______

11 ______

16 ______

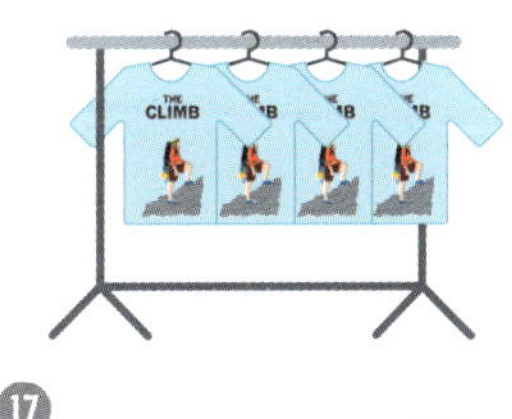

17 ______

22 ______

23 ______

advertising agency slogan / tagline

copywriter online survey leaflet / flyer

door-to-door sales logo brand

radio advertising promote

merchandise poster consumer

television advertising sales pitch

~~direct mail~~ billboard word of mouth

free sample coupons

unique selling point / USP sponsor

market research social media

17 Marketing a product

You can use a variety of adjectives and adverbs to describe the key features when marketing a product or service. Not all adjectives can be modified in the same way.

New language Adjectives and adverbs
Vocabulary Descriptive adjectives
New skill Modifying descriptions of products

17.1 WRITE THE WORDS FROM THE PANEL IN THE CORRECT GROUPS

EXTREME	ABSOLUTE	CLASSIFYING
enormous	*true*	*metal*

electronic terrible wrong brilliant furious ~~enormous~~ scientific woolen perfect fascinating equal ~~true~~ impossible industrial exhausted organic ~~metal~~ unique empty rural awful

17.2 MARK THE SENTENCES THAT ARE CORRECT

The test was absolutely impossible. ☑
The test was fairly impossible. ☐

1. The factory was totally destroyed. ☐
   The factory was very destroyed. ☐
2. I was thoroughly tired this morning. ☐
   I was thoroughly exhausted this morning. ☐
3. The warehouse is almost empty. ☐
   The warehouse is very empty. ☐
4. Jon is an absolutely good speaker. ☐
   Jon is an extremely good speaker. ☐
5. Peter is nearly good at Spanish. ☐
   Peter is fairly good at Spanish. ☐
6. The project is largely complete. ☐
   The project is very complete. ☐
7. Sian is a fairly brilliant swimmer. ☐
   Sian is an utterly brilliant swimmer. ☐

17.3 RESPOND OUT LOUD TO THE AUDIO, FILLING IN THE GAPS USING THE WORDS IN THE PANEL

Where are most of our products sold?

Our customer base is ___largely___ Chinese.

1. Are you certain you sent the report?

   ______________ certain. I think I sent it yesterday.

2. Our new product range is really good!

   Yeah, it's absolutely ______________ . I love it.

3. Did you like Claude's presentation?

   It was very impressive, but ______________ identical to mine!

4. I've never seen a watch like yours before!

   Yes, it's totally ______________ . I have the only one.

5. Our new manager seems very popular.

   That's right. ______________ everyone likes him.

6. Did you enjoy the movie?

   No. It was ______________ awful. I almost fell asleep.

7. How was the event?

   It was practically ______________ . There were only a few people there.

fantastic | Nearly | almost | ~~largely~~ | unique | absolutely | empty | Fairly

17.4 LISTEN TO THE AUDIO AND ANSWER THE QUESTIONS

Huong, the manager of a clothing brand, is being interviewed by Philippa, a journalist.

The employees at Huong's company are...
fairly confident. ☐
pretty happy. ☑
completely miserable. ☐

1 Philippa thought the press release was...
absolutely fantastic. ☐
fairly interesting. ☐
totally ridiculous. ☐

2 Philippa says that Huong's idea is...
utterly ordinary. ☐
largely unoriginal. ☐
utterly original. ☐

3 Huong says that jogging during the day is...
almost impossible. ☐
always possible. ☐
absolutely plausible. ☐

4 Huong says that during the day, people are...
very busy. ☐
absolutely exhausted. ☐
extremely bored. ☐

5 According to Huong, exercise is...
utterly essential. ☐
pretty important. ☐
extremely important. ☐

6 Huong developed a line that was...
very expensive. ☐
totally organic. ☐
completely new. ☐

7 The stickers on the "NightJogging" line are...
highly reflective. ☐
wholly metallic. ☐
pretty unusual. ☐

8 To begin with, promoting the line was...
pretty difficult. ☐
practically impossible. ☐
extremely easy. ☐

9 Since a sports star offered support, it has been...
absolutely amazing. ☐
absolutely exhausting. ☐
completely perfect. ☐

10 Philippa thinks the idea is...
pretty confusing. ☐
really complicated. ☐
really clever. ☐

11 Huong thinks that launching in China is...
thoroughly impractical. ☐
fairly certain. ☐
extremely unlikely. ☐

18 Advertising and branding

When you want to tell people about your company, product, or brand, intensifiers like "enough," "too," "so," and "such" can help communicate your point.

New language Intensifiers
Aa Vocabulary "Enough," "too," "so," and "such"
New skill Adding emphasis to descriptions

18.1 LISTEN TO THE AUDIO AND MARK WHICH THINGS ARE DESCRIBED

1 

2 

3 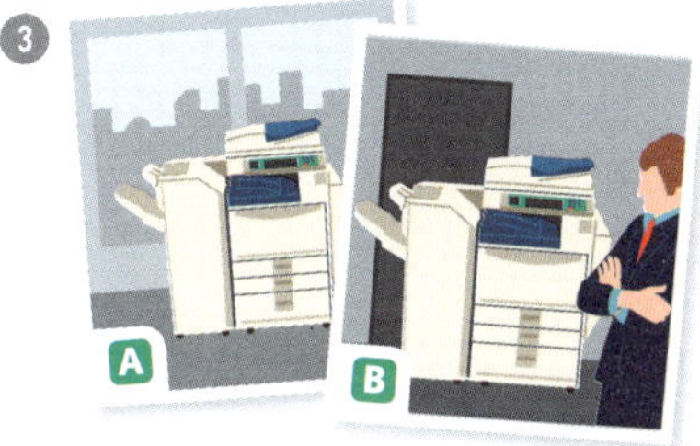

4 

5 

18.2 FILL IN THE GAPS WITH "SO" OR "SUCH"

 I work with *such* interesting people.

1  There was ______ a large crowd outside.

2  The results were ______ disappointing.

3  We've had ______ a fantastic year.

4  The price for the hotel was ______ high.

5  The week seems to pass ______ slowly.

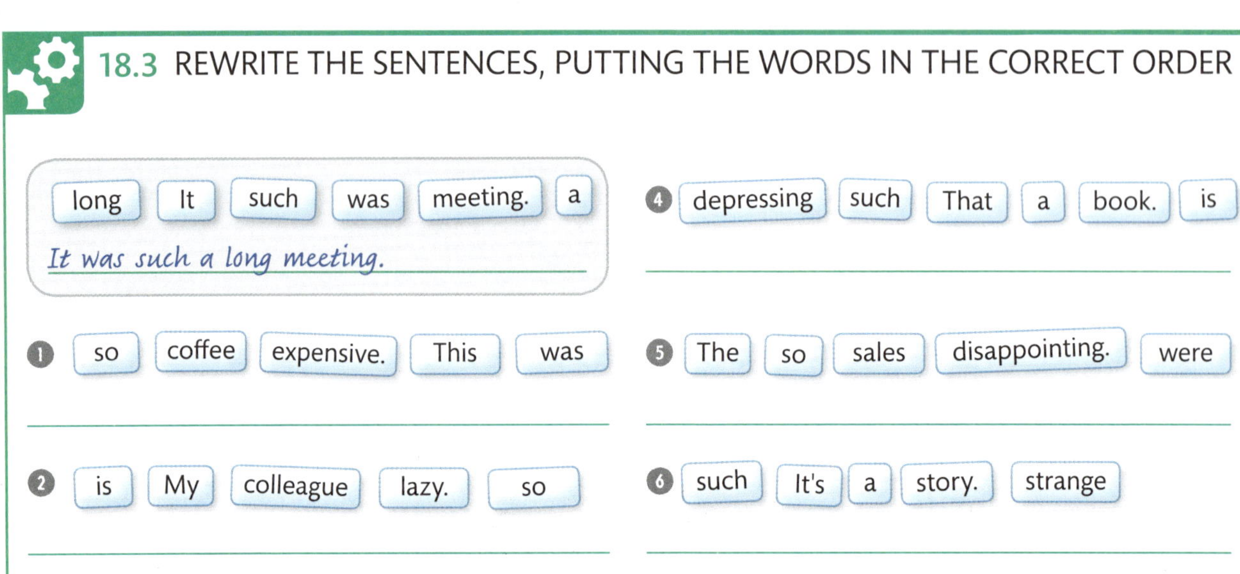

18.3 REWRITE THE SENTENCES, PUTTING THE WORDS IN THE CORRECT ORDER

long | It | such | was | meeting. | a

It was such a long meeting.

1. so | coffee | expensive. | This | was

2. is | My | colleague | lazy. | so

3. so | Clara's | was | interesting. | presentation

4. depressing | such | That | a | book. | is

5. The | so | sales | disappointing. | were

6. such | It's | a | story. | strange

7. on | It's | to | important | time. | so | be

18.4 READ THE ARTICLE AND ANSWER THE QUESTIONS

The ad is for an athletics club.
True ☐ False ☑ Not given ☐

1. Gym members receive a free T-shirt.
True ☐ False ☐ Not given ☐

2. Most adults think they don't get enough exercise.
True ☐ False ☐ Not given ☐

3. The gym offers a flexible timetable.
True ☐ False ☐ Not given ☐

4. Most people think they don't swim well enough.
True ☐ False ☐ Not given ☐

5. The gym offers swimming lessons for children.
True ☐ False ☐ Not given ☐

WELLNESS AND LIFESTYLE

Fellingdon Health & Sport

Feeling tired? Feeling low? Summer is here, and it's time for you to get fit, get healthy, and feel totally amazing with a free one-day pass to our gym and swimming pool in central Fellingdon.

In a recent survey 75 percent of adults said that they either don't get enough exercise, are too busy, or think that a gym would be too expensive. But our gym is affordable, and our timetable is flexible enough to fit the busiest schedule. And for those 23 percent of people who think they don't swim well enough, we offer training and expert advice. Get in touch now for a free quote!

18.5 CROSS OUT THE INCORRECT WORD IN EACH SENTENCE, THEN SAY THE SENTENCES OUT LOUD

I'd never seen ~~so~~ / such a big number of customers in the store before.

1. Our senior managers think the price of our products is enough / too high.
2. This room won't be big enough / too for this afternoon's meeting.
3. The team is such / so excited about tonight's awards ceremony.
4. I thought today's meeting was such / so a waste of time.
5. Jim doesn't speak loudly enough / too. I can barely hear him.
6. Our IT system is enough / so old. It's time we invested in a new one.
7. The new intern works so / such slowly. She prefers talking on the phone.
8. Our products were so / too expensive to appeal to middle-market customers.
9. Mary is such / so an ambitious woman. She wants to be a CEO by the age of 30.
10. You shouldn't drive enough / too quickly when you're in this part of town.
11. The strikes have caused such / enough a problem for our employees who commute.
12. The marketing campaign was so / too boring to appeal to young people.

19 Advice and suggestions

English uses modal verbs such as "could," "should," and "must" for advice or suggestions. They can be used to help co-workers in difficult or stressful situations.

New language Modal verbs for advice
Aa Vocabulary Workplace pressures
New skill Giving advice

19.1 MATCH THE SITUATIONS TO THE CORRECT ADVICE

I earn less than most of my colleagues. → You ought to ask for a raise.

1. I have no energy and am tired of my job.
2. I find the new IT system very confusing.
3. I'm feeling sleepy.
4. Peter hasn't answered any of my emails.
5. We don't have much coffee left.

- You shouldn't work so hard.
- You should get some fresh air.
- You ought to ask for a raise.
- You should order some more.
- You could do a training course.
- You must give him a call.

19.2 CROSS OUT THE INCORRECT WORDS IN EACH SENTENCE

You really **shouldn't** / ~~ought~~ eat your lunch in front of your computer.

1.  You **could** / **shouldn't** try delegating the task to your team. I'm sure they'd do a great job.
2.  Greg **ought to** / **ought** apologize to his team for his behavior. He was very rude.
3.  Antonio really **ought to** / **shouldn't** employ some new staff, or we'll never meet our deadline.
4.  We **should** / **should to** organize a training course for the interns.
5.  The secretary really **should** / **couldn't** ask her boss for a raise. She works very hard.

19.3 FILL IN THE GAPS USING THE PHRASES IN THE PANEL

Cath *should move* if she lives too far from the office.

1. You ______ to work if the train is canceled.
2. You ______ the IT desk about your new password.
3. You ______ your lunch at your desk. Go to a café instead.
4. You ______ your manager when you want to book time off.
5. Clare ______ a break if she's tired of her job.
6. You ______ an English course if you want to learn English.
7. Dave ______ home if he's not feeling well.
8. Pete ______ to the public about company secrets.

could do
must tell
~~should move~~
ought to call
shouldn't eat
ought to go
shouldn't talk
should walk
ought to take

19.4 READ THE EMAIL AND MARK THE CORRECT SUMMARY

1. Vikram strongly advises Clara to make a list of her most important tasks. He suggests she might take a break from work for a week. ☐
2. Vikram says Clara must delegate her tasks to her team, and suggests she might ask another manager to help her complete her work. ☐
3. Vikram strongly advises Clara to list all her duties, and suggests she might ask a team member to complete half her work. ☐
4. Vikram strongly advises Clara to make a list of all her tasks, and suggests that she might ask her clients for more time. ☐

To: Clara McMillan

Subject: Re: Workload

Hi Clara,

Thanks for your email. I hope you're not finding the new position too stressful. Here's some advice that should help you to deal with your workload.

Firstly, you must make a list of all your duties and tasks, so you have a clear idea of what you have to do. You shouldn't try to do everything yourself. You could definitely delegate more work to your team. I also think you ought to ask the client for more time to finish the project.

Remember that you shouldn't worry too much! This situation is quite typical for new employees here.

Best regards,

Vikram

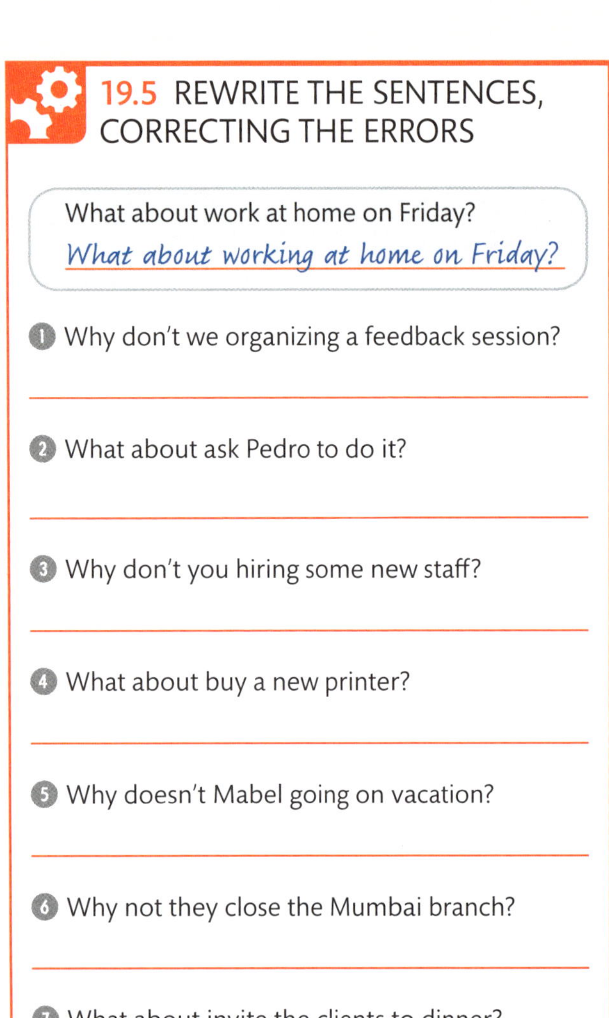

19.5 REWRITE THE SENTENCES, CORRECTING THE ERRORS

What about work at home on Friday?
What about working at home on Friday?

1. Why don't we organizing a feedback session?
2. What about ask Pedro to do it?
3. Why don't you hiring some new staff?
4. What about buy a new printer?
5. Why doesn't Mabel going on vacation?
6. Why not they close the Mumbai branch?
7. What about invite the clients to dinner?

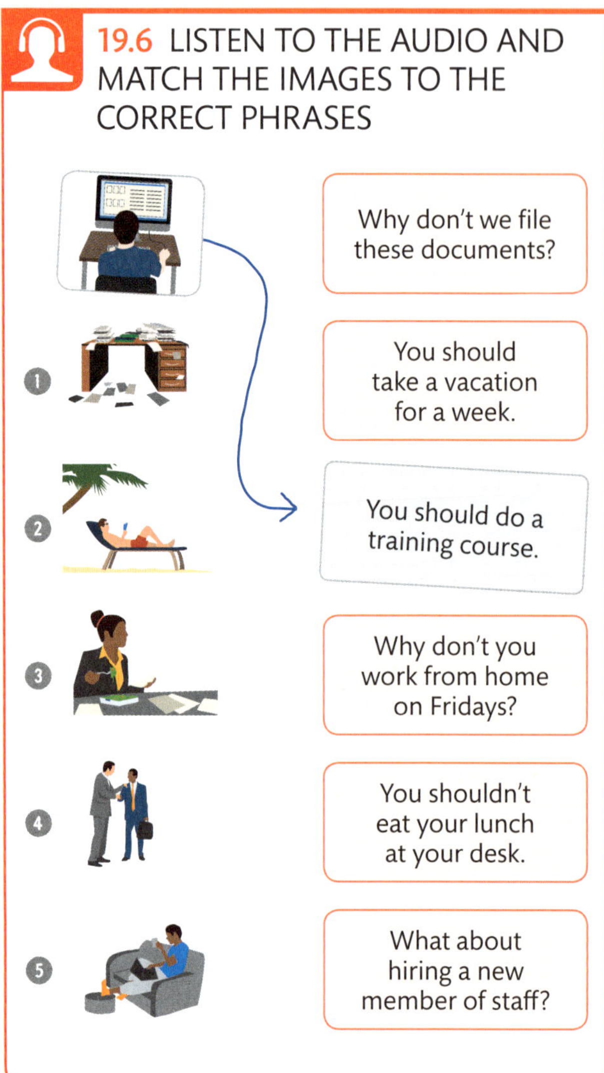

19.6 LISTEN TO THE AUDIO AND MATCH THE IMAGES TO THE CORRECT PHRASES

Why don't we file these documents?

You should take a vacation for a week.

You should do a training course.

Why don't you work from home on Fridays?

You shouldn't eat your lunch at your desk.

What about hiring a new member of staff?

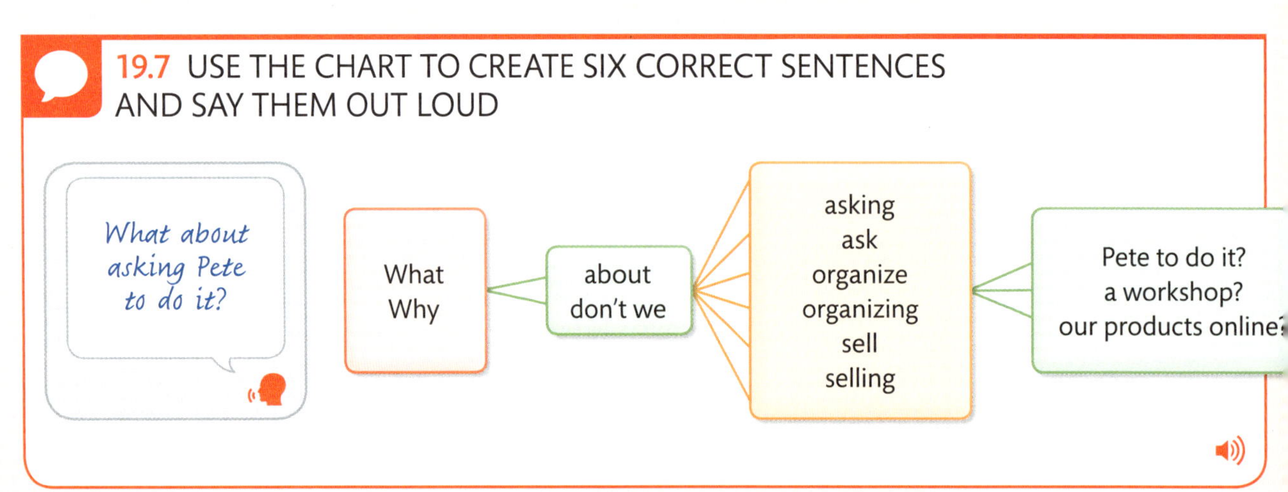

19.7 USE THE CHART TO CREATE SIX CORRECT SENTENCES AND SAY THEM OUT LOUD

What about asking Pete to do it?

What Why	about don't we	asking ask organize organizing sell selling	Pete to do it? a workshop? our products online?

19.8 MARK THE SENTENCES THAT ARE CORRECT

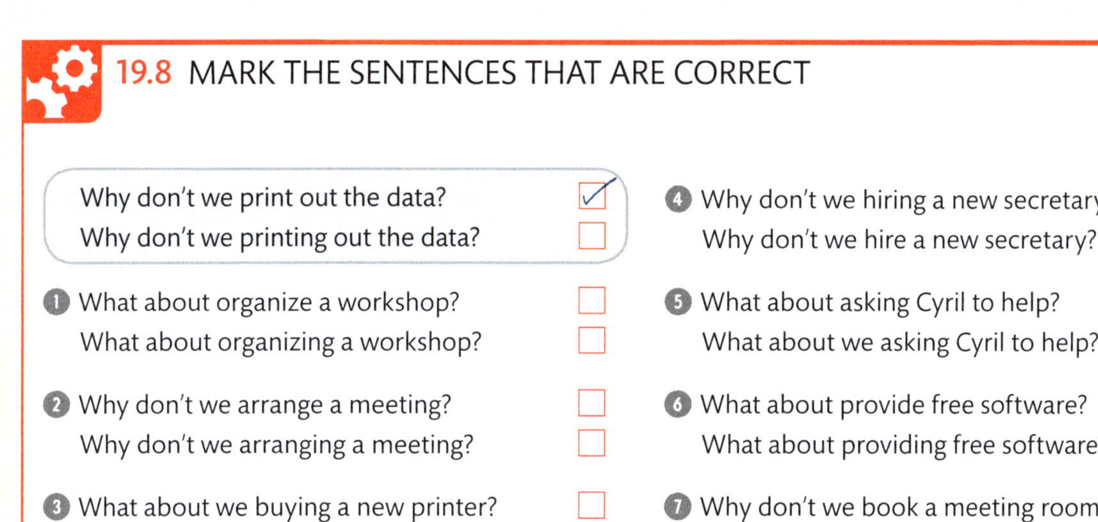

Why don't we print out the data? ☑
Why don't we printing out the data? ☐

1. What about organize a workshop? ☐
   What about organizing a workshop? ☐
2. Why don't we arrange a meeting? ☐
   Why don't we arranging a meeting? ☐
3. What about we buying a new printer? ☐
   What about buying a new printer? ☐
4. Why don't we hiring a new secretary? ☐
   Why don't we hire a new secretary? ☐
5. What about asking Cyril to help? ☐
   What about we asking Cyril to help? ☐
6. What about provide free software? ☐
   What about providing free software? ☐
7. Why don't we book a meeting room? ☐
   Why we don't book a meeting room? ☐

19.9 REWRITE THE SENTENCES, PUTTING THE WORDS IN THE CORRECT ORDER

so | on | You | the | work | weekend. | shouldn't | hard

You shouldn't work so hard on the weekend.

1. ask | You | to | the | for | clients | time. | ought | more

2. your | talking | to | about | co-workers | problems? | How | your | about

3. next | new | year. | We | interns | some | could | hire

4. don't | quit | you | like | you | job | don't | if | it? | your | Why

5. the | complete | deadline. | the | project | should | You | before

20 Vocabulary

Aa 20.1 **MANAGEMENT AND LEADERSHIP** WRITE THE PHRASES FROM THE PANEL UNDER THE CORRECT DEFINITIONS

To give a task to somebody

to allocate a task

1 Money added to a person's wages as a reward for good performance

____

4 To give work or tasks to a person in a position junior to you

____

5 How well a person carries out tasks

____

Aa 20.2 **SKILLS AND ABILITIES** WRITE THE PHRASES FROM THE PANEL UNDER THE CORRECT PICTURES

initiative

1 __________

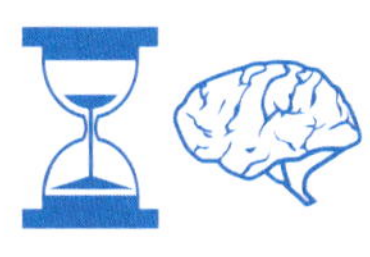

2 __________

3 __________

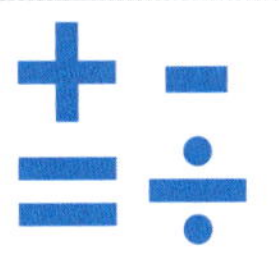

6 __________

7 __________

8 __________

9 __________

12 __________

13 __________

14 __________

15 __________

2 An interview to discuss an employee's performance

3 To officially confirm something meets the required standards

6 To be given a more senior position within a company

to delegate
to approve
to be promoted
an appraisal / a performance review
performance
a bonus
~~to allocate a task~~

4 ______

5 ______

10 ______

11 ______

16 ______

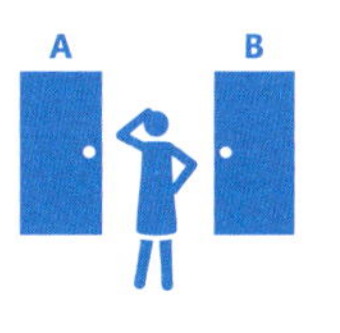

17 ______

IT / computing
written communication
data analysis
research
able to drive
fast learner
~~initiative~~
teamwork
work well under pressure
organization
decision-making
numeracy
public speaking
problem-solving
leadership
telephone manner
attention to detail
time management

21 Talking about abilities

To talk about people's skills, for example in a performance review, you can use various modal verbs to express present, past, and future ability.

New language Modal verbs for abilities
Aa Vocabulary Workplace skills
New skill Describing abilities

21.1 FILL IN THE GAPS USING "CAN" OR "CAN'T"

Jenny has great people skills. She ___can___ talk to all sorts of people.

1. Tom ______ fix your car this afternoon. It will be ready at 5:00.
2. Karl ______ drive. He failed his driving test again.
3. Jon used to be really nervous, but now he ______ give presentations.
4. She ______ type really quickly. She types over 60 words per minute.
5. I ______ work the new photocopier. It's too difficult.
6. Hansa is a really good cook. She ______ cook really nice Indian food.
7. Ali ______ read my handwriting. He says it's really messy.
8. Ania ______ speak French. She learned it in college.
9. Petra ______ manage her staff any more. They do what they like.
10. Parvesh ______ write clear reports. They are easy to read.

21.2 LISTEN TO THE AUDIO AND MARK WHETHER EACH PICTURE SHOWS PRESENT OR PAST ABILITY

21.3 REWRITE THE SENTENCES, CORRECTING THE ERRORS

George can't understand the old CEO because she had a strong accent.
George couldn't understand the old CEO because she had a strong accent.

1. Janice can tell me if sales are up until she gets the final reports in.

2. Phil loves meeting new people, so he can't work in the HR department.

3. Saira can't type fast, but now she can type 60 words a minute.

4. Ed can't write reports very well. I'm going to ask him to help me write mine.

5. Keira could use the database, but now she trains people in how to use it.

6. For years Alex can't speak Arabic, but now he has done a beginners' course.

21.4 READ THE PERFORMANCE REVIEW AND ANSWER THE QUESTIONS

Matt has worked at Pietro's for five years.
True ☐ False ☑ Not given ☐

1. Matt has made little progress in his time at Pietro's.
True ☐ False ☐ Not given ☐

2. He was a confident assistant chef.
True ☐ False ☐ Not given ☐

3. He particularly enjoys cooking Italian food.
True ☐ False ☐ Not given ☐

4. Matt has worked as head chef for four years.
True ☐ False ☐ Not given ☐

5. He can create exciting menus.
True ☐ False ☐ Not given ☐

6. He could be an excellent trainer of young chefs.
True ☐ False ☐ Not given ☐

Matt has worked for Pietro's for four years and has made good progress in that time. He joined us as an assistant chef and was rather unconfident in his cooking abilities then.

He didn't feel he could reach the standards required of a professional kitchen, but soon showed he was a very competent chef.

He was promoted two years ago to the position of head chef after proving he can create interesting and exciting menus with new dishes. His manager and I think he could be an excellent trainer of young chefs. We believe he would make a great mentor to talented young chefs.

21.5 MATCH THE PAIRS OF SENTENCES

Carrie is a great team member. → She would work well in any team.	She could train staff to do them.
1. Jim is quite shy.	He could be head of the department.
2. Clare couldn't manage her old team.	She would work well in any team.
3. Carl is more confident now.	She can manage her new team much better.
4. Bea is good at giving presentations.	She wouldn't be a good trainer.
5. Jola is very impatient.	Before, he wouldn't talk in public.
6. Sam is very talented.	He would do well in a smaller team.

21.6 MARK THE SENTENCES THAT ARE CORRECT

You're an excellent team member and you would do well on the sales team. ☑
You're an excellent team member and you can't do well on the sales team. ☐

1. David has given his team excellent training. Now they can't do anything. ☐
   David has given his team excellent training. Now they can do anything. ☐

2. Have you seen his brilliant designs? He can create our banners. ☐
   Have you seen his brilliant designs? He couldn't create our banners. ☐

3. No one couldn't read the boss's handwriting. It was terrible. ☐
   No one could read the boss's handwriting. It was terrible. ☐

4. Sebastian is a very proactive person and would do well in marketing. ☐
   Sebastian is a very proactive person and couldn't do well in marketing. ☐

21.7 CROSS OUT THE INCORRECT WORD IN EACH SENTENCE, THEN SAY THE SENTENCES OUT LOUD

If Jorge keeps on working hard, he ~~would~~ / **could** be area manager one day.

1. We think you are very talented and **would** / **couldn't** be a great addition to our department.

2. I don't know what is wrong with the coffee machine. I **can** / **can't** get it working.

3. My confidence is much better now. Before, I **couldn't** / **could** give presentations.

4. Laila couldn't negotiate with her old boss, but she **can't** / **can** with her new boss.

22 Comparing and contrasting

In team discussions, discourse markers can ease the flow of conversation. They can help link similar or contrasting ideas, or connect an action to a result.

New language Discourse markers
Aa Vocabulary Teamwork and team building
New skill Expressing your ideas

22.1 CROSS OUT THE INCORRECT WORDS IN EACH SENTENCE

Team A enjoyed the task a lot. Team B found it very rewarding as well / ~~however~~.

1  This training is really interesting. It is a lot of fun, also / too.

2  Team-building days are useful. They are also / too fun.

3  Some people always wash their coffee cups, while / as well others don't.

4  However / Although Team A did the task quickly, Team B didn't finish it.

5  Team A built the bridge very quickly. Team B was as well / equally successful.

6  Team A helped each other, while / as well Team B disagreed with each other.

7  Hard work is an excellent trait in a team, equally / whereas laziness is terrible.

8  Yesterday's training was useful. However / Although, this morning's task was pointless.

9  Some people want to lead a team, as well / while others are happy to be team members.

10  It is important to say what we all think. We should listen to each other as well / equally.

11  This training is very useful. It is equally / as well a good way to get to know people.

22.2 MARK THE SENTENCES THAT ARE CORRECT

We learned a lot from that training session, whereas it was a lot of fun. ☐
We learned a lot from that training session. It was a lot of fun, too. ☑

1. However, Sam went to the training day, he didn't learn anything new. ☐
   Although Sam went to the training day, he didn't learn anything new. ☐

2. Team A solved the problem really quickly. Team B was equally successful. ☐
   Team A solved the problem really quickly. Team B was as well successful. ☐

3. This training is useful for managers. It is too useful for team members. ☐
   This training is useful for managers. It is also useful for team members. ☐

4. Some people want to be managers, while others want to be team members. ☐
   Some people want to be managers, as well others want to be team members. ☐

5. Laziness is a terrible trait for a team member, whereas honesty is excellent. ☐
   Laziness is a terrible trait for a team member, also honesty is excellent. ☐

6. We'd like all staff to follow our usual dress code for the training. Please be on time, however. ☐
   We'd like all staff to follow our usual dress code for the training. Please be on time, too. ☐

22.3 LISTEN TO THE AUDIO, THEN NUMBER THE SENTENCES IN THE ORDER THAT YOU HEAR THEM

A team leader is giving feedback on her team's performance in a task.

A. Team A was the first to complete the task. ☐
B. This was a very challenging task. 1
C. Creative thinking can be equally useful. ☐
D. It is important to read instructions carefully. ☐
E. However, Team B worked well together, too. ☐
F. We hope you also found it very rewarding. ☐

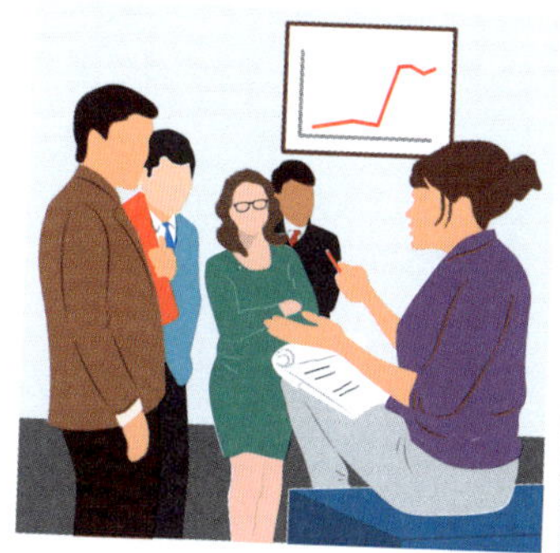

22.4 REWRITE THE SENTENCES, PUTTING THE WORDS IN THE CORRECT ORDER

people | in | Some | prefer | while | team, | others | working | enjoy | alone. | a | working

Some people enjoy working in a team, while others prefer working alone.

1. was | The | and | it | useful | lot | task | also | of | was | team-building | fun. | a

2. to | pizza. | had | Team A | a | build | make | had | a | Team B | bridge, | whereas | to

3. some | had | the | Team B | completed | While | task | problems. | first, | they

4. often | as well. | really | they | are | courses | and | fun | are | Training | useful

5. was | Team A | cooperative. | equally | together | Team B | worked | as | well. | very

6. identify | This | your | task | weaknesses, | also | strengths. | will | your | but

7. a | team | However, | didn't | cake. | the | activity | baked | matter. | Our

8. worked | other | Although | we | came | first, | together. | the | team | well

9. easy, | today's | Yesterday's | difficult. | more | task | was | task | was | while

10. the | finished | its | took | Team A | whereas | task | time. | quickly, | Team B

22.5 MATCH THE PAIRS OF SENTENCES

The team worked well together. → As a result, they completed the task.

1. The course taught me how to manage people.
2. Team Orange completed the challenge first.
3. I'd never driven a forklift truck before.
4. The training days are useful.
5. Jess learned a lot from the training.

- Consequently, they all won a medal.
- As a result, everyone attends them.
- As a result, they completed the task.
- Consequently, she was promoted last week.
- As a consequence, I am now a team leader.
- For this reason, I was very nervous.

22.6 SAY THE SENTENCES OUT LOUD, FILLING IN THE GAPS USING THE WORDS IN THE PANEL

The task taught us how to run a team. As a *result*, I now lead a team of ten.

1. Team-building days are great for morale. ________, the atmosphere in our office is good.
2. We have regular IT training sessions. For this ________, everyone has good computer skills.
3. We do team building every year. As a ________, we work really well together.
4. During team building we meet new staff. ________ reason, we know our co-workers well.

For this | consequence | Consequently | ~~result~~ | reason

23 Planning events

Many English verbs that are used to give opinions or talk about plans, intentions, and arrangements are followed by a gerund or an infinitive.

New language Verb patterns
Aa Vocabulary Corporate entertainment
New skill Talking about business events

23.1 CROSS OUT THE INCORRECT WORDS IN EACH SENTENCE

We must keep ~~to remind~~ / reminding customers of our new product range.

1. We plan to launch / launching our new product range at the conference.
2. Would you consider to organize / organizing the accommodation for the visitors?
3. I really enjoy to take / taking clients out for dinner at famous restaurants.
4. Jenny has offered to meet / meeting our visitors at the airport.
5. I keep to suggest / suggesting that we should have a staff training session.

23.2 REWRITE THE SENTENCES, CORRECTING THE ERRORS

I really enjoy to give presentations.
I really enjoy giving presentations.

1. Our clients expect receive good customer service.

2. Would you consider to make the name badges for the delegates?

3. Colin has offered organizing the training program for the new staff.

4. I hope impressing our clients when I show them around the new office.

23.3 READ THE ARTICLE AND ANSWER THE QUESTIONS

CORPORATE EVENTS

RED GIRAFFE EVENTS PLANNING

How we can plan the ideal event for your company

Kayaking is one of the team-building events that Red Giraffe will offer soon.

Red Giraffe is an international events management business. We are one of the biggest events organizers in the US, and our clients range from start-up businesses to large corporations. We enjoy all aspects of the job, but the most enjoyable is entertaining clients. Our clients expect to receive excellent service and we pride ourselves on meeting their every requirement. We often take clients out for lunch during the planning phase to talk about their requirements. It's good to do this over a meal as they say what they really want when they are relaxed and enjoying the food.

After lunch, we have a brainstorming session in groups. When all the clients have arrived, we serve coffee as it helps to get the ideas flowing. All kinds of things come up in these sessions. For instance, when we planned a launch for a media company, the employees kept saying we should have a boat trip on the river. But some people didn't like this idea because their competitors had done the same, so we went for a covered venue in a converted warehouse. Next year, we plan to start offering team-building events, such as sports days and treasure hunts. We expect these to be very popular with our clients.

What clients does Red Giraffe work with?
- **Small start-up businesses** ☐
- **Only big corporate clients** ☐
- **All sizes of business** ☑

1. What do the company's employees enjoy?
   - **Entertaining clients** ☐
   - **Organizing refreshments** ☐
   - **Having great accommodation** ☐

2. What do the company's clients expect?
   - **To have a free lunch** ☐
   - **To receive good customer service** ☐
   - **To eat a planned dinner** ☐

3. Why should you go out for a meal with clients?
   - **They like eating great food** ☐
   - **They like talking about the food** ☐
   - **They give their honest opinion** ☐

4. Why didn't one client want to have a boat trip?
   - **They wanted an outdoor venue** ☐
   - **Their competitors had had one** ☐
   - **Their CEO didn't like boats** ☐

5. What does Red Giraffe plan to do next year?
   - **Offer team-building events** ☐
   - **Go on a treasure hunt** ☐
   - **Become popular with clients** ☐

23.4 FILL IN THE GAPS USING THE WORDS IN THE PANEL

Did you remember ___to call___ the hotel about the catering?

1. I regret ______________ you that I can't take the clients out for dinner. I'm very sorry.
2. Do you remember ______________ Dan last month? He has a question about a discount you offered.
3. Sue stopped ______________ the program for the launch event. It looked really interesting!
4. He regrets ______________ her his idea for the event because she copied it.
5. David gave his presentation, and went on ______________ about new events.
6. I stopped ______________ my presentation because the CEO had a question.

to talk	giving	telling	calling	to read	~~to call~~	to tell

23.5 LISTEN TO THE AUDIO, THEN NUMBER THE PICTURES IN THE ORDER THEY ARE DESCRIBED

A ☐

B [1]

C ☐

D ☐

E ☐

F ☐

G ☐

H ☐

23.6 REWRITE THE SENTENCES, PUTTING THE WORDS IN THE CORRECT ORDER

visitors | at | has | the | to | our | offered | airport. | Kelly | meet

Kelly has offered to meet our visitors at the airport.

1. entertaining | I | clients. | enjoy | really | new

2. invited | the | Sandra | overseas | to | conference. | me | sales | attend

3. book | My | the | asked | to | accommodation. | manager | me

4. him | Tom | manager | a | soon. | expects | promotion | his | to | give

5. me | recent | My | to | give | sales. | him | asked | an | on | boss | update

6. our | come | We | to | all | to | party. | invited | customers | our

23.7 USE THE CHART TO CREATE 16 CORRECT SENTENCES AND SAY THEM OUT LOUD

I enjoy entertaining our clients.

I	enjoy	entertaining	our clients.
She	remembered	to meet	accommodation.
We	enjoys	to book	
They			

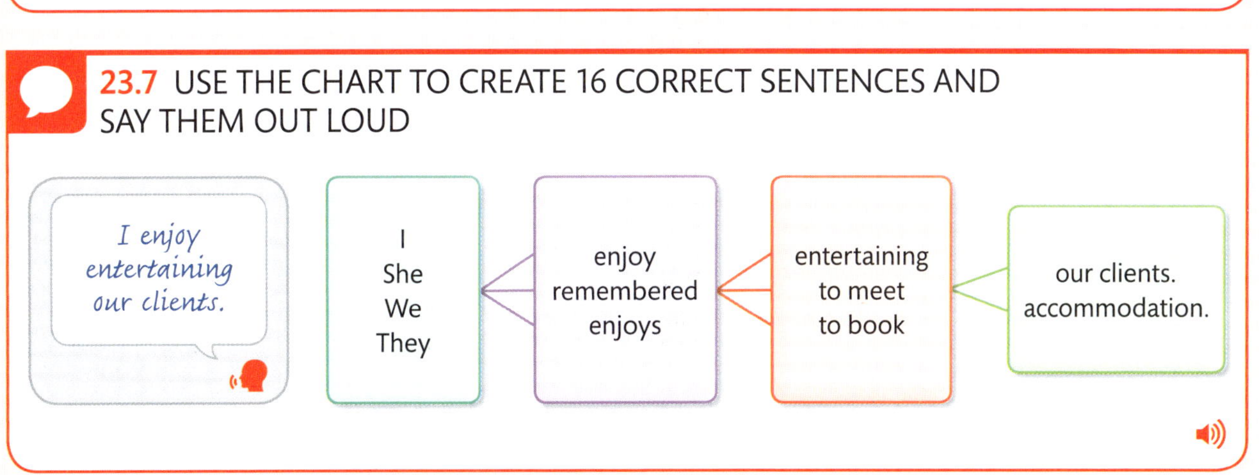

24 Vocabulary

Aa 24.1 MEETINGS WRITE THE PHRASES FROM THE PANEL UNDER THE CORRECT DEFINITIONS

To conclude

to sum up

❶ To write a record of what was said during a meeting

❸ To answer questions

❹ To be not present

❻ To have no more time left to do something

❼ A plan for achieving a particular goal

❾ Proposals for specific action to be taken

❿ To present information to a group of people

⓬ To say something before someone else has finished speaking

⓭ People who have been to or are going to a meeting

⓯ When everyone agrees

⓰ To look again at the written record of a past meeting

2 To consider or focus on something

5 To come to an agreement about an issue

8 The primary aim

11 To send a plan for what will be discussed

14 To put forward an idea or plan for others to discuss

17 A vote made by raising hands in the air to show agreement

a show of hands — attendees — action points — to give a presentation — to take minutes — to suggest / propose — to send out an agenda — to look at — ~~to sum up~~ — to review the minutes — main objective — to interrupt — to be absent — unanimous agreement — a strategy — to reach a consensus — to run out of time — to take questions

25 What people said

When telling co-workers what someone else said, you can take what they said (direct speech) and rephrase it accurately and clearly. This is called reported speech.

New language Reported speech
Aa Vocabulary Meetings
New skill Reporting what someone said

25.1 MATCH THE DIRECT SPEECH TO THE REPORTED SPEECH

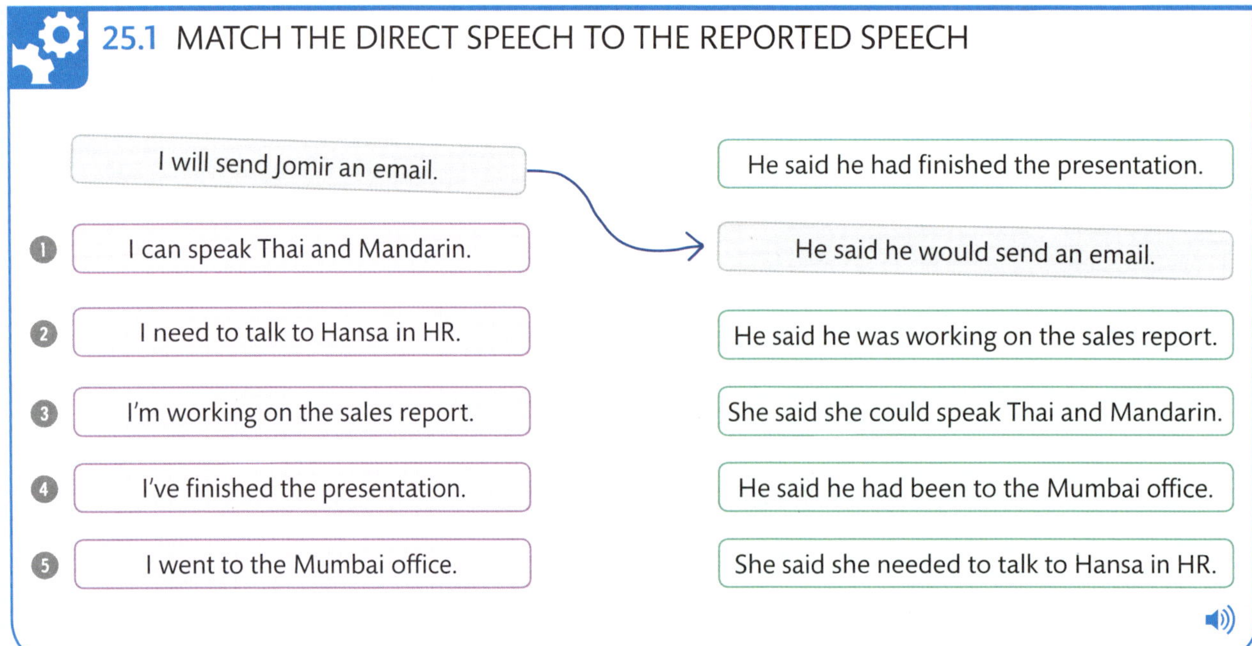

25.2 REWRITE THE SENTENCES AS REPORTED SPEECH USING "SAID"

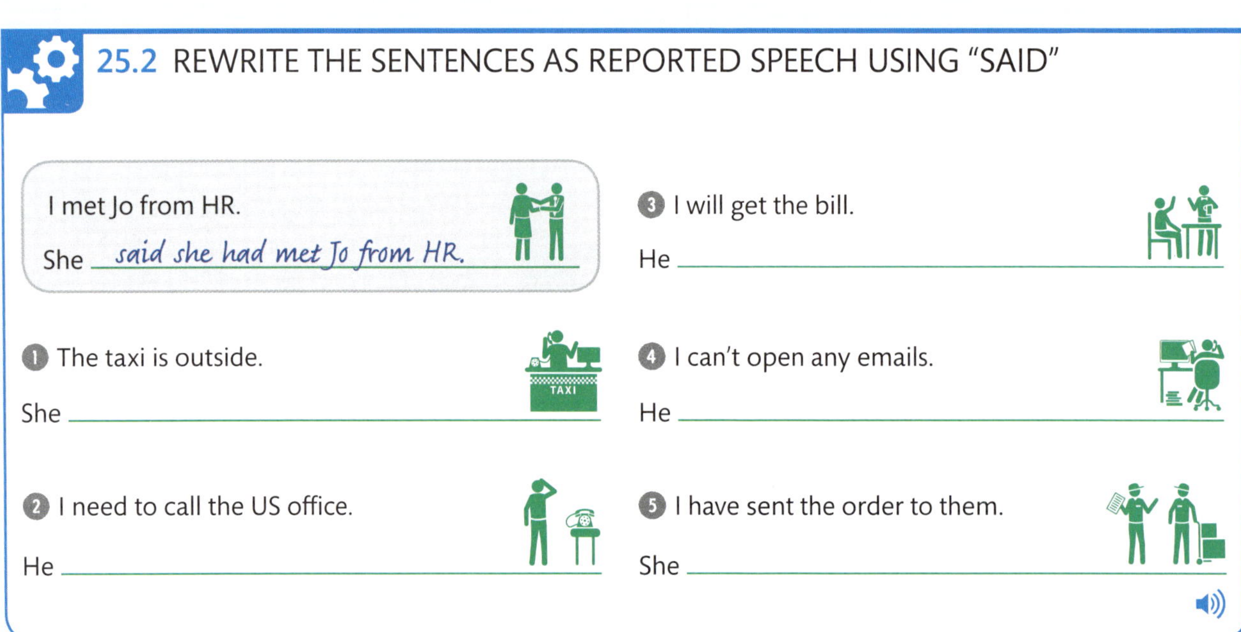

25.3 REWRITE THE SENTENCES, PUTTING THE WORDS IN THE CORRECT ORDER

said | He | figures! | couldn't | those | believe | he

He said he couldn't believe those figures!

1. busy | she | that | was | She | afternoon. | said

2. his | like | He | that | he | didn't | boss. | said | new

3. received | said | hadn't | the | they | delivery. | They

4. was | He | to | in | week. | Tokyo | that | going | said | be | he

5. to | new | had | product | They | been | the | said | launch. | they

6. invoice | She | away. | right | would | she | an | said | issue

7. give | company | said | 5 percent | the | could | discount. | a | He

8. said | she | the | had | well | gotten | interviewer. | along | She | with

9. said | They | were | they | range. | a | new | designing

25.4 LISTEN TO THE AUDIO, THEN NUMBER THE REPORTED SENTENCES IN THE ORDER YOU HEAR THEM AS DIRECT SPEECH

Suzanne is talking to a co-worker throughout the day.

- **A** Suzanne said she'd send him the report the following day. ☐
- **B** Suzanne said she had met the new CEO in the Miami office that week. [1]
- **C** Suzanne said her laptop wasn't working that day. ☐
- **D** Suzanne said she could help Alemay prepare her presentation that afternoon. ☐
- **E** Suzanne said she had come into work early that morning. ☐
- **F** Suzanne said she had to stay late and call the Mexico office that evening. ☐
- **G** Suzanne said she was going to design a new app with Tim the week after. ☐

25.5 CROSS OUT THE INCORRECT WORDS IN EACH SENTENCE

Jake ~~told~~ / said that he wanted a promotion before the end of the year.

1. He said / told me that he'd been to China twice.

2. She suggested / said that she was going to Montreal.

3. He promised / told that he wouldn't be late for the train.

4. He explained / promised that he didn't know how to use the photocopier.

5. He denied / told that he had broken the coffee machine.

6. She promised / complained that the food was cold when the waiter brought it.

7. He confirmed / announced that the tickets had been booked.

25.6 REPORT THE DIRECT SPEECH IN THE AUDIO OUT LOUD, FILLING IN THE GAPS USING THE WORDS IN THE PANEL

I am not the person in charge of this project.

He *denied* that he was the person in charge of that project.

1. I'll definitely call you back after 2:30 this afternoon.

   She ____________ to call me back after 2:30 that afternoon.

2. I need a printout, and I will also need a copy of Simon's report about the year-end accounts.

   He ____________ that he needed a copy of Simon's report about the year-end accounts.

3. The new all-in-one printer isn't difficult to use.

   She ____________ that the new all-in-one printer wasn't difficult to use.

4. Yes, that's right. I'd like to buy 100 units of the new product.

   He ____________ that he'd like to buy 100 units of the new product.

5. I'm not happy with the customer service I have experienced.

   He ____________ that he wasn't happy with the customer service he had experienced.

6. How about asking Ameera what she thinks?

   She ____________ that we should ask Ameera what she thought.

explained | promised | suggested | complained | added | ~~denied~~ | confirmed

26 What people asked

You can use reported questions to tell someone what someone else has asked. Direct questions and reported questions have different word orders.

New language Reported questions
Aa Vocabulary "Have," "make," "get," "do"
New skill Reporting what someone asked

26.1 REWRITE THE SENTENCES, PUTTING THE WORDS IN THE CORRECT ORDER

how | Kevin | gone. | asked | negotiations | me | the | had

Kevin asked me how the negotiations had gone.

1. where | Selma | put | me | you | annual | the | report. | asked | had

2. wanted | Krishnan | why | was | know | I | late | again. | to | for | work

3. asked | My | what | I | the | IT | new | about | me | system. | boss | thought

4. me | asked | Hans | would | where | we | have | the | afternoon. | presentation | this

5. wasn't | he | Sophie | Claude | why | at | meeting. | asked | the

6. me | Tabitha | who | cell | taken | her | phone. | asked | had

7. the | Fiona | to | had | know | who | minutes. | wanted | taken

26.2 LISTEN TO THE AUDIO AND ANSWER THE QUESTIONS

Sam is telling Shelly about a conversation that he had with Doug.

Doug is feeling confident about the conference.
True ☐ **False** ☑ **Not given** ☐

1. Shelly has booked the flights for Monday.
True ☐ **False** ☐ **Not given** ☐

2. The Hotel Belle Vue is fully booked.
True ☐ **False** ☐ **Not given** ☐

3. Shelly has booked the rooms for three nights.
True ☐ **False** ☐ **Not given** ☐

4. The Classic Inn includes breakfast.
True ☐ **False** ☐ **Not given** ☐

5. There are meeting facilities at the Classic Inn.
True ☐ **False** ☐ **Not given** ☐

6. Doug is planning to bring his family.
True ☐ **False** ☐ **Not given** ☐

7. Shelly has finished the promotional materials.
True ☐ **False** ☐ **Not given** ☐

8. Shelly also has to prepare a presentation.
True ☐ **False** ☐ **Not given** ☐

9. Ted can help Shelly with her work.
True ☐ **False** ☐ **Not given** ☐

26.3 MATCH THE DEFINITIONS TO THE COLLOCATIONS

explain to someone what they have done wrong → have a word

1. offer advice or ideas
2. lose your job because of misconduct
3. misunderstand, or do something incorrectly
4. try as hard as you can
5. help someone without thought of reward
6. find work
7. investigate a topic, or discover information
8. write down information during a meeting

- make a suggestion
- make a mistake
- have a word
- get fired
- do someone a favor
- make notes
- do research
- do your best
- get a job

26.4 REWRITE THE SENTENCES, TURNING THEM INTO REPORTED QUESTIONS

Who took the minutes yesterday?

She *asked me who had taken the minutes yesterday.*

1. How many people work in the company?

   She ____________________

2. Why did you hand in the report so late?

   He ____________________

3. Who got promoted?

   He ____________________

4. Who is the new senior manager?

   He ____________________

5. Which candidate did you choose?

   She ____________________

6. How long have you worked here?

   He ____________________

7. Why were you so late this morning?

   She ____________________

8. What time do you get home?

   He ____________________

9. Where did you have the appointment?

   He ____________________

10. Which printer do you prefer?

    She ____________________

26.5 SAY THE DIRECT QUESTIONS OUT LOUD, TURNING THEM INTO REPORTED QUESTIONS

Did you make notes during the meeting?

He *asked me if I had made notes during the meeting.*

1. Did the package arrive safely?

   He ______.

2. Can you do me a favor?

   She ______.

3. Can I have a word with you later?

   He ______.

4. Have you finished writing the report yet?

   She ______.

5. Can I make a suggestion?

   He ______.

6. Did you read last year's report?

   She ______.

7. Are you coming to the awards ceremony on Saturday?

   He ______.

8. Did you enjoy the presentation?

   She ______.

9. Have you booked a table at the restaurant?

   He ______.

27 Reporting quantities

In presentations and reports, you may need to talk about how much of something there is. The words you can use to do this depend on the thing you are describing.

New language "Few," "little," and "all"
Aa Vocabulary Meetings
New skill Talking about quantity

27.1 READ THE REPORT AND ANSWER THE QUESTIONS

Sales have grown fast in the last year.
True ☐ False ☑ Not given ☐

1. China has been a strong competitor over the last year.
True ☐ False ☐ Not given ☐

2. There is not much chance of a quick solution.
True ☐ False ☐ Not given ☐

3. The company should reduce its prices dramatically.
True ☐ False ☐ Not given ☐

4. The most expensive product made in China costs $25.
True ☐ False ☐ Not given ☐

5. The brand is well known among older people.
True ☐ False ☐ Not given ☐

6. The brand is unpopular with teenagers.
True ☐ False ☐ Not given ☐

7. The company's advertising campaign is old.
True ☐ False ☐ Not given ☐

8. The company needs to open more stores in Asia.
True ☐ False ☐ Not given ☐

9. It costs less to open stores in Asia than Europe.
True ☐ False ☐ Not given ☐

10. Asia is not a very valuable market for the company.
True ☐ False ☐ Not given ☐

REPORT

Problem:
Over the past 12 months, our overseas sales have fallen dramatically. Competition from Asia, particularly China, is intense.

Proposed solutions:
There is little we can do to turn this situation around in the next couple of months. However, if we take a long-term view, there are a few solutions.

1) We can lower our prices a little. This will make our products more price-competitive. Currently, our products are 15–25% more expensive than China-made products.

2) We can launch a new advertising campaign. Our research suggests that few people over the age of 50 have heard of our brand. This is a big market we can access if we get our advertising message right. At the other end of the market, very few teenagers seem interested in our products. We need to position our advertising to make our brand appear current and fashionable.

3) We have very few stores in Asia. We can consider opening a few more stores in Asia so that we can become a more familiar brand in this important market.

27.2 MARK THE SENTENCES THAT ARE CORRECT

There's little bit of money left in the budget to redesign the website. ☐
There's a little bit of money left in the budget to redesign the website. ☑

1. Unfortunately, we have few problems with our production line. ☐
   Unfortunately, we have a few problems with our production line. ☐

2. Regrettably, few people have the skills necessary to run a multinational company. ☐
   Regrettably, a few people have the skills necessary to run a multinational company. ☐

3. So few of our customer reviews are positive that it's becoming a problem. ☐
   So a few of our customer reviews are positive that it's becoming a problem. ☐

4. I have a little doubt that the conference will be a success. ☐
   I have little doubt that the conference will be a success. ☐

27.3 CROSS OUT THE INCORRECT WORD IN EACH SENTENCE, THEN SAY THE SENTENCES OUT LOUD

We have very **few** / ~~little~~ rooms left on the 12th of December.

1. **A little** / **Few** employees have worked for the company for as long as Sofia.
2. We have **little** / **a little** bit of time before the meeting ends.
3. So **few** / **a few** companies offer this service that demand is sure to be high.
4. Very **few** / **little** can be done to improve facilities in the short term.
5. We can expect **a few** / **a little** increase in profits over the summer season.
6. It's great that you have **few** / **a few** ideas about how we can improve sales.

27.4 REWRITE THE SENTENCES, PUTTING THE WORDS IN THE CORRECT ORDER

well | in | goes | the | all | boss. | your | I | meeting | hope | with

I hope all goes well in your meeting with the boss.

1. will | customer. | be | sure | to | all | you've | spoken | I'm | well | once | the

2. know | late. | that | the | All | I | order | is | is

3. that | need? | all | Is | you

4. is | for | wait | we | do | a | the | can | client. | response | All | from

27.5 MATCH THE PAIRS OF SENTENCES THAT MEAN THE SAME THING

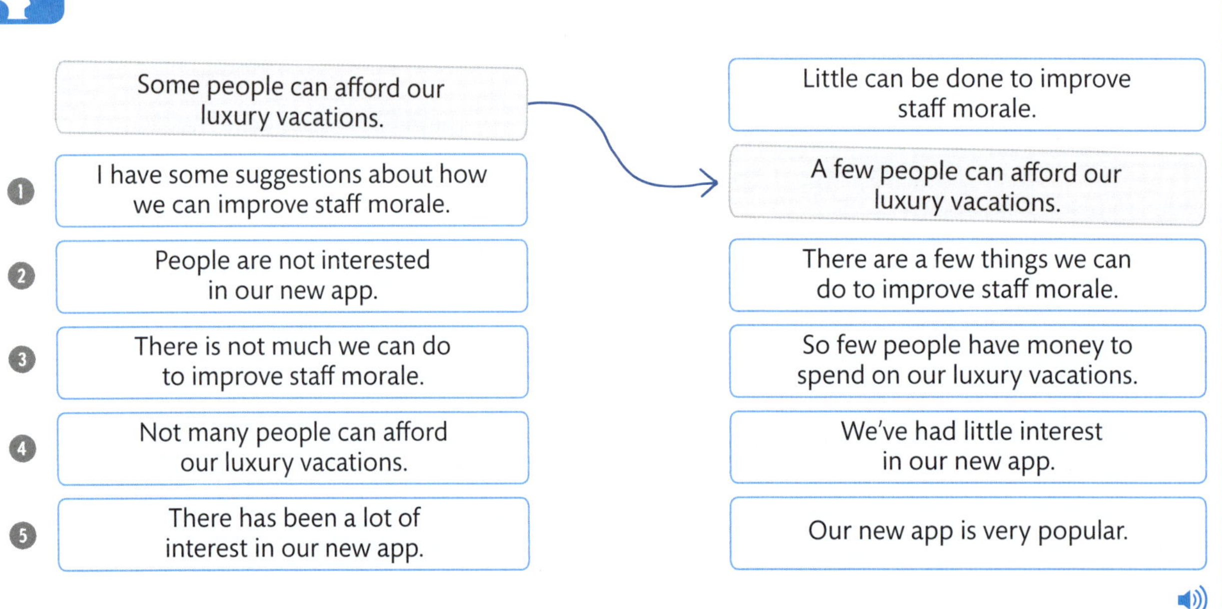

Some people can afford our luxury vacations. → A few people can afford our luxury vacations.

1. I have some suggestions about how we can improve staff morale.
2. People are not interested in our new app.
3. There is not much we can do to improve staff morale.
4. Not many people can afford our luxury vacations.
5. There has been a lot of interest in our new app.

- Little can be done to improve staff morale.
- A few people can afford our luxury vacations.
- There are a few things we can do to improve staff morale.
- So few people have money to spend on our luxury vacations.
- We've had little interest in our new app.
- Our new app is very popular.

28 Checking information

Sometimes you may need to clarify whether you have understood a point. There are a number of ways to politely check information in conversation.

New language Subject questions, question tags
Aa Vocabulary Polite checks and echo questions
New skill Checking information

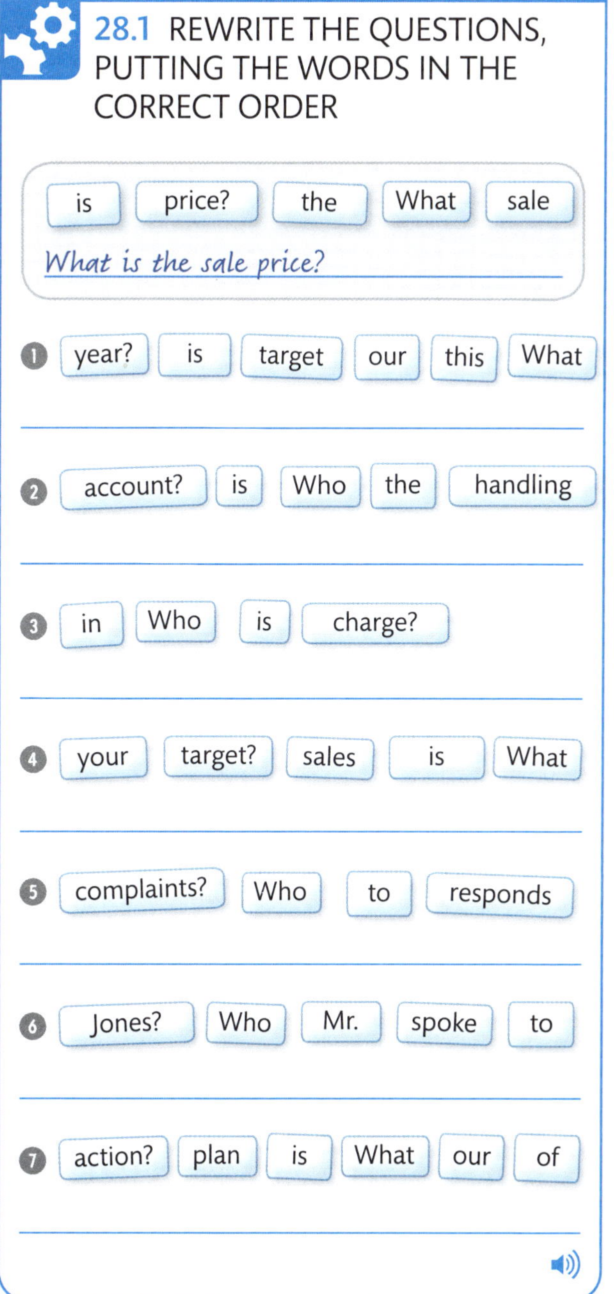

28.1 REWRITE THE QUESTIONS, PUTTING THE WORDS IN THE CORRECT ORDER

is | price? | the | What | sale

What is the sale price?

1. year? | is | target | our | this | What
2. account? | is | Who | the | handling
3. in | Who | is | charge?
4. your | target? | sales | is | What
5. complaints? | Who | to | responds
6. Jones? | Who | Mr. | spoke | to
7. action? | plan | is | What | our | of

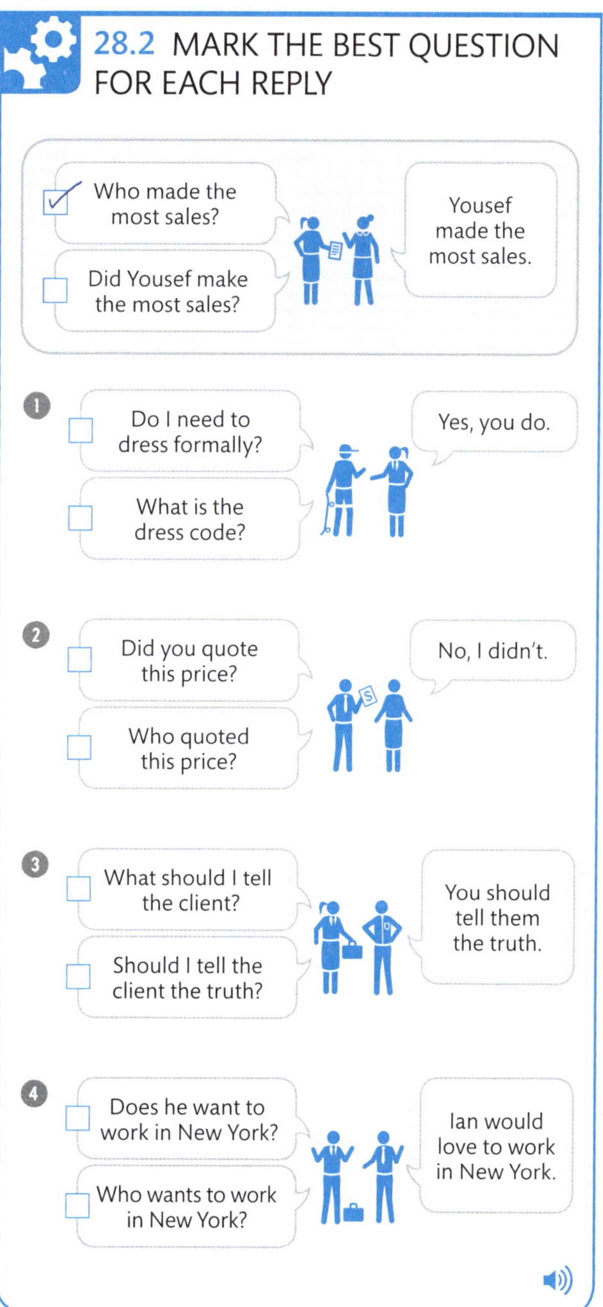

28.2 MARK THE BEST QUESTION FOR EACH REPLY

☑ Who made the most sales?
☐ Did Yousef make the most sales?
Yousef made the most sales.

1. ☐ Do I need to dress formally?
☐ What is the dress code?
Yes, you do.

2. ☐ Did you quote this price?
☐ Who quoted this price?
No, I didn't.

3. ☐ What should I tell the client?
☐ Should I tell the client the truth?
You should tell them the truth.

4. ☐ Does he want to work in New York?
☐ Who wants to work in New York?
Ian would love to work in New York.

28.3 MATCH THE BEGINNINGS OF THE SENTENCES TO THE CORRECT ENDINGS

Joel is our best negotiator, → isn't he?

1 We should increase our margins,

2 I didn't send you the report,

3 She'll be a great manager,

4 I'm not getting a raise,

5 We haven't made a loss,

6 We're going to win the award,

7 Louis has worked here since 2012,

8 Brett worked late last night,

am I?

did I?

isn't he?

didn't he?

aren't we?

shouldn't we?

have we?

won't she?

hasn't he?

28.4 FILL IN THE GAPS USING THE CORRECT QUESTION TAGS

I've made a mistake, *haven't I?*

1 We could launch our product early, ________

2 Jakob ordered the samples, ________

3 We can't cut prices any further, ________

4 We haven't achieved our target, ________

5 We need to improve product quality, ________

6 We're not ready for the meeting, ________

7 They are opening a new store, ________

8 You weren't in London last week, ________

9 You traveled to Paris by train, ________

10 I'm writing the proposal, ________

11 I emailed the right person, ________

28.5 LISTEN TO THE AUDIO AND ANSWER THE QUESTIONS

A sales assistant is calling his manager to check a few details and confirm information.

Anya is very busy when Mike calls.
True ☐ False ☑ Not given ☐

1. The conference takes place every year.
True ☐ False ☐ Not given ☐

2. Mike's plan is to put out 100 seats.
True ☐ False ☐ Not given ☐

3. Only five people have replied to the invitation.
True ☐ False ☐ Not given ☐

4. Anya thinks they should put out 140 seats.
True ☐ False ☐ Not given ☐

5. Pauline is dealing with the food and drink.
True ☐ False ☐ Not given ☐

6. Anya wants her guests to feel welcome.
True ☐ False ☐ Not given ☐

7. Anya will contact Francesca about catering.
True ☐ False ☐ Not given ☐

28.6 CROSS OUT THE INCORRECT WORDS IN EACH SENTENCE, THEN SAY THE SENTENCES OUT LOUD

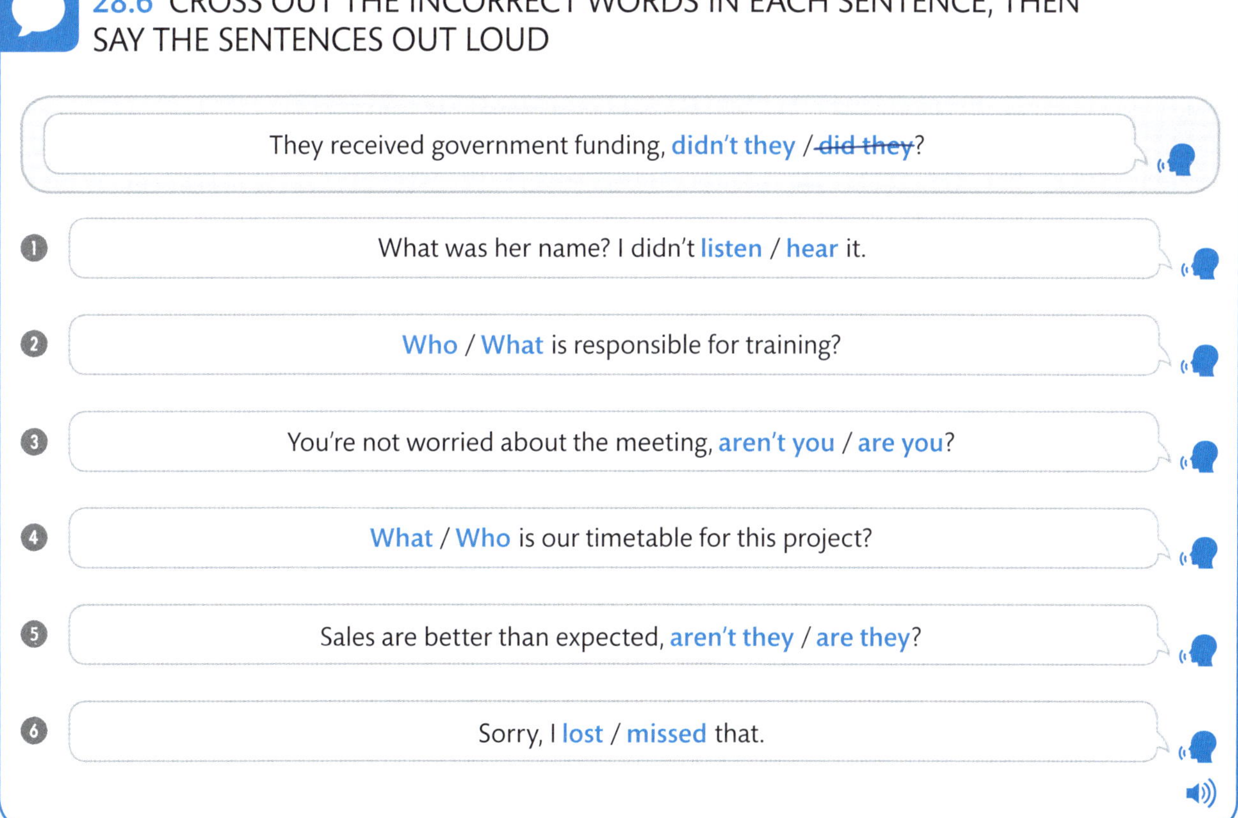

They received government funding, didn't they / ~~did they~~?

1. What was her name? I didn't listen / hear it.

2. Who / What is responsible for training?

3. You're not worried about the meeting, aren't you / are you?

4. What / Who is our timetable for this project?

5. Sales are better than expected, aren't they / are they?

6. Sorry, I lost / missed that.

29 Vocabulary

Aa 29.1 **INDUSTRIES** WRITE THE WORDS FROM THE PANEL UNDER THE CORRECT PICTURES

shipping

1 ______

2 ______

3 ______

4 ______

5 ______

6 ______

7 ______

8 ______

9 ______

10 ______

11 ______

12 ______

13 ______

14 ______

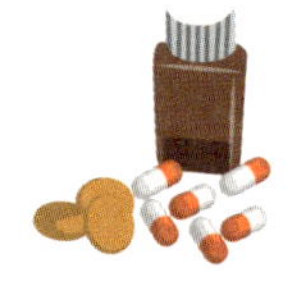
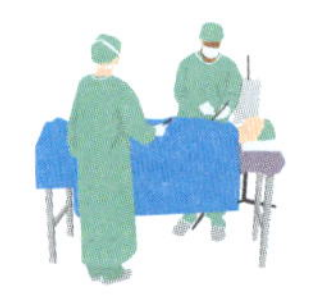

15 ______

16 ______

17 ______

18 ______

19 ______

fashion catering / food tourism recycling transportation hospitality energy manufacturing finance agriculture / farming electronics ~~shipping~~ chemical healthcare real estate (US) / property (UK) fishing education pharmaceutical mining entertainment

Aa 29.2 **PROFESSIONAL ATTRIBUTES** WRITE THE WORDS FROM THE PANEL UNDER THE CORRECT PICTURES

flexible

1 ____________

2 ____________

3 ____________

4 ____________

5 ____________

6 ____________

7 ____________

8 ____________

9 ____________

10 ____________

11 ____________

12 ____________

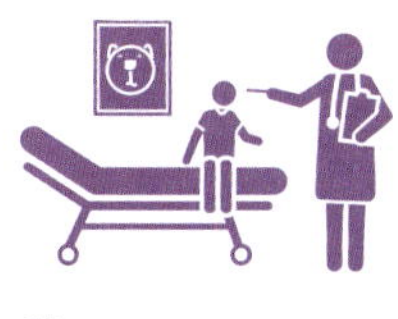

13 ____________

14 ____________

15 ____________

creative reliable practical professional ~~flexible~~
motivated confident ambitious accurate team player
organized energetic responsible punctual innovative calm

30 Job descriptions

English uses "a" or "an" in descriptions of jobs and to introduce new information. The zero article refers to general things, and "the" refers to specific things.

New language Articles
Aa Vocabulary Job descriptions and applications
New skill Describing a job

30.1 CROSS OUT THE INCORRECT WORDS IN EACH SENTENCE

I applied for a job as ~~a~~ / an / ~~the~~ IT engineer. ~~A~~ / ~~An~~ / The salary is really good.

1. I want to apply for a / an / the job in a / an / the office.
2. I've got a / an / the interview next week for a / an / the job I told you about.
3. A / An / The ideal candidate enjoys working in a / an / the team.
4. A / An / The deadline for applications for a / an / the job in IT is next Monday.
5. Please complete a / an / the form on a / an / the job page on our website.

30.2 LISTEN TO THE AUDIO, THEN NUMBER THE PICTURES IN THE ORDER THEY ARE DESCRIBED

A ☐

B 1

C ☐

D ☐

E ☐

F ☐

G ☐

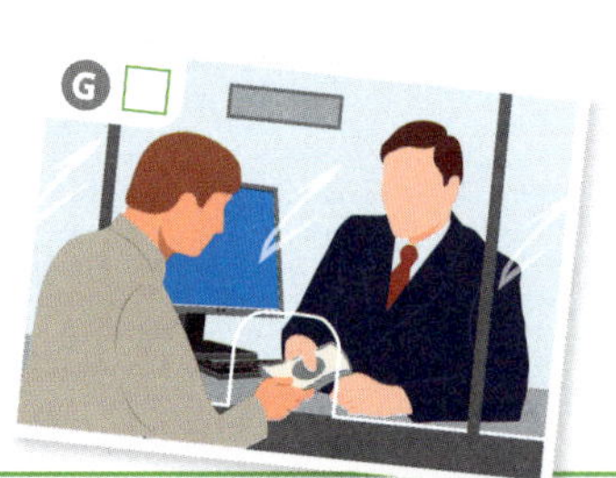

H ☐

30.3 MARK THE SENTENCES THAT ARE CORRECT

Mark loves teaching students. The students he teaches at the college are all adults. ☑
Mark loves teaching the students. Students he teaches at the college are all adults. ☐

1. The nurses often have to work very long hours. They are the very important people. ☐
   Nurses often have to work very long hours. They are very important people. ☐

2. Working hours are from 8:30 to 5:00. Lunch is from 1:00 to 2:00. ☐
   The working hours are from 8:30 to 5:00. The lunch is from 1:00 to 2:00. ☐

3. Vale loves giving training sessions. The training sessions she gave yesterday were amazing. ☐
   Vale loves giving the training sessions. Training sessions she gave yesterday were amazing. ☐

4. Job I applied for is based in Madrid. It's in the sales and marketing. ☐
   The job I applied for is based in Madrid. It's in sales and marketing. ☐

5. The people who interviewed me for the job were really nice. They were managers. ☐
   People who interviewed me for the job were really nice. They were the managers. ☐

6. I have just applied for a job in finance department at your company. ☐
   I have just applied for a job in the finance department at your company. ☐

7. The salary for this job is not very good. I don't think I'll apply for it. ☐
   Salary for this job is not very good. I don't think I'll apply for it. ☐

8. The successful candidate will have three years' experience branding new products. ☐
   Successful candidate will have three years' experience branding the new products. ☐

9. Our company is currently recruiting more the staff for Paris office. ☐
   Our company is currently recruiting more staff for the Paris office. ☐

10. I have the meetings with CEO and some of our new clients today. ☐
    I have meetings with the CEO and some of our new clients today. ☐

11. Marisha is good at pitching products. It's the thing she enjoys most about her job. ☐
    Marisha is good at pitching the products. It's thing she enjoys most about her job. ☐

12. This job requires in-depth knowledge of business trends in the wider world. ☐
    This job requires the in-depth knowledge of the business trends in wider world. ☐

30.4 READ THE JOB DESCRIPTION AND ANSWER THE QUESTIONS

The job is a sales and marketing role.
True ☑ False ☐

1. No previous experience is needed.
True ☐ False ☐

2. The job involves giving presentations.
True ☐ False ☐

3. The job requires market-specific knowledge.
True ☐ False ☐

4. No leadership experience is needed.
True ☐ False ☐

5. The successful candidate will have training.
True ☐ False ☐

VACANCIES

Arctic Foods

Sales and Marketing Manager

Do you have a passion for selling new ideas? Then we could have the job for you.

Arctic Foods is looking for a dynamic sales and marketing manager. You will have previous experience in a sales and marketing role, preferably in the frozen food sector. You will be good at giving presentations and fully up to date with market trends. Previous experience leading a sizeable team is essential.

Full product training will be given to the successful candidate.

30.5 CROSS OUT THE INCORRECT WORDS IN EACH SENTENCE, THEN SAY THE SENTENCES OUT LOUD

At the second-round interview, you will meet ~~HR manager~~ / the HR manager.

1. We need someone who is willing to travel, and can speak the Spanish / Spanish.

2. Tara works in the finance department / finance department of an advertising agency.

3. Marc and Samantha often travel to China on business / on the business.

4. The company is based in the UK, but it does business throughout EU / the EU.

5. I started looking for a job as an engineer / the engineer after I finished college.

31 Applying for a job

Cover letters for job applications should sound fluent and confident. Using the correct prepositions after verbs, nouns, and adjectives can help you achieve this.

New language Dependent prepositions
Aa Vocabulary Cover-letter vocabulary
New skill Writing a cover letter

31.1 MATCH THE PICTURES TO THE CORRECT SENTENCES

I am fully trained in all aspects of health and safety.

1 

I have several years of experience in the catering industry.

2 

I graduated from college in June 2016 with a degree in chemistry.

3 

I am writing to apply for the role of head chef.

4 

I heard about the job on your website.

31.2 CROSS OUT THE INCORRECT WORDS IN EACH SENTENCE

At college, I focused ~~in~~ / on / ~~at~~ business studies. It has been very useful in my career.

1. Jim graduated **from** / **at** / **out** college with a degree in physics. Now he is a research scientist.
2. He is fully trained **to** / **with** / **in** all aspects of sales and marketing. I think he'll do a great job.
3. In my role as Senior Program Developer, I reported **in** / **on** / **to** the Director of IT.
4. Tanya has applied **at** / **for** / **on** a job in the marketing department of our company.
5. I worked **at** / **of** / **for** the owner of a leading hairdressing salon. I learned a lot from him.

31.3 READ THE COVER LETTER AND WRITE ANSWERS TO THE QUESTIONS AS FULL SENTENCES

Why is Ellie writing the letter?

To apply for the role of Head of Marketing.

1. How long has Ellie worked in marketing?

____

2. What did she develop in her previous jobs?

____

3. What did she introduce last year?

____

4. What is she responsible for in her current job?

____

5. Which region does she look after?

____

6. How does she describe herself?

____

Dear Ms. Jenkins,

I am writing to apply for the position of Head of Marketing as advertised on your company website.

I have more than ten years' experience in marketing, and I have worked in the marketing departments of several big companies, where I developed award-winning campaigns in key markets. Last year I was responsible for introducing a new customer-focused branding initiative.

In my current position, I am responsible for training junior members of staff. I run the sales and marketing operations for the Europe region. This includes setting the sales and marketing strategy for the region.

I would welcome the opportunity to learn new skills. I am also energetic, dynamic, and extremely reliable.

Please find attached my résumé and references. I look forward to hearing from you.

Yours sincerely,

Ellie Abrahams

Aa 31.4 MATCH THE DEFINITIONS TO THE WORDS AND PHRASES

	Definition	Word or phrase
	honest and trustworthy → reliable	a position
1	a set of abilities resulting from experience	reliable
2	a fixed regular payment	to report to someone
3	a job	skills
4	to make an official request for a job	salary
5	to have someone in charge of you	a team
6	the group of people you work with	a résumé
7	a document detailing your skills	an opportunity
8	a chance to do something	to amount to
9	to equal a total number	to apply for a job

31.5 READ THE COVER LETTER AND CROSS OUT THE INCORRECT WORDS

3257 Gateway Drive
Portland, OR
March 29, 2014

Dear Mr. Chang,

I am writing to ~~apply to~~ / **apply for** the position of Senior Sales Consultant, as advertised on your website.

I have **worked on** / **worked in** the sales industry for more than eight years, and am **trained in** / **trained of** selling a range of products to varied markets. In my current position, I am **responsible of** / **responsible for** sales to Asian markets, and last year I **looked up** / **looked after** the new market of China, where sales **amounted to** / **amounted on** more than $10 million.

I am **passionate for** / **passionate about** working in the sales industry and welcome the opportunity to learn new skills. I run the training program for new staff members and ten of the junior sales consultants **report to** / **report on** me. In their training, I **focus in** / **focus on** developing awareness of the most effective sales strategies.

Please find my résumé and references attached. I look **forward at** / **forward to** hearing from you.

Yours sincerely,
Deepak Singh

32 Job interviews

In a job interview, it is important to describe your achievements in a specific and detailed way. You can use relative clauses to do this.

New language Relative clauses
Aa Vocabulary Job interviews
New skill Describing your achievements in detail

32.1 CROSS OUT THE INCORRECT WORDS IN EACH SENTENCE

This is the app ~~who~~ / that / ~~what~~ I designed for the new client.

1  The person who / what / which I admire the most in the company is the Sales Manager.

2  The office that / which / where I work is a tall, modern building.

3  The customers what / who / why gave us feedback were all very positive.

4  The team that / what / where I lead is fully qualified and highly motivated.

32.2 MATCH THE BEGINNINGS OF THE SENTENCES TO THE CORRECT ENDINGS

	We work with clients → who want innovative products.	that are designed by IT specialists.
1	We sell apps	who have high standards.
2	We are based in an office	who want innovative products.
3	I work with clients	where we sell the most.
4	This is the reason	that is in the business park.
5	Spain and Italy are the countries	that I applied for this job.

32.3 REWRITE THE SENTENCES, CORRECTING THE ERRORS

In my previous job, what was in sales, I learned a lot from my boss.

In my previous job, which was in sales, I learned a lot from my boss.

1. Training staff, that is my favorite part of the job, is really interesting.

2. In my current job, who I serve lots of customers, I have learned how to deal with complaints.

3. My boss, which is very understanding, encourages me to leave the office on time.

4. While I was in college I worked in a café, what taught me a lot about customer service.

32.4 LISTEN TO THE AUDIO, THEN NUMBER THE PICTURES IN THE ORDER THEY ARE DESCRIBED

A ☐

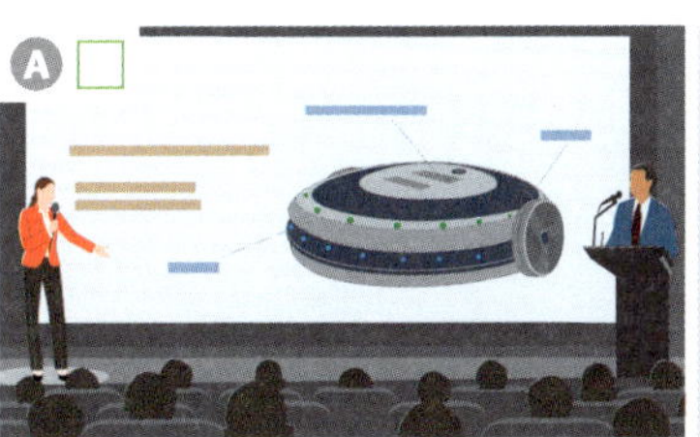

B ☐

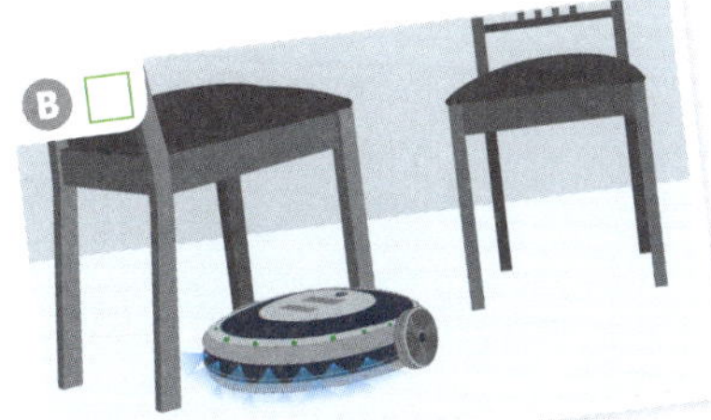

C *1*

D ☐

E ☐

F ☐

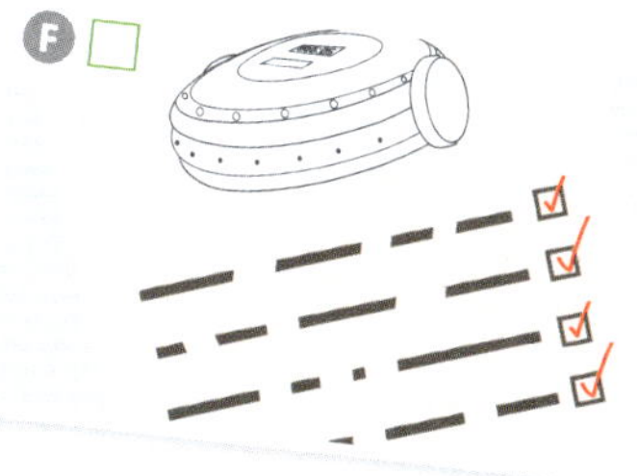

32.5 FILL IN THE GAPS USING THE WORDS IN THE PANEL

The sales team, ___whose___ staff work very hard, always meet their targets.

1. Last summer, ______________ I had just graduated, I worked as an intern in a bank.
2. My teacher, ______________ was an amazing person, inspired me to study law.
3. My apprenticeship, ______________ I completed in 2016, was in IT.
4. The place ______________ I want to work as a tour guide is New York.

who	where	~~whose~~	which	when

32.6 MARK THE SENTENCES THAT ARE CORRECT

In 2014, when I had just graduated, I worked as an intern. ☑
In 2014, which I had just graduated, I worked as an intern. ☐

1. Tom's team, who staff are hard-working, hit their sales targets last month. ☐
   Tom's team, whose staff are hard-working, hit their sales targets last month. ☐
2. In my previous job, which was in sales, I learned to give presentations. ☐
   In my previous job, what was in sales, I learned to give presentations. ☐
3. I sometimes work from home as it is the place which I can concentrate best. ☐
   I sometimes work from home as it is the place where I can concentrate best. ☐
4. My clients, who expect good customer service, said my work was excellent. ☐
   My clients, whose expect good customer service, said my work was excellent. ☐

32.7 RESPOND OUT LOUD TO THE AUDIO, FILLING IN THE GAPS USING THE WORDS IN THE PANEL

What experience do you have of customer service?

I work with clients *who expect* excellent service at all times.

1. What do you like most about your job?

   The thing ______ me excited is when we hit our sales targets.

2. What would you say is your biggest strength?

   People ______ me well say I am customer-focused and give good customer service.

3. What do you think you would bring to our company?

   I have a can-do attitude, ______ that I get things done.

4. What are your salary expectations?

   I would hope to receive more than my current salary, ______ $45,000 a year.

5. How soon can you start, supposing we offer you the job?

   My boss, ______ quite understanding, would allow me to leave after a month's notice.

that gets | who know | ~~who expect~~ | which is | who is | which means

33 Vocabulary

Aa 33.1 **BUSINESS IDIOMS** WRITE THE PHRASES FROM THE PANEL UNDER THE CORRECT DEFINITIONS

To agree totally

to see eye to eye

❶ To talk to someone briefly in order to catch up or get an update

❸ A strategy worked out beforehand

❹ To be in agreement about something

❻ Operating properly

❼ Simply and succinctly

❾ To start doing a job or role that someone else has just left

❿ Original and a big departure from what was there before

⓬ To stop the current activity

⓭ To do something in a cheaper or easier way, at the expense of high standards

⓯ A rough estimate

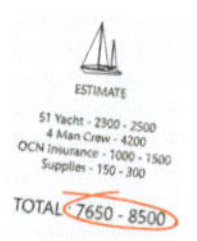

⓰ To do something strictly according to the rules

2 An increase or decrease in speed from what is normal

5 Uncertain and undecided

8 To make more effort than is usually expected

11 To confirm or settle an agreement or contract

14 To be ahead of your competitors in a certain field

17 To have control of a particular market

a ballpark figure
to touch base
in a nutshell
to go the extra mile
a change of pace
to corner the market
to be ahead of the game
to cut corners
~~to see eye to eye~~
to clinch the deal
to fill someone's shoes
groundbreaking
to do something by the book
a game plan
up in the air
to be on the same page
up and running
to call it a day

34 Working relationships

Phrasal verbs are commonly used to talk about relationships with co-workers and clients. It is important to use the correct word order with phrasal verbs.

New language Three-word phrasal verbs
Vocabulary Social media
New skill Social networking

34.1 FILL IN THE GAPS USING THE WORDS IN THE PANEL

My team looks *up* to me.

1. Alex comes up ______ great ideas.
2. Hal looks down ______ his co-workers.
3. I'm ______ forward to the launch.
4. Fred ______ up with a lot of noise.
5. She comes ______ as rather superior.
6. The printer has run ______ of paper.
7. Jim's staff get ______ with being late.
8. Shona has to ______ up to poor sales.
9. We need to ______ up with the schedule.

across, face, with, puts, ~~up~~, on, keep, away, looking, out

34.2 REWRITE THE SENTENCES, PUTTING THE WORDS IN THE CORRECT ORDER

them. / down / looks / on / John
John looks down on them.

1. my / team. / get / with / I / along
2. friendly. / across / She / as / comes
3. with / I / put / music! / up / can't / his
4. with / good / comes / ideas. / He / up
5. gets / with / lot. / Tom / away / a
6. out / We / run / have / of / coffee.
7. to / We / facts. / must / up / face

34.3 READ THE WEB PAGE AND WRITE ANSWERS TO THE QUESTIONS AS FULL SENTENCES

Business Tips

HOME | ENTRIES | ABOUT | CONTACT

Keeping up with competitors

Some companies have been slow to get up to speed with using social media to strengthen their brand. Some even look down on using social media as trivial and having no value in the business world, but they do so at their own risk. With social media you can reach out to a wider audience and keep up with the latest trends.

Here at ABC Foods we use social media to tell our customers our news. We have previews of our TV ads, so subscribers feel they are keeping up with our news and developments.

We also run competitions that make us stand out from our competitors. Last month, we asked our subscribers to post recipes they had come up with using their favorite ABC foods. We then had customers like their favorite recipes and the best three won prizes.

Using social media in such ways allows us to build loyal customer relationships. Customer loyalty is key to us as loyal customers make repeat purchases. We have to constantly be coming up with new features for our social media activity. Perhaps you have an idea for our next competition!

What can social media help you do?
It can help you strengthen your brand.

1. Why don't some companies like social media?

2. Why is it a risk to ignore social media?

3. Why does ABC Foods use social media?

4. What does ABC Foods have previews of?

5. Why does the company do this?

6. Why does ABC Foods run competitions?

7. Why is customer loyalty so important?

34.4 REWRITE THE SENTENCES USING OBJECT PRONOUNS

You must check out their website.
You must check it out.

1. I'll look up our competitors online.
2. Can you fill in this form?
3. I'd like you to take on this task.
4. I can't let down our clients.
5. Can we talk over your problem?
6. Could you look over my résumé?
7. We are giving away free books.
8. I need to call off our meeting.
9. I can't figure out these sales figures.
10. The taxi will pick up Tom.
11. I keep putting off writing my report.
12. Yola turned down the job offer.

34.5 LISTEN TO THE AUDIO AND ANSWER THE QUESTIONS

Bilal is giving a presentation on using social media in business.

What should you encourage clients to do?
Look at your website ☑
Take on difficult tasks ☐
Sell your products ☐

1. What do you need to do regularly?
   Be in the news ☐
   Update your website ☐
   Focus on selling ☐

2. What do customers expect from business social media sites?
   To find new ideas for your product ☐
   To buy more of your products ☐
   To read old news stories ☐

3. What is vital for small businesses?
   Missing out on opportunities ☐
   Translating social media use into sales ☐
   Advertising on social media ☐

4. How do successful businesses engage with their target customers?
   Uploading photos of their products ☐
   Entering competitions ☐
   Sharing users' questions and answers ☐

34.6 MATCH THE PICTURES TO THE CORRECT SENTENCES

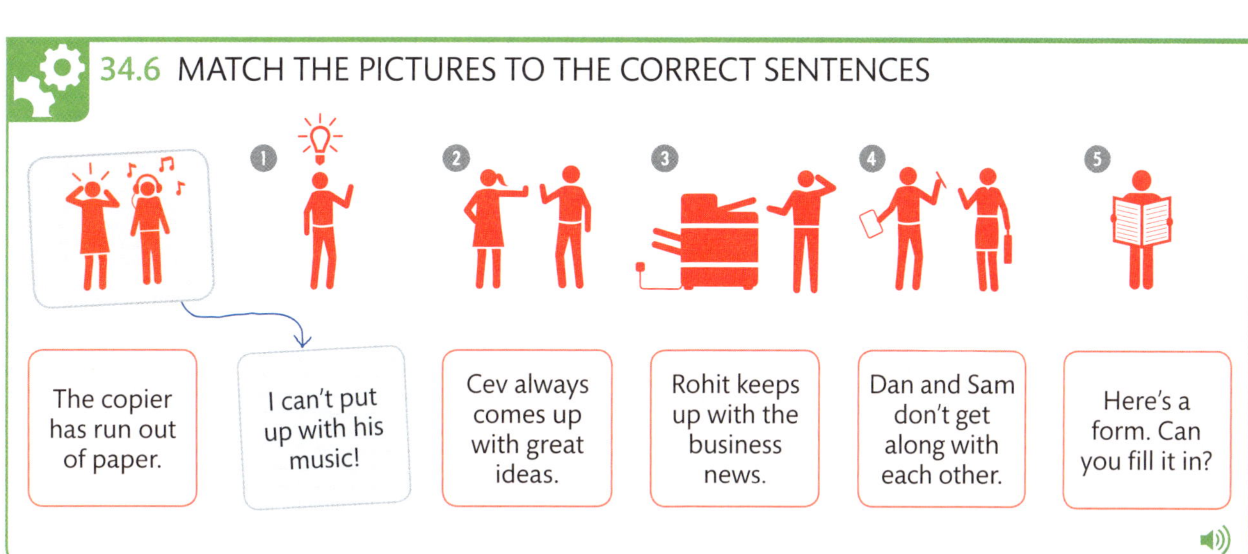

34.7 CROSS OUT THE INCORRECT WORDS IN EACH SENTENCE, THEN SAY THE SENTENCES OUT LOUD

They have a new website. Can you ~~check out it~~ / **check it out**?

1. I looked **up** / **to** the candidates on social media. They all looked very talented.
2. Kennedy's team **gets away with** / **gets with away** a lot. It's not fair on the others.
3. You're leading an important pitch today. Please don't **let down me** / **let me down**.
4. Can you take **on** / **off** writing the sales report today, or are you too busy?
5. We're giving **down** / **away** free books to customers. We hope it will increase sales.

35 Career outcomes

To talk about possible future events, such as career development and promotion, use "will," "might," and "won't" to say how likely something is to happen.

New language Modal verbs for possibility
Aa Vocabulary Career development
New skill Talking about the future

35.1 MATCH THE PAIRS OF SENTENCES

Katya is really hard-working. → She will add a great deal to the team.

1. Julia has been promoted.
2. You have not met your sales targets.
3. Adam is great with new staff.
4. We are understaffed right now.
5. Ella made a lot of mistakes in her report.

- We may have to fire her.
- You won't get a bonus.
- She will add a great deal to the team.
- We might need to recruit more staff.
- She will get a raise in her new position.
- We may ask him to become a mentor.

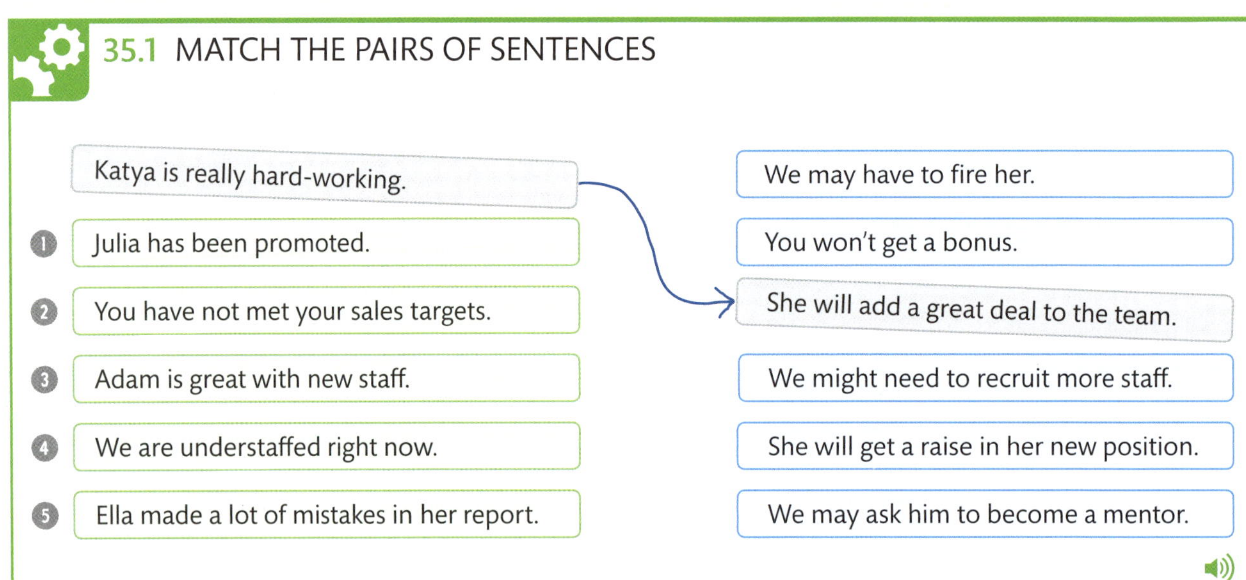

35.2 LISTEN TO THE AUDIO AND ANSWER THE QUESTIONS

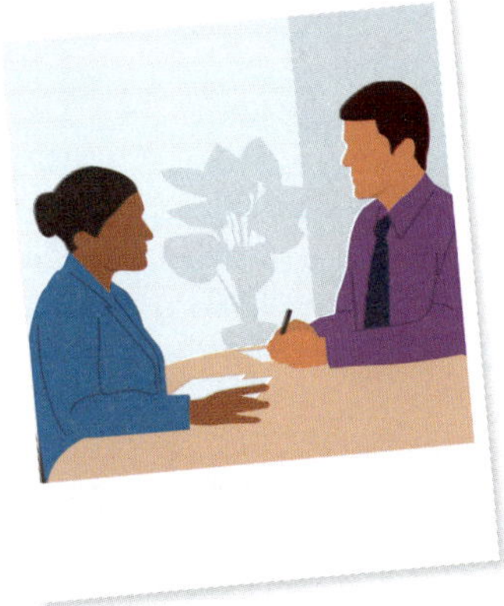

Ruth is having her annual performance review with her manager, Tim.

Ruth won't meet her sales targets.
True ☐ False ☑

1. Ruth will be promoted this year.
True ☐ False ☐
2. Ruth may get a company car.
True ☐ False ☐
3. Ruth might not be a team leader.
True ☐ False ☐
4. Ruth will travel outside the US for work.
True ☐ False ☐
5. Ruth might work in the Dallas office.
True ☐ False ☐

35.3 MARK THE SENTENCES THAT ARE CORRECT

The company has made a loss this year. You will get a bonus. ☐
The company has made a loss this year. You might not get a bonus. ☑

1. Our staff can't use the new database. We might have to provide more training. ☐
   Our staff can't use the new database. We won't have to provide more training. ☐

2. David has over 15 years' experience and he will lead our marketing department. ☐
   David has over 15 years' experience and he won't lead our marketing department. ☐

3. I need your report by Thursday. You need might to work overtime. ☐
   I need your report by Thursday. You might need to work overtime. ☐

4. Anna's laptop is broken. She wills get a new one this week. ☐
   Anna's laptop is broken. She will get a new one this week. ☐

5. There is a pay freeze at the moment, so you won't get a raise. ☐
   There is a pay freeze at the moment, so you will get a raise. ☐

6. If Rita's work doesn't get better, we won't have to fire her. ☐
   If Rita's work doesn't get better, we may have to fire her. ☐

7. We have some meetings in France. You may have to go to Paris. ☐
   We have some meetings in France. You don't may have to go to Paris. ☐

8. We can't hire any staff at the moment, so you don't might get an assistant until March. ☐
   We can't hire any staff at the moment, so you might not get an assistant until March. ☐

9. If your presentation goes well, the CEO might ask you to give it to the board. ☐
   If your presentation goes well, the CEO won't ask you to give it to the board. ☐

10. Tanya has been promoted. She will lead a team next year. ☐
    Tanya has been promoted. She will to lead a team next year. ☐

11. Dev has had a bad trading year. He will meet his sales targets. ☐
    Dev has had a bad trading year. He won't meet his sales targets. ☐

12. Paula always goes the extra mile. She will make a great addition to the team. ☐
    Paula always goes the extra mile. She won't make a great addition to the team. ☐

35.4 REWRITE THE SENTENCES, PUTTING THE WORDS IN THE CORRECT ORDER

will | bonus | probably. | You | a | get

You will probably get a bonus.

1. promoted. | will | definitely | He | be

2. probably | raise. | You | a | will | get

3. need | She | training. | probably | won't

4. bonus. | They'll | a | get | definitely

5. I | go | won't | vacation. | probably | on

6. I | jobs. | definitely | change | won't

7. We | intern. | hire | an | probably | will

8. He | meet | probably | clients. | won't

9. sell | It | definitely | well. | will

35.5 SAY THE SENTENCES OUT LOUD, PUTTING THE MODIFIER IN THE CORRECT PLACE

You won't be promoted. **[definitely]**

You definitely won't be promoted.

1. You will be promoted. **[probably]**

2. He will get the job. **[definitely]**

3. She won't get a raise. **[definitely]**

4. They will get a bonus. **[probably]**

5. I won't get a new laptop. **[probably]**

6. You will get a company car. **[definitely]**

7. I will move to the head office. **[probably]**

8. You won't need much training. **[probably]**

9. We will hire a new assistant soon. **[definitely]**

35.6 CROSS OUT THE INCORRECT WORDS IN EACH SENTENCE

Everything's up in the air right now. We might not / ~~will definitely~~ meet our deadline.

1. Katrina doesn't have much experience. She will probably / definitely won't need more training.
2. Meliz has to travel to see clients. She definitely won't / will probably get a company car.
3. Mr. Cox has complained about our service. He probably won't / definitely will use us again.
4. The negotiations are going quite well. We definitely won't / might clinch the deal tomorrow.
5. You're doing a great job, but our profits are down. You might not / definitely will get a raise.

35.7 READ THE PERFORMANCE REVIEW AND WRITE ANSWERS TO THE QUESTIONS AS FULL SENTENCES

What is Isaac's work like?
Isaac's work is very thorough.

1. What did Isaac do this year?
____

2. What might happen to Isaac next year?
____

3. Who will Isaac mentor from next month?
____

4. Where will Isaac start selling products?
____

5. What might Isaac need in his new role?
____

6. How does the company think he will perform?
____

Name: Isaac Hawkins
Position: Sales adviser
Subject: Performance review

Isaac has worked in our sales department for four years and has a positive attitude. His work is very thorough and he never cuts corners. He met all his sales targets this year, so he will be considered for promotion next year. He is great with new staff and will mentor two new employees from next month. Isaac has shown himself to be a confident and competent sales adviser and from next month will take on sales to Asia after working in the European department for two years. We may need to give Isaac additional training in this field and I am confident he will perform well in this role.

36 Vocabulary

Aa 36.1 **OFFICE AND PRESENTATION EQUIPMENT** WRITE THE WORDS FROM THE PANEL UNDER THE CORRECT PICTURES

1 ____________

2 ____________

3 ____________

4 ____________

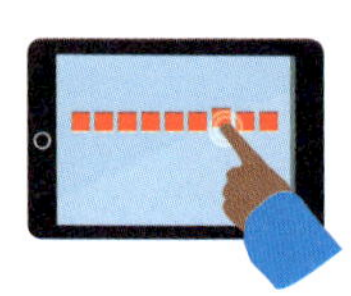

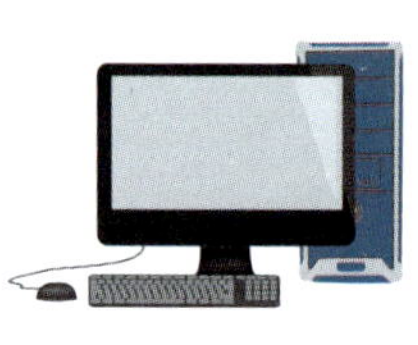

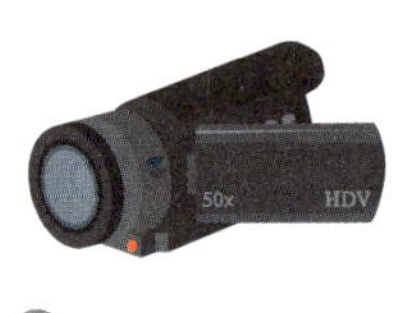

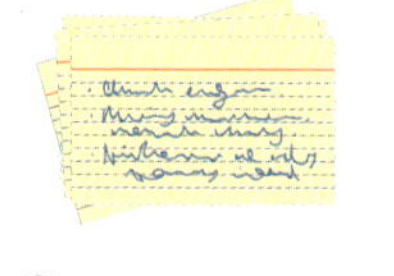

18 ____________

19 ____________

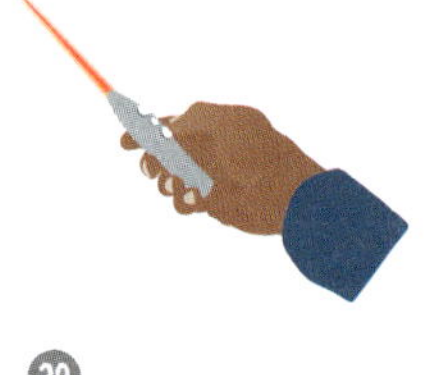
20 ____________

21 ____________

22 ____________

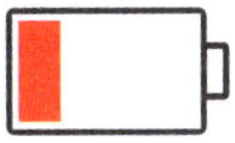

5 ______

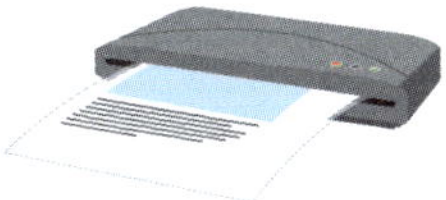

11 ______

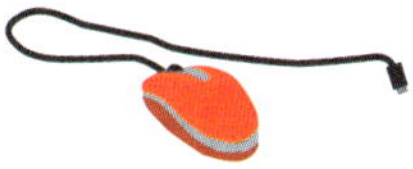

17 ______

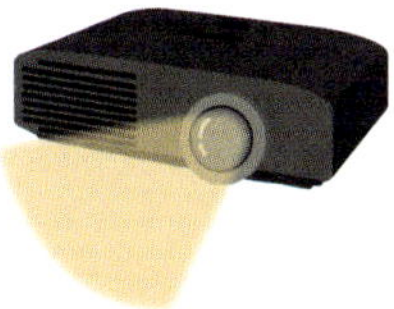

23 ______

printer

handout projector

USB drive / flash drive

keyboard speakers

router voice recorder

low battery cue cards

pointer webcam

~~projector screen~~ lectern

video camera cursor

touch screen laptop

computer mouse

microphone laminator

power cable chairs

Aa 36.2 PRESENTING DATA

WRITE THE WORDS FROM THE PANEL UNDER THE CORRECT PICTURES

table

1 ______

2 ______

3 ______

4 ______

flow chart

pie chart

report

~~table~~

graph

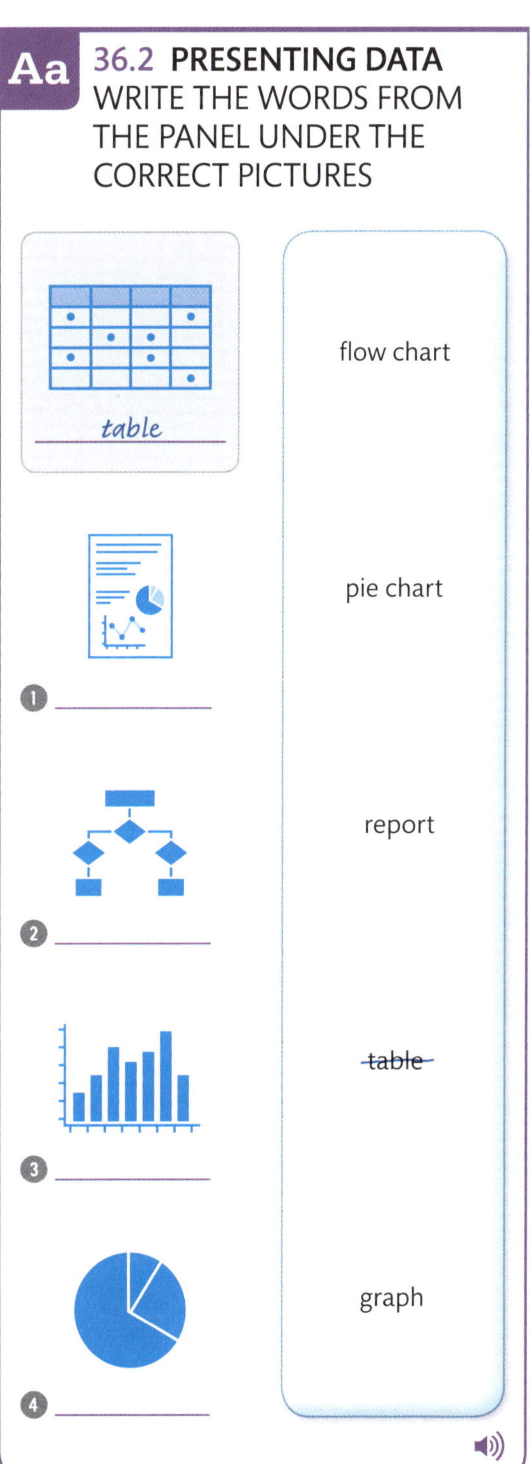

37 Structuring a presentation

When you are presenting to an audience, it is important to structure your talk in a way that is clear and easy to understand. Certain set phrases can help you do this.

New language Signposting language
Aa Vocabulary Presentation types
New skill Structuring a presentation

37.1 REWRITE THE SENTENCES, PUTTING THE WORDS IN THE CORRECT ORDER

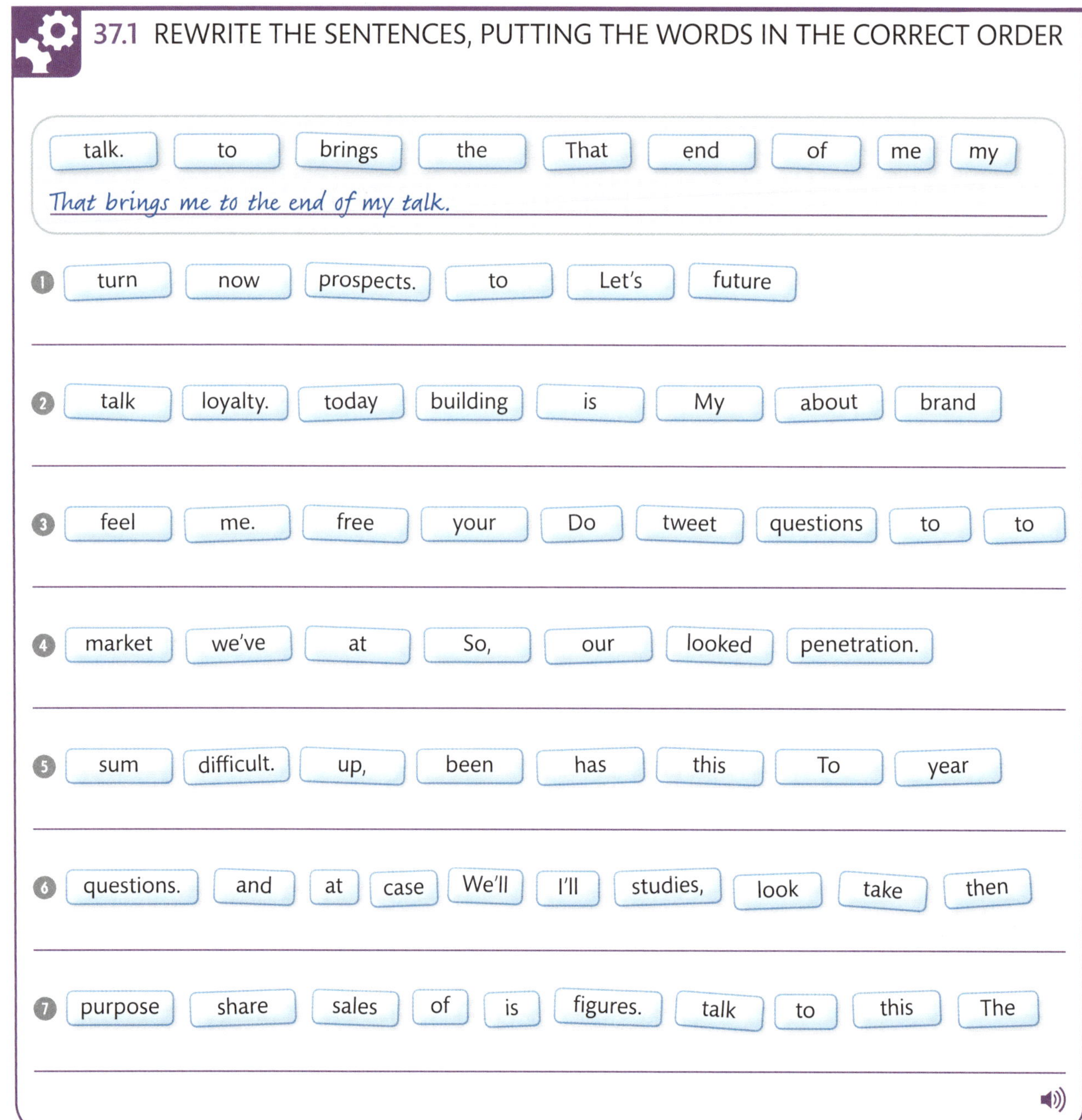

37.2 SAY THE SENTENCES OUT LOUD, FILLING IN THE GAPS USING THE WORDS IN THE PANEL

I'll quickly explain the latest proposal, and ___then___ I'll go through some case studies.

1. To ______________ up, it's been a very successful year for us.
2. We'll ______________ at the competitor's products, then I'll introduce our new product.
3. Do ______________ free to interrupt if you'd like to comment.
4. So, we've ______________ at problems we need to overcome.
5. Now let's ______________ to the solutions to those problems.

feel	look	~~then~~	looked	sum	turn

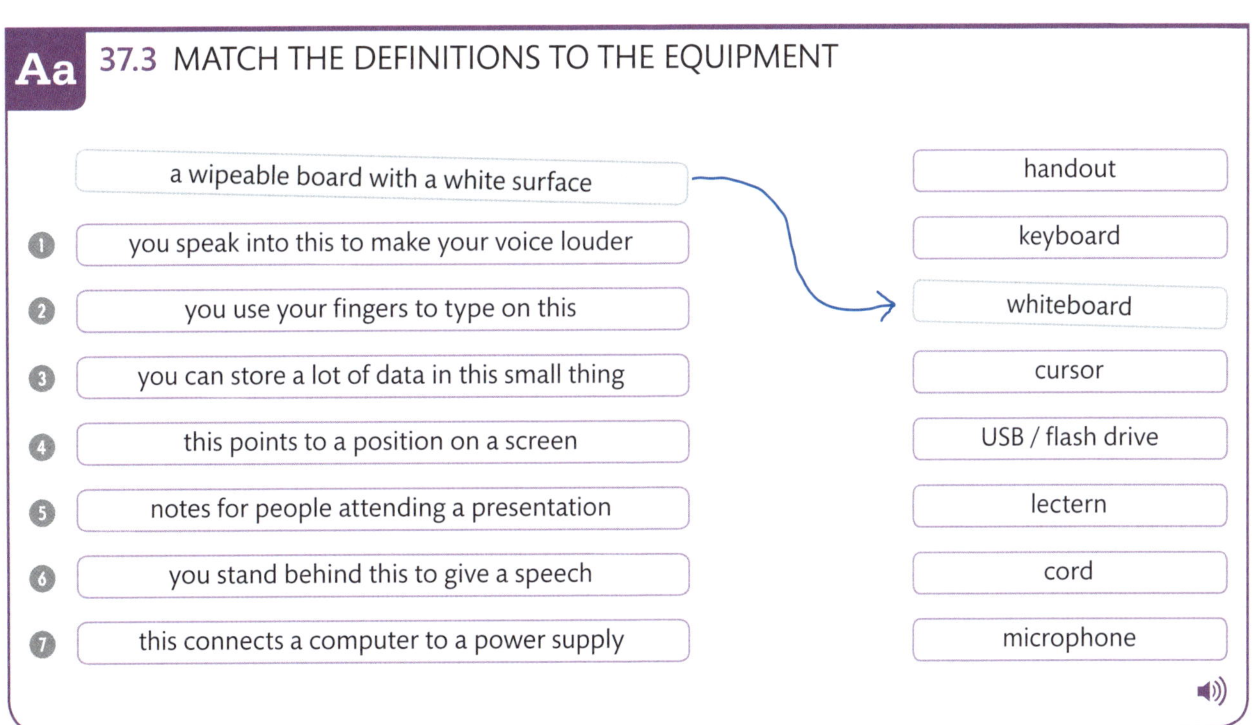

37.3 MATCH THE DEFINITIONS TO THE EQUIPMENT

a wipeable board with a white surface → whiteboard

1. you speak into this to make your voice louder
2. you use your fingers to type on this
3. you can store a lot of data in this small thing
4. this points to a position on a screen
5. notes for people attending a presentation
6. you stand behind this to give a speech
7. this connects a computer to a power supply

- handout
- keyboard
- whiteboard
- cursor
- USB / flash drive
- lectern
- cord
- microphone

37.4 READ THE ARTICLE AND ANSWER THE QUESTIONS

Presentation equipment is always a good idea.
True ☐ **False** ☑ **Not given** ☐

1. Most people do not practice their presentations.
True ☐ **False** ☐ **Not given** ☐

2. It is not important to practice your presentation.
True ☐ **False** ☐ **Not given** ☐

3. It doesn't take long to check your equipment.
True ☐ **False** ☐ **Not given** ☐

4. You should not use built-in cameras too often.
True ☐ **False** ☐ **Not given** ☐

5. The aim of a presentation is to convey a message.
True ☐ **False** ☐ **Not given** ☐

6. It is not always necessary to use lots of equipment.
True ☐ **False** ☐ **Not given** ☐

23 PUBLIC SPEAKING

WELL PRESENTED

Using equipment in presentations can be useful, but it can also make you look unprofessional if you don't know how to use it correctly.

- Practice! Don't leave it until the day to work out how to use the projector screen. Have two or three dry runs to resolve any problems so that your presentation is smooth and professional.
- Make sure equipment is working! Charge any batteries, make sure cords are plugged into sockets and test built-in cameras to make sure they are working, especially if you only use them now and again.
- Don't forget the handouts. High-tech equipment may be great, but the most important thing is that your audience understands the message.
- Sometimes, less is more. If you're not familiar with presentation software, and you fumble when using the remote and pointers, you may be better off not using any visual aids at all. Make your presentation interesting, and whatever you use should be enough.

37.5 LISTEN TO THE AUDIO, THEN NUMBER THE SENTENCES IN THE ORDER YOU HEAR THEM

An HR manager is talking to staff about changes in the company's technology policies.

A. They're small, they're light, and they have a built-in camera. ☐
B. Many of you need to respond to emails out of the office. ☐
C. That's the end of my talk. Do feel free to ask any questions. ☐
D. Let's now turn to how this will happen. You will receive an email with a time allocation. ☐
E. Good morning, everyone. On your chairs, you should have a handout. [1]
F. Now, all of you already have company laptops. Next month you'll also be issued with tablets. ☐
G. To sum up, we want to make it as easy and efficient as possible for you to do your jobs. ☐

38 Developing an argument

When you are making a presentation, there are several key phrases you can use to develop your argument, and make your audience aware of what is coming.

New language Useful presentation language
Aa Vocabulary Presentations
New skill Developing an argument

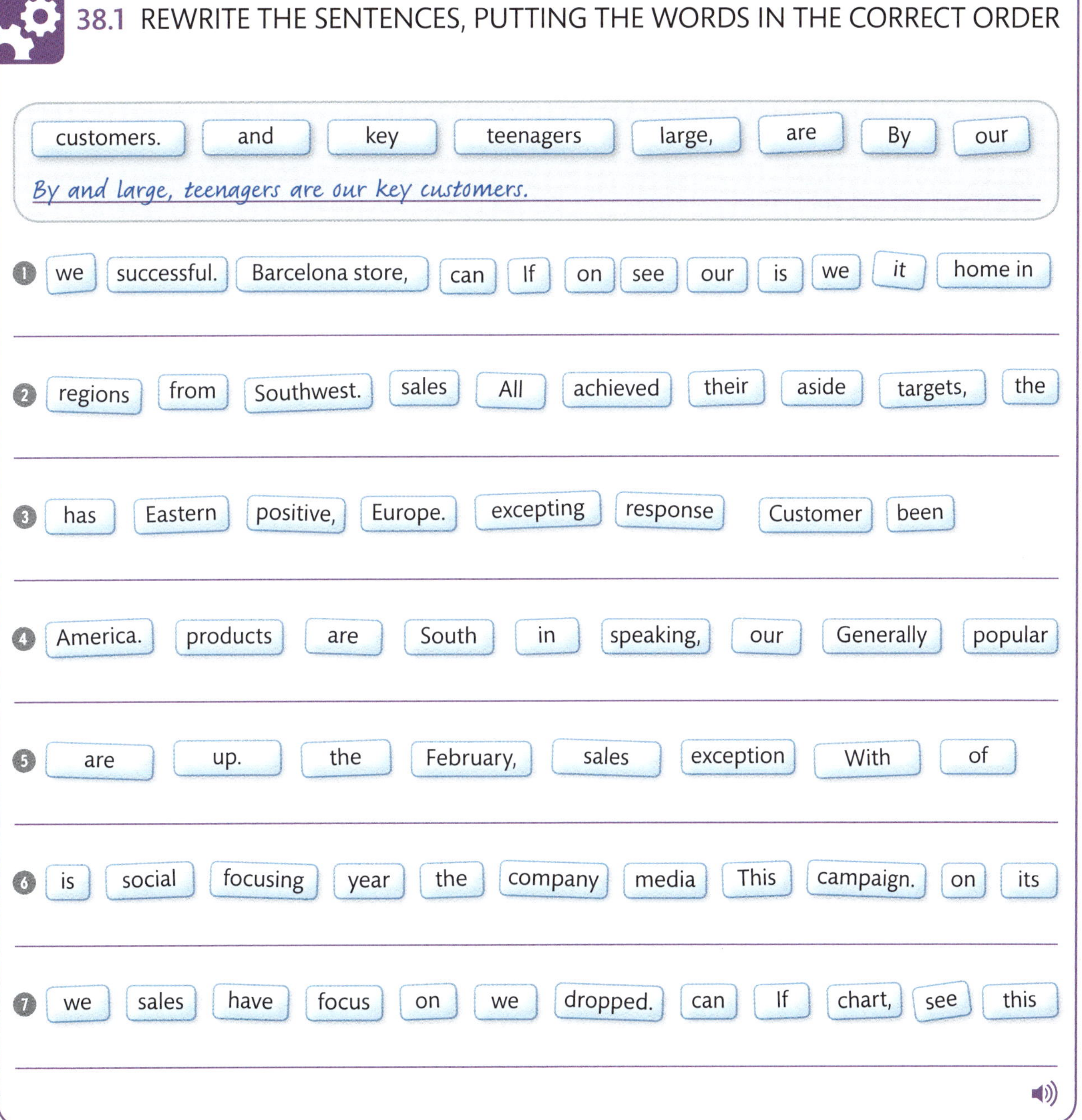

38.2 MATCH THE BEGINNINGS OF THE SENTENCES TO THE CORRECT ENDINGS

If we focus on these results → we can see a general trend downward.

1. Excepting East Asia, our sales
2. In actual fact, the consumer group said
3. As a matter of fact, I don't think
4. For instance, we've had a lot of positive
5. In general, the number of subscribers
6. Concentrating on the basics, there are
7. Jorge needs to improve key skills such

- to our magazines is falling.
- as dealing with customers.
- we can see a general trend downward.
- they really liked our prototype.
- many areas where we can improve.
- have grown by more than 10 percent.
- feedback about our menswear.
- Alyssa is suitable for the role.

38.3 CROSS OUT THE INCORRECT WORDS IN EACH SENTENCE, THEN SAY THE SENTENCES OUT LOUD

~~Except for~~ / On the whole, customers are very loyal to our brand.

1. In exception / reality, there is no way of knowing what sales will be like next year.
2. In fact / whole, we need to hire about 10 more staff this year.
3. Except for / However, we can't really afford to hire more staff.
4. In general / Except for Janice, all staff in this department deserve a raise.
5. Actually / Actual fact, there is little we can do to increase production.
6. If we focus on / Generally, staff seem very happy with working conditions.

38.4 READ THE ARTICLE AND ANSWER THE QUESTIONS

At the start of a presentation, give a summary.
True ☑ False ☐ Not given ☐

1. It's important to pack your talk full of details.
True ☐ False ☐ Not given ☐

2. It's best to speak in a dramatic way.
True ☐ False ☐ Not given ☐

3. You can end your presentation by giving advice.
True ☐ False ☐ Not given ☐

4. You should invite the audience to ask questions.
True ☐ False ☐ Not given ☐

5. The ideal length for a presentation is 5 minutes.
True ☐ False ☐ Not given ☐

6. Quality is more important than quantity.
True ☐ False ☐ Not given ☐

70 Business Insider

PRESENTING PROFESSIONALLY

Your boss asks you to give a presentation, but you don't know where to start. Here are our top tips.

✓ On the whole, you should begin your presentation with a summary statement: explain what issue you are addressing and what your presentation will contain.

✓ Home in on key trends. By and large, you don't need to talk about every single detail of an issue. In fact, it's much better to summarize the most important information, or the most dramatic results.

✓ In general, you should end with a recommendation or conclusion. What do you think your company should do in the future? How can they solve a problem or work more efficiently? You can also ask your audience a question: give them something to think about.

✓ Keep it brief. It's much better to give an excellent 5-minute presentation than to give a boring talk for 30 minutes.

38.5 FILL IN THE GAPS USING THE WORDS IN THE PANEL

In actual *fact*, Simone has never been late.

1. If we ______ in on profits, we can see growth.
2. If we focus ______ prices, it's clear they're too high.
3. ______ and large, our T-shirts are our bestseller.
4. In ______, there's no way we can recover.
5. As a ______ of fact, I am very disappointed.
6. Except ______ Korea, I've been to most of Asia.
7. ______ general, China is our biggest market.

reality | matter | In | home | ~~fact~~ | on | for | By

39 Pitching a product

When describing a product to a potential client, it is useful to compare the product with competitors using comparative and superlative adjectives.

New language Comparatives and superlatives
Aa Vocabulary Product marketing
New skill Comparing products

39.1 CROSS OUT THE INCORRECT WORDS IN EACH SENTENCE

Our new tablet is **slimmer** / ~~more slim~~ than any other tablet on the market.

1  This sports car is **the fastest** / **the most fast** car on sale today.

2  Our leather jackets are **fashionable** / **more fashionable** than our competitors' jackets.

3  This digital camera is **the best** / **best** model ever.

4  Our new microwave oven is more efficient **than** / **then** any other model.

5  This ice cream maker is **easyer** / **easier** to use than any other on the market.

6  Our customers said our sofa is **more comfortable** / **comfortabler** than other models.

7  Our organic vegetables are **more fresher** / **fresher** than supermarket vegetables.

8  Book a train trip with us in advance to get **the most cheapest** / **the cheapest** fares.

9  Our cake range was voted **the tastiest** / **tastiest** on the market in a recent survey.

10   These batteries last **more long** / **longer** than the leading brand.

11  We think our new winter coat is **the most warm** / **the warmest** on the market.

39.2 LISTEN TO THE AUDIO AND MATCH THE PRODUCTS TO THE PHRASES THAT DESCRIBE THEM

1

2

3

4

more energy-efficient

the most comfortable

the biggest

more stylish

cheaper

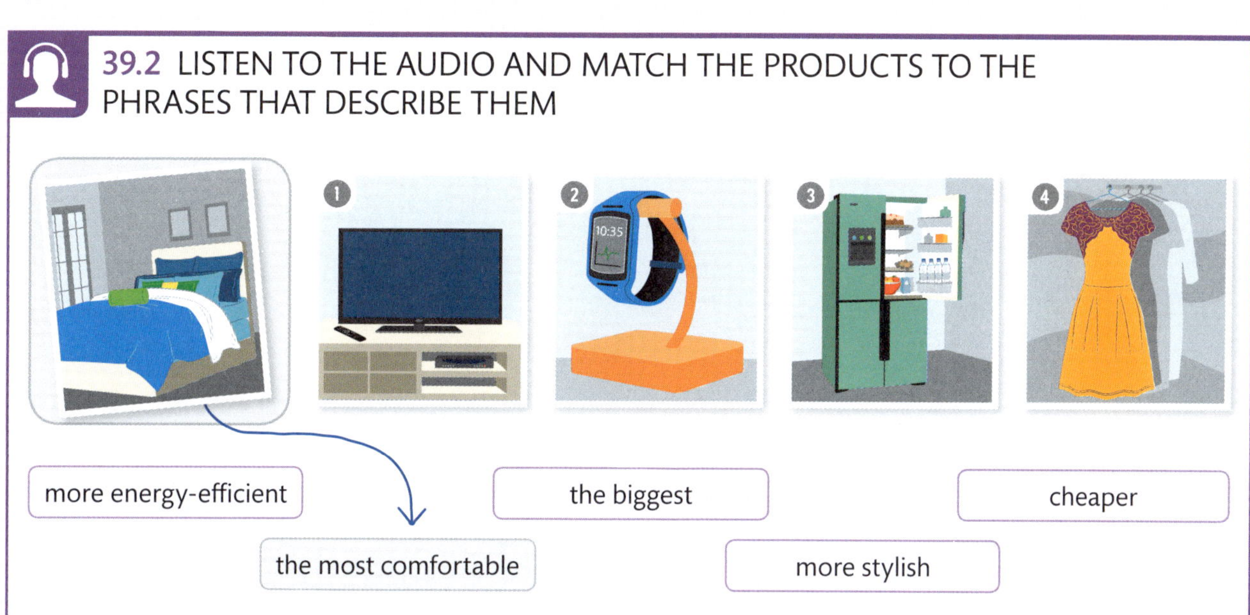

39.3 SAY THE SENTENCES OUT LOUD, FILLING IN THE GAPS USING THE WORDS IN THE PANEL

We think it is *the best* tablet on the market today.

1. We will create ______________ flowers for the tables and the bride's bouquet.
2. Our drink is ______________ than that brand because it has a natural caffeine substitute.
3. Our fitness tracker is ______________ more expensive models, but is cheaper.
4. We offer ______________ other cell phone companies do.

just as effective as | healthier | the most beautiful | ~~the best~~ | better technical support than

39.4 REWRITE THE SENTENCES, PUTTING THE WORDS IN THE CORRECT ORDER

detergent | as | effective | expensive | just | is | Our | as | brands. | more | laundry

Our laundry detergent is just as effective as more expensive brands.

1. tasty | cheaper. | is | as | much | the | This | leading | pizza | but | brand, | as

____

2. other | budget | is | as | the | brands | Our | market. | stylish | on | clothing | as

____

3. are | good | leader. | dishwasher | the | tablets | These | as | market | as | store-brand

____

4. is | seen. | action | movie | as | Our | anything | you've | as | exciting | latest | ever

____

5. not | eco-friendly | good | brand. | liquid | This | is | as | the | leading | dishwashing | as

____

39.5 REWRITE THE HIGHLIGHTED PHRASES, CORRECTING THE ERRORS

more exciting

1. ______________________________
2. ______________________________
3. ______________________________
4. ______________________________
5. ______________________________
6. ______________________________

FOOD MONTHLY

SALAD BOX

Receive delicious vegetables, dressings, and a recipe to make **excitinger** salads each week!

In our boxes, you'll find all you need to make salads **as exciting** they can be. We also provide you with a recipe card that tells you how to make five different salads. What could be **more simpler**? Enjoy a **convenienter** way to dine in at home.

Our salads are among **the healthyest** on the market. Every box comes with a nutritional information leaflet so you know you are enjoying **the most good** food. Our recipe boxes are **just as cheaper than** shopping in your local supermarket. So what are you waiting for? Place your order today.

40 Talking about facts and figures

When you are making a presentation or writing a report, it is important to describe changes and trends with precise language that sounds natural.

New language Collocations
Aa Vocabulary Business trends
New skill Describing facts and figures

40.1 LISTEN TO THE AUDIO, THEN NUMBER THE TRENDS IN THE ORDER THEY ARE DESCRIBED

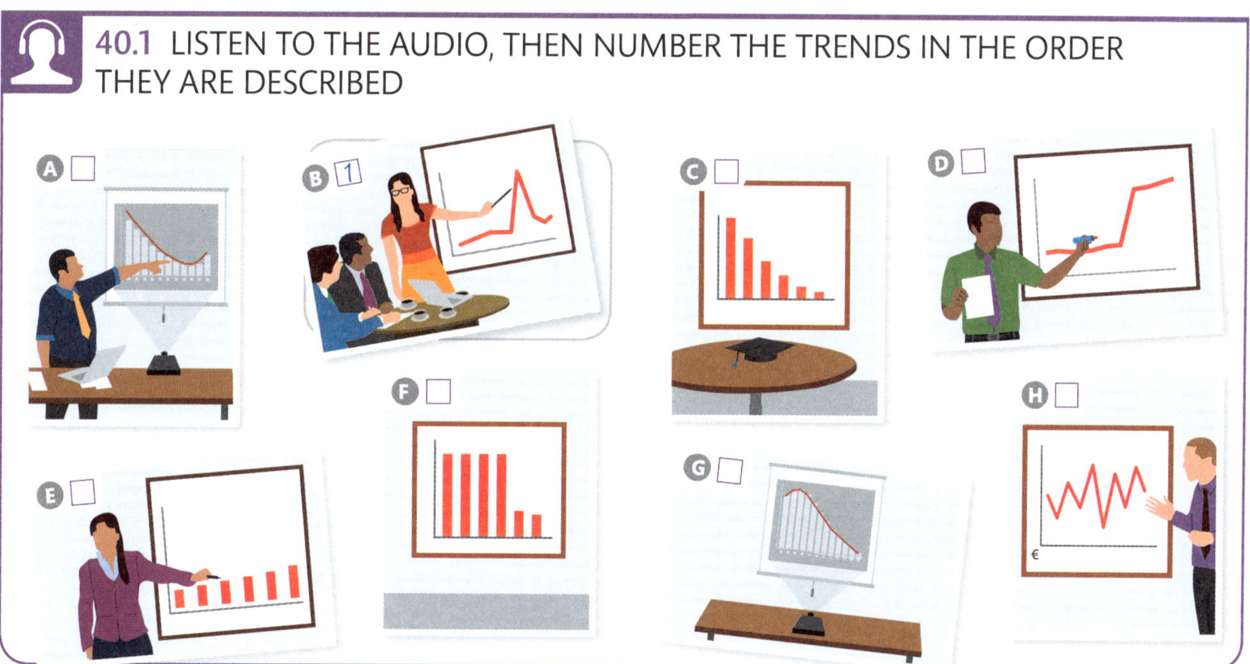

40.2 MATCH THE PAIRS OF SENTENCES THAT MEAN THE SAME THING

	There are fewer customer complaints. →	We expect a considerable drop in prices.
1	Customer complaints are more common.	The share value has rallied slightly.
2	Prices peaked, then fell.	Customer complaints have fallen steadily.
3	The price is going up and down a lot.	There was a sharp rise in the share value.
4	Prices are likely to fall significantly.	The price is fluctuating wildly.
5	The share value increased dramatically.	There has been an increase in complaints.
6	The share value has improved a bit.	There was a dramatic spike last year.

40.3 CROSS OUT THE INCORRECT WORD IN EACH SENTENCE

There was a fall of / ~~on~~ more than 13 percent.

1. Staff numbers went for / from 120 to 150.
2. Between / To 15 and 18 percent of stock is unsold.
3. We've experienced a boom of / at 56 percent.
4. Profits have fallen by / at 11 percent.
5. The share price peaked on / at $22.
6. Complaints doubled in / on the last quarter.
7. Our sale was from / between May and June.

40.4 READ THE REPORT AND ANSWER THE QUESTIONS

Profits have fallen because of the political situation.
True ☑ False ☐ Not given ☐

1. Mayvis Homes was established 12 years ago.
True ☐ False ☐ Not given ☐
2. Mayvis Homes' share price dropped in the first quarter.
True ☐ False ☐ Not given ☐
3. People think Mayvis Homes' share price will climb in the next few months.
True ☐ False ☐ Not given ☐
4. Customers do not like the latest houses built by Mayvis Homes.
True ☐ False ☐ Not given ☐
5. Last year, there was a sharp rise in Rushington Construction's share price.
True ☐ False ☐ Not given ☐
6. Most of Rushington Construction's work comes from the government.
True ☐ False ☐ Not given ☐

INDUSTRY AND TECHNOLOGY

Gloom in construction sector

The construction sector experienced a difficult first quarter, with share prices in the leading construction companies declining considerably. It is believed that worries about recent political events have contributed to a considerable drop in profits in the sector.

Mayvis Homes, which specializes in residential property for the over-60s, saw its share price fall by 12 percent in the first quarter, and there are fears that it could fall further before the end of the year. CEO Stan Gilmore said that customers are adopting a "wait and see" approach before making the decision to buy.

Going against the general trend is Rushington Construction PLC, which focuses on the education and healthcare sectors. Although the company's share price fluctuated slightly last year, the first quarter saw a return to stability, with the company's share price rallying slightly in the first quarter. The company relies on government contracts for between 60 and 85 percent of its work, and therefore is not so affected by short-term market trends.

40.5 RESPOND OUT LOUD TO THE AUDIO, FILLING IN THE GAPS USING THE WORDS IN THE PANEL

What are you doing about customer service staff?

We are increasing our customer service staff from 10 to 15.

1. What's happening to the price of rice?

   There's been a ______ because of a poor harvest.

2. When was your best sales period last year?

   Our sales ______ $200,000 a day in December.

3. Your production facility seems very efficient.

   Yes, malfunctions have ______ since last year.

4. How much of the stock is on sale?

   Between ______ percent of our stock is on sale.

5. Are you happy with our profits this year?

   Yes, they've ______ since last year.

6. Why have our costs gone up?

   There was an ______ 10 percent in the cost of electricity.

~~10 to 15~~ | 20 and 30 | dramatic spike | fallen steadily | increase of | peaked at | rallied slightly

41 Plans and suggestions

English uses modal verbs to make suggestions, and indirect questions or the passive voice to politely request information or point out a mistake.

New language Indirect questions
Aa Vocabulary Business negotiations
New skill Negotiating politely

Aa 41.1 MATCH THE BEGINNINGS OF THE SENTENCES TO THE CORRECT ENDINGS

Would you mind bringing → the delivery date forward by a week?

1. Are you able to pay
2. We might move forward with the contract
3. I would like to resolve this issue
4. Maybe we could discuss some
5. We were thinking
6. I'm afraid I was hoping for

- our fee in installments?
- as soon as possible.
- the delivery date forward by a week?
- that you could design our new logo.
- if you would consider buying in bulk.
- something more innovative.
- alternative options for the design.

41.2 LISTEN TO THE AUDIO, THEN NUMBER THE SENTENCES IN THE ORDER YOU HEAR THEM

Pippa is negotiating with a client over her contract to redecorate his store.

A. Well, we were hoping for something more modern. ☐
B. I'm afraid we need it sooner. ☐
C. I was wondering what sort of look you want. 1
D. Would you mind waiting until next month for payment? ☐
E. I was thinking we could use the company colors. ☐
F. Are you able to pay in installments? ☐

41.3 REWRITE THE INDIRECT QUESTIONS, PUTTING THE WORDS IN THE CORRECT ORDER

tell | Could | expect | me | you | deliver | order? | to | you | our | when

Could you tell me when you expect to deliver our order?

1. try | wondering | I | these | on. | was | where | clothes | I | can

2. me | sample | you | tell | will | when | ready? | designs | be | the | Could

3. I | to | Samia's | I | about | if | you | was | talk | performance. | could | wondering

4. tell | store? | product | you | me | I | order | Could | this | in | whether | can

5. have | whether | invoice | was | my | you | wondering | paid | yet. | I

6. tell | the | Could | is? | me | warranty | you | period | what

7. how | new | from | was | the | I | product | is | one. | wondering | old | different | the

8. when | you | price | available? | will | me | the | Could | be | tell | list

9. able | be | I | offer | if | was | a | wondering | to | me | discount. | would | you

41.4 REWRITE THE SENTENCES USING THE PASSIVE VOICE

I'm afraid you didn't pay our invoice on time.
I'm afraid our invoice wasn't paid on time.

1. I'm afraid you missed our deadline.
2. It looks as if you sent the wrong size.
3. It seems that you did not apply the discount.
4. I'm afraid you delivered our order to the wrong address.
5. It looks as if you calculated the price incorrectly.
6. It seems that you do not train your employees very well.
7. I'm afraid you did not satisfy our customers.
8. It seems that you lost my order while it was being delivered.
9. I'm afraid you did not cook my steak properly.
10. It looks as if you have made a mistake.
11. It seems that you still haven't fixed the printer.
12. I'm afraid you did not check the document thoroughly enough.

41.5 CROSS OUT THE INCORRECT WORDS IN EACH SENTENCE, THEN SAY THE SENTENCES OUT LOUD

Could / ~~Do~~ you tell me when my order will be ready?

1. I was wondering if you could / could you look at my presentation.
2. Could you tell / telling me when my order will be dispatched?
3. I was wondering if you do / would be free to meet tomorrow.
4. Could you tell me when can we / we can expect our invoice to be paid?
5. I was wondering what time does the store open / the store opens.
6. Could you tell me / know how much the new product should retail for?

41.6 READ THE EMAIL AND MARK THE CORRECT SUMMARY

1. Juanita has only paid 25 percent of Brendan's invoice because she is not happy with the service she received. She wants the staff to receive training. ☐
2. Juanita has not paid Brendan's invoice because she is unhappy with the service that she received. She does not think Brendan has trained his staff well. ☐
3. Brendan has not invoiced Juanita for the bikes because his staff were rude to Juanita. He is going to give them training in customer service. ☐
4. Brendan has sent a revised invoice for the bikes because the order was delivered two weeks late. He is going to look into training his staff. ☐

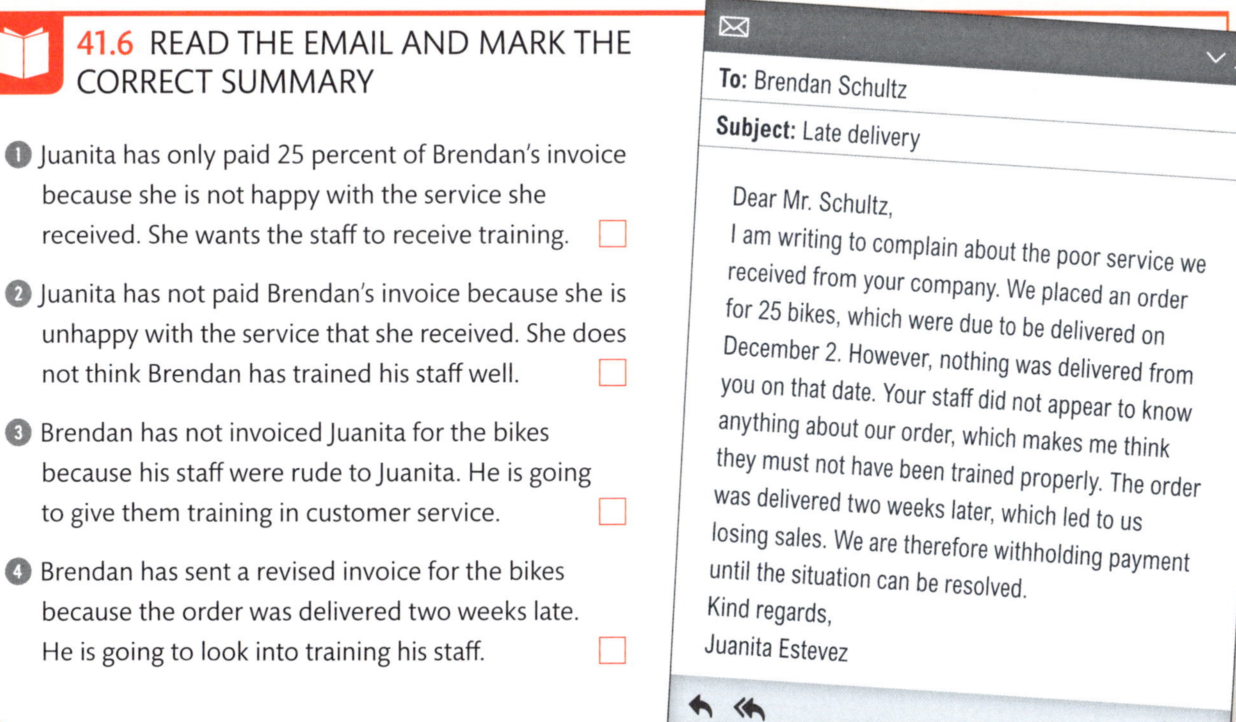

To: Brendan Schultz

Subject: Late delivery

Dear Mr. Schultz,

I am writing to complain about the poor service we received from your company. We placed an order for 25 bikes, which were due to be delivered on December 2. However, nothing was delivered from you on that date. Your staff did not appear to know anything about our order, which makes me think they must not have been trained properly. The order was delivered two weeks later, which led to us losing sales. We are therefore withholding payment until the situation can be resolved.

Kind regards,

Juanita Estevez

42 Emphasizing your opinion

There are many English phrases for politely emphasizing your point of view. These are useful when you are dealing with disagreement in the workplace.

New language Discourse markers for emphasis
Aa Vocabulary Workplace disagreement
New skill Emphasizing your opinion

42.1 MARK THE SENTENCES THAT ARE CORRECT

What we need is an up-to-date delivery schedule from you. ☑
What need is an up-to-date delivery schedule from you. ☐

1. If I ask you, you won't find a better deal ☐
   If you ask me, you won't find a better deal. ☐

2. Actually, we are waiting for the factory to send us more of that product. ☐
   We are waiting actually for the factory to send us more of that product. ☐

3. The most thing is that we agree on schedule dates. ☐
   The main thing is that we agree on schedule dates. ☐

4. What I'm saying is that I can offer free delivery on orders over a hundred. ☐
   What I say is that I can offer free delivery on orders over a hundred. ☐

42.2 LISTEN TO THE AUDIO AND ANSWER THE QUESTIONS

Tia is negotiating with a store manager, Roger, who she hopes will sell her new product.

Roger is happy with Tia's asking price.
True ☐ False ☑ Not given ☐

1. The raincoats sell for $30 in the store.
   True ☐ False ☐ Not given ☐

2. Roger is happy with Tia's revised deal.
   True ☐ False ☐ Not given ☐

3. Roger places an order for 200 raincoats.
   True ☐ False ☐ Not given ☐

4. The raincoats are the cheapest on the market.
   True ☐ False ☐ Not given ☐

5. Tia would sell the raincoats in another store.
   True ☐ False ☐ Not given ☐

42.3 RESPOND OUT LOUD TO THE AUDIO, FILLING IN THE GAPS USING THE PHRASES IN THE PANEL

Unfortunately, I can't do the job until next month.

That's OK. The main thing is that we have the right person to do the job.

1. Could you send some sample designs for us to look at?

   ______, we sent you an email with them this morning.

2. Is there any way you could offer a reduced asking price?

   I'm afraid not. If ______, this is a great deal.

3. We'd like to sign the contract today if that is possible.

   What ______ an assurance that you can meet our schedule dates.

4. Would you consider offering us a discount?

   The ______ that we agree on a price that allows enough profit.

5. Can we say a price of $50 per unit?

   ______ your asking price is too high. Can we say $40 a unit?

I'm afraid | Actually | ~~The main thing is~~ | you ask me | main thing is | we need is

43 Discussing conditions

English often uses the first and second conditionals for negotiating with clients and co-workers, and the zero conditional to talk about general truths.

New language Conditionals
Aa Vocabulary Negotiating and bargaining
New skill Discussing possibilities

43.1 FILL IN THE GAPS BY PUTTING THE VERBS IN THE CORRECT FORMS TO MAKE SECOND CONDITIONAL SENTENCES

If the contract ___was___ (be) clearer, we ___would sign___ (sign) it now.

1. If they ______________ (give) us a discount, we ______________ (place) an order.
2. If the product ______________ (be) cheaper, we ______________ (buy) it.
3. If they ______________ (move) the deadline, we ______________ (meet) it.
4. I ______________ (reply) to the email now if I ______________ (have) more time.
5. We ______________ (sell) more online if our website ______________ (be) faster.
6. We ______________ (send) the package tomorrow if you ______________ (order) before 9 tonight.
7. If the agency ______________ (send) us better temps, we ______________ (use) them again.
8. If I ______________ (work) late every night, I ______________ (finish) my report for Friday.
9. I ______________ (apply) for the job if the hours ______________ (not be) so long.

43.2 LISTEN TO THE AUDIO AND ANSWER THE QUESTIONS

Andrés is negotiating with a painting and decorating company about his home improvements.

The team can start in December.
True ☐ **False** ☑ **Not given** ☐

1 The team might finish by the end of January.
True ☐ **False** ☐ **Not given** ☐

2 There are six painters on the team.
True ☐ **False** ☐ **Not given** ☐

3 Andrés asks the team to repaint all the rooms.
True ☐ **False** ☐ **Not given** ☐

4 Andrés knows what colors he wants.
True ☐ **False** ☐ **Not given** ☐

5 Andrés wants to see more wallpaper samples.
True ☐ **False** ☐ **Not given** ☐

6 Andrés won't see new designs until next week.
True ☐ **False** ☐ **Not given** ☐

43.3 REWRITE THE ZERO CONDITIONAL SENTENCES, PUTTING THE WORDS IN THE CORRECT ORDER

they're | Products | quality. | sell | really | good | if | well

Products sell really well if they're good quality.

1 a | customers | pay | 15 | late fee. | we | don't | on | charge | If | time, | percent

2 need | open | helpline | to | 8pm | if | from | is | you | Our | help. | 8am

3 double | get | employees | time. | weekends, | When | they | work | paid

4 we | 5 | a | give | If | you | a | customer, | percent | you | discount. | are | regular

5 after | we | a | day. | payment | credit | next | 3pm, | we | it | If | the | receive

43.4 MATCH THE BEGINNINGS OF THE SENTENCES TO THE CORRECT ENDINGS

If you book 100 places, → we'll give you a 5 percent discount.

1. If you need help with your computer,
2. We would move production to Europe,
3. We will issue a full refund
4. If clients are regular customers,
5. If our receptionist was rude to you,

- we would give her a verbal warning.
- if it was cheaper to do that.
- we'll give you a 5 percent discount.
- we give them a 5 percent discount.
- you can call the IT department.
- if you return the product to one of our stores.

43.5 REWRITE THE FIRST CONDITIONAL SENTENCES, CORRECTING THE ERRORS

If you **will order** before 9pm, we'll deliver your goods the following day.
If you order before 9pm, we'll deliver your goods the following day.

1. If you **not** pay on time, we won't send you your order.

2. We'll issue a full refund if **you won't be** happy with our products.

3. If you **will book** two nights in our hotel, we'll give you a third night for free.

4. If Alan's presentation **will go** well, he will get promoted next month.

5. We won't charge you for your stay if you **won't** get a good night's sleep.

6. If you **ordering** over 100 units, we'll give you a discount.

43.6 RESPOND OUT LOUD TO THE AUDIO, FILLING IN THE GAPS USING THE PHRASES IN THE PANEL

Our standard price for this new model is $200 per unit.

Well, if you lowered the price, *I would buy* 50 units.

1. We'd like the renovations to be finished by the end of next month.

   Well, if you pay for the overtime, ______ the job by then.

2. Is there any possibility you can give us a discount?

   Yes. If ______ 100 units or more, we give them a 5 percent discount.

3. I'm not happy with the quality of your product.

   If you return it to us within 28 days, ______ a full refund.

4. Our new tablet retails for $79 in all major stores. We can do you a price of $69 per unit.

   If ______ a price of $59 per unit, we'd sell it in our stores.

5. Your product is not very good quality.

   We're sorry to hear that. If a customer makes a complaint, ______ it very seriously.

6. We love your product. We'd like to place an order for 100 units a month.

   We can't do that yet. If ______ on extra staff, we'd be able to increase production.

we take | we will issue | ~~I would buy~~ | clients buy | we took | we will finish | you could do

44 Discussing problems

English uses the third conditional to talk about an unreal past, or events that did not happen. This is useful for talking about workplace mistakes.

New language Third conditional
Aa Vocabulary Workplace mistakes
New skill Talking about past mistakes

44.1 FILL IN THE GAPS BY PUTTING THE VERBS IN THE CORRECT FORMS TO MAKE THIRD CONDITIONAL SENTENCES

If you *had worked* (work) late, you *would have finished* (finish) the presentation.

1. We ______ (sign) the contract if the deadline ______ (not be) so tight.
2. If we ______ (leave) earlier, we ______ (not miss) the train.
3. If the waitress ______ (not be) so rude, we ______ (not complain).
4. If we ______ (order) before 3pm, we ______ (receive) the goods today.
5. We ______ (not lose) the client if we ______ (deliver) the report on time.
6. If you ______ (repair) the printer, we ______ (not cancel) the contract.
7. If I ______ (know) how expensive it was, I ______ (put) it in the safe.
8. The boss ______ (not shout) if you ______ (admit) your mistake.
9. If you ______ (be) more prepared, you ______ (give) a better presentation.
10. We ______ (give) you free delivery if you ______ (pay) on time.
11. If I ______ (know) our competitor's price, I ______ (offer) a bigger discount.
12. We ______ (meet) our deadline if we ______ (employ) more staff.
13. If you ______ (not be) off sick, we ______ (invite) you to the meeting.
14. We ______ (pay) the full amount due if you ______ (not miss) our deadline.
15. If you ______ (sell) more products last time, we ______ (ask) you to lead the pitch.

44.2 LISTEN TO THE AUDIO AND MARK WHICH THINGS ACTUALLY HAPPENED

1

2

3

4
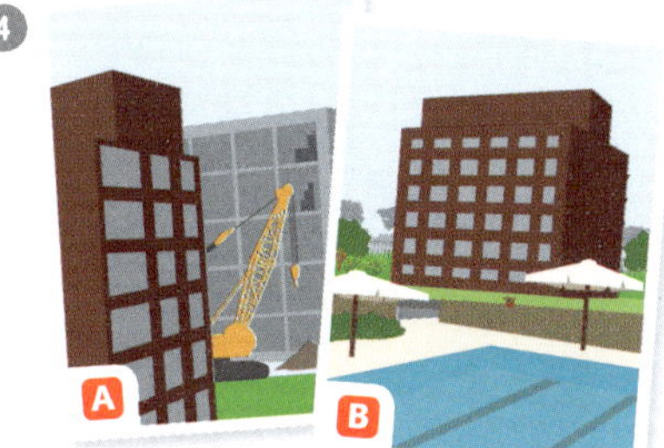

5
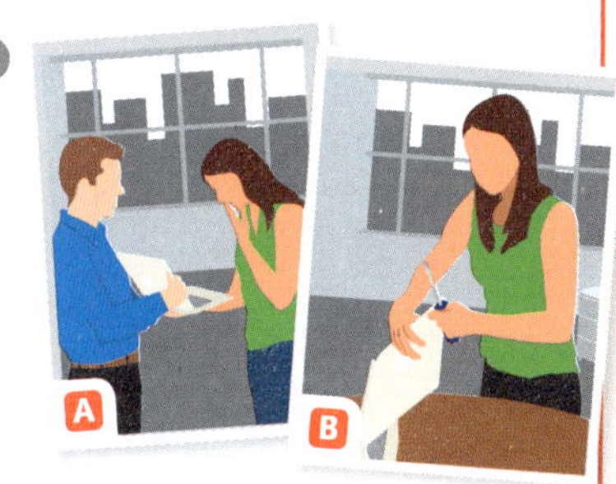

44.3 MATCH THE BEGINNINGS OF THE SENTENCES TO THE CORRECT ENDINGS

If you'd left earlier → you wouldn't have missed the meeting.

1. If I'd used the spell check,
2. If she'd told the boss about her mistake,
3. If they'd paid on time,
4. If I'd used the latest sales data,
5. If he'd checked the order was right,
6. If you'd ordered more units,
7. If he'd wanted an older model,

- we wouldn't have canceled their order.
- he wouldn't have been so angry.
- you wouldn't have missed the meeting.
- my report would have been up to date.
- he would have asked for one.
- we would have given you a discount.
- my work wouldn't have had so many errors.
- his clients wouldn't have complained.

44.4 REWRITE THE SENTENCES USING "UNLESS"

If you don't order 500 units, we won't be able to give you a discount.
Unless you order 500 units, we won't be able to give you a discount.

1. Clive will get a verbal warning if his timekeeping doesn't improve.

2. If you don't pay by the end of today, we will cancel the contract.

3. We won't win the contract if we can't offer a better price.

4. I won't get promoted this year if I don't impress the boss.

5. Your warranty will not be valid if you don't register your product.

6. If I don't sell to 100 new customers, I won't meet my sales targets.

7. We won't make many sales if we don't beat our competitors' prices.

8. If I don't work overtime, I'm not going to meet the deadline.

9. His presentation will be boring if he doesn't add special effects.

10. The CEO won't be happy if we don't win the contract.

11. If you don't lower the price, we won't order any more units.

12. We will miss the train if we don't leave now.

44.5 READ THE REPORT AND ANSWER THE QUESTIONS

The clients were happy with the product.
True ☐ False ☑ Not given ☐

1. Customers wanted recipes from around the world.
True ☐ False ☐ Not given ☐

2. Future Foods didn't offer traditional dishes.
True ☐ False ☐ Not given ☐

3. Customers wanted evening deliveries.
True ☐ False ☐ Not given ☐

4. Customers thought that the price was too high.
True ☐ False ☐ Not given ☐

5. Future Foods will develop more international dishes.
True ☐ False ☐ Not given ☐

PROGRESS REPORT

Ten months ago we launched our new recipe service, Future Foods, where we send customers the ingredients to cook a new recipe. Sales have been very disappointing, and feedback on the service was not as good as we expected.

WHY? Customers said that they prefer to try a range of dishes from around the world. If we had known that, we would have had less of a focus on traditional meals. They also said that the price could be lower.

WHAT NOW? Unless we reduce the price of our service and listen to customers' feedback, we won't make as many sales as we want. We need to offer a more international, affordable range of foods and recipe packs.

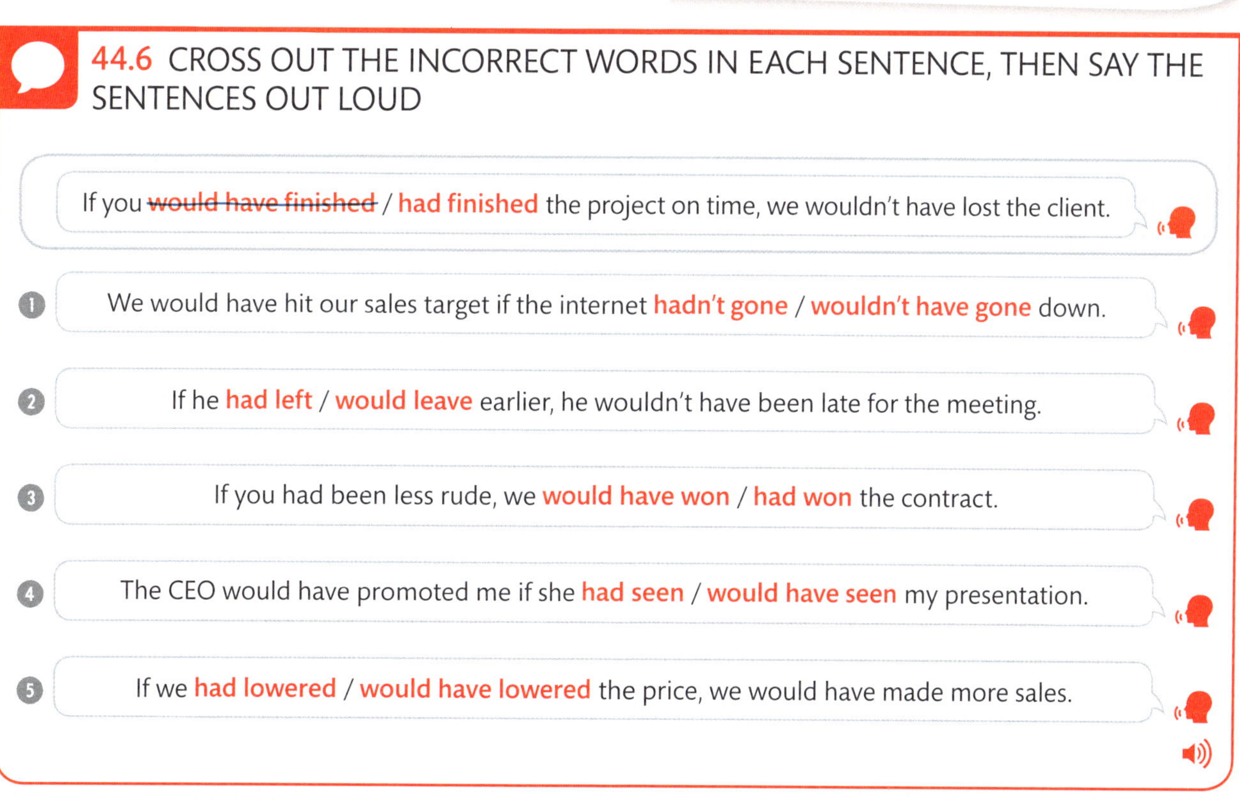

44.6 CROSS OUT THE INCORRECT WORDS IN EACH SENTENCE, THEN SAY THE SENTENCES OUT LOUD

If you ~~would have finished~~ / had finished the project on time, we wouldn't have lost the client.

1. We would have hit our sales target if the internet hadn't gone / wouldn't have gone down.

2. If he had left / would leave earlier, he wouldn't have been late for the meeting.

3. If you had been less rude, we would have won / had won the contract.

4. The CEO would have promoted me if she had seen / would have seen my presentation.

5. If we had lowered / would have lowered the price, we would have made more sales.

Answers

01

1.1

1. I'd like to **introduce** you to Marco from IT.
2. You **must** be Paola from Madrid.
3. Gloria, **meet** Julia, our new secretary.
4. Have you two **met** each other before?
5. Great to **see** you again!
6. **Nice** to meet you, Antonio.
7. Sanjay has **told** me all about you.
8. I don't **think** we've met before, have we?
9. It's a **pleasure** to meet you.

1.2

1. Simone, I'd like to introduce you to **Gerald, our new sales manager.**
2. Hello. I don't think we've **met. My name's Jana.**
3. You must be Selma from the **Chicago branch. Great to meet you.**
4. Hi, Omar. I think we **met at the conference in Dubai last year.**
5. My boss has told me **so much about your work.**
6. This is Colin from IT. **Colin, meet Liam. He's joining our team soon.**

1.3

1. False
2. True
3. Not given
4. True
5. False
6. False

1.4

1. I **catch** the train to work at 8:15am each morning.
2. We **have** a new printer that is difficult to use.
3. I **am** working at the Guangdong branch all this August.
4. Sanchez **knows** Katie because they worked together.
5. **Are** you enjoying this presentation? I think it's great.
6. Tim **doesn't know** Anna from the Montevideo branch.
7. Marek **likes** the new furniture we bought for the office.
8. How **do you spell** your name?
9. The meeting usually **takes** only half an hour.
10. Doug is really **enjoying** the conference this year.
11. I'd like **to** introduce you to my manager, José Rodriguez.
12. Clara **works** from 8:30 to 4:30 on Thursdays and Fridays.

1.5

1. Our company **is having** some difficulties at the moment.
2. Pablo, I'd like you to **meet** my wife, Elvira.
3. I usually hate conferences, but I **am enjoying** this one a lot.
4. I **have** two children, a son and a daughter.
5. Michael, **I'd like** to introduce you to Michelle.
6. I **don't think** we've met before, have we?
7. It's so great **to see** you again after such a long time.
8. How **do you pronounce** your last name?
9. You must **be** Harold from Copenhagen. Nice to meet you.
10. Hi, I think we met in Oslo, **didn't we**?

02

2.1

1. I was preparing for the presentation.
2. Did Greg work in the New York branch?
3. Akira was living in Kyoto in 1998.
4. I didn't understand the presentation.
5. Pete was reading a book at 9pm yesterday.
6. I was feeling exhausted at work, so I left.
7. Did you enjoy the presentation?
8. Were you working in IT then?
9. Kai wasn't feeling well, so he went home.
10. I found a new job in France.

2.2

A 6
B 1
C 5
D 7
E 4
F 3
G 2
H 8

2.3

1 Daniel **has worked** for more than five different law firms.
2 I **have taken** the bus to work all my working life.
3 The company **has employed** five new people since September.
4 Peter is a terrible waiter. He **has started** looking for a different job.
5 Andrea **has worked** here since she graduated in 1999.
6 The factory **has produced** 15,000 machines this year.
7 Tim's really happy. He **has finished** his presentation for tomorrow.
8 We **have sold** our products in more than 25 countries.
9 I **have walked** to work since my car broke down.
10 I **have decided** that I'm going to retire next year.
11 Dave **has taken** more time than we expected.
12 I **have worked** at this office for more than 25 years now.
13 Chris **has visited** more than 50 countries so far.

2.4

1 Jim was preparing a presentation **when his boss entered the room**.
2 I've worked at this company **for more than ten years**.
3 Chris had to wait for a taxi for **more than an hour**.
4 Tim moved to New York **when he was transferred to the US office**.
5 I ran my own software company **before I started working here**.
6 In 2013, our company **bought a smaller Canadian software firm**.

2.5

1 True
2 True
3 False
4 True
5 Not given
6 True

2.6

1 At 3pm yesterday, I **was discussing** the new software with our IT team.
2 While Susan **was eating** lunch, her team was working hard.
3 Karl moved to Berlin when he **lost** his job in Paris.
4 Alan **was traveling** to work when he received a call from his wife.
5 In 2007, I **was working** in the company headquarters in Geneva.
6 I **have lived** in San Francisco since 2003.
7 Peter **was sleeping** at his desk when his phone rang.
8 They **have been** based in Frankfurt since 1994.
9 While I **was living** in France, I worked as a waiter.
10 Derek **bought** his first house in 2009.
11 What **were you doing** at 4pm this afternoon?
12 I **was studying** in college when I decided to work as a lawyer.
13 Who was in the meeting room when you **entered**?
14 We **sold** our first machine in China in 2003.

03

3.1

1 Human Resources (HR)
2 Information Technology (IT)
3 Sales
4 Public Relations (PR)
5 Legal
6 Facilities / Office Services
7 Administration
8 Research and Development (R&D)
9 Accounts / Finance
10 Marketing
11 Production

3.2

1 assistant
2 Chief Executive Officer (CEO)
3 Chief Financial Officer (CFO)
4 employee
5 manager

3.3

1 to work for
2 to work as
3 to be responsible for
4 to be in charge of
5 to work in

04

4.1

1 Claude is used to working weekends.
2 Did Paul use to work in San Francisco?
3 I am not used to working in such heat.
4 The team used to go out for lunch.
5 We didn't use to have so many meetings.
6 I used to live in a house near the office.
7 Did you use to work in Paris?
8 I'm used to the new software now.
9 I'll never get used to this operating system.
10 Kerry is used to commuting a long way.

4.2

A 7
B 1
C 5
D 6
E 2
F 4
G 3

4.3

1 We didn't use to have so much free time.
2 I'll never get used to driving on the left.
3 Did Anthony use to work in the Frankfurt branch?
4 I am used to having to get up at 6am.
5 Derek isn't used to commuting so far to work.
6 The team hasn't got used to the new operating system.
7 We used to have lunch in the café near the park.
8 Danielle isn't used to giving presentations.
9 Pam used to work in the branch in Cologne.
10 Phil isn't used to wearing a uniform for work.

4.4

1 She's not used to working long hours.
2 I used to work as a doctor.
3 Dan's used to driving on the left.
4 She's used to getting up early.
5 I'm not used to spicy food.
6 I'll never get used to English weather.
7 I'm not used to working so late.
8 We're getting used to the new boss.

4.5

1 No, thanks. I'm fine.
2 I'm not used to this hot weather!
3 That would be great!
4 I haven't yet. Is it any good?
5 I'm getting used to the traffic.

4.6

1 Are you **used to** living in a tropical country yet?
2 I **used to** travel to work on foot before they built the metro.
3 When I lived in Berlin, we **used to** live in an apartment downtown.
4 **Did you use to** work in the Edinburgh branch?
5 I grew up in Japan, so I'm **used to** driving on the left.
6 Arnold's **used to** waking up at 5am every morning.
7 I **am used to** working for a demanding boss.
8 When I was a child, I didn't **use to** like going to school.
9 We **used to** go to Florida each year on vacation.
10 My father **used to** work in a factory until it closed down.

05

5.1

1 Staff must not smoke in the building.
2 We don't have to go to work tomorrow.
3 I have to go home early on Thursday.
4 You have to do this assignment today.
5 We need to increase sales this year.
6 Jim doesn't have to attend the meeting.
7 The team must not forget their timesheets.
8 Paolo has got to sign up for the course.

9 We will need to hire new staff this fall.
10 We must improve our productivity.

5.2

1 False
2 True
3 False
4 False
5 False
6 Not given
7 True
8 True
9 Not given

5.3

1 Would you give Peter a copy of the minutes, please?
2 All visitors must leave their passes at reception.
3 Could you take this letter to the post office, please?
4 Ramon needs to work harder if he wants a promotion.
5 Sharon needs to sign up for the training course.
6 Could you leave a copy of the agenda on my desk, please?
7 You must complete the enrolment form before 5pm on Friday.
8 Staff must not smoke inside the building.
9 Would you send an email to everyone about the meeting?
10 You must finish the project by Wednesday evening.

5.4

1 The company must change **if it wants to survive**.
2 I need you to finish **the presentation by Friday**.
3 Could you keep a **record of everything you spend this week**?
4 Would you inform **the team about the recent changes, please**?
5 The company has got to **invest more in training**.
6 You don't have **to finish the assignment today**.
7 We need to think **about closing some of our branches**.

5.5

1 True
2 False
3 Not given
4 False
5 False

5.6

1 No, I **don't need** you to finish it today.
2 I'm sorry, Mike. We really **must** have it by Friday.
3 I'm sorry, but members of the public **must not** enter the building.
4 We need them tomorrow. **Could** you call the supplier, please?
5 No, you **don't have** to. The deadline is next week.
6 Well, I **need** it by 1pm today.

06

6.1

1 to make a loss
2 to undercut competitors
3 an overdraft
4 overheads
5 sales figures
6 to get into debt
7 to break even
8 an economic downturn
9 income
10 expenditure / outlay
11 an upturn in the market
12 accounts
13 to drop
14 cash flow
15 to peak
16 the exchange rate
17 to go out of business

07

7.1

1 Sales **were** good because we **had organized** a good marketing campaign.
2 Sales **had fallen** sharply, so we **decided** to withdraw the product.
3 Aditya **wanted** to try a program that the team **hadn't used / had not used** before.
4 After Peter **had finished** the report, he **wanted** to go on vacation.

7.2

1 Ramon **had written** ten pages of the report when his computer **crashed**.
2 Many of our employees **had not** visited the factory before and **were** very impressed.
3 Bob's speech **was** disappointing because he **hadn't prepared** well.
4 Nobody **had told** the conference delegates where their hotel **was**.
5 I **hadn't delegated** tasks to Kai before, but I **thought** he did a good job.

7.3

1 The **following** report will explore our new sales strategy.
2 As can be **seen** in the table, we have invested $4 million this year.
3 Some of our customers have **stated** that they are not satisfied with the result.
4 Our initial investigation **suggests** that this is not true.
5 Our **initial** recommendation is to reduce the budget by 50 percent.
6 We **consulted** a number of focus groups for this report.

7.4

1 The purpose of our report **is to review our current sales strategy**.
2 The following report presents **a summary of our findings**.
3 Our clients stated that **they were unhappy with the changes**.
4 Based on the initial research, **we should invest more in R&D**.
5 Our principal recommendation is to **proceed with the sale of the subsidiary**.

7.5

1 20 miles from downtown
2 Rail connections to other cities
3 It is affordable in Alchester
4 Stay in Alchester for over ten years
5 A decision has not yet been made

7.6

1 The purpose of this report is to compare the two factories.
2 Focus groups had been consulted before we implemented the policy.
3 Sales of our products had fallen in comparison with the previous quarter.
4 Our principal recommendation is to increase investment in R&D.
5 Profits had risen by more than 20 percent in the first half of 2015.

7.7

1 In this report we will **present** the findings of our research.
2 The **purpose** of this report is to investigate the pros and cons of the new software.
3 This bar chart **compares** the sales figures for the last two years.
4 Our customers **stated** that they had been disappointed with the product.

08

8.1

1 Of course. Let me see what I can do.
2 Certainly. It's ZX42 9JL.
3 We've been having difficulties with our software.
4 We'll offer you a discount on your next order.

8.2

1 Could you **tell me** your reference number?
2 **Let's see** what we can do.
3 **We'll offer** you a full refund.
4 Our driver **has been experiencing** problems.
5 Could you **hold the line**, please?
6 I'm very **sorry to hear** that.
7 Can you **look into** this issue?
8 **We'll send you** a replacement.
9 Of course I can **help** you.

8.3

1 I'm very **sorry** to hear that, sir.
2 Certainly. Let's **see** what I can do.
3 Could you tell me your **reference** number, please?
4 Could you please **hold** the line?
5 I'm sorry. Our IT system's been **experiencing** difficulties.
6 My order **arrived** dirty and broken.
7 Can you **offer** any compensation?
8 Of course. We'll give you a **discount** on your next order.

8.4

1. Could you look **into** the problem for me?
2. The company **has** been experiencing difficulties recently.
3. Please **hold** the line for a moment.
4. I've been **waiting** all day for my order to arrive.

8.5

Note: Answers to 1, 2, and 4 can also be written in contracted form.

1. We **have been preparing** a proposal all evening.
2. Our website **has been experiencing** difficulties this morning.
3. Chris **has been working** on that project for three months now.
4. Our products **have not been selling** well so far this year.

8.6

1. Peter has been talking for more than 25 minutes.
2. Have you been getting good feedback from the clients?
3. The company has been losing money for years.
4. Juan hasn't been working at our company for long.

8.7

A 4
B 2
C 6
D 5
E 1
F 3

8.8

4

09

9.1

1. social media
2. a website
3. automated
4. to access
5. to work online
6. up to date
7. user-friendly
8. to back up
9. a conference call
10. breaking up
11. to download an app
12. a mobile device
13. to work offline
14. an email has bounced
15. to charge
16. a username and password
17. a network

10

10.1

1. I hope all's well **with you and the team in Tokyo**.
2. Would you be free **on Thursday July 7 at 4pm**?
3. Please give me a call **if you can't make it**.
4. Please see the schedule **for next week's conference attached**.
5. If you have any questions, **don't hesitate to get in touch**.

10.2

1. I was **wondering** if you could help me prepare my presentation.
2. Would you be free to **meet** on Thursday evening?
3. I'm **copying** Sanjay and Anita in on this email.
4. I **hope** all's well with you and the team in Delhi.
5. Please see the minutes of yesterday's meeting **attached**.
6. If you have any **questions**, please let me know.
7. How **about** joining us at the pizza place later this evening?

10.3

1. I just wanted **to** check that you're coming to the presentation.
2. Would you **be** free next Wednesday morning at 11:30?
3. Please find a copy of the report **attached**.
4. If you **have** any questions, please let me know.
5. I'm **copying** Ricardo in on this.

10.4

4

11

11.1

1. Mohammed **is meeting** the new supplier to discuss a new deal.
2. Jola **is talking** to Sales this afternoon to agree new discounts.

3. They **are aiming** to have the presentation ready by 5:00pm.
4. I **am writing** to inform you that there is a delay with the part you need.
5. We **are still waiting** to hear from the Chinese partners.

11.2

1. Future 2. Future
3. Future 4. Present

11.3

1. hesitate
2. obtain
3. confirm
4. inform
5. prefer
6. assure

11.4

1. Will you be attending the launch of the new products?
2. I was wondering if we could put our meeting back to tomorrow.
3. We are aiming to send the new designs by Friday.
4. Will you be paying for the order in cash or by card?
5. I was wondering if you would take the clients out for dinner.

11.5

1. We are still putting together the final sales report.
2. Will you be giving the presentation at tomorrow's conference?
3. We were wondering if we could postpone our meeting.

11.6

1. Not given 2. True
3. False 4. False

12

12.1

1. Can you deal **with** the cleaners, please? The kitchen is a mess.
2. Can we catch **up** later this morning at around 11:00?
3. Is the fridge broken again? I'll **look** into that now.
4. Have we run **out** of paper? There's none in the photocopier.

12.2

1. Can we **fix up** a meeting with Marketing and Sales?
2. Have you asked Surina to **fill out** all the paperwork?
3. The printer has **run out** of ink again.
4. I can't **figure out** what Dave wants me to do.
5. I need to **bring up** the topic of punctuality with you.

12.3

1. I need to **back** my files **up**.
2. Can you **give** the agenda **out**?
3. Can we **call** tomorrow's meeting **off**?
4. Can you **pass** my message **on** to her?
5. Let me **hand** the minutes **out**.
6. I want to **put** my tie **on**.
7. Can you **fix** another meeting **up**?
8. I need to **send** an email **out**.
9. We are **taking** new staff **on**.
10. Can you **set** the projector **up**?
11. I'd like to **talk** the sales plan **over**.

12.4

1. She hasn't backed them up
2. Thursday afternoon
3. Write a report about feedback
4. Deal with some of Amanda's emails
5. A message
6. His best suit and tie

12.5

1. Jamil's flight is delayed. I think we'll have to call our meeting with him **off**.
2. All employees have to put an apron **on** before entering the kitchen.
3. We're hoping to give **out** samples of our work at the exhibition.
4. It's really important to back your files **up** every night or you could lose work.

12.6

1. Khalil has **filled the form** out.
2. She has just **hung up** on me without saying goodbye!
3. He **put his tie on** because he had an important meeting.
4. He gave **his report out** to everyone at the meeting.
5. They **set a meeting** up for later in the week.

13

13.1

1. packaging
2. product testing
3. handmade
4. a one-off production
5. labor-intensive
6. stock
7. product approval
8. raw materials
9. a prototype
10. a production line
11. a warehouse
12. shipping
13. ethically sourced
14. overproduction
15. a factory
16. mass production
17. a supplier

14

14.1

1. The media **had been** told about the press launch and were out in force.
2. New models **are being** created to coincide with the premiere of the movie.
3. The design has been **patented** so nobody can copy it.
4. Our coffee is **produced** using the finest coffee beans from Kenya.
5. It is thought that the sandwich **was** invented in 1762.

14.2

A 4
B 1
C 7
D 8
E 2
F 5
G 3
H 6

14.3

Model Answers

1. Our accounts are audited every May by a separate department.
2. The coffee blends we produce are approved by our professional coffee tasters.
3. All passengers' luggage is scanned by security staff when they go through Departures.
4. All our marketing material for the Asia office is designed by Jane.
5. All the orders are checked by our packing department before delivery.
6. The database is updated with customers' details by Stephen.
7. All our ingredients are bought from Fair Trade suppliers by our cosmetics buyer.
8. New lines are added to our women's fashion range on a regular basis by Nicola.
9. The new product tracking app for customers was invented by Jason.
10. Our new website was launched by our marketing team in January.

14.4

1. False
2. False
3. True
4. Not given
5. True

14.5

1. These toys can't have been checked.
2. A discount should have been given.
3. The order can't have been taken by her.
4. A free bag can be given to every customer.
5. Faults in the products shouldn't be ignored.
6. Our prices can't be beaten.
7. His order must have been placed late.

14.6

1. Next, the ingredients **are mixed** together to make a cake mixture.
2. Then the cake mixture **is poured** into cake pans.
3. Next, the cakes **are put** in a hot oven.
4. When the cakes are cooked, they **are taken** out of the oven.
5. The cakes **are left** to cool on a wire cooling rack.
6. Finally, the cakes **are assembled** and decorated with icing.

15

15.1

OPINION:
fantastic, **amazing**, **excellent**
SIZE:
huge, **tiny**, **large**
AGE:
ancient, **modern**, **state-of-the-art**
COLOR:
magenta, **crimson**, **black**
NATIONALITY:
Indian, **Turkish**, **Chinese**
MATERIAL:
leather, **metal**, **plastic**

15.2

1 It's made by a fabulous, young Indian designer.
2 I love these fantastic, small, blue china bowls.
3 We're launching an outstanding new range of clothes.

15.3

1 What a lovely **stylish** desk you have!
2 Sam asked me to design a **classic** brown chair.
3 I brought back some delicious **Turkish** candy from my trip.
4 Do you like this **pretty** crimson watch for ladies?
5 Do you like our cute **green** teddy bear for our new children's range?
6 Our competitors are selling **unfashionable** black suits.
7 Our team is developing an innovative **leather** interior for our executive car.
8 I love buying large **yellow** flowers for the office.
9 Jane has bought an **expensive** classic car at an auction.
10 We have an amazing **Italian** coffee machine in our office.
11 I have ordered some of those fabulous **double-sided** business cards.
12 We have an amazing **grey** oven in our staff kitchen.
13 This is our new **lightweight** digital camera.

15.4

1 B
2 A
3 B
4 A
5 B

15.5

1 False
2 True
3 True
4 False
5 Not given

15.6

1 Their website is easy to use because it has a **simple**, effective style.
2 Zander's Pizzeria makes **delicious**, oven-baked pizzas.
3 I love this **comfortable**, leather armchair.
4 The new, **full-color** brochure is very bright and attractive.
5 I like the **clean**, new rooms in that hotel.
6 Those small, **diamond** earrings are beautiful.
7 My dad drives a **huge**, black truck.
8 Ella makes high-quality, **cotton** curtains.
9 We aim to give **excellent** customer service.
10 We offer a **unique**, personal experience.
11 I don't like those ugly, **wooden** desks. They're hideous!
12 This modern, **Japanese** car is much faster than my old one.
13 What a **gorgeous**, big photo of all the team!

16

16.1

1 logo
2 slogan / tagline
3 brand
4 radio advertising
5 billboard
6 poster
7 sponsor
8 door-to-door sales
9 copywriter
10 word of mouth
11 coupons
12 free sample
13 market research
14 consumer
15 promote
16 sales pitch
17 merchandise
18 social media
19 unique selling point / USP
20 television advertising
21 online survey
22 leaflet / flyer
23 advertising agency

17

17.1

EXTREME:
enormous, **terrible**, **brilliant**, **furious**, **fascinating**, **exhausted**, **awful**
ABSOLUTE:
true, **wrong**, **perfect**, **equal**, **impossible**, **unique**, **empty**
CLASSIFYING:
metal, **electronic**, **scientific**, **woolen**, **industrial**, **organic**, **rural**

17.2

1. The factory was totally destroyed.
2. I was thoroughly exhausted this morning.
3. The warehouse is almost empty.
4. Jon is an extremely good speaker.
5. Peter is fairly good at Spanish.
6. The project is largely complete.
7. Sian is an utterly brilliant swimmer.

17.3

1. **Fairly** certain. I think I sent it yesterday.
2. Yeah, it's absolutely **fantastic**. I love it.
3. It was very impressive, but **almost** identical to mine!
4. Yes, it's totally **unique**. I have the only one.
5. That's right. **Nearly** everyone likes him.
6. No. It was **absolutely** awful. I almost fell asleep.
7. It was practically **empty**. There were only a few people there.

17.4

1. absolutely fantastic.
2. utterly original.
3. almost impossible.
4. very busy.
5. extremely important.
6. completely new.
7. highly reflective.
8. practically impossible.
9. absolutely amazing.
10. really clever.
11. fairly certain.

18

18.1

1. B
2. A
3. A
4. B
5. A

18.2

1. There was **such** a large crowd outside.
2. The results were **so** disappointing.
3. We've had **such** a fantastic year.
4. The price for the hotel was **so** high.
5. The week seems to pass **so** slowly.

18.3

1. This coffee was so expensive.
2. My colleague is so lazy.
3. Clara's presentation was so interesting.
4. That is such a depressing book.
5. The sales were so disappointing.
6. It's such a strange story.
7. It's so important to be on time.

18.4

1. Not given
2. True
3. True
4. False
5. Not given

18.5

1. Our senior managers think the price of our products is **too** high.
2. This room won't be big **enough** for this afternoon's meeting.
3. The team is **so** excited about tonight's awards ceremony.
4. I thought today's meeting was **such** a waste of time.
5. Jim doesn't speak loudly **enough**. I can barely hear him.
6. Our IT system is **so** old. It's time we invested in a new one.
7. The new intern works **so** slowly. She prefers talking on the phone.
8. Our products were **too** expensive to appeal to middle-market customers.
9. Mary is **such** an ambitious woman. She wants to be a CEO by the age of 30.
10. You shouldn't drive **too** quickly when you're in this part of town.
11. The strikes have caused **such** a problem for our employees who commute.
12. The marketing campaign was **too** boring to appeal to young people.

19

19.1

1. You shouldn't work so hard.
2. You could do a training course.
3. You should get some fresh air.
4. You must give him a call.
5. You should order some more.

19.2

1. You **could** try delegating the task to your team. I'm sure they'd do a great job.
2. Greg **ought to** apologize to his team for his behavior. He was very rude.
3. Antonio really **ought to** employ some new staff, or we'll never meet our deadline.
4. We **should** organize a training course for the interns.
5. The secretary really **should** ask her boss for a raise. She works very hard.

19.3

1. You **should walk** to work if the train is canceled.
2. You **ought to call** the IT desk about your new password.
3. You **shouldn't eat** your lunch at your desk. Go to a café instead.
4. You **must tell** your manager when you want to book time off.
5. Clare **ought to take** a break if she's tired of her job.
6. You **could do** an English course if you want to learn English.
7. Dave **ought to go** home if he's not feeling well.
8. Pete **shouldn't talk** to the public about company secrets.

19.4

4

19.5

1. Why don't we **organize** a feedback session?
2. What about **asking** Pedro to do it?
3. Why don't you **hire** some new staff?
4. What about **buying** a new printer?
5. Why doesn't Mabel **go** on vacation?
6. Why **don't** they close the Mumbai branch?
7. What about **inviting** the clients to dinner?

19.6

1. Why don't we file these documents?
2. You should take a vacation for a week.
3. You shouldn't eat your lunch at your desk.
4. What about hiring a new member of staff?
5. Why don't you work from home on Fridays?

19.7

1. What about asking Pete to do it?
2. What about organizing a workshop?
3. What about selling our products online?
4. Why don't we ask Pete to do it?
5. Why don't we organize a workshop?
6. Why don't we sell our products online?

19.8

1. What about organizing a workshop?
2. Why don't we arrange a meeting?
3. What about buying a new printer?
4. Why don't we hire a new secretary?
5. What about asking Cyril to help?
6. What about providing free software?
7. Why don't we book a meeting room?

19.9

1. You ought to ask the clients for more time.
2. How about talking to your co-workers about your problems?
3. We could hire some new interns next year.
4. Why don't you quit your job if you don't like it?
5. You should complete the project before the deadline.

20

20.1

1. a bonus
2. an appraisal / a performance review

3 to approve
4 to delegate
5 performance
6 to be promoted

20.2

1 telephone manner
2 fast learner
3 IT / computing
4 data analysis
5 attention to detail
6 numeracy
7 written communication
8 problem-solving
9 time management
10 work well under pressure
11 able to drive
12 public speaking
13 teamwork
14 research
15 organization
16 leadership
17 decision-making

21

21.1

1 Tom **can** fix your car this afternoon. It will be ready at 5:00.
2 Karl **can't** drive. He failed his driving test again.
3 Jon used to be really nervous, but now he **can** give presentations.
4 She **can** type really quickly. She types over 60 words per minute.
5 I **can't** work the new photocopier. It's too difficult.
6 Hansa is a really good cook. She **can** cook really nice Indian food.
7 Ali **can't** read my handwriting. He says it's really messy.
8 Ania **can** speak French. She learned it in college.
9 Petra **can't** manage her staff any more. They do what they like.
10 Parvesh **can** write clear reports. They are easy to read.

21.2

1 Past
2 Present
3 Present
4 Past

21.3

1 Janice **can't** tell me if sales are up until she gets the final reports in.
2 Phil loves meeting new people, so he **can** work in the HR department.
3 Saira **couldn't** type fast, but now she can type 60 words a minute.
4 Ed **can** write reports very well. I'm going to ask him to help me write mine.
5 Keira **couldn't** use the database, but now she trains people in how to use it.
6 For years Alex **couldn't** speak Arabic, but now he has done a beginners' course.

21.4

1 False
2 False
3 Not given
4 False
5 True
6 True

21.5

1 He would do well in a smaller team.
2 She can manage her new team much better.
3 Before, he wouldn't talk in public.
4 She could train staff to do them.
5 She wouldn't be a good trainer.
6 He could be head of the department.

21.6

1 David has given his team excellent training. Now they can do anything.
2 Have you seen his brilliant designs? He can create our banners.
3 No one could read the boss's handwriting. It was terrible.
4 Sebastian is a very proactive person and would do well in marketing.

21.7

1 We think you are very talented and **would** be a great addition to our department.
2 I don't know what is wrong with the coffee machine. I **can't** get it working.
3 My confidence is much better now. Before, I **couldn't** give presentations.
4 Laila couldn't negotiate with her old boss, but she **can** with her new boss.

22

22.1

1 This training is really interesting. It is a lot of fun, **too**.
2 Team-building days are useful. They are **also** fun.
3 Some people always wash their coffee cups, **while** others don't.
4 **Although** Team A did the task quickly, Team B didn't finish it.
5 Team A built the bridge very quickly. Team B was **equally** successful.
6 Team A helped each other, **while** Team B disagreed with each other.
7 Hard work is an excellent trait in a team, **whereas** laziness is terrible.
8 Yesterday's training was useful. **However**, this morning's task was pointless.
9 Some people want to lead a team, **while** others are happy to be team members.
10 It is important to say what we all think. We should listen to each other **as well**.
11 This training is very useful. It is **equally** a good way to get to know people.

22.2

1 Although Sam went to the training day, he didn't learn anything new.
2 Team A solved the problem really quickly. Team B was equally successful.
3 This training is useful for managers. It is also useful for team members.
4 Some people want to be managers, while others want to be team members.
5 Laziness is a terrible trait for a team member, whereas honesty is excellent.
6 We'd like all staff to follow our usual dress code for the training. Please be on time, too.

22.3

A 3
B 1
C 6
D 5
E 4
F 2

22.4

1 The team-building task was useful and it was also a lot of fun.
2 Team A had to build a bridge, whereas Team B had to make a pizza. / Team B had to build a bridge, whereas Team A had to make a pizza.
3 While Team B completed the task first, they had some problems.
4 Training courses are really useful and they are often fun as well.
5 Team A worked together very well. Team B was equally cooperative. / Team B worked together very well. Team A was equally cooperative.
6 This task will identify your weaknesses, but also your strengths.
7 Our team baked a cake. However, the activity didn't matter.
8 Although the other team came first, we worked well together. / Although we came first, the other team worked well together.
9 Yesterday's task was easy, while today's task was more difficult.
10 Team A finished the task quickly, whereas Team B took its time. / Team B finished the task quickly, whereas Team A took its time.

22.5

1 As a consequence, I am now a team leader.
2 Consequently, they all won a medal.
3 For this reason, I was very nervous.
4 As a result, everyone attends them.
5 Consequently, she was promoted last week.

22.6

1 Team-building days are great for morale. **Consequently**, the atmosphere in our office is good.
2 We have regular IT training sessions. For this **reason**, everyone has good computer skills.
3 We do team building every year. As a **consequence**, we work really well together.
4 During team building we meet new staff. **For this** reason, we know our co-workers well.

23

23.1

1 We plan **to launch** our new product range at the conference.
2 Would you consider **organizing** the accommodation for the visitors?
3 I really enjoy **taking** clients out for dinner at famous restaurants.
4 Jenny has offered **to meet** our visitors at the airport.
5 I keep **suggesting** that we should have a staff training session.

23.2

1 Our clients expect **to** receive good customer service.
2 Would you consider **making** the name badges for the delegates?
3 Colin has offered **to organize** the training program for the new staff.
4 I hope **to impress** our clients when I show them around the new office.

23.3

1 Entertaining clients
2 To receive good customer service
3 They give their honest opinion
4 Their competitors had had one
5 Offer team-building events

23.4

1 I regret **to tell** you that I can't take the clients out for dinner. I'm very sorry.
2 Do you remember **calling** Dan last month? He has a question about a discount you offered.
3 Sue stopped **to read** the program for the launch event. It looked really interesting!
4 He regrets **telling** her his idea for the event because she copied it.
5 David gave his presentation, and went on **to talk** about new events.
6 I stopped **giving** my presentation because the CEO had a question.

23.5

A 4
B 1
C 6
D 8
E 2
F 7
G 5
H 3

23.6

1 I really enjoy entertaining new clients.
2 Sandra invited me to attend the overseas sales conference.
3 My manager asked me to book the accommodation.
4 Tom expects his manager to give him a promotion soon.
5 My boss asked me to give him an update on recent sales.
6 We invited all our customers to come to our party.

23.7

1. I enjoy entertaining our clients.
2. I remembered entertaining our clients.
3. I remembered to meet our clients.
4. I remembered to book accommodation.
5. She remembered entertaining our clients.
6. She remembered to meet our clients.
7. She remembered to book accommodation.
8. She enjoys entertaining our clients.
9. We enjoy entertaining our clients.
10. We remembered entertaining our clients.
11. We remembered to meet our clients.
12. We remembered to book accommodation.
13. They enjoy entertaining our clients.
14. They remembered entertaining our clients.
15. They remembered to meet our clients.
16. They remembered to book accommodation.

24

24.1

1 to take minutes
2 to look at
3 to take questions
4 to be absent
5 to reach a consensus
6 to run out of time
7 a strategy
8 main objective
9 action points
10 to give a presentation
11 to send out an agenda
12 to interrupt
13 attendees

14. to suggest / propose
15. unanimous agreement
16. to review the minutes
17. a show of hands

25

25.1

1. She said she could speak Thai and Mandarin.
2. She said she needed to talk to Hansa in HR.
3. He said he was working on the sales report.
4. He said he had finished the presentation.
5. He said he had been to the Mumbai office.

25.2

1. She **said (that) the taxi was outside**.
2. He **said (that) he needed to call the US office**.
3. He **said (that) he would get the bill**.
4. He **said (that) he couldn't open any emails**.
5. She **said (that) she had sent the order to them**.

25.3

1. She said she was busy that afternoon.
2. He said that he didn't like his new boss.
3. They said they hadn't received the delivery.
4. He said he was going to be in Tokyo that week.
5. They said they had been to the new product launch.
6. She said she would issue an invoice right away.
7. He said the company could give a 5 percent discount.
8. She said she had gotten along well with the interviewer.
9. They said they were designing a new range.

25.4

A. 5
B. 1
C. 4
D. 6
E. 3
F. 7
G. 2

25.5

1. He **told** me that he'd been to China twice.
2. She **said** that she was going to Montreal.
3. He **promised** that he wouldn't be late for the train.
4. He **explained** that he didn't know how to use the photocopier.
5. He **denied** that he had broken the coffee machine.
6. She **complained** that the food was cold when the waiter brought it.
7. He **confirmed** that the tickets had been booked.

25.6

1. She **promised** to call me back after 2:30 that afternoon.
2. He **added** that he needed a copy of Simon's report about the year-end accounts.
3. She **explained** that the new all-in-one printer wasn't difficult to use.
4. He **confirmed** that he'd like to buy 100 units of the new product.
5. He **complained** that he wasn't happy with the customer service he had experienced.
6. She **suggested** that we should ask Ameera what she thought.

26

26.1

1. Selma asked me where you had put the annual report.
2. Krishnan wanted to know why I was late for work again.
3. My boss asked me what I thought about the new IT system.
4. Hans asked me where we would have the presentation this afternoon.
5. Sophie asked Claude why he wasn't at the meeting.
6. Tabitha asked me who had taken her cell phone.
7. Fiona wanted to know who had taken the minutes.

26.2

1. False
2. True
3. False
4. Not given
5. True
6. Not given
7. False
8. True
9. True

26.3

1. make a suggestion
2. get fired
3. make a mistake
4. do your best
5. do someone a favor
6. get a job
7. do research
8. make notes

26.4

1. She **asked me how many people worked in the company**.
2. He **asked me why I had handed in the report so late**.
3. He **asked me who had gotten / got promoted**.
4. He **asked me who the new senior manager was**.
5. He **asked me which candidate I had chosen**.
6. He **asked me how long I had worked here**.
7. She **asked me why I had been so late this / that morning**.
8. He **asked me what time I got home**.
9. He **asked me where I had had the appointment**.
10. She **asked me which printer I preferred**.

26.5

1. He **asked me if / whether the package had arrived safely**.
2. She **asked me if / whether I could do her a favor**.
3. He **asked me if / whether he could have a word with me later**.
4. She **asked me if / whether I had finished writing the report yet**.
5. He **asked me if / whether he could make a suggestion**.
6. She **asked me if / whether I had read last year's report**.
7. He **asked me if / whether I was coming to the awards ceremony on Saturday**.
8. She **asked me if / whether I had enjoyed the presentation**.
9. He **asked me if / whether I had booked a table at the restaurant**.

27

27.1

1. True
2. True
3. False
4. Not given
5. False
6. True
7. Not given
8. True
9. Not given
10. False

27.2

1. Unfortunately, we have a few problems with our production line.
2. Regrettably, few people have the skills necessary to run a multinational company.
3. So few of our customer reviews are positive that it's becoming a problem.
4. I have little doubt that the conference will be a success.

27.3

1. **Few** employees have worked for the company for as long as Sofia.
2. We have **a little** bit of time before the meeting ends.
3. So **few** companies offer this service that demand is sure to be high.
4. Very **little** can be done to improve facilities in the short term.
5. We can expect **a little** increase in profits over the summer season.
6. It's great that you have **a few** ideas about how we can improve sales.

27.4

1. I'm sure all will be well once you've spoken to the customer.
2. All I know is that the order is late.
3. Is that all you need?
4. All we can do is wait for a response from the client.

27.5

1. There are a few things we can do to improve staff morale.
2. We've had little interest in our new app.
3. Little can be done to improve staff morale.
4. So few people have money to spend on our luxury vacations.
5. Our new app is very popular.

28

28.1

1. What is our target this year?
2. Who is handling the account?
3. Who is in charge?
4. What is your sales target?
5. Who responds to complaints?
6. Who spoke to Mr. Jones?
7. What is our plan of action?

28.2

1. Do I need to dress formally?
2. Did you quote this price?
3. What should I tell the client?
4. Who wants to work in New York?

28.3

1. We should increase our margins, **shouldn't we**?
2. I didn't send you the report, **did I**?
3. She'll be a great manager, **won't she**?
4. I'm not getting a raise, **am I**?
5. We haven't made a loss, **have we**?
6. We're going to win the award, **aren't we**?
7. Louis has worked here since 2012, **hasn't he**?
8. Brett worked late last night, **didn't he**?

28.4

1. We could launch our product early, **couldn't we**?
2. Jakob ordered the samples, **didn't he**?
3. We can't cut prices any further, **can we**?
4. We haven't achieved our target, **have we**?
5. We need to improve product quality, **don't we**?
6. We're not ready for the meeting, **are we**?
7. They are opening a new store, **are they**?
8. You weren't in London last week, **were you**?
9. You traveled to Paris by train, **didn't you**?
10. I'm writing the proposal, **aren't I**?
11. I emailed the right person, **didn't I**?

28.5

1. Not given
2. True
3. False
4. False
5. False
6. True
7. False

28.6

1. What was her name? I didn't **hear** it.
2. **Who** is responsible for training?
3. You're not worried about the meeting, **are you**?
4. **What** is our timetable for this project?
5. Sales are better than expected, **aren't they**?
6. Sorry, I **missed** that.

29

29.1

1. tourism
2. finance
3. energy
4. mining
5. recycling
6. manufacturing
7. agriculture / farming
8. catering / food
9. hospitality
10. fashion
11. electronics
12. real estate (US) / property (UK)
13. chemical
14. entertainment
15. pharmaceutical
16. healthcare

17 fishing
18 transportation
19 education

29.2

1 organized
2 team player
3 practical
4 responsible
5 motivated
6 calm
7 confident
8 reliable
9 innovative
10 punctual
11 accurate
12 ambitious
13 professional
14 energetic
15 creative

30

30.1

1 I want to apply for **a** job in **an** office.
2 I've got **an** interview next week for **the** job I told you about.
3 **The** ideal candidate enjoys working in **a** team.
4 **The** deadline for applications for **the** job in IT is next Monday.
5 Please complete **the** form on **the** job page on our website.

30.2

A 8
B 1
C 7
D 5
E 3
F 6
G 2
H 4

30.3

1 Nurses often have to work very long hours. They are very important people.
2 Working hours are from 8:30 to 5:00. Lunch is from 1:00 to 2:00.
3 Vale loves giving training sessions. The training sessions she gave yesterday were amazing.
4 The job I applied for is based in Madrid. It's in sales and marketing.
5 The people who interviewed me for the job were really nice. They were managers.
6 I have just applied for a job in the finance department at your company.
7 The salary for this job is not very good. I don't think I'll apply for it.
8 The successful candidate will have three years' experience branding new products.
9 Our company is currently recruiting more staff for the Paris office.
10 I have meetings with the CEO and some of our new clients today.
11 Marisha is good at pitching products. It's the thing she enjoys most about her job.
12 This job requires in-depth knowledge of business trends in the wider world.

30.4

1 False
2 True
3 True
4 False
5 True

30.5

1 We need someone who is willing to travel, and can speak **Spanish**.
2 Tara works in **the finance department** of an advertising agency.
3 Marc and Samantha often travel to China **on business**.
4 The company is based in the UK, but it does business throughout **the EU**.
5 I started looking for a job as **an engineer** after I finished college.

31

31.1

1 I graduated from college in June 2016 with a degree in chemistry.
2 I am writing to apply for the role of head chef.
3 I heard about the job on your website.
4 I am fully trained in all aspects of health and safety.

31.2

1. Jim graduated **from** college with a degree in physics. Now he is a research scientist.
2. He is fully trained **in** all aspects of sales and marketing. I think he'll do a great job.
3. In my role as Senior Program Developer, I reported **to** the Director of IT.
4. Tanya has applied **for** a job in the marketing department of our company.
5. I worked **for** the owner of a leading hairdressing salon. I learned a lot from him.

31.3

Model Answers

1. Ellie has worked in marketing for more than ten years.
2. She developed award-winning campaigns in key markets.
3. She introduced a new customer-focused branding initiative.
4. She is responsible for training junior members of staff.
5. She looks after the Europe region.
6. She describes herself as energetic, dynamic, and extremely reliable.

31.4

1. skills
2. salary
3. a position
4. to apply for a job
5. to report to someone
6. a team
7. a résumé
8. an opportunity
9. to amount to

31.5

Dear Mr. Chang,

I am writing to **apply for** the position of Senior Sales Consultant, as advertised on your website.

I have **worked in** the sales industry for more than eight years, and am **trained in** selling a range of products to varied markets. In my current position, I am **responsible for** sales to Asian markets, and last year I **looked after** the new market of China, where sales **amounted to** more than $10 million.

I am **passionate about** working in the sales industry and welcome the opportunity to learn new skills. I run the training program for new staff members and ten of the junior sales consultants **report to** me. In their training, I **focus on** developing awareness of the most effective sales strategies.

Please find my résumé and references attached. I look **forward to** hearing from you.

Yours sincerely,
Deepak Singh

32

32.1

1. The person **who** I admire the most in the company is the Sales Manager.
2. The office **where** I work is a tall, modern building.
3. The customers **who** gave us feedback were all very positive.
4. The team **that** I lead is fully qualified and highly motivated.

32.2

1. We sell apps **that are designed by IT specialists**.
2. We are based in an office **that is in the business park**.
3. I work with clients **who have high standards**.
4. This is the reason **that I applied for this job**.
5. Spain and Italy are the countries **where we sell the most**.

32.3

1. Training staff, **which** is my favorite part of the job, is really interesting.
2. In my current job, **where** I serve lots of customers, I have learned to deal with complaints.
3. My boss, **who** is very understanding, encourages me to leave the office on time.
4. While I was in college I worked in a café, **which** taught me a lot about customer service.

32.4

Ⓐ 3
Ⓑ 5
Ⓒ 1
Ⓓ 6
Ⓔ 2
Ⓕ 4

32.5

1 Last summer, **when** I had just graduated, I worked as an intern in a bank.
2 My teacher, **who** was an amazing person, inspired me to study law.
3 My apprenticeship, **which** I completed in 2016, was in IT.
4 The place **where** I want to work as a tour guide is New York.

32.6

1 Tom's team, whose staff are hard-working, hit their sales targets last month.
2 In my previous job, which was in sales, I learned to give presentations.
3 I sometimes work from home as it is the place where I can concentrate best.
4 My clients, who expect good customer service, said my work was excellent.

32.7

1 The thing **that gets** me excited is when we hit our sales targets.
2 People **who know** me well say I am customer-focused and give good customer service.
3 I have a can-do attitude, **which means** that I get things done.
4 I would hope to receive more than my current salary, **which is** $45,000 a year.
5 My boss**, who is** quite understanding, would allow me to leave after a month's notice.

33

33.1

1 to touch base
2 a change of pace
3 a game plan
4 to be on the same page
5 up in the air
6 up and running
7 in a nutshell
8 to go the extra mile
9 to fill someone's shoes
10 groundbreaking
11 to clinch the deal
12 to call it a day
13 to cut corners
14 to be ahead of the game
15 a ballpark figure
16 to do something by the book
17 to corner the market

34

34.1

1 Alex comes up **with** great ideas.
2 Hal looks down **on** his co-workers.
3 I'm **looking** forward to the launch.
4 Fred **puts** up with a lot of noise.
5 She comes **across** as rather superior.
6 The printer has run **out** of paper.
7 Jim's staff get **away** with being late.
8 Shona has to **face** up to poor sales.
9 We need to **keep** up with the schedule.

34.2

1 I get along with my team.
2 She comes across as friendly.
3 I can't put up with his music!
4 He comes up with good ideas.
5 Tom gets away with a lot.
6 We have run out of coffee.
7 We must face up to facts.

34.3

Model Answers

1 Some companies think social media is trivial.
2 Social media helps you keep up with trends.
3 ABC Foods uses social media to tell customers news about the company.
4 ABC Foods has previews of its TV ads.
5 The company does this so that subscribers feel they are keeping up with company news.

6 Competitions make ABC Foods stand out from its competitors.
7 Customer loyalty means customers make repeat purchases.

34.4

1 I'll look **them** up online.
2 Can you fill **it** in?
3 I'd like you to take **it** on.
4 I can't let **them** down.
5 Can we talk **it** over?
6 Could you look **it** over?
7 We are giving **them** away.
8 I need to call **it** off.
9 I can't figure **them** out.
10 The taxi will pick **him** up.
11 I keep putting **it** off.
12 Yola turned **it** down.

34.5

1 Update your website
2 To find new ideas for your product
3 Translating social media use into sales
4 Sharing users' questions and answers

34.6

1 Cev always comes up with great ideas.
2 Dan and Sam don't get along with each other.
3 The copier has run out of paper.
4 Here's a form. Can you fill it in?
5 Rohit keeps up with the business news.

34.7

1 I looked **up** the candidates on social media. They all looked very talented.
2 Kennedy's team **gets away with** a lot. It's not fair on the others.
3 You're leading an important pitch today. Please don't **let me down**.
4 Can you take **on** writing the sales report today, or are you too busy?
5 We're giving **away** free books to customers. We hope it will increase sales.

35

35.1

1 She will get a raise in her new position.
2 You won't get a bonus.
3 We may ask him to become a mentor.
4 We might need to recruit more staff.
5 We may have to fire her.

35.2

1 True
2 True
3 False
4 False
5 True

35.3

1 Our staff can't use the new database. We might have to provide more training.
2 David has over 15 years' experience and he will lead our marketing department.
3 I need your report by Thursday. You might need to work overtime.
4 Anna's laptop is broken. She will get a new one this week.
5 There is a pay freeze at the moment, so you won't get a raise.
6 If Rita's work doesn't get better, we may have to fire her.
7 We have some meetings in France. You may have to go to Paris.
8 We can't hire any staff at the moment, so you might not get an assistant until March.
9 If your presentation goes well, the CEO might ask you to give it to the board.
10 Tanya has been promoted. She will lead a team next year.
11 Dev has had a bad trading year. He won't meet his sales targets.
12 Paula always goes the extra mile. She will make a great addition to the team.

35.4

1 He will definitely be promoted.
2 You will probably get a raise.
3 She probably won't need training.
4 They'll definitely get a bonus.
5 I probably won't go on vacation.
6 I definitely won't change jobs.
7 We will probably hire an intern.
8 He probably won't meet clients.
9 It will definitely sell well.

35.5

1. You will **probably** be promoted.
2. He will **definitely** get the job.
3. She **definitely** won't get a raise.
4. They will **probably** get a bonus.
5. I **probably** won't get a new laptop.
6. You will **definitely** get a company car.
7. I will **probably** move to the head office.
8. You **probably** won't need much training.
9. We will **definitely** hire a new assistant soon.

35.6

1. Katrina doesn't have much experience. She **will probably** need more training.
2. Meliz has to travel to see clients. She **will probably** get a company car.
3. Mr. Cox has complained about our service. He **probably won't** use us again.
4. The negotiations are going quite well. We **might** clinch the deal tomorrow.
5. You're doing a great job, but our profits are down. You **might not** get a raise.

35.7

Model Answers

1. Isaac met all his sales targets this year.
2. Isaac might be promoted next year.
3. Isaac will mentor two new employees from next month.
4. Isaac will start selling products in Asia.
5. Isaac might need additional training.
6. The company thinks Isaac will perform well.

36

36.1

1. microphone
2. USB drive / flash drive
3. voice recorder
4. cursor
5. low battery
6. power cable
7. touch screen
8. handout
9. speakers
10. computer
11. laminator
12. video camera
13. lectern
14. keyboard
15. printer
16. cue cards
17. mouse
18. laptop
19. webcam
20. pointer
21. router
22. chairs
23. projector

36.2

1. report
2. flow chart
3. graph
4. pie chart

37

37.1

1. Let's now turn to future prospects.
2. My talk today is about building brand loyalty.
3. Do feel free to tweet your questions to me.
4. So, we've looked at our market penetration.
5. To sum up, this year has been difficult.
6. We'll look at case studies, and then I'll take questions.
7. The purpose of this talk is to share sales figures.

37.2

1. To **sum** up, it's been a very successful year for us.
2. We'll **look** at the competitor's products, then I'll introduce our new product.
3. Do **feel** free to interrupt if you'd like to comment.
4. So, we've **looked** at problems we need to overcome.
5. Now let's **turn** to the solutions to those problems.

37.3

1. microphone
2. keyboard
3. USB / flash drive
4. cursor
5. handout
6. lectern
7. cord

37.4

1. Not given
2. False
3. Not given
4. Not given
5. True
6. True

37.5

A 4
B 3
C 7
D 5
E 1
F 2
G 6

38

38.1

1. If we home in on our Barcelona store, we can see it is successful.
2. All regions achieved their sales targets, aside from the Southwest.
3. Customer response has been positive, excepting Eastern Europe.
4. Generally speaking, our products are popular in South America.
5. With the exception of February, sales are up.
6. This year the company is focusing on its social media campaign.
7. If we focus on this chart, we can see sales have dropped.

38.2

1. Excepting East Asia, our sales **have grown by more than 10 percent**.
2. In actual fact, the consumer group said **they really liked our prototype**.
3. As a matter of fact, I don't think **Alyssa is suitable for the role**.
4. For instance, we've had a lot of positive **feedback about our menswear**.
5. In general, the number of subscribers **to our magazines is falling**.
6. Concentrating on the basics, there are **many areas where we can improve**.
7. Jorge needs to improve key skills such **as dealing with customers**.

38.3

1. In **reality**, there is no way of knowing what sales will be like next year.
2. In **fact**, we need to hire about 10 more staff this year.
3. **However**, we can't really afford to hire more staff.
4. **Except** for Janice, all staff in this department deserve a raise.
5. **Actually**, there is little we can do to increase production.
6. **Generally**, staff seem very happy with working conditions.

38.4

1. False
2. Not given
3. True
4. Not given
5. Not given
6. True

38.5

1. If we **home** in on profits, we can see growth.
2. If we focus **on** prices, it's clear they're too high.
3. **By** and large, our T-shirts are our bestseller.
4. In **reality**, there's no way we can recover.
5. As a **matter** of fact, I am very disappointed.
6. Except **for** Korea, I've been to most of Asia.
7. **In** general, China is our biggest market.

39

39.1

1. This sports car is **the fastest** car on sale today.
2. Our leather jackets are **more fashionable** than our competitors' jackets.
3. This digital camera is **the best** model ever.
4. Our new microwave oven is more efficient **than** any other model.
5. This ice cream maker is **easier** to use than any other on the market.
6. Our customers said our sofa is **more comfortable** than other models.
7. Our organic vegetables are **fresher** than supermarket vegetables.
8. Book a train trip with us in advance to get **the cheapest** fares.

9 Our cake range was voted **the tastiest** on the market in a recent survey.
10 These batteries last **longer** than the leading brand.
11 We think our new winter coat is **the warmest** on the market.

39.2

1 the biggest
2 cheaper
3 more energy-efficient
4 more stylish

39.3

1 We will create **the most beautiful** flowers for the tables and the bride's bouquet.
2 Our drink is **healthier** than that brand because it has a natural caffeine substitute.
3 Our fitness tracker is **just as effective as** more expensive models, but is cheaper.
4 We offer **better technical support than** other cell phone companies do.

39.4

1 This pizza is as tasty as the leading brand, but much cheaper.
2 Our budget clothing is as stylish as other brands on the market.
3 These store-brand dishwasher tablets are as good as the market leader.
4 Our latest action movie is as exciting as anything you've ever seen.
5 This eco-friendly dishwashing liquid is not as good as the leading brand.

39.5

1 as exciting as
2 more simple / simpler
3 more convenient
4 the healthiest
5 the best
6 just as cheap as / cheaper than

40

40.1

A 3
B 1
C 4
D 2
E 8
F 5
G 6
H 7

40.2

1 There has been an increase in complaints.
2 There was a dramatic spike last year.
3 The price is fluctuating wildly.
4 We expect a considerable drop in prices.
5 There was a sharp rise in the share value.
6 The share value has rallied slightly.

40.3

1 Staff numbers went **from** 120 to 150.
2 **Between** 15 and 18 percent of stock is unsold.
3 We've experienced a boom **of** 56 percent.
4 Profits have fallen **by** 11 percent.
5 The share price peaked **at** $22.
6 Complaints doubled **in** the last quarter.
7 Our sale was **between** May and June.

40.4

1 Not given
2 True
3 False
4 Not given
5 False
6 True

40.5

1 There's been a **dramatic spike** because of a poor harvest.
2 Our sales **peaked at** $200,000 a day in December.
3 Yes, malfunctions have **fallen steadily** since last year.
4 Between **20 and 30** percent of our stock is on sale.
5 Yes, they've **rallied slightly** since last year.
6 There was an **increase of** 10 percent in the cost of electricity.

41

41.1

1. Are you able to pay **our fee in installments**?
2. We might move forward with the contract **if you would consider buying in bulk**.
3. I would like to resolve this issue **as soon as possible**.
4. Maybe we could discuss some **alternative options for the design**.
5. We were thinking **that you could design our new logo**.
6. I'm afraid I was hoping for **something more innovative**.

41.2

A 3
B 4
C 1
D 6
E 2
F 5

41.3

1. I was wondering where I can try these clothes on.
2. Could you tell me when the sample designs will be ready?
3. I was wondering if I could talk to you about Samia's performance.
4. Could you tell me whether I can order this product in store?
5. I was wondering whether you have paid my invoice yet.
6. Could you tell me what the warranty period is?
7. I was wondering how the new product is different from the old one.
8. Could you tell me when the price list will be available?
9. I was wondering if you would be able to offer me a discount.

41.4

1. I'm afraid **our deadline was missed**.
2. It looks as if **the wrong size was sent**.
3. It seems that **the discount was not applied**.
4. I'm afraid **our order was delivered** to the wrong address.
5. It looks as if **the price was calculated** incorrectly.
6. It seems that **your employees are not very well trained**.
7. I'm afraid **our customers were not satisfied**.
8. It seems that **my order was lost** while it was being delivered.
9. I'm afraid **my steak was not cooked** properly.
10. It looks as if **a mistake has been made**.
11. It seems that **the printer still hasn't been fixed**.
12. I'm afraid **the document was not checked** thoroughly enough.

41.5

1. I was wondering if **you could** look at my presentation.
2. Could you **tell** me when my order will be dispatched?
3. I was wondering if you **would** be free to meet tomorrow.
4. Could you tell me when **we can** expect our invoice to be paid?
5. I was wondering what time **the store opens**.
6. Could you **tell me** how much the new product should retail for?

41.6

2

42

42.1

1. If you ask me, you won't find a better deal.
2. Actually, we are waiting for the factory to send us more of that product.
3. The main thing is that we agree on schedule dates.
4. What I'm saying is that I can offer free delivery on orders over a hundred.

42.2

1. True
2. True
3. False
4. Not given
5. False

42.3

1 **Actually**, we sent you an email with them this morning.
2 I'm afraid not. If **you ask me**, this is a great deal.
3 What **we need is** an assurance that you can meet our schedule dates.
4 The **main thing is** that we agree on a price that allows enough profit.
5 **I'm afraid** your asking price is too high. Can we say $40 a unit?

43

43.1

Note: All answers can also use the contracted form of "would."

1 If they **gave** us a discount, we **would place** an order.
2 If the product **was** cheaper, we **would buy** it.
3 If they **moved** the deadline, we **would meet** it.
4 I **would reply** to the email now if I **had** more time.
5 We **would sell** more online if our website **was** faster.
6 We **would send** the package tomorrow if you **ordered** before 9 tonight.
7 If the agency **sent** us better temps, we **would use** them again.
8 If I **worked** late every night, I **would finish** my report for Friday.
9 I **would apply** for the job if the hours **weren't** so long.

43.2

1 True
2 Not given
3 False
4 False
5 True
6 False

43.3

1 If customers don't pay on time, we charge a 15 percent late fee.
2 Our helpline is open from 8am to 8pm if you need help.
3 When employees work weekends, they get paid double time.
4 If you are a regular customer, we give you a 5 percent discount.
5 If we receive a payment after 3pm, we credit it the next day.

43.4

1 If you need help with your computer, **you can call the IT department**.
2 We would move production to Europe **if it was cheaper to do that**.
3 We will issue a full refund **if you return the product to one of our stores**.
4 If clients are regular customers, **we give them a 5 percent discount**.
5 If our receptionist was rude to you, **we would give her a verbal warning**.

43.5

1 If you **don't / do not** pay on time, we won't send you your order.
2 We'll issue a full refund if **you're not / you are not** happy with our products.
3 If you **book** two nights in our hotel, we'll give you a third night for free.
4 If Alan's presentation **goes** well, he will get promoted next month.
5 We won't charge you for your stay if you **don't / do not** get a good night's sleep.
6 If you **order** over 100 units, we'll give you a discount.

43.6

1 Well, if you pay for the overtime, **we will finish** the job by then.
2 Yes. If **clients buy** 100 units or more, we give them a 5 percent discount.
3 If you return it to us within 28 days, **we will issue** a full refund.
4 If **you could do** a price of $59 per unit, we'd sell it in our stores.
5 We're sorry to hear that. If a customer makes a complaint, **we take** it very seriously.
6 We can't do that yet. If **we took** on more staff, we'd be able to increase production.

44

44.1

Note: All answers can also use contracted positive forms and long negative forms.

1 We **would have signed** the contract if the deadline **hadn't been** so tight.
2 If we **had left** earlier, we **wouldn't have missed** the train.
3 If the waitress **hadn't been** so rude, we **wouldn't have** complained.
4 If we **had ordered** before 3pm, we **would have received** the goods today.
5 We **wouldn't have lost** the client if we **had delivered** the report on time.
6 If you **had repaired** the printer, we **wouldn't have canceled** the contract.
7 If I **had known** how expensive it was, I **would have put** it in the safe.
8 The boss **wouldn't have shouted** if you **had admitted** your mistake.
9 If you **had been** more prepared, you **would have given** a better presentation.
10 We **would have given** you free delivery if you **had paid** on time.
11 If I **had known** our competitor's price, I **would have offered** a bigger discount.
12 We **would have met** our deadline if we **had employed** more staff.
13 If you **hadn't been** off sick, we **would have invited** you to the meeting.
14 We **would have paid** the full amount due if you **hadn't missed** our deadline.
15 If you **had sold** more products last time, we **would have asked** you to lead the pitch.

44.2

1 B
2 A
3 B
4 A
5 B

44.3

1 If I'd used the spell check, **my work wouldn't have had so many errors**.
2 If she'd told the boss about her mistake, **he wouldn't have been so angry**.
3 If they'd paid on time, **we wouldn't have canceled their order**.
4 If I'd used the latest sales data, **my report would have been up to date**.
5 If he'd checked the order was right, **his clients wouldn't have complained**.
6 If you'd ordered more units, **we would have given you a discount**.
7 If he'd wanted an older model, **he would have asked for one**.

44.4

1 Clive will get a verbal warning **unless his timekeeping improves**.
2 **Unless you pay** by the end of today, we will cancel the contract.
3 We won't win the contract **unless we can** offer a better price.
4 I won't get promoted this year **unless I impress** the boss.
5 Your warranty will not be valid **unless you register** your product.
6 **Unless I sell** to 100 new customers, I won't meet my sales targets.
7 We won't make many sales **unless we beat** our competitors' prices.
8 **Unless I work** overtime, I'm not going to meet the deadline.
9 His presentation will be boring **unless he adds** special effects.
10 The CEO won't be happy **unless we win** the contract.
11 **Unless you lower** the price, we won't order any more units.
12 We will miss the train **unless we leave** now.

44.5

1 True
2 False
3 Not given
4 True
5 True

44.6

1. We would have hit our sales target if the internet **hadn't gone** down.
2. If he **had left** earlier, he wouldn't have been late for the meeting.
3. If you had been less rude, we **would have won** the contract.
4. The CEO would have promoted me if she **had seen** my presentation.
5. If we **had lowered** the price, we would have made more sales.

Acknowledgments

The publisher would like to thank: Amy Child, Dominic Clifford, Devika Khosla, and Priyansha Tuli for design assistance; Dominic Clifford and Hansa Babra for additional illustrations; Sam Atkinson, Vineetha Mokkil, Antara Moitra, Margaret Parrish, Nisha Shaw, and Rohan Sinha for editorial assistance; Elizabeth Wise for indexing; Jo Kent for additional text; Scarlett O'Hara, Georgina Palffy, and Helen Ridge for proofreading; Christine Stroyan for project management; ID Audio for audio recording and production; David Almond, Gillian Reid, and Jacqueline Street-Elkayam for production assistance.

DK would like to thank the following for their kind permission to use their photograph:
33 **123RF.com**: Federico Rostagno / ilfede (top left)

For more information, please visit **www.dkimages.com**.